Cultures of Taste/Theories of Appetite: Eating Romanticism

Cultures of Taste/Theories of Appetite: Eating Romanticism

Edited by

Timothy Morton

palgrave
macmillan

First published 2004 by
PALGRAVE MACMILLAN™
175 Fifth Avenue, New York, N.Y. 10010 and
Houndmills, Basingstoke, Hampshire, England RG21 6XS
Companies and representatives throughout the world

PALGRAVE MACMILLAN is the global academic imprint of the Palgrave
Macmillan division of St. Martin's Press, LLC and of Palgrave Macmillan Ltd.
Macmillan® is a registered trademark in the United States, United Kingdom
and other countries. Palgrave is a registered trademark in the European
Union and other countries.

ISBN 0–312–29301–1 hardback
ISBN 0–312–29304–6 paperback

Library of Congress Cataloging-in-Publication Data
    Cultures of taste/theories of appetite / [edited] by Timothy Morton.
        p. cm.
    Includes bibliographical references and index.
    ISBN 0–312–29301–1 (hc)—ISBN 0–312–29304–6 (pbk)
      1. Food habits. 2. Food preferences. 3. Taste. 4. Appetite. 5. Food habits
    in literature. 6. Dinners and dining in literature. I. Morton, Timothy, 1968–

    GT2850.C86 2004
    394.1′2—dc22   2003058081

A catalogue record for this book is available from the British Library.

Design by Newgen Imaging Systems (P) Ltd., Chennai, India.

First edition: January, 2004
10 9 8 7 6 5 4 3 2 1

Printed in the United States of America.

Contents

List of Illustrations

Acknowledgments

First and foremost, I would like to thank Denise Gigante for her inspiring and unstinting work on early drafts of this book. Thanks to my superb and varied contributors for their constant attention to their work. My discussions with David Clark have been particularly spirited and I extend my gratitude to him for his warmth and encouragement. I would like to thank the University of Colorado and in particular the Graduate Committee on the Arts and Humanities for their award of a Faculty Fellowship during the academic year 2001–02, during which I had the chance to do major work on this project. I have also been supported by a generous subvention from the Dean's Committee on Excellence to help with reproduction costs. This book was seen into production by the consistent expertise of Kristi Long, Melissa Nosal, Rose Raz, and Ian Steinberg.

An earlier version of Denise Gigante's essay was published in *Romanticism on the Net* (2002) and *Studies in Romanticism* (2001). An earlier version of Tim Fulford's essay was published in *European Romantic Review* (Fall 2000).

I would like to thank David Simpson for his unfailing support and cogent, insightful advice. I am grateful to Jeffrey Cox and the Center for the Humanities and the Arts at CU Boulder for their timely invitation to me to present my work for this volume at their work-in-progress seminar: in particular I would like to thank the participants Bud Coleman, Andrew Cowell, Steven Epstein, Bruce Holsinger, and John Stevenson. I would also like to thank Brad Johnson and Alice den Otter. Jamie Oliver's recipe books provided much of my culinary reading and practice while I was preparing this volume: can I recommend his very fine risottos? Finally, my head and stomach would have come apart long before now if it had not been for the inspiration of my wife Kate, who has worked with me well beyond the call of duty.

Notes on Contributors

PENNY BRADSHAW is Lecturer in English at St. Martin's College, Lancaster. She has published articles on women writers of the Romantic period in *Women's Writing* and *Romanticism on the Net*, and has contributed to *The Encyclopaedia of the Romantic Era, 1760–1850* (forthcoming). She is currently working on a study of nineteenth-century women writers and Unitarianism.

DAVID CLARK is Professor of English Literature at McMaster University. His work includes *Regarding Sedgwick: Essays on Queer Culture and Critical Theory* (2002), *New Romanticisms: Theory and Critical Practice* (1994), and *Intersections: Nineteenth-Century Philosophy and Contemporary Theory* (1994).

TIM FULFORD is a professor at Nottingham Trent University. Among his many books are *Landscape, Liberty and Authority* (1996) and *Romanticism and Masculinity* (1999). He is the coeditor of *Travels, Explorations and Empires*, an eight-volume anthology of travel writing from the period 1770–1830. He has also completed the first scholarly edition of Southey's *Thalaba* and cowritten a study of Romanticism and Imperial Science. Long-term projects include a book on British perceptions of Native Americans.

DENISE GIGANTE, Assistant Professor of English at Stanford, has just completed a book on taste and appetite from Milton through Romanticism, parts of which are available in *diacritics* (2001) and *Studies in Romanticism* (2002).

NICK GROOM is Reader in English Literature and Director of the Centre for Romantic Studies at the University of Bristol. Among his books are *The Making of Percy's Reliques* (1999), *Introducing Shakespeare* (2001), and *The Forger's Shadow: How Forgery Changed the Course of Literature* (2002). He has edited Thomas Chatterton's poems (2003) and Percy's Reliques (forthcoming), and is currently again working on the English ballad tradition.

PETER J. KITSON is Chair of English at the University of Dundee. He is the editor of *Romantic Criticism, 1800–25* (1989) (with T. N. Corns), *Coleridge and the Armoury of the Human Mind: Essays on His Prose Writings* (1991), *Coleridge, Keats and Shelley: Contemporary Critical Essays* (1996) (with Tim Fulford) *Romanticism and Colonialism: Writing and Empire, 1780–1830* (1998), and (with Debbie Lee) *Slavery, Abolition and Emancipation: Writings in the British Romantic Period* (1999). He has published several essays on the relationship between the English and French Revolutions.

PETER MELVILLE recently received his Ph.D. from McMaster University. His publications include recent and forthcoming articles in *European Romantic Review, Mosaic, The Dalhousie Review*, and *Arachne*. He is currently a Social Sciences and Humanities Research Council of Canada postdoctoral fellow at Cornell University.

TIMOTHY MORTON is Professor of Literature and the Environment at the University of California, Davis. He is author of three books on food and eating: *The Poetics of Spice: Romantic Consumerism and the Exotic* (Cambridge, 2000); *Radical Food: The Culture and Politics of Eating and Drinking, 1780–1830* (Routledge, 2000); and *Shelley and the Revolution in Taste: The Body and the Natural World* (Cambridge, 1994). He is also coauthor, with Nigel Smith, of *Radicalism in British Literary Culture, 1650–1830: From Revolution to Revolution* (Cambridge, 2002).

ARKADY PLOTNITSKY is Professor of English and a University Faculty Scholar at Purdue University, where he also directs the Theory and Cultural Studies Program. He is the author of several books and many articles on English and European Romanticism, Continental Philosophy, and the relationships among literature, philosophy, and science. His most recent books are *The Knowable and the Unknowable: Modern Science, Nonclassical Thought, and the "Two Cultures"* (2002), and *Reading Bohr: Physics and Philosophy* (2004). He is currently completing the book entitled *Minute Particulars: Romanticism, Science and Epistemology*.

TILOTTAMA RAJAN is Canada Research Chair in English and Theory at the University of Western Ontario. She is the author of *Dark Interpreter: The Discourse of Romanticism* (1980); *The Supplement of Reading: Figures of Understanding in Romantic Theory and Practice* (1990); and *Deconstruction and the Remainders of Phenomenology: Sartre, Derrida, Foucault, Baudrillard* (2002); the editor of Mary Shelley's *Valperga* (1998); and the coeditor of

Intersections: Nineteenth-Century Philosophy and Contemporary Theory (1995); *Romanticism, History, and the Possibilities of Genre* (Cambridge, 1998); and *After Poststructuralism: Writing the Intellectual History of Theory* (2002). Her further projects include a book on Romantic Narrative, and a book on encyclopedism and interdisciplinarity of which the present essay will form a part.

NICHOLAS ROE's most recent books are *Romanticism: An Oxford Guide* and *Samuel Taylor Coleridge and the Sciences of Life*. He teaches at the University of St. Andrew's.

JANE STABLER is Lecturer in English at the University of Dundee. She is the editor of the *Longman Byron Critical Reader* (1998) and the author of *Burke to Byron, Barbauld to Baillie*, 1790–1830 (2001) and *Byron, Poetics and History* (2002).

PAUL YOUNGQUIST is Associate Professor of English Literature at Penn State University, and writes on British Romanticism, science fiction, and Black music. He is the author of *Monstrosities: Bodies and British Romanticism* (2003) and *Madness and Blake's Myth* (1989).

Preface

The reason the poet in Samuel Taylor Coleridge's "Kubla Khan" becomes taboo in the final stanza is quite simply what the poem says: he is enjoying, and showing the symptoms of it. He is no longer entirely a self-possessed subject. He has consumed, and been consumed by, those Dionysian, ecstatic foods, milk and honey. His eyes do not merely look, passively, but actively "flash." His hair is really enjoying itself, floating like Robert Smith's of the British pop band The Cure. Is this a metaphor for opium intoxication? Is intoxication here a metaphor for poetics? What Coleridge is offering here is the image of a *de-sublimation*. The poet will make a poem about Kubla Khan's pleasure dome—a sublime prospect— but the real reason people are in "dread" of him is his having eaten and drunk. Coleridge was fascinated with states that fall out of the aesthetic.

All too briefly, the kinds of observation I have just made map out the areas that occupy this collection of essays. *Cultures of Taste / Theories of Appetite* is a study of the ways in which food and eating appears in the Romantic period. It casts as wide a net as possible in its attempt to catch different types of literary, philosophical and cultural phenomenon. The essays in this volume are surprisingly wide-ranging: from deconstrution to historicism, from cultural criticism to close reading.

Cultures of Taste / Theories of Appetite contributes both to literary theoretical and cultural-historical approaches to literature. In doing so it breaks with the habit in contemporary criticism of drawing boundaries between these areas of sudy, as is visible in the various panel titles and personnel of conferences on the Romantic period. This rich, varied collection is of value simply for the range of scholars that it has grouped together. It is, however, more than that. As the scholars assmbled here cross various disciplinary boundaries, a startling picture emerges of the many ways in which food and eating was not simply an empirical reality in the Romantic period, but a mixture of ideas, practices, figures, debates, and philosphical speculations.

In developing the current negotiation between philosophical and historical approaches to literature, this volume does not resolve contradictions so much as illuminate their tensions and paradoxes. This collection is more than a medley of essays on food, a merely haphazard arrangement. On the other hand, to theorize is not necessarily to integrate under a single rubric. Walter Benjamin has shown how collage and juxtaposition can have surprising, helpful effects. For Theodor Adorno "A successful work, from the perspective of imminent criticism, is not one which resolves objective contradictions in a spurious harmony, but one which expresses the idea of harmony negatively by embodying contradictions, pure and uncompromised, in its innermost structure."[1] It is a pity that the finely nuanced Marxism of the Frankfurt School is so little taken up in post-structuralism, as Michel Foucault himself complained.[2] Despite the export of post-structuralism from English Departments into the humanities and even the social sciences at large, history has not fully attended to the material and the physical in Marx, Nietzsche, and Freud.[3] Studies in the history and culture of food have meanwhile often taken refuge in the magical realness of food as a holdout against theory, thus establishing an opposition between empiricism and "theory."

The collision between philosophy and history is a symptom of the period investigated in this book. Let us look briefly and directly. The figure of the Prince Regent embodies the productive asymmetry between taste and appetite. Alan Bewell noted in his study of dietary figures that he is *the* consumer of the 1790s.[4] The Regent is often portrayed in ways that emphasize the bodily aspect of appetite. Richard Davenport-Hines observed that this man put laudanum in his breakfast along with beef and pigeon pie, white wine, champagne, and brandy.[5] But look at his face: he is lost in speculation, or not. Is it contemplation or dyspepsia? To what extent *is* contemplation itself a form of dyspepsia? What kinds of dyspepsia—the hunger of the workers for example—are ignored by a mild, overstuffed, contemplative gaze? James Gillray's cartoon shoves thought awkwardly against the physical world.

To have bourgeois taste is to know how to recoil in horror. Where is the horror in *A Voluptuary Under the Horrors of Digestion*? The Regent is not himself experiencing revulsion. The horror is in the eyes of the middle-class consumer who cannot quite match his aristocratic rites of consumption. The wistful contemplation in the Regent's eye more nicely suits a Romantic poet than a tyrannical gourmand. It was an awkward wistfulness for a radical such as Shelley, keen in his own dietary habits to differentiate himself from this kind of body image; or Byron, whose diet of lettuce and

James Gillray, *A Voluptuary under the Horrors of Digestion* (London, 1792). Copyright the British Museum, London.

vinegar was designed to stave off the fat and attract the ladies. In Tenniel's illustration to Lewis Carroll's "The Walrus and the Carpenter" the walrus is weeping and contemplating the sentience of oysters precisely at the moment at which he has devoured them. Philosophy bites.

Food enabled Gillray's satire to cut in different directions. In *Temperance Enjoying a Frugal Meal*, he placed the Regent's father next to a boiled egg and a copy of the writings of George Cheyne, vegetarian doctor to Samuel Richardson. Is George III being compared with his son lovingly or contemptuously? Are diet books being mocked, or is Cheyne there as a politicized admonition? It gets a little easier to read things in *French Liberty and British Slavery*: in typical Burkean manner, Gillray juxtaposes French theory with British organicism, a starving carrot-eater with a plump John Bull. Gillray's cartoons exemplify the reified ways in which his society tried to think mind and body, theory and history. Moreover the issue of reification itself revolves around ideas and practices of food and eating. The study of sensibility has produced detailed accounts of the history of the physiology of nerves but frequently imagines its field as a scene of classical epistemology. The view of the body as bombarded by sense data could become a form of reification reproducing an asymmetrical world of subjects coming to know objects.

To summarize this volume is a trepidatious task indeed: there are so many different guests at this symposium. Normatively empiricist histories of food jostle awkwardly with cultural materialist studies seeking to explore the ideological comportment of eating. The study of eating in philosophy traces how eating complicates such basic metaphysical assumptions as the difference between an inside and an outside—something every oyster should ponder as it slips down the throat of a sentimental poet. The introduction establishes two parameters for examining food and eating: the performative idea of "consumerism" (a role emerging in the Romantic period), and a structuralist model that lays bare four sets of binary oppositions pertaining to specific representations of food and eating in the period.

It has not been easy to divide the essays into subgroups, but for the sake of clarity in indicating the volume's major concerns, I have separated them into three parts. Part I, "Constructions, Simulations, Cultures" features those essays that most strongly indicate trends that we would associate with culture—broadly understood as the context in which texts may be read, whether literary or not. Here the reader will find Nick Groom's pioneering work on fish and chips as a construct of the Romantic imagination. Before the railways brought potatoes from Lancashire to London and fish in the opposite direction in the 1840s, this simulated-English meal had been imagined in poetic language. Indeed, Groom establishes that fish and chips symbolized the French Revolution. Timothy Fulford analyzes the figuration of breadfruit in colonial language about the South Sea Islands. In delineating the particular ideological landscape of those islands in the British colonial imaginary, Fulford reveals that "Romantic nature first took shape not at home but in the distant tropics of the mind" (49). This idea of nature was palpable, sensual, and focused upon the breadfruit as a

James Gillray, *Temperance Enjoying a Frugal Meal* (London, 1792). Copyright the British Museum, London.

symbol of the racialized innocence that the colonial project constructed. Penny Bradshaw furthers the investigation of the sociopolitical implications of food by showing how Charlotte Smith uses food imagery to relate consumerism and consumer values more closely to the development of a market economy. Peter J. Kitson investigates Romantic representations of cannibalism. Kitson's essay engages with the anthropological cultural criticism of current scholars, such as Nicholas Thomas, and examines how late eighteenth- and early nineteenth-century concepts of "race" were informed by discussion of eating and diet. Specifically Kitson shows how the Enlightenment classification of the peoples of Oceania into the divisions of Polynesian and Melanesian was interwoven with an assessment of such peoples' practice of or tendency to anthropophagy. For Kitson, Byron's late poem *The Island*, which depicts a fictionalized version of the Bounty mutiny, is complicit in this politics of diet and demonisation in the "South Seas" of the European scientific and cultural imagination.

Nicholas Roe's study of foot and mouth disease shows how the culture that grew up around the recent epidemic in Britain had strong Romantic overtones. Roe discovers the lineages of a suburban pastoral aesthetic that depends upon figures of food and eating, of H. P. Sauce and Heinz Ketchup, for its ironic effects. One of these ironies is the simultaneous presence and absence of extreme violence toward animals and industrial farming techniques that are carefully managed in preserving an image of English pastoral. The very countryside of Britain is shaped by figures of food and eating.

Part II is entitled "Waiter, There's a Trope in My Soup: Close Readings." It is a selection of varied ways in which a close attention to Romantic-period texts can yield striking and surprising results in the field of diet studies. I have deliberately chosen here to make no distinction as to whether it is specifically literature or philosophy that is being close-read. I believe that in doing so this collection is not only in line with the postmodern or deconstructive approaches to the text such as Jacques Derrida's, but also to interdisciplinary cultural studies that mix history, literature, and philosophy. David Clark opens the section with a fine-grained reading of figures of meat-eating and masculinity in Hegel. His essay proceeds by identifying the ways in which Schelling engaged Hegel's idealism, which like the omnivorous vacuum cleaner in the Beatles film *Yellow Submarine*, sucks up everything in its way. Jane Stabler reads closely the poetry of Byron, discovering that poet's particular engagement with figures of milk and blood, and his interest in generic and literal mixed dishes. These figures have wide implications in cultural representations of diet in the Romantic period. Finally, Arkady Plotnitsky's essay on Keats and Shelley examines the significance of the idea and imagery of excessive consumption in their late poetry. This examination leads him to consider the extent to which their poetic engagement with excessive consumption causes problems for normative ideas of the sublime and of literature itself.

Part III, "Disgust, Digestion, Thought," accounts for the ways in which eating appears in, and falls out of, Romantic philosophy. For example, it can be shown that the idea of the aesthetic is subtended by disgust at the idea of appetite. This disgust is as it were the little piece of grit that irritates philosophy into making the pearl of the aesthetic. Disgust is thus both "inside" and "outside" the realm of what counts as proper philosophy. Eating not only troubles the neat boundaries of speculative thought—it produces them. Denise Gigante opens this section with a detailed account of the figure of disgust in Romantic literature. Through the study of allusion, her essay boldly associates the work of Keats with that of Sartre and Beckett. Peter Melville's essay on Kant's view of group eating is a queer theory close reading, a valuable contribution to our understanding of that philosopher's figuration of what it means to inhabit a community. Tilottama Rajan's essay on Hegel focuses upon the idea of digestion, exploring the relationship between the idealist Hegel and materialist philosophy. This leads to a discussion of ideas about the "constitution" of bodies in Hegel and in materialist science, giving rise to an even wider analysis of the idea of disease in Romantic literature and culture. Paul Younquist investigates the ways in which Mary Wollstonecraft's writing is formed and deformed by ideas about digestion. To this task he brings the long history of modern thinking on digestion and excretion, from John Locke onward.

The Afterword outlines the range and scope of the study of food and eating, focusing upon the specific conditions that affect the study of the Romantic period. It develops the idea of a broad and critical approach to this kind of scholarship: "diet studies." It makes a case for the value of studying the interrelated issues of materialism and ideology.

Notes

1. Theodor Adorno, "Cultural Criticism and Society," in *Prisms* (Cambridge, Mass.: MIT Press, 1981), 32.
2. Michel Foucault, *Politics, Philosophy, Culture: Interviews and Other Writings, 1977–1984*, tr. Alan Sheridan and others, ed. Lawrence D. Kritzman (New York: Routledge, 1988), 27.
3. See David Simpson, *The Academic Postmodern and the Rule of Literature: A Report on Half-Knowledge* (Chicago and London: Chicago UP, 1995).
4. Alan Bewell, *Romanticism and Colonial Disease* (Baltimore: Johns Hopkins UP, 2000), 132.
5. I am grateful to Denise Gigante for discussing this with me. See Richard Davenport-Hines, *The Pursuit of Oblivion: A Global History of Narcotics 1500–2000* (London: Weidenfeld, 2001).

Introduction ∽

CONSUMPTION AS PERFORMANCE: THE EMERGENCE OF THE CONSUMER IN THE ROMANTIC PERIOD

Timothy Morton

ousseau's phrase, misattribued to a condescending Marie Antoinette, "Let them eat cake!"; the food riots precipitated in England during the wartime embargo;[1] the fact that Napoleon and Wellington had meals named after them; all indicate the diverse significance of food in the Romantic period. All periods have their styles of eating, their table manners, their preferred dishes and styles of recipe writing.[2] But when we consider what in the realm of food and diet defines the period between the American Revolution and the passing of the Reform Act we begin to notice significant patterns and structures. One of the culinary creations of that era, the French fry, is still politicized. Before the invasion of Iraq in 2003, the American congress, angry at what they saw as betrayal by the French at the United Nations and inspired by actions in the southern states, renamed their restaurant's French fries "freedom fries." Charlotte Smith's novel *Desmond*, the subject of Penny Bradshaw's essay in this volume (chapter 4), remarks on the politics of fried fish, sister of the French fry. Early in the novel, the conversation between two reactionary English gentlemen about French manners is in part an attack on fried fish.[3]

By the Romantic period "the consumer" had been born as an economic subject, and as a style of individuality. Neil McKendrick, John Brewer and J. H. Plumb have demonstrated the rise of consumer society throughout the eighteenth century, charting the growth of an "unprecedented propensity to consume": "the first of the world's consumer societies had unmistakably emerged by 1800."[4] After 1750 a quarter of all English families had incomes between £50 and 400, and between 1785 and 1800 the consumption of excised commodities in mass demand increased twice as fast as the population; a democratization of consumption that generated a broad increase in spending (24, 29). One could take this notion too far: other social forces were in play. For example, the rise in the price of meat meant that the working class risked deterioration. In the seventeenth century the high price of bread was not vitally important to the lower classes: they lived on other sorts of cheap food and occupied the land. But now, as William Godwin observed, they could hardly afford meat, while tea and white bread had become necessities.[5]

It became possible to take various consumer and literary positions within emerging consumer society. Although diet is not listed in the index of Colin Campbell's *The Romantic Ethic and the Spirit of Modern Consumerism* one can use as a template his performative model of different forms of consumer identity.[6] Observing that imitative behavior is not necessarily emulative, Campbell qualifies Thorstein Veblen's influential thesis that the lower classes only emulate upper class acts of "conspicuous consumption," as if what we find in research on consumption are merely trickle-down effects.[7] Consumption was performance (45), a selection of choices and acts from a repertoire of roles. Performativity implies different styles, and more: in the Romantic period the notion of consumption as performance became reflexive, generating such specific roles as that of the bohemian, a consumer who consumes for the sake of experiencing some general essence of consumption itself (52–5).

Along with bohemianism Campbell identifies three others: sensibility— the maintenance of one's good name through a fusion of ethics and aesthetics (48–9); aristocracy—a nonchalant style of all-round accomplishment which nevertheless eschews sensuousness because of its connotations of femininity (49–51); and dandyism—peudo-aristocratic refinements of extreme self-control. It is the hedonism of the Romantic, reflexive, bohemian style which Campbell identifies as having spawned modern forms of consumption. Significantly, this bohemian style is not emulative. The ways in which Romantic writers such as Keats, a reflexive consumer if ever there was one, represented such items as spice, often associated with luxury and aristocracy, take on fresh, ironic, and sometimes subversive meanings.[8] Reflexivity can carry a critical charge. Moreover this is where the study of poetics can be superadded to Campbell's view. As window shoppers, we are now all potential De Quinceys, Baudelaires, flâneurs.

Someone could *be* a consumer, highlighting their role in the theater of consumption through self-reflection. Thomas Love Peacock wrote about "the consumer" in *Melincourt* through the person of Mr. Forester. This Shelleyan figure opposes the consumption of sugar that supports the slave trade. The choice *not* to consume was in itself a self-reflexive way of defining oneself as a consumer:

> I never suffer an atom of West Indian produce to pass my threshold. I have no wish to resemble those pseudo-philanthropists...who are very liberal of words which cost them nothing...If I wish seriously to exterminate an evil, I begin by examining how far I am myself...an accomplice in the extension of its baleful influence. My reform begins at home...How can I seriously call myself an enemy to slavery, while I indulge in the luxuries that slavery acquires? How can the consumer of sugar pretend to throw on the grower of it the burden of their participated criminality? How can he wash his hands, and say with Pilate: "*I am innocent of this blood, see ye to it?*"[9]

Mr. Forester is not just a figment of Peacock's imagination, nor indeed of Percy Shelley's. His language echoes the Bluestockings, William Fox, and Samuel Taylor Coleridge, who had proposed boycotting sugar to end slavery, as Sidney Mintz, Charlotte Sussman and myself have noted. Robert Southey wrote sonnets on the subject; not to mention the slaves themselves, whose poetic forms pitted the artifice of sugar against an organicist notion of what we would now think of as "soul food."[10] As Keith Sandiford has shown, sugar in the Romantic period crystallized a range of cultural and political forms.[11]

Mr. Forester joins an "Anti-Saccharine Society" of like-minded consumers (65); an Anti-Saccharine fête is held (volume 2, chapter 17). Peacock's use of "the consumer" is a hair's breadth away from its more recent semantic range as an economic category. The cynical Sir Telegraph sums up the Romantic posture of consumer politics, whereby the sense of subjective power is in inverse proportion to objective impotence, the feeling that Caspar David Friedrich evokes in depictions of Romantic gentlemen surveying a vast cloudy chasm. In this case the chasm is capitalist production. "I may do that," declares Sir Telegraph, speaking of giving up sugar to benefit the cause, "without any great effort of virtue" (65). Similar feelings confront "green" consumers today. Will buying organic food save the planet? Sidney Mintz has observed that choice was simultaneously broadened and narrowed in this theater of consumption.[12] Such notions of choice, giving rise to utopian "dreams of satisfaction," indicated social deadlocks as well as possibilities (271).

We should add to Cambpell's list reflexive working-class consumption. Their demand for red meat and fine white bread, as opposed to potatoes, represented a desire not only for satisfaction but also for respect, and indeed for a radical revision of those social structures that inhibited such satisfaction and respect. In London, as Roger Wells declares, "White bread, like printed cotton-clothes, enabled the poor to challenge the wealthy's consumerist monopoly."[13] This was a function of what E. P. Thompson called "the moral economy of the crowd," a set of traditions and social norms that generated the food riots of the 1790s.[14] Regarding meat, "The working-class housewife not only wanted to buy [it]; she wanted to be seen shopping in the shambles" (20). Indeed, there were working-class campaigns against sugar. The black transatlantic activist Robert Wedderburn, author of *The Axe Laid to the Root*, advocated nonviolent revolution and radically recontextualized "The Slaves, an Elegy": "The drops of blood, the horrible manure / That fills with luscious juice the teeming can[e]."[15] Such facts put paid to simplistic and classist Bourdeauian models of "Kantian" and "non-Kantian" forms of consumption. For Kantian, read middle and upper class; for non-Kantian, the working class: it is not only the upper classes who can be reflexive.

Henry Hunt's "Radical Breakfast Powder" demonstrates further the period's politicization of diet. Based on roasted corn, it was recommended as a substitute for tea or coffee: a way of boycotting taxed foods. The mouth became a barricade: "Now that we are deprived of arms, the revenue is the only effectual manner in which we can overthrow the junto by whom we are so miserably enth[r]alled."[16] Aesthetic pleasure is raised to a height of politicized concretion. The underground publisher Richard Carlile liked the breakfast powder but commented that it was not as good as coffee "further than as a war upon revenue."[17] What price resistance?

> there are many grasses and herbs in this country that make an excellent tea if carefully gathered and dried. The common meadow hay is . . . preferable to the roasted grain, to make a beverage pleasant and nutritious, where the mind can be raised above the prejudice of habit. Those who love milk, butter, and cheese, need not feel a prejudice towards the use of grass or hay; whatever is nutritious in the former, is scarce any thing but a chemical solution of the latter. (12)

Carlile's use of "common" compresses two senses. It evokes class weakness and oppression: the reduction of diet to basic survival instincts, cattle food. But "common" also metonymically suggests the common land. Carlile's wit, mixing pedantry and outrage in a vegetarian inversion of Swift's cannibalistic "Modest Proposal," is based in his understanding of radical diet.

He praised vegetarianism in a review of Percy Shelley's popularly pirated radical didactic poem, *Queen Mab*, whose passage on vegetarianism included a call for politicized abstinence; such politicizations were the reason why Joseph Ritson's republican atheist vegetarianism was lambasted in the reactionary *Edinburgh Review*.[18,19]

Following Keith Thomas's *Man and the Natural World* Stephen Mennell sketched the long history that contributed to the flourishing of a truly popular vegetarianism in the Romantic period (304–10). Desires to abstain from cruelty to animals and humans were articulated as claims to encompass a wider circle of social inclusion. Vegetarianism's medical benefits were also a social issue. Modernity and capitalism encroached upon the body and consumption; people started wanting to hone their body image. The permanent revolutionary quality of capitalist productive forces demands lean and mean, flexible members of the workforce who are capable of being hired and fired at a stroke. Foucault would have made much of the desire expressed by prison reformers to feed prisoners vegetarian food. The Jacobin Robert Pigot situated himself to the left of John Howard, who had advocated vegetarianism for prisoners: prevention was better than cure.[20] But in prison, those incarcerated should be kept from alcohol ("liquid fire") and "any kind of animal food or flesh, as further means to soften their hardened character, and render it more mild and sensible; but [place] them on that wholesome and natural regimen of bread, water, and vegetables, as the only means to restore them to their lost senses and knowledge of their crimes."[21] The circle of inclusion could become one of surveillance and pacification. General John "Walking" Stewart, who cured his gangrene on a diet of roast apples and bread, advocated vegetarianism as part of an enlightened but counter-revolutionary regime: "Nations, or the whole species of mankind, must ultimately sympathize with their fellow-beings the brute species; for while cruelty and violence of any kind is inflicted in this wide relation of self, there can be no peace or repose for human nature."[22] A self-educated poet who traveled in Asia, Africa, and North America, Stewart held soirées for a variety of progressive publishers, philosophers, and writers.

There is yet another dialectical twist in the cultural logic of vegetarianism. The increasingly global view promulgated by capitalism—even by the Romantic period—encouraged a greater environmental awareness. Lest we assume that this awareness simply pertains to a natural world "outside" society we should observe that vegetarian arguments indicated how human domination of nature could affect the "inside" of the human body and mind. Percy Shelley addresses "exhalations from chemical processes" and "the pollutions of man and his inventions" as medical problems in his vegetarian prose: problems, in other words, which affect the interior of organisms.[23] The discourses of diet connected interior and exterior. Since the circle of inclusion-surveillance could include chemical processes and tropical diseases—both encountered as risks because of advancing social processes—one could argue that a higher level of surveillance established a more comprehensive form of social critique. Historically detailed forms of ecocritical analysis could interanimate arguments hitherto pigeonholed among historical and philosophical forms of criticism.

Vegetarianism was a specifically *Romantic* ideological practice. Middle-class reformist and radical responses to the culture of luxury, based upon the surpluses accumulated during the gigantic wave of commercial capitalist expansion throughout the long eighteenth century, developed temperate forms of consumption and/or "Romantic" forms of consumerism that challenged or parodied the official forms of nascent consumerism. Percy Shelley, ideologically tied to upper-class reformism while supporting more radical kinds of social change, posited vegetarianism as a critical practice, at once expressing and subverting forms of social meaning. The vegetarian body was like the paper money he despised elsewhere: light, easily exchangeable, empty of the symbolic trappings of feudal power. In this sense, vegetarianism is on the cutting edge of capitalist ideology. But vegetarianism also belonged to more radical forms of praxis among the emergent working class. The vegetarian visionary Richard Brothers reimagined Eden as a public park in a millenarian state.[24]

Vegetarianism also persisted in religious discourse in the lineage of the radical seventeenth century. Behmenism, the Diggers and other formations had envisioned a sacred world. Mennell has demonstrated influence of Puritanism on British cooking.[25] The ideological determinations of anthropology, from Montaigne's "Des Cannabales" onward, was another aspect of the inconsistent kernel of vegetarian fantasies. Anthropology rewrote the rules of historiography: synchronic, profane, concerned with the low rather than the high, with family structures and diet rather than with kings and battles.[26] Some vegetables, however, could make one feel more equal than others. To borrow Igor Kopytoff's term meat was an "enclaved" marker of cultural value, used in the ideology of John Bull and the Roast Beef of Old England, a figure with a genealogy in the early eighteenth century in writers such as John Arbuthnot.[27] The pamphlet *Rare News for Old England! Beef a Shilling a Pound!* declared that the government was attempting to starve the potentially revolutionary people. When they tried this on the French, they simply made bread out of "*rotten wood* and *soap lather*" and soup out of "old hats and shoes."[28] Wage increases encouraged the working class to consume meat but *per capita* consumption probably fell from 1790 to 1840.[29] Charles Pigott's *Political Dictionary*, for the publication of which Daniel Isaac Eaton was imprisoned, contains this entry: "*Famine*—For the existence of this word, we are indebted to the *magnanimous* exploits of CONQUERORS and KINGS" (28). In this light "natural diet" appeals to a conceptual bonding with the poor. Later in the nineteenth century, vegetarianism settled more comfortably within the rhetoric of bourgeois humanitarianism. Henry Salt established a humanitarian and environmental legacy for Shelley's writing about diet, to some extent detaching it from its more urgent and radical class associations.[30]

Let us consider one vegetable in particular. R. N. Salaman and Catherine Gallager have explored the social history and semiotic connotations of the potato in the Romantic period.[31] Pigot argued in their favor, along with other grains, in a French address that sought to circumvent the predominance of bread—a sensible political move in a time of English Corn Laws; Pigot praises Irish and Scots non-wheat diets.[32] English radical representations were more negative. *The Black Dwarf* contained a poetic letter *From a Potatoe to a Sirloin of Beef*:

> DEAR SIRLOIN, (For spite of the fashion and state
> Which has kept you from all your old comrades of late
> You are still *dear* to us,) I have taken my pen
> To implore you to visit our hovels again.
> . . .
>
> If you like just to come in the old fashioned mood
> To the cottage of industry, all well and good:
> Sam says if you *won't*, why he'll stick like a Cato,
> To Freedom, a crust, and
> Your Friend, A POTATOE.[33]

The reply from "Sir Loin" simultaneously removes meat from the reach of the working class while banishing the potato, thus giving vent to the contradictory pains of being someone who cannot afford the former and despises the latter:

> So my good friend Potato, if *friend* you must be,
> You had better return to your home d' ye see!
> From Brazil, I think it is said you was [*sic*] brought,
> To where with your ancient formality fraught,
> Go and teach humble slaves on your favour to dine,
> But never think more to approach a SIRLOIN. (1.588)

The idealized fantasy meat of the working classes, here personified as their noble champion, defeats the ideological and real root of government domination. The products of agriculture serve as the very figures of class fantasy. We may thus confirm Slavoj Žižek's theory that the social real is incarnated in fantasy, and that the critical task is tracing these fantasies and isolating those substances that cause fantasy to resonate, the better to undermine the ideology they inconsistently substantiate. The potato was a figurative readymade that could be engaged in various fantasy forms, as Nick Groom shows.

Diet studies must account for the role of gender. Sarah Moss is investigating the ways in which gender and social status figured in the representation of food in Romantic-period novels.[34] In an essay on women's reading practices and radicalism in the long eighteenth century, Sussman relates certain styles of silent reading to the emergence of coffee houses and the eating and fasting practices of women prophets and antislavery groups.[35] The modern association between vegetarianism and femininity—for instance warmth toward the natural world—is only part of the picture. Queer theory could reinterpret Thomas Trotter's vegetarian medical work. Trotter attacks the risks to masculinity posed by capitalist modernity. Worrying like Edward Gibbon about the modern state's integrity, Trotter asks "could an army of man-milliners defend the British islands against the ruffians of Bonaparte?"[36] Trotter sees a decadent Stock Exchange based on fantasy as a cause of fear and hypochondria (165, 156–7, 147). Modern sexual relations are too highly mediated, tortuous and feminized (9, 33). Later, J. H. Kellogg devised vegetarian corn flakes in part to assuage the masturbatory feminization of boys.

The British ruling class, in Marx's words, fed like a vampire upon the other class. The figure's genealogy is the "blood sugar" topos of Romantic-period antislavery poetry: "Capital is dead labour which, vampire-like lives only by sucking living labour, and lives the more, the more it sucks."[37] The asymmetry between the voracious disembodied appetite for otherness of universalizing consumerism, and the particularized life of actual human cultures, reproduces that between the classes. Daniel Isaac Eaton published *The History of a Good Bramin*, a text of universal reason in which nations scorn each other for their diet: a domino theory of cultural difference in which dung-eating Brahmins castigate meat-eating Europeans.[38] "The consumer" was Janus-faced. On the one hand tremendous empowerment is reflected in the idea of boycotting. In refusing to eat sugar or meat or consume alcohol, vegetarians and antislavery activists in the period thought they were making a point, performing a certain kind of consumerist script. On the other hand the reduction of the subject of the social structure to the increasingly quantitative subject of economics, "the consumer," fails fully to encapsulate other forms of social performance.

Dietary Representation

Diet scholarship is currently questioning approaches based on structural anthropology. Campbell wishes to replace a purely semiotic model with one attuned to various consumer roles, and must thus negotiate a difficult but fruitful line between autonomous un-authored signs and notions of full intentional subjects existing prior to history. The method of sorting things into binaries is itself a feature of the discourses of luxury and necessity; the bourgeois subject becomes like a Spenserian knight, relentlessly distinguishing between true and false, acceptable and unacceptable. Nevertheless, antique as they are, semiotic models can serve the interests of clarity. Let us consider, then, the following sets of categories as the repertoire from which performances of consumption could draw: excess and discipline; production and consumption; marked and unmarked; near and far.

Excess and Discipline

This is Georges Bataille's contrast between restricted and general economy, between systems that are self-contained and those that are not. It is also the bourgeois choice between freedom and unfreedom, conceived and practiced often as the restriction of the body in the name of the mind's liberty: asceticism, the category into which the aesthetic collapses in the vegetarian prose of Schopenhauer. Such figurations was common among middle-class representations, though the artisanal class, keen to hone its image, could also fall into this axis.

Discourses of taste appear along this axis. Distinctions resonate between fat and lean—radical asceticism and Regency rioting. The excesses of the Regent were constantly satirized.[39] Many predicted famine in Ireland if the potato monoculture were to persist.[40] Famines in England—though some writers balk at describing them as such—arose from the combination of nature and culture in the shape of crop failures and the corn laws.[41] Marx's history of colonialism and imperialism accounts for the "inexhaustible mines" of capital potential in opium and other exotic products: his metaphor depicts a world open to the hungry maw of business.[42] Marx establishes that "Between 1769 and 1770, the English created a famine [in India] by buying up all the rice and refusing to sell it again, except at fabulous prices" (917). Mike Davis's *Victorian Holocausts* examines the ways in which imperialism affected Indian starvation rates.[43]

Aesthetic discipline has a history. Early in *Ars Poetica*, Horace enjoins, "Medea must not butcher her children in the presence of the audience, nor the monstrous Atreus cook his dish of human flesh within public view... I shall turn in disgust from anything of this kind that you show me."[44] William King's *The Art of Cookery* (1709) translated Horace into English and into the kitchen with detailed instructions on presentation. As in the case of carving, monstrosity now had a (hidden) place.

De Quincey was consuming opium and writing about it, turning his own text into an addictive vortex, parodying both Coleridge and Wordsworth. For De Quincey, Thomas Trotter, and Robert MacNish, another writer on alcohol, addiction was new territory. As the nineteenth century continued, the role of the addict joined the repertoire of consumer performances. According to Virginia Berridge and Griffith Edwards, it was formulated at around the same time as the category of homosexuality.[45] Like homosexual identity, addiction tied paradoxical knots in old progressive notions of free choice. As Eve Sedgwick puts it, "From being the *subject* of her own perceptual manipulations or indeed experimentations, she is installed as the proper *object* of compulsory institutional disciplines, legal and medical, which, without actually being able to do anything to 'help' her, nonetheless presume to know her better than she can know herself."[46] To be stigmatized as an addict is to be imprisoned in a biologically determined role. Joshua Wilner has explored De Quincey's painful slippage from subject to object.[47] Anya Taylor's pioneering work on Romantic-period drinking shows how, without the category of addiction, drinkers could distinguish themselves from effeminate dandies precisely in their capacity for masculine choices.[48] Percy Shelley asserts that abstaining both from meat and alcohol will render the subject more capable of cool reflection and rational decision making (*Vindication* 10–12).

Immanuel Kant distinguished aesthetic beauty from the "spicy." Spice is a linking point in the third critique. Kant focuses upon the idea of taste as discipline. Spicy food resembles the beautiful, but not much: it is like beauty but too cheap, too corny. It evokes not a contemplative liking but something more active: we *want* to eat. Spice does however have an unreasonable uselessness about it which allies with the beautiful proper: it appeals to our senses but not to our reason, as when we consider, as Kant nicely puts it, the "consequences" of a spicy meal.[49] Kant associates spice with such undetermined aesthetic phenomena as "Flowers, free designs, lines aimlessly intertwined and called foliage: these have no significance, depend on no determinate concept, and yet we like ... them" (49). There is no clearer picture of Romantic consumption than this. For the middle class, not preoccupied with emulating the aristocracy but lumbered with their codes, spice—and supplements, and supplementarity in general—was a perennial problem.

How should one—should one—consume such irrational meaningless signifiers? Kant's aesthetics, a discipline for training the middle-class mind and body, encounters not only the obstacle of the disgusting and tasteless, but also the useless and supplementary. The excess of sheer flavor is not subject to rational explanation: "if our sole aim were enjoyment, it would be foolish to be scrupulous about the means for getting it" (50).

Production and Consumption

This pair includes the body in pain and pleasure. We could understand the production/consumption binary in terms of transformation, as metabolism. Consider the vegetarian demonstrative rhetoric of slaughter and butchery, and the subsequent forensic rhetoric of "silent eloquence"; and "blood sugar," the crasis of slave blood and tea sugar in sentimental antislavery writing. Production and consumption combine two categories that Lévi-Strauss prizes apart: raw and cooked, sweet and sour. A similar poetics could emerge around the contemporary use of slaves in chocolate production.

In a shockingly novel metaphor, William Fox's best-selling pamphlet against slavery equates sugar consumption with the drinking of the blood of slaves. Fox renders this reality with the chilling language of mathematical proportion, evidence of how commercial capitalism divided scenes of production from scenes of consumption. In this environment the feminized consumer could be upset by bland mathematical discourse with its transparent equals sign: for every pound of sugar two ounces of human flesh are consumed.[50] Violent juxtaposition illuminates the realm in which blood and sugar are equivalent—capitalism. A modern poetics of *ambience*, of describing a medium or atmosphere, emerges both in the poetics of capitalism, for instance in eighteenth-century trade panegyrics, and in anti-capitalist rhetoric. Here is Coleridge:

> if the inspired Philanthropist of Galilee were to revisit earth and be among the feasters as at Cana he would...convert the produce into the things producing...Then with our fleshly eye should we behold what even now truth-painting Imagination should exhibit to us—instead of sweetmeats Tears and Blood, and Anguish—and instead of Music groaning and the loud Peals of the Lash.[51]

The slaves appear only as drops of liquid and as breath. The impersonal ambience is a negative picture of the alienation and exploitation of actual people, a monstrous version of Hegel's dark night of sheer identity in which bloody heads swim around undigested, like the floating butcher's shop of Blake's calculating Urizen.[52] The only thing permitted an identity in this perverted medium is capital itself. It can flow around the globe: "The treasures captured outside Europe by undisguised looting, enslavement and murder flowed back to the mother-country and were turned into capital there" (*Capital* 1.918).

Vegetarian rhetoric, appearing since Thomas Tryon alongside antislavery language, shows the silencing of the suffering body and its subsequent guilt-inducing eloquence.[53] The literary precedent is Ovid's description of the rape of Philomela, her enforced silence (her tongue is cut out) and the pictographic eloquence with which she indicts King Tereus. John Oswald's *The Cry of Nature* figures the inarticulate but eloquent animal suffering, a sentimentalized empiricism: facts "spoke" in invisible writing, as if engraved on their insides with a bar code.[54] The learned *Cry of Nature* combined Hindu spiritualism with David Hartley's psychological theory of associationism. Oswald interprets a hymn to Rama as portraying the "felicity of the golden age." "The Hindoo...beholds in every creature, a kinsman" in a kinship born of sympathetic vibrations: "may we learn to recognize and to respect in other animals the feelings which vibrate on ourselves."[55] Orientalized Hinduism encounters Adam Smith's *Theory of Moral Sentiments*.

Marked and Unmarked

This is associated with the perennial bourgeois political–economic opposition between luxury and necessity, the special and the generic. The "foodiness" of food, its status *as* food, falls into this category. On the one hand the poetics of spice denotes capitalist value as food in a cunning mix of generic and special (*species* is the etymological root both of *specie* and *spice*). On the other hand the liberal use of "spice" in poetic description denotes no specific flavor, figuring as it were the flavor of the general. By the Romantic period, this rhetoric had become capitalist kitsch. The marked/unmarked axis opposes genuine and fake. One could accuse vegetarian writers of a strategic form of what Derrida calls "carnologocentrism," elevating meat into a transcendental signifier: in subverting this false god, vegetarianism bestows "marked" status upon it; conversely, vegetarian society would remain unmarked by symptoms of violence and the violence of the symptom.

In the Romantic period alum frequently thinned out flour. The issue of adulteration was politically sensitive: the working class was demanding fine white bread instead of the potatoes they were being forced to eat.

The flyleaf of Friedrich Accum's chemical and medical treatise on adulterations features a spider, an old symbol for textuality lurking amidst a web framed or encircled by not one but *eight* amphisbaenas. The snakes are symbols both of medicine (Hermes' Caduceus) and of poison. The image encapsulates the uncertainty and anxiety around food in modern society. This is the logic of what Derrida has called the pharmakon, the ambiguous Greek term for a scapegoat, combining both medicine and poison. Molloy's sucking stones, analyzed in Denise Gigante's study of Beckett and Sartre as inheritors of the Romantic problematic of taste and appetite, resemble what appeared in the period as a cure for cancer: mineral water. For William Lambe, Shelley's vegetarian doctor, water with a trace of stone in it is as neutral, natural, and unmarked as one could wish: the height of good taste, for it does not have one. There are no zero degrees of diet, no pure foods, *pace* the Hare Krishnas and their idea of sattvic food. Mineral water (Lambe recommends Malvern, still commercially available) combined the categories of "raw," "lean," "plain," and "genuine."[56]

Genuine and fake, natural and unnatural, figure in Samuel Jackson Pratt's *Bread*. Bread was a bone of ideological contention: the staff of life ("Give us this day our daily bread") and a working class fantasy object. Pratt's medievalism is a post–Agricultural Revolution lament for a lost Eden.[57] The extreme discrepancy between rich and poor is figured through diet (41). In a feudal idyll reminiscent of what Chaucer says about the rain of meat in the Franklin's house, the fake cottages of the *nouveaux riches* are stuffed with "cherry-bounce," "Hung beef," "relish," "tempting brawn," "rich *Noyaux*" (44). Pratt includes a premonition of the famine that threatened England in 1813. He imagines capitalism as a "paper-kite" that can easily get carried away on the currents, a clever imaging of paper money (56). Food becomes a gravitational attractor toward an earthy organicism in opposition to capitalism's ambient air.

Near and Far

Consider the oppositions between domestic and "oriental," Pacific or African scenery, which affect such culinary representations such as cannibalism and breadfruit, as discussed by Peter J. Kitson and Tim Fulford. Colonialism, orientalism, and imperialism are vital to the study of modernity. A deep kernel of consumer ideology is figured in the poetics of spice—the fantasy image of infinite (and often infantile) consumption. Britain's first curry house was the Hindustani Coffee House, which opened in Portman Square in London, 1809. By the Victorian period, such hybrid constructions as kedgeree and mulligatawny soup were emerging. In a hybridization generated by global trade, chiles had arrived in Indian cuisine via the West Indies. Curry has now been christened as the British national dish. In Australia, "bush tucker" emerged from indigenous foods and is now classified as condiments.[58] Is this actually a more complex form of exoticization: that as imperialism advances, the exotic becomes available as a consumer role for the bohemian or Romantic consumerist?

"Near and far" affected representations of French revolutionaries. Gillray condemned them as queer eaters, occupying an impossible ideological space, an inconsistent blend of vegetarianism and cannibalism. "Near and far" also influenced distinctions between "now" and "then." The domestic-national antique had emerged and with it the "new antique" as Susan Stewart puts it: the simulation of pastness.[59] Antiquarian studies of food such as Richard Warner's exoticized medieval food through tales of wonder, extensive quotations from long ekphrastic descriptions of medieval banquets. Nick Groom's essay (chapter 1) observes that fish and chips was a (fake) antique, a simulation.

Notes

1. "Enfin je me rappelai le pis-aller d'une grande princesse à qui l'on disait que les paysans n'avaient pas de pain, et qui répondit: Qu'ils mangent de la brioche." Jean-Jacques Rousseau, *Confessions*, chapter 6.
2. The history of European table manners has been charted in Norbert Elias, *The History of Manners* (*The Civilizing Process*, vol. 1), tr. Edmund Jephcott (New York: Pantheon, 1978).
3. Charlotte Smith, *Desmond*, ed. Antje Blank and Janet Todd (London: Pickering and Chatto, 1997), 44.
4. Neil McKendrick, John Brewer, and J. H. Plumb, *The Birth of a Consumer Society: The Commercialization of Eighteenth-Century England* (Bloomington: Indiana UP, 1982), 11.
5. William Godwin, *Of Population: An Enquiry Concerning the Power of Increase in the Numbers of Mankind, Being an Answer to Mr. Malthus's Essay on that Subject* (London: Longman, Hurst, Rees, Orme and Brown, 1820), 490–2.
6. See Colin Campbell, *The Romantic Ethic and the Spirit of Modern Consumerism* (Oxford and New York: Basil Blackwell, 1987).
7. Colin Campbell, "Understanding Traditional and Modern Patterns of Consumption in Eighteenth-Century England," in *Consumption and the World of Goods*, ed. John Brewer and Roy Porter (London and New York: Routledge, 1993), 40–57 (40).
8. See Timothy Morton, *The Poetics of Spice: Romantic Consumerism and the Exotic* (Cambridge and New York: Cambridge UP, 2000), 148–70.
9. Thomas Love Peacock, *Melincourt: By the Author of Headlong Hall*, 3 vols. (London: printed for T. Hookham Jr. and Co. and Baldwin, Cradock and Joy, 1817), 1.52–3.

10. See Charlotte Sussman, *Consuming Anxieties: Consumer Protest, Gender, and British Slavery, 1713–1833* (Stanford: Stanford UP, 2000), 110–29; Timothy Morton, "Blood Sugar," in *Romanticism and Colonialism*, ed. Timothy Fulford and Peter J. Kitson (Cambridge and New York: Cambridge UP, 1998), 87–106; Sidney Mintz, "Tasting Food, Tasting Freedom," in *Slavery in the Americas*, ed. Wolfgang Binder (Würzburg: Königshausen & Neumann, 1993), 257–75.

11. Keith A. Sandiford, *The Cultural Politics of Sugar: Caribbean Slavery and the Narratives of Colonialism* (Cambridge and New York: Cambridge UP, 2000).

12. Sidney Mintz, "The Changing Roles of Food in the Study of Consumption," in *Consumption and the World of Goods* 269.

13. Roger Wells, *Wretched Faces: Famine in Wartime England, 1793–1801* (Gloucester: Alan Sutton and New York: St. Martin's Press, 1988), 13, 14–15.

14. E. P. Thompson, "The Moral Economy of the Crowd," in *Customs in Common: Studies in Traditional and Popular Culture* (New York: New Press, 1991), 185–258.

15. Timothy Morton, "The Plantation of Wrath," in *Radicalism in British Literary Culture, 1650–1830: From Revolution to Revolution*, ed. Timothy Morton and Nigel Smith (Cambridge and New York: Cambridge UP, 2002), 64–85 (76–7).

16. *The Medusa; or, Penny Politician* 1 (1820), 360.

17. *The Republican* 6 (May–December 1822), 12.

18. *The Edinburgh Review* 2.128–35.

19. *The Republican* 1 (27 August 1819–7 January 1820), 213; *The Republican* 5 (January–May 1822), 148.

20. John Aikin, *A View of the Character and Public Services of the Late John Howard* (London, 1792), 212.

21. Robert Pigot, *The Liberty of the Press: A Letter Addressed to the National Assembly of France, by Robert Pigot, Esquire, Late of Chetwynd in Shropshire, and Published by Their Order, with Notes and Supplement afterwards Added; and Offered to the Consideration of Every Englishman* (Paris, 1790), 30–1.

22. John Stewart, *Opus Maximum; or, the Great Essay to Reduce the Moral World from Contingency to System, in the Following Sciences: Psyconomy; or, the Science of the Moral Powers; in Two Parts: 1st, Containing the Discipline of the Understanding; 2nd, the Discipline of the Will: Mathemanomy; or, the Laws of Knowledge: Logonomy; or, the Science of Language: Anagognomy; or the Science of Education: Ontonomy; or, the Science of Being* (London: printed for J. Ginger, 1803), 20, 90–3.

23. Percy Bysshe Shelley, note to *Queen Mab*, in *Shelley: Poetical Works*, ed. Thomas Hutchinson (London and New York: Oxford UP, 1970), 828; *A Vindication of Natural Diet*, in *The Complete Works*, ed. R. Ingpen and W. E. Peck, 10 vols. (London and New York: Ernest Benn, 1926–30), 6.9.

24. Timothy Morton, "The Plantation of Wrath" 69.

25. Stephen Mennell, *All Manners of Food: Eating and Taste in England and France from the Middle Ages to the Present*, 2nd ed. (Urbana and Chicago: University of Illinois Press, 1985, 1996).

26. See Maureen McLane, *Romanticism and the Human Sciences* (Cambridge and New York: Cambridge UP, 2000).

16 ∽ *Timothy Morton*

27. See Arjun Appadurai, ed., *The Social Life of Things: Commodities in Cultural Perspective* (Cambridge: Cambridge UP, 1986), 22; John Arbuthnot, *An Essay Concerning the Nature of Aliments, and the Choice of them, According to the Different Constitutions of Human Bodies. In which the Different Effects, Advantages, and Disadvantages of Animal and Vegetable Diet, are Explain'd,* 2nd ed., with *Practical Rules of Diet in the Various Constitutions and Diseases of Human Bodies* (London: printed for J. Johnson, 1732).
28. Anon., *Rare News for Old England! Beef a Shilling a Pound!* (London, ca. 1795), 2.
29. E. P. Thompson, *The Making of the English Working Class* (Harmondsworth: Penguin, 1988), 349.
30. See William Stroup, "Henry Salt on Shelley: Literary Criticism and Ecological Identity," in "Romanticism and Ecology," *Romantic Circles Praxis Series,* ed. James Mckusick (http://www.rc.umd.edu/praxis/ecology/stroup/stroup.html).
31. R. N. Salaman, *The History and Social Influence of the Potato* (Cambridge: Cambridge UP, 1949; repr. 1986); Catherine Gallagher, "The Potato in the Materialist Imagination," in *Practicing New Historicism* ed. Catherine Gallagher and Stephen Greenblatt (Chicago and London: U of Chicago P, 2000), 110–35.
32. Robert Pigot, *Discours Prononcé dans la Société des Amis de la Constitution de Dijon, par R. Pigot, Anglois, Citoyen françois, contre le grand usage du pain* (?Paris, 1792), 3–4.
33. *The Black Dwarf* (3 September 1817), 1.511.
34. Sarah Moss, "Do You Run or Fly?: Eating and Gender in the Novels of Susan Ferrier," in *Eating Culture: The Poetics and Politics of Food,* ed. Tobias Doring, Susanne Mühleisen, and Markus Heide, (unpublished collection).
35. Charlotte Sussman, "Women's Private Reading and Political Action, 1649–1838," in *Radicalism in British Literary Culture, 1650–1830,* 133–50.
36. Thomas Trotter, *A View of the Nervous Temperament* (Newcastle and London: printed for Longman, Hurst, Rees, and Orme, 1807), 150.
37. For example, see Karl Marx, *Capital,* tr. Ben Fowkes, 3 vols. (Harmondsworth: Penguin, 1976, 1990), 1.342, 367, 416; Timothy Morton, "Blood Sugar."
38. Anon., *The History of a Good Bramin: To which is Annexed, an Essay on the Reciprocal Contempt of Nations, Proceeding from their Vanity* (London, 1795), 7–8.
39. Venetia Murray, *High Society: A Social History of the Regency Period 1788–1830* (London and New York: Viking Penguin, 1998).
40. See *The Republican* 6 (24 May–27 December 1822), 315–17.
41. See Salaman, *Potato* 501; Scrivener, *Radical Shelley* 18; Roger Wells, *Wretched Faces* 13–15.
42. Marx, *Capital* 1.917.
43. Mike Davis, *Late Victorian Holocausts: El Niño Famines and the Making of the Third World* (London and New York: Verso, 2001).
44. Horace, *Ars Poetica,* in Aristotle Horace Longinus, *Classical Literary Criticism* (Harmondsworth: Penguin, 1965, 1984), 85.
45. Virginia Berridge and Griffith Edwards, *Opium and the People: Opiate Use in Nineteenth-Century England,* 2nd ed. (New Haven: Yale UP, 1987).

46. Eve Kosovsky Sedgwick, "Epidemics of the Will," in *Incorporations (Zone 6)*, ed. Jonathan Crary and Sanford Kwinter (New York: Urzone, 1992), 582–95 (582).

47. Joshua Wilner, "Autobiography and Addition: The Case of De Quincey," *Genre* 14 (Winter 1981), 493–503; "The Stewed Muse of Prose," *MLN* (December 1989), 1085–98.

48. Anya Taylor, *Bacchus in Romantic England: Writers and Drink, 1780–1830* (London: Macmillan and New York: St. Martin's Press, 1999), 197–8.

49. Immanuel Kant, *Critique of Judgment: Including the First Introduction*, tr. Werner S. Pluhar (Indianapolis: Hackett, 1987), 50.

50. William Fox, *An Address to the People of Great Britain, on the Utility of Refraining from the Use of West India Sugar and Rum* (London, 1791), 3.

51. Samuel Taylor Coleridge, *The Collected Works of Samuel Taylor Coleridge*, vol. 1 (*Lectures 1795 on Politics and Religion*), ed. L. Patton and P. Mann (London: Routledge and Kegan Paul and Princeton: Princeton UP, 1971), 248.

52. See Timothy Morton, "The Pulses of the Body: Romantic Vegetarian Rhetoric and its Cultural Contexts," in *1650–1850: Ideas, Aesthetics, and Inquiries in the Early Modern Era*, vol. 4, ed. Kevin Cope (New York: AMS Press, 1998), 53–88.

53. See my "The Plantation of Wrath" and Ginnie Smith, "Thomas Tryon's Regimen for Women: Sectarian Health in the Seventeenth Century," in *The Sexual Dynamics of History: Men's Power, Women's Resistance* (London and Leichhardt: Pluto Press, 1983), 47–65.

54. See Jacques Derrida, *Of Grammatology*, tr. Gayatri Chakravorty Spivak (Baltimore and London: Johns Hopkins UP, 1987), part 1.

55. John Oswald, *The Cry of Nature; or, an Appeal to Mercy and to Justice, on Behalf of the Persecuted Animals* (London: printed for J. Johnson, 1791), 64, 5, 82.

56. William Lambe, *A Medical and Experimental Inquiry, into the Origin, Symptoms, and Cure of Constitutional Diseases. Particularly Scrophula, Consumption, Cancer, and Gout* (London: printed for J. Mawman, 1805), 35.

57. Samuel Jackson Pratt, *Bread; or, the Poor. A Poem. With Notes and Illustrations* (London: printed for Longman, Rees and Becket, 1802), 4, 17.

58. I am grateful to Kate Evans for pointing this out to me.

59. Susan Stewart, "Notes on Distressed Genres," in *Crimes of Writing: Problems in the Containment of Representation* (Oxford and New York: Oxford UP, 1991), 66–101.

Part I ∽

CONSTRUCTIONS, SIMULATIONS, CULTURES

Chapter 1 ∾

WILLIAM HENRY IRELAND: FROM FORGERY TO FISH 'N' CHIPS

Nick Groom

> The critics often invent authors: they select two dissimilar works—the *Tao Te Ching* and the *1001 Nights*, say—attribute them to the same writer and then determine most scrupulously the psychology of this interesting *homme de lettres*. . .
>
> —Jorge Luis Borges, "Tlön, Uqbar, Orbis Tertius"[1]

William Henry Ireland, "otherwise Shakspeare," was a late eighteenth-century literary forger. By the time he was twenty-one he had produced a substantial archive of Shakespearean manuscripts, had his supposedly original new Shakespeare play *Vortigern* performed at Drury Lane, confessed to the forgery, been disowned by his father, revealed to be the illegitimate child of the housekeeper, and written his autobiography. He spent the remainder of his life as a Grub Street hack, counterfeiting his Shakespearean forgeries for collectors of curiosities. He died in 1835.

This, in a nutshell, is the common account of William Henry Ireland's career and constitutes the critical ground on which he is assessed.[2] Ireland has suffered in precisely the same way as the "marvellous Boy" Thomas Chatterton, identified with one dubious cultural project (Shakespeare) eradicating his subsequent *œuvre* and effectively removing him from the canon. One critic suggests that Ireland "might have made an honourable name for himself as a contemporary of Coleridge and the other romantic writers," but that "it is scarcely to be wondered at that nobody took an impostor

seriously as a writer."[3] But Ireland *was* a contemporary, and he had his suc-
cesses and certainly influence.[4] This chapter, however, will barely discuss
Shakespeare, forgery, Chatterton, or Richard Savage, Ireland's other great
influence. Instead, it develops these points by examining a particular
moment in Ireland's post-Shakespearean career and the ways in which it
challenges the Romantic conception of authorship, accounting in part for
his subsequent critical neglect.

Even in the 1820s, Ireland still inhabited a sort of romantic (with a small
"r") Augustan Grub Street. In a sense he is a *lost* Romantic, shadowing the
other writers of his generation: in 1801, for example, Biggs and Cottle of
Bristol had published Ireland's own book of lyrical ballads. Yet he haunted
himself with his own literary past, as if caught in an auto-anxiety of influence
or a belated, revisionary phase of his own "visionary" Shakespeare produc-
tions. Nevertheless, Ireland is a remarkable and uncontainable example of
diversity: poet, novelist, playwright, satirist, historian, translator, revolutionary
librarian, bookbinder (and, bigamist). By the time of his death in 1835, the
sixty-year-old Ireland had published at least sixty-seven original works. If the
sense of unity created among potentially disparate works constitutes not only
Romantic literary *œuvres* but eventually the whole model of authorship in
the period, then Ireland's restless and exuberant polygraphy perhaps offers a
prototype for reconsidering the coherence of Romantic authorship.

Bernard Grebanier devotes a single chapter of *The Great Shakespeare
Forgery* to the last forty years of Ireland's career, unfairly entitling his brief
survey "Sputtering Candle." The redoubtable Montague Summers has given
the best account of Ireland's range in *The Gothic Quest*, but Summers focuses
on Ireland's novels, in particular *Gondez, The Monk*, a "Monk" Lewis-like
celebration of thirteenth-century Inquisitorial torture and execution.
Summers has little truck with Ireland's poetry, despite its prevalence in
Gondez. For example, Ireland declares in his preface:

> You'll doubtless ask me, and with some surprize,
> What merit has the work that's framed on lies?
> What wholesome information can be found,
> Where ev'ry character treads magic ground?[5]

This is half a century on from the Richardson-Fielding debate on whether
morals can be taught by fiction, and looks forward to the "Newgate
Novels" row of the mid-nineteenth century. The sentiments also confirm
Mario Praz's account of the Romantic "agony" as "magic," "suggestive,"
"nostalgic," and "above all . . . expressing states of mind which cannot be

described . . . The essence of Romanticism consequently comes to consist in that which cannot be described."[6] And yet with Ireland, a forger, things are never so simple. The first chapter of *Gondez* has as an epigraph a ten-line Shakespearean speech, " 'Twas there I learn'd the untun'd song of war . . .," which at second glance turns out to be from *Henry II* (by William Henry Ireland, "otherwise Shakspeare," as he continued to sign himself as the fancy took him). This epigraph is followed by two genuine lines from Shakespeare; all the epigraphs to all the chapters of *Gondez* are by one of the Williams Shakespeare or Henry Ireland.

This auto-inter-textual complexity is further compounded by other repeated elements within *Gondez*. A manuscript is found in a convent library, giving the text and provenance of the

Legend of the Little Red Woman, written by the Monk Ingulphus, at the Instigation of that Holy Father and Ghostly Confessor, Geronimo, Abbot of the Monastery of Saint Columba, in the Island of Oronza; Wherein was displayed this Bloody Tragedy, in the Year of Grace 1152. (1.173–83)

This ballad had already appeared two years previously in Ireland's *Rhapsodies*, as "The Little Red Woman, A Legendary Tale, From the Romance of the Abbot of Oronza, which will speedily be published" (44–56). It is a sprightly nursery rhyme: the Little Red Woman is a witch with a foul black cat called Vinegar Tom. After various adventures (for instance, they feast upon the decapitated head of a child) she sells her soul. On going to confession to try to escape her fate, the Little Red Woman discovers that the Abbot who has been praying for her is really the Devil. Now, even if Ireland is merely trying to eke out such sensationalist verse, he is still playing hide-and-seek with authenticity. And although both *Rhapsodies* and *Gondez* were published under his own name, these games become more intricate in other dubious and semi-fraudulent texts penned pseudonymously and anonymously: *A Ballade Wrotten on the Feastynge and Merrimentes of Easter Maunday Laste Paste* and *Effusions of Love from Chatelar to Mary Queen of Scotland. Translated from a Gallic Manuscript, in the Scotch College, at Paris.*

It may be that part of the reason for not admitting Ireland to the "honourable" company of Coleridge et al. is that his writing does not easily fit recognizable critical traditions or notions of Romantic authorship. He is a sort of radical *bricoleur*. *Bricolage* became a byword of postmodernism, but Claude Lévi-Strauss defines it in *The Savage Mind* as something more magical and primitive: a *bricoleur* is "someone who works with his hands and uses devious means comparable to those of a craftsman."[7] There is a quality of manual craftedness and craftiness in much of Ireland's writings. Nevertheless, forgery should not be allowed to tyrannize Ireland's writings, even if Ireland himself was seldom far from the subject, repeatedly and unrepentantly confessing his guilt in a spiralling process of self-mythologization. In the tradition of Savage and Chatterton (his "two angels"), Ireland developed simple forgery into a model of plurality. This babbling polyvalence enabled him to challenge emergent notions of authorship. Like forgery but more so, in these authorial scenarios the name of the author ceases to function as a useful means of classification. Ireland used at least sixteen different pseudonyms throughout his writing life (including "Paul Persius," "Henry Boyle," "Charles Clifford," "Flagellator," "Satiricus Sculptor, Esq.," "Anser-Pen-Drag-On, Esq.," and "Baron Karlo Excellmanns"); he is less an author-function than a rhizomic author-collective, spreading like a tuber.

Every so often Ireland did try to establish a single writerly identity. In the prologue to his first novel after the Shakespeare fiasco (*The Abbess*), Ireland has a vision of a hostile band of critics watching a youth foundering in a vessel; it breaks and "She splits, and to the bottom sinks the chest: / The spurious papers are consign'd to rest." Consequently shipwrecked, he dreams not of other writers, but:

> Such fancies did not sooth the Author's brain:
> He wander'd not amidst the Muses' train,
> But views a British female bland and fair,
> Who, smiling, offers him her fost'ring care:
> "Hear me, O youth," she cries;"my counsels keep;
> Or better hadst thou perished in the deep.
> No longer tread that dangerous path for fame;
> Never again assume another's name:
> As your works merit, let them stand or fall,
> Be either pitied or admir'd by all . . ."[8]

Which is good Romantic advice, offered by a traditional Muse—and which Ireland did not heed at all. For him, the name does not contain, separate, define, identify the text. Rather, the writer is engaged in espionage against all such authorial formations, either by habitually masking itself, or by gadding about with no name at all.

Ireland's writing does tend to gad about. His *Confessions* (which he actually wrote in two versions, the first draft, a great hostage to fortune, entitled *An Authentic Account*) is a text entirely out of joint, mixing

Shakespeareanisms, critical quotations, and his own poetry in a compendious confusion consistent only in its inconsistency. The range of his publication is equally erratic. He wrote *Mutius Scævola*, a Roman play, and edited a children's chapbook, *Youth's Polar Star or The Beacon of Science*. He composed "Lines" on a balloon flight, "Johannes Taurus, the Don Juan of England by Byronus Secundus,"[9] and at the request of Princess Elizabeth daughter of George III he provided (under the name of "Cervantes") a birthday pantomime for Frogmore Fete, replete with jokes, songs, comic foreigners, and a concluding prophecy delivered by Merlin. He attacked slavery in *All the Blocks* and patriotism in *The State Doctors*. In *France for The Last Seven Years* he wrote a history of that country interlaced with personal reminiscences, satires, street songs, and society conversation, and as "Henry Boyle," editor of *The Universal Chronologist* (a history of the eighteenth century), he suggested that the performance of *Vortigern* "caused the greatest ferment in the world of literature." As "Anser Pen-Drag-On, Esq." he satirized Southey, Burns, Scott, Byron, Coleridge and Wordsworth in *Scribbleomania, or The Printer's Devil's Polichronicon* (he also included himself, as Ireland, for good measure), and, in a similar anti-genealogical compendium of folly, *Stultifera Navis* (*The Modern Ship of Fools*), he described everyone from "Venal Fools" to "Fools who do not understand a Game, and yet will play," and ultimately "The Folly of all the World." He translated Voltaire's *La Pucelle d' Orléans* into English verse, and as "Satiricus Sculptor" in *Chalcographimania* he charted "Infatuations of Every Description," taking a cross section of print-selling and connoisseurship. This panorama runs from pornography to "Nicknackatarian Mania":

> Samples we have of some, whose hopes
> Concentrate in the *hangman's* ropes:
> One rusty *armour* buys amain,
> Or painted window's shatter'd pane;
> The skins of birds, of beasts, and fishes,
> Cups, saucers, tea-pots, old Delft dishes.

Every collector, from the erotic print hoarder to the archivist of the gallows, was footnoted, including his own father (an etcher of the picturesque and a Hogarthian), and again himself:

> That *Ir–l–nd*, fam'd for picturesque,
> And fond of *Hogarth's* keen burlesque . . .
> To parent now the *son* let's add,
> Of ancient lore, *impostor lad* . . .

Evidently Ireland moonlighted as his own gang of Boswells, adding one version of himself as the Shakespeare forger to the satires and histories he penned in other names, as other people, a conundrum that has stymied serious research beyond the Shakespeare papers. "Ireland" was not even his real name, just the monicker of the forger, only about a twentieth of his eventual person. His father had adopted the name; he was christened "Irwin," but this man was still not W. H.'s real father anyway: William Henry was in fact the housekeeper's son, perhaps by a dissolute aristocrat— possibly one reason he later identified with the bastard Savage.

So Ireland's is a defeatist egotism. He had not one or two pseudonyms, open secrets like Walter Scott or James Hogg, Charles Lamb, or Thomas De Quincey, but maybe a dozen and a half. He dissolves himself as a single author at the moment at which the Wordsworthian "Poet" is stirring. As the professional author was increasingly defined as a legal entity and a speculator in intellectual property, as well as a textual identity and an authentic human quantity, the multifarious authorship that Ireland promulgated looks irrepressibly illegal, illegitimate, cataclysmically overinvested, and oddly reminiscent of the old Grub Street of Daniel Defoe and Alexander Pope. Indeed, he invokes old Grub Street when wondering about the fate of the sheets of his first novel, *The Abbess*:

Perhaps to chandler's shop thou wilt be ta'en,
And for each customer be rent in twain,
    To fold the double Gloucester's slice;
Perhaps when in the cupboard lying,
Toward the cheese some wand'rers straying,
    Will nibble thee—I mean the mice. (*Rhapsodies* 11)

The Dunciad notwithstanding, this is of course quite the image of those notorious *manuscrits trouvés*, the Shakespeare papers, and could launch a discussion of authorship and transience, sentimental narratives of recovery, antiquarianism, and so forth. But in this collection one is alerted to the "double Gloucester's slice." The remainder of this essay will savor a culinary perspective in the work of William Henry Ireland and in the nature of "Irish" authorship by investigating something even more quintessentially English than Double Gloucester.[10] Ireland forged more than literature; by the same techniques he forged a national dish.

The Fisher Boy, A Poem Comprising His Several Avocations, During the Four Seasons of the Year was published by Ireland under the initials "H. C. Esq." It is a portrait of a year in the lives of a mother and child: "Jane the maniac"—seduced, abandoned, and in consequence lunatic—and her illegitimate son, Ned. In the course of one melancholy passage, Ireland offers a lively Thomsonian account of fishing methods, exhibiting such a fetching sympathy for "the finny race" he verges on animal rights: "it is apparent that their corporeal sufferings," he says in one footnote, "must be of the most acute kind."[11] This is noticeably different from Wordsworth's attitude to fishing in *The Excursion*, in which the catch is described as "A splendid sight" (8.568), or in Shelley's *Peter Bell the Third*:

> In the death hues of agony
>> Lambently flashing from a fish,
> Now Peter felt amused to see
> Shades like a rainbow's rise and flee,
>> Mixed with a certain hungry wish. (127)

The Fisher Boy is a late georgic. The eponymous hero prepares his mother's supper—he is frying tonight:

> And for his parent's eating dab supplies,
> Which cleans'd—in dripping pan he dextrous fries;
> Then adds potatoes slic'd, thin, crisp, and brown,
> Whereto he sets his silent mother down;
> Praises the dish, to coax her to the meal,
> The highest earthly transport he can feel.

From the title page of *The Cottage Girl*, a later georgic in the same series and also attributed to "H. C. Esq.," it transpires that *The Fisher Boy* must have been written prior to 1810, probably in 1808. It is by a very long way the first English poem to describe the preparation of fish 'n' chips.

The potato had been grown in Ireland (appropriately enough) since the 1640s in County Wicklow. The crop thrived in the rainy climate, proved to be reliable winter food, and was, as Redcliffe Salaman argues in his classic *The Social History and Influence of the Potato*, cultivated as much as stabilizing social ballast as a dish for the dinner table. In England, the best potatoes were grown in Lancashire, but the tuber was barely considered to be a foodstuff at all; they were generally recommended for fattening pigs.[12] Even in the mid–eighteenth century, boiled potatoes were only rarely served with meat, and some farmers were still reluctant to feed the things to their livestock. Among some rural workers, they were hated with a venom normally reserved for Catholics. In Lewes in Suffolk, where an effigy of the Pope is still burnt annually on 5 November, the call went up during a 1765 election, "No Potatoes, No Popery." Others were almost entirely apathetic: in the same year in Horsted Keynes in Sussex, there was nobody who knew how to plant potatoes, and an old man from outside the county used to visit each year on Old Ladyday to do so (Salaman 120, 437).

Much of this may be put down to superstition, derived from seventeenth-century rumors spreading across Europe—for example that the potato (because of its irregular skin) caused leprosy and scrofula and should be planted by moonlight (Salaman 112, 114). However, Salaman argues that such superstitions had more serious roots than simply innate conservatism:

> the potato was a new type of food, the like of which had not been seen previously in Europe. To eat of it, was not merely a venture in dietetics, but an audacious break with common tradition, a tradition which in Europe was permeated through and through by the Bible . . . akin to eating the forbidden fruit of Eden, a sinful act which, even if its effects were physically harmless, was bound to create a feeling of personal guilt, which demanded some kind of expiation lest the individual be smitten with some dreaded disease. (116)

Potatoes were of the earth and water, subterranean and covert, massy, rhizomic: examples of vegetal otherness as potentially as exotic as the banana, but more sinister because less spectacularly alien, with eyes and skin disconcertingly human. Thomas Tryon, the late seventeenth-century radical vegetarian and potato-eater, admitted the humoral problems of the plant, but claimed that they were not as sublunary as more traditional root vegetables: "Turnips and Potatoes etc. that grow almost on the top and surface of the earth are better than other roots and more familiar to our natures than such as grow deeper in the ground, because they participate more of the influences both of the air and sun than the others" (quoted in Salaman 113).

This is an early sounding of what became *the* critical dietary debate of the late eighteenth century: whether the staple food of the working classes should be bread or potatoes. As Salaman demonstrates, the potato became increasingly central to working-class diets not because of the impact of nutritional arguments, but as a consequence of economic change and social policy (456). Wheat had a completely different symbolic vocabulary: it was golden, swayed in the air, and ripened in the sun; it was the Biblical staple enshrined in the Lord's Prayer, a prayer enacted at a domestic level every day in the miraculous, metamorphic, living process of breadmaking.[13] Wheat also had a powerful social cachet. By the middle of the eighteenth century, the lower classes had become progressively gentrified, at teatime at least: white bread and tea, previously a reliable indicator of class, had gradually become affordable to a mass market. Once the lower classes had tasted such meagre crumbs of comfort, they were extremely reluctant to surrender them for spuds, and especially to return to old, coarse bread. Salaman describes the extent of this prejudice thus: "after 1770, as provisions began to get scarcer and dearer, and meat had all but vanished from their tables, it was white wheaten, and not a cheaper and coarser barley loaf, which together with cheese, constituted the staple food of the masses... It was felt to be better to make use of the Irishman's potato, or even the coolie's rice, both the food of peoples regarded socially as little better than slaves, than to return to a coarse and coloured loaf" (481).

The debate peaked in the 1790s and 1830s, when grain supplies were dangerously low, and the government was actively promoting the economic advantages of potato cultivation. But it was the staple of Ireland and the food of immigrant Irish laborers: it symbolized Ireland, and therefore Catholicism ("No Popery"), and therefore France, the old enemy, where they allegedly had all-potato cookbooks and Marie Antoinette wore potato flowers in her hair—the potato's spreading tuber roots were themselves symbolic of the nefarious spread of Catholicism. It has also been suggested that the Inca name "papa" meant that the potato became the "pope's fruit," or even the "pope-ato."[14]

The Irish had, however, perfected the preparation of the tater by this time, and the opulent "Irish Stew" was being noted as early as 1673 (Salaman 239). For more modest tables, potatoes were boiled in their skins with a little water in family cauldrons, and drained in wicker "skeehogues," from which they were eaten by hand. They were sometimes also parboiled, mashed, and made them into cakes that were then fried in butter. More luxurious and rare dishes included colcannon (turnips or cabbage mashed with potatoes) and cobbledy (potatoes and onion with milk, butter, and seasoning). By the early nineteenth century, the Irish staple was boiled potatoes and milk, occasionally enlivened with small amounts of meat or fish. They consequently ate potatoes in vast quantities: an average of five pounds per person per day, according to Edward Wakefield, who researched Irish eating habits from 1809–11.[15] W. H. T. Hawley's survey of laborers' diets (1839) gave the male diet then as 4–5 lbs potatoes per day, consisting of potatoes and milk, and occasionally herrings, oatmeal, lard, dripping, eggs, butter, or onions.[16] By 1845, the year of the catastrophic Blight, nearly forty percent of the Irish population lived chiefly on potatoes.

In England, potato recipes were noted by John Evelyn as early as 1664: "the root being roasted under the ecula or otherwise, opened with a knife, the pulp is buttered in the skin, of which it will take up a good quantity, and is seasoned with a little salt and pepper. Some eat this with sugar together in the skin, which has a pleasant crispness; they are also stewed and baked in pies," but it was a century before the potato began to gain in popularity as a side dish, roasted with the meat.[17] The vegetarian Joseph Ritson reluctantly ate potatoes roasted in mutton fat during his tour of Scotland in 1786–87. More adventurous recipes were gradually published, tending to endorse Evelyn's suggestion to supplement potatoes with sugar. In the 1796 edition of Hannah Glasse's *Art of Cooking Made Plain and Easy* there are no less than eleven potato recipes; almost half added sugar and sweeteners like oranges or candied lemon peel, and among such "sweet" recipes were potatoes panfried with sugar—sweetmeats.[18] Even so, Timothy Morton quotes a poetic address "From a Potatoe to a Sirloin of Beef" from as late as 1817, in which the potato is dismissed as being an unsuitable accompaniment to the old English roast: potatoes are foreign muck (Brazilian, in this text) and the staple food of "humble slaves" rather than the choice of John Bull and a fit companion to the bloody meat.[19]

Potatoes were also served with fish. In 1814, Patrick Colquhoun recommended an established Cornish dish for the "inferior classes": corned fish and boiled potato.[20] The potato had been cultivated in Devon and Cornwall with some enthusiasm, and by 1795, when the Board of Agriculture was urging the rest of the country to make potato bread, this concoction was an established Devonian staple.[21] William Cobbett noticed this later, discovering that in the West Country the potato was replacing bread "to a very great extent."[22] For Cobbett, this reduced the English laborers to the level of the Irish: slavish, bestial, forever facing famine and poverty. The potato was a measure of national confidence and well-being. Adding fish to potatoes simply added insult to injury. William Lovett remembered his uncle's appetite in the first decade of the nineteenth century:

> The first question when he came home at noon, was to ask his mistress what she had got for dinner. If it happened to be baked potatoes, pork, and pie-crust—a favourite dinner with him—Uncle Jeremy would kneel down and make a long grace over it; but if it was a dinner of fish and potatoes, Uncle Jeremy could never be induced to say grace; for he always persisted that "God Almighty never ordained fish and potatoes for a working man's dinner."[23]

For Uncle Jeremy, the offer of a dinner of fish and potatoes is a diabolical liberty: wholly insufficient fare for a proud worker—food by implication feminized (the prejudice remains to this day). Moreover, the meal is not merely unmanly: in contrast to the hearty Anglo-Saxon pork and piecrust, it is un-English.

But salt-pickled fish with boiled potatoes has only a passing resemblance to Ireland's *Fisher Boy* recipe of fried flat fish and "potatoes slic'd, thin, crisp, and brown." We need to look over the Channel for his inspiration. French agricultural workers roasted potatoes in embers before salting them to their taste; the bourgeoisie parboiled, sliced, and fricasseed potatoes with onion or in wine, or made batters for them; they were also eaten sliced thinly, floured, and fried in oil or butter; as Larry Zuckerman says, this latter is "the french fry's ancestor."[24] And this is where Ireland learnt his cooking. He had lived for some four years in France as a child, and in the *Confessions* speaks of this as "The happiest period of my life." The Ireland family were republicans and supporters of Bonaparte (another reason, incidentally, for Edmond Malone's energetic attack on the Shakespeare papers[25]). Ireland visited France with his newly wedded wife from 1804–05, and *Effusions of Love* (1805) was, as noted above, supposedly translated from a manuscript held in Paris. It is possible that he also visited around 1806, a year in which he does not appear to have published anything in Britain, and then they moved to Devon, where a connection with northern France was well established. Possibly he ran a prison for French prisoners of war; in any case, he was again in France with his family from 1814 to 1823. Ireland greeted Napoleon on his return from Elba and was made a librarian in the National Library. He was nominated for the Legion of Honor just before Waterloo, and was subsequently made a member of the Atheneum of Sciences and Arts in Paris. Ireland wrote, edited, and translated a number of books on Napoleon, his "hero," including his will, and after his return to England, translated *The King of Holland* (published under Napoleon's own name).

The sociological history of fish 'n' chips has previously been understood in terms of the industrial revolution and urbanization, rather than in terms of Anglo-French cultural relations. Baked-potato-men began to appear in London in the 1820s; according to Henry Mayhew in *London Labour and the London Poor* (1861), they proliferated throughout the 1830s. By 1851 there were some three hundred on the streets.[26] They hired ovens from bakers to bake potatoes in tins, which were then stored in what were effectively heated brass chimneys on wheels. They sold from street corners to passersby, many of whom might become regulars (a practice revived in Britain a few years ago). The trade clearly benefited from rapid urbanization and the fact that such cheap dishes could not be prepared at home. Baked potatoes became popular and joined with another fast food: fried fish.

In *Oliver Twist* (serialized 1837–39), Charles Dickens describes a fried-fish warehouse in what has been considered the archetypal English fish and chip shop:

> Near to the spot on which Snow Hill and Holborn Hill meet, there opens, upon the right hand as you come out of the city, a narrow and dismal alley leading to Saffron Hill. In its filthy shops are exposed for sale huge bunches of second-hand silk handkerchiefs of all sizes and patterns—for here reside the traders who purchase them from pickpockets. Hundreds of these hand-kerchiefs hang dangling from pegs outside the windows, or flaunting from the door-posts; and the shelves within are piled with them. *Confined as the limits of Field Lane are, it has its barber, its coffee-shop, its beer-shop, and its fried-fish warehouse.* It is a commercial colony of itself, the emporium of petty lar-ceny, visited at early morning and setting-in of dusk by silent merchants, who traffic in dark back-parlours, and go as strangely as they came. Here, the clothes' man, the shoe-vamper, and the rag-merchant display their goods as signboards to the petty thief; and stores of old iron and bones ... rust and rot in the grimy cellars.[27]

Mayhew also describes itinerant fish fryers:

> The fish fried by street dealers is known as "plaice dabs" and "sole dabs," which are merely plaice and soles—dab being a common word for any flat fish...the fish is cooked in ordinary frying pans...The fried fish sellers live in some out-of-the-way alley, and not infrequently in garrets...A gin-drinking neighbourhood, one coster said, suits best, for people hasn't their smell so correct there.[28]

Fried fish was sold in paper bags and by mid-century was being eaten with a baked potato; deep-fried sliced potatoes only appeared in the cities in the 1860s, enabled by specialist cauldrons and automatic potato-peelers. (For some reason, the oil used was cottonseed rather than the rapeseed used for fish, although today chefs such as Keith Floyd recommend the more opu-lent beef dripping.) As Winston Churchill later declared, the two went together like "good companions."[29]

Ireland's *Fisher Boy* implies that fried fish and chipped potatoes was a lower-class fisherman's staple eaten possibly in Devon at the beginning of the nineteenth century, long before the dish was popularized, perhaps inde-pendently, in the cities. Moreover, Ireland's account of proto-fish 'n' chips (which even favors a frying pan, and cooks with dripping rather than oil or butter) was probably influenced by his gastronomic experiences in France.

It was also recorded in a poem so popular that it went into a second edition; it therefore outsold anything published by Keats or Shelley during their lifetimes. There are some surprising implications here for theories of Romantic authorship and Shakespearean forgery.

"*Der Mensch ist, was er isst*."[30] In cultural terms, ingestion redefines the body, and in the arts has long been thought to have direct influence on the creative imagination. Ireland's "angel" Chatterton professed vegetarianism and temperance, often refusing dinner because "he had work in hand, and he must not make himself more stupid than God had made him," though he had a penchant for aphrodisiacs such as gingerbread and narcotics such as opium, both of which shimmer through his verse.[31] Robert Burns's creativity, on the other hand, seemed to rely upon alcoholic self-destructiveness. Wordsworth famously fretted in "Resolution and Independence" about the effects of the twin demons Chatterton and Burns upon Coleridge: could the forger and/or the drunkard compose authentic inspired poetry, or was their verse simply symptomatic of incipient suicidal madness? The analysis was uncharacteristically simple for Coleridge, who was in effect "pot-valiant": he lumped James Hogg with his countryman Burns precisely because of their shared love of the water of life: "Your whisky has made you original."[32]

For Ireland, fish 'n' chips is just one concoction that makes him original. In 1818, Cobbett, a late commentator on the Shakespeare forgeries, attacked the culture of the potato in *A Year's Residence, in the United States of America*:

> It is the fashion to extol potatoes, and to eat potatoes. Everyone joins in extolling potatoes, and all the world like potatoes, or pretend to like them, which is the same thing in effect. Indeed it is the fashion to extol the virtues of potatoes, as it has been to admire the writings of Milton and Shakespear.[33]

Cobbett argues that potatoes are instruments of oppression, maintaining the poor as if they were livestock. They are as "fashionable" (or rather, as *ideological* and by implication as English) as Shakespeare is. But this also means that (if you will forgive the phrase) potatoes can be read against the grain: they can be subverted—as Catherine Gallagher puts it in "The Potato in the Materialist Imagination": "the potato did not restrict itself to one meaning; it was ambivalent, arbitrary, historically overdetermined, and opaque as any signifier" (112). Ireland himself had already rewritten Shakespeare, and in *The Fisher Boy* accomplished the same feat with fried fish and potatoes: taking a revolutionary supper and presenting it within a folkloric tableau of Merrie England. He was profoundly more successful cooking up a new national dish than in cooking the books of the Bard of Avon. *The Fisher Boy* is mythopoeic, but mischeviously so: Ireland attributed to fish and chips an Olde Worlde pedigree, which he liberally salted with revolutionary republicanism and vinegared with continental democracy.

Fish 'n' chips appears as a natural and original dish. Gallagher argues that the potato has a "medieval" association in the modern mind: "despite its very late arrival on the scene, the potato represents something like an Ur-food even in the northern European imagination" (110). It is fashionably primitivist: it can be prepared swiftly and eaten on the move because it does not require an oven and a baking process; it self-consciously lacks supplementary spices in cooking and appeals to purist tendencies in dietary theory. As Morton points out, bland food was favored by eighteenth-century vegetarians and dieticians: "[George] Cheyne emphasised that the blander food was, the better"—and it is also worth noting that fish, like offal, was considered by some to be effectively a vegetable.[34] Moreover, the potato's autochthonous quality means that it is outside the genealogical model of monarchic society: its legitimacy as a staple foodstuff is in question. Compared with wheat it has no pedigree; it is effectively a usurper or a revolutionary. Ireland saw that the national dish, the enthroned Roast Beef of Old England, could be ambushed by Francophile bandits: the quick, vernacular Robin-Hood radicalism of fysshe & chippes.

The contradictions that William Henry Ireland cooks up in his skillet, in which fashionable French fries and feminine fish are transformed into traditional and sustaining sturdy English fare, are part of his wider craving for self-identity, innovation, and cultural nutrition through invention. Ireland's new-but-historical fish 'n' chips, like his authentic-yet-original Shakespeare and the multiple self-representations, rethinks English history and Englishness, making it restless and incoherent, contextually contingent, and necessarily impermanent. This itself presents a radical challenge: it is in unity, whether in law or psychiatry or artistic composition (especially in terms of Romantic authorship), that the self becomes legal, sane, and authentic, and this unity is expressed as a repetition of salient elements: in signatures and lineage, personality function, style, and so forth (although the *perfect* copy is considered counterfeit in the case of the signature, a monstrous clone in the case of breeding, in psychiatry neurosis and dementia, and in literature plagiarism). Ireland was a man of repetitions, but the wrong sort of repetition—not of his self, but of another: "the *second* Chatterton," or "*Shakspeare* Ireland"; he was nicknamed "Sam" after an older, dead (step?-)brother and after his adoptive father; he wrote his inconsistent autobiography twice. He also maintains the wrong sort of repetition in the breadth of his writing and the catalogue of his names, only rarely managing any coherency across more than a few works. This sort of behavior could be deemed illegal, insane, inauthentic, or unliterary because it queries prevalent canons of originality, authenticity, and modes of artistic composition.

Recent attempts to define Romanticism have focused on the notion of authorial presence in questions of editing, especially in assessing the editorial status permitted to revisions and drafts. The problem is that the editorial rationale of Greg-Bowers (constructing the text of original authorial intentions) is an idealizing critical engagement that replicates the prevailing Romantic ideology that literary composition should be pure and spontaneous, and therefore authentic.[35] Zachary Leader shows that Wordsworth was acutely aware that he had a theory of composition to promote that championed "the so-called primary-process claims of originality, spontaneity, authenticity, inspiration"; his best poetry sizzled. Despite claiming sustained poetical "labour," the poet sounds more like a celebrity chef: "in literary historical terms the Wordsworth who is remembered is the Wordsworth of 'spontaneous overflow,' of verses 'written at a heat,' 'fresh from the brain,' 'piping hot' and free of any merely 'mechanical' adoption of tropes or figures" (24).[36] Wordsworth editing should at least acknowledge, if it cannot resist, the temptation to go to work in Romanticism's own ideological kitchen. Wordsworth almost seems to think that poetry might be made as one might go at a pie—no wonder his verse appealed to New Critics who believed that "Judging a poem is like judging a pudding." Ireland is doing something quite different.[37]

To return to the lines from *The Fisher Boy*:

> And for his parent's eating dab supplies,
> Which cleans'd—in dripping pan he dextrous fries;
> Then adds potatoes slic'd, thin, crisp, and brown,
> Whereto he sets his silent mother down;
> Praises the dish, to coax her to the meal,
> The highest earthly transport he can feel.

Ned is doing precisely what Uncle Jeremy refused to do: make a long grace over the dish (reminding this reader at least of Christ's prodigious charitable miracle with the loaves and fishes, the Biblical archetype of fish 'n' chips). In doing so he is glossing the text of the meal, explicitly preparing his mother—and the reader—to take pleasure in its fraudulence: a meal that, according to some, "God Almighty never ordained," a meal that is disgustingly French, but a meal that is nevertheless feeding his crazy mother and giving voice to the "highest earthly transport" Ned can feel, which may well be another way of saying, "he tells lies about the food." In offering this explicatory condiment Ireland is explicitly writing poetry that restlessly regards and chatters about itself. He creates a fugitive context, or rather a succession of perspectives, within which the verses keep shifting; the effect is experienced in miniature in this passage as the hyperactive vitality of movement and morbid empirical intensity, but is also endemic to his entire *œuvre*.

This shiftingness (and shiftiness) actually articulates the fraught question of personal identity in the eighteenth century, which promulgated an essential relationship between individual subjectivity and authenticity. Leader quotes John Clendon, who in 1710 confirmed Boethius's definition of "A person" as "the individual substance of a rational view" as precisely "*Authentick*, and in Effect held ever since" (316 ff.; my italics). All of Ireland's writing is fundamentally about the fear that he has no authentic existence beyond the page—or, as it transpires, beyond the pages of his own inauthenticities. He is ideally inauthentic, and his own *Authentic Account* was speedily mocked in the press as a fine species of inauthenticity:

> An apology, as it lately came from IRELAND.—
>> "I confess I am an impostor, and therefore I expect you will be prepared to believe every word I say."
>> Another.—["] *Shakespear* did not write these plays, *therefore* I did.—I imposed upon you before, *therefore* I speak truth now.—You have detected me already, *therefore* I am above suspicion at present."[38]

Any word from Ireland's lips, or any line from Ireland's pen (or any forkful from his plate) is already a lie-in-waiting, demonstrating his inauthentic status. Rather than construct a watertight literary identity, he wars against the whole mode of coherent authorship. Ireland's works, taken *en masse*, are supremely heteronomous, encapsulating the century-old personal heresy first formulated by John Locke.

Locke's attack on Cartesian being arrives with the 1694 edition of his *Essay Concerning Human Understanding*, which questions the validity of material and immaterial definitions of identity, locating it in "*consciousness*" (a word Locke himself coined):

> If the same *Socrates* waking and sleeping do not partake of the same *consciousness*, *Socrates* waking and sleeping is not the same Person. And to punish *Socrates* waking, for what sleeping *Socrates* thought, and waking *Socrates* was

never conscious of, would be no more of Right, than to punish one Twin for what his Brother-Twin did, whereof he knew nothing, because their outsides were so alike.[39]

The problem facing the law, for Locke, is that it cannot distinguish "what is real, what is counterfeit." On the one hand, if a crime is committed by one *not himself*, intoxicated or somnambulating, "the ignorance in Drunkenness or Sleep is not admitted as a plea" (Locke's only consolation is that at the Day of Judgment, "no one shall be made to answer for what he knows nothing of," 344). On the other hand, it is consciousness that unites the disparate traces of memory, experience, sensation, perception, and so forth into identity: "Nothing but consciousness can unite remote Existences into the same Person" (344). The practical necessity of governing by a theory of identity a person construed through physical bodily continuity therefore defines and restricts the nature of the self, and profoundly delineates its responsibilities.

Locke's model of consciousness was potentially destabilizing to the self because it seemed to permit the possibility that the same body could be different persons at different times. David Hume elaborated this in *A Treatise on Human Nature*, in which the self is supposedly "nothing but a bundle or collection of different perceptions, which succeed each other with an inconceivable rapidity, and are in a perpetual flux and movement... The mind is a kind of theatre, where several perceptions successively make their appearance; pass, re-pass, glide away, and mingle in an infinite variety of postures and situations."[40] Leader glosses Hume's position, in which continued existence is constructed as a fiction or a *feint* of continued existence: "It is the imagination that does the feigning" (320). This imagination, in the hands of later philosophers as diverse as David Hartley and Immanuel Kant—and clearly through the poetry of Wordsworth and Coleridge (and their editors)—ultimately provided the groundwork for a new Christian morality and a consistent sense of self, incorporating a profound stability of character that could now relish the Humean flux precisely because it was centered. The problem with William Henry Ireland's clatter of voices, however, is that they casually and rather adroitly move Lockean decenteredness into a complete mode of being.

Hence Ireland reinvents his bastard self perpetually through a succession of names and writing identities—a revolutionary creative force warring against the imposition of centralized history (and especially pertinent, perhaps, after the Act of Oblivion of Louis XVIII in 1815). It would be easy simply to say that he was mad, something that contemporaries such as

Robert Southey were intent to prove in the pressing canonical case of Chatterton, in order to contain his transgressive suicide. But if Ireland was dead literary meat, he refused to lie down and refused to stop writing.[41] He defied the definition of the author, and what was to become a specifically *Romantic* author, whether expressed through the teleology of chronology, by the evolutionary process of authorial revision, or by subsequent editorial and critical construction. The writings of William Henry Ireland are protean and duplicitous, making sorties against the new orthodoxies of authorship and composition by spinning lines from the recent radical past of Savage and Chatterton and Revolutionary France, whether by cod-Elizabethan Shakespeare forgeries or the fish 'n' chippification of national identity, and still he has yet more fish to fry.

Notes

1. Jorge Luis Borges, *Labyrinths: Selected Stories and Other Writings*, ed. Donald A. Yates and James E. Irby (Harmondsworth: Penguin, 1970), 37.
2. See, for example, "Samuel Ireland" entry in *DNB*; John Mair, *The Fourth Forger: William Henry Ireland and the Shakespeare Papers* (London: Cobden-Sanderson, 1938); Bernard Grebanier, *The Great Shakespeare Forgery* (London: Heinemann, 1966); Samuel Schoenbaum, *Shakespeare's Lives* (Oxford: Clarendon Press, 1970); and Jeffrey Kahan, *Reforging Shakespeare: The Story of a Theatrical Scandal* (London: Associated UP, 1998).
3. F. E. Halliday, *The Cult of Shakespeare* (London: Duckworth, 1957), 108, 109.
4. Nick Groom, *The Forger's Shadow: How Forgery Changed the Course of Literature* (London: Picador, 2002), 217–55.
5. William Henry Ireland, *Gondez, The Monk. A Romance, of the Thirteenth Century*, 4 vols. (London, 1805), 1.viii.
6. Mario Praz, *The Romantic Agony* (London and New York: Oxford UP, 1970), 14.
7. Claude Lévi-Strauss, *The Savage Mind*, 2nd ed. (London: Weidenfeld and Nicolson, 1972), 16–20; see also Jacques Derrida, *Writing and Difference* (Chicago: University of Chicago Press, 1978), 279–95.
8. William Henry Ireland, *The Abbess. A Romance*, 4 vols. (London, 1799), 1. xviii, xxi–xxii.
9. Byron had reviewed Ireland's *Neglected Genius*.
10. Owen Junior describes the Shakspeare papers as "the Irish Shakespeare" in *Chalmeriana: or A Collection of Papers Literary and Political, entitled, Letters, Verses, &c. occasioned by reading a late heavy Supplemental Apology for the Believers in the Shakespeare Papers by George Chalmers, F.R.S.S.A.*, ed. Owen Junior and Jasper Hargrave (London, 1800), 5.
11. "H. C. Esq." [William Henry Ireland], *The Fisher Boy, a Poem Comprising his several Avocations, during the four Seasons of the Year* (n.p., n.d.), 23n.

12. Redcliffe N. Salaman, *The History and Social Influence of the Potato*, rev. J. G. Hawkes (Cambridge: Cambridge UP, 1985), 453, 486.

13. See Catherine Gallagher, "The Potato in the Materialist Imagination," in *Practicing New Historicism*, ed. Catherine Gallagher and Stephen Greenblatt (Chicago and London: University of Chicago Press, 2000), chapter 4 (113–14).

14. Stewart Lee Allen, *In the Devil's Garden: A Sinful History of Forbidden Food* (Edinburgh: Canongate, 2002), 137, 21 (no source given).

15. Larry Zuckerman, *The Potato: From the Andes in the Sixteenth Century to Fish and Chips; the Story of How a Vegetable Changed History* (Basingstoke and Oxford: Macmillan, 1999), chapter 2 and passim. It has been suggested that it was Thomas Jefferson who took the *pomme frite* from Paris to America in 1802 (Elizabeth Rozin, *The Primal Cheeseburger* (New York: Penguin, 1994), 133–52). Jefferson was certainly keen to cultivate the potato, writing to John Taylor on 29 December 1794, "The first step towards the recovery of our lands is to find substitutes for corn & bacon. I count on potatoes, clover, & sheep." Thomas Jefferson, *Writings* (New York: Library of America, n.d.), 1021; see also "lucerne and potatoes" 1014, and history of the potato 1205.

16. L. A. Clarkson and E. Margaret Crawford, *Feast and Famine: Food and Nutrition in Ireland 1500–1920* (Oxford: Oxford UP, 2001), 71–3.

17. See John Evelyn, *Sylva. Tena. Pomona acetaria and Kalendarium Hortense* (1664), quoted by Salaman 446.

18. Such dishes may be making a comeback. "Orangey Duchesse Potatoes" are suggested in *Christmas from the Freezer* (Home and Freezer Digest: British European Associated Publications Limited, 1985), although the recipe lacks the tangy sweetness of Glasse's.

19. Timothy Morton, *Shelley and the Revolution in Taste: The Body and the Natural World* (Cambridge: Cambridge UP, 1994), 14.

20. See Patrick Colquhoun, *Treatise on the Wealth, Power and Resources of the British Empire* (1814), quoted by Salaman 521.

21. See David Henry, *The Complete English Farmer* (1771), quoted in Salaman 487, 504.

22. See William Cobbett, *A Treatise on Cobbett's Corn* (1828), quoted in Salaman 521.

23. See William Lovett, *The Life and Struggles of William Lovett, in his Pursuit of Bread, Knowledge and Freedom; with some Short Account of the Different Associations he Belonged to, and of the Opinions he Entertained* (1876), quoted in Morton (1994), 14.

24. Zuckerman 71.

25. Jonathan Bate, "Faking It: Shakespeare and the 1790s," in *Essays and Studies 1993*, ed. Nigel Smith, 63–80.

26. Redcliffe Salaman describes them from personal experience, 597.

27. Charles Dickens, *Oliver Twist, or, The Parish Boy's Progress*, ed. Philip Horne (London: Penguin, 2002), 204–5 (my italics). Incidentally, Ireland, who was incarcerated for debt at least twice—once in York castle (1811), and later in London (ca. 1820; "because I could not get my MS. executed on time") and

locked in a sponging house; he wrote begging his friend George Virtue for £1—lived the last years of his life in the stews of Southwark, and could conceivably have been known to Dickens, who also tramped those streets. In 1835, Ireland was buried in the common ground of St. George the Martyr, the closest church to the Marshalsea; many who died in prison were buried there. Little Dorrit sleeps in St. George's when she is locked out, and eventually marries Arthur Clennam there.

28. Henry Mayhew, *London Labour and the London Poor* (1851), quoted by *Fish Trades Gazette* 5 November 1910 and by John K. Walton, *Fish and Chips and the British Working Class* (Leicester, London, and New York: Leicester UP, 1992), 55.

29. Zuckerman, *The Potato* 247.

30. "A man is what he eats," Ludwig Feuerbach, *Blätter für Literarische Unterhaltung*, 12 November 1850.

31. See *The Forger's Shadow* ch. 4.

32. Anya Taylor, *Bacchus in Romantic England: Writers and Drink, 1780–1830* (London: Macmillan, 1999), 57.

33. William Cobbett, *A Year's Residence, in the United States of America* (1818), paragraphs 270–1, 278–85.

34. Timothy Morton, *The Poetics of Spice: Romantic Consumerism and the Exotic* (Cambridge: Cambridge UP, 2000), 124.

35. See, for example, Jerome McGann, *The Romantic Ideology: A Critical Investigation* (Chicago and London: University of Chicago Press, 1983); Robert Brinkley and Keith Hanley, eds., *Romantic Revisions* (Cambridge: Cambridge UP, 1992); and Zachary Leader, *Revision and Romantic Authorship* (Oxford: Oxford UP, 1996).

36. Leader provides the sources for these references, but does not comment on their place in the kitchen.

37. W. K. Wimsatt Jr. and Monroe C. Beardsley, "The Intentional Fallacy," in *Authorship: From Plato to the Postmodern, A Reader*, ed. Séan Burke (Edinburgh: Edinburgh UP, 1995), 91.

38. Clipping pasted in copy of Ireland's *An Authentic Account of the Shaksperian Manuscripts, &c.* (London: Debrett, 1796), British Library 642.d.29(2).

39. John Locke, *An Essay Concerning Human Understanding*, ed. P. H. Nidditch (Oxford: Clarendon Press, 1975), 342 (ch. 27: "Identity and Diversity").

40. David Hume, *A Treatise of Human Nature*, ed. L. A. Selby Bigge, rev. P. H. Nidditch (Oxford: Clarendon Press, 1978), 252–3.

41. See my unpublished essay, "Love and Madness: Southey Editing Chatterton," in *Robert Southey and the Contexts of English Romanticism*, ed. Lynda Pratt (Aldershot: Ashgate, forthcoming).

Chapter 2 ❧

THE TASTE OF PARADISE: THE FRUITS OF ROMANTICISM IN THE EMPIRE

Timothy Fulford

In the late eighteenth century the South Pacific was a new delicacy on the menu of European intellectuals. Tahiti and the other Society Islands, "discovered" only in 1767, were a new New World, greeted with all the wonder that had attended the fifteenth-century arrival in America. Polynesia was, in effect, flavor of many a month, as Europe's explorers raved to fascinated readers about Edenic gardens of nature in which food was so plentiful that the natives could live, strong and healthy, merely by plucking fruit ripe from the trees. Prime among the many delicious fruits was the breadfruit. This remarkable plant seemed a miracle food because it was so plentiful and nutritious that it freed the islanders from the biblical curse—it was a form of bread that man did not have to work in the sweat of his brow to make.

The breadfruit was not unknown to travelers in the East, but only became a Europe-wide sensation after the voyage of Cook on the *Endeavour* (1768–71).[1] Discussed in voyage narratives, pictured in watercolors and engravings, represented on stage, collected in museums and botanic gardens, it was received, whole, dried, and on paper, by a public who saw it as a synecdoche for the Polynesian islands on which it flourished. Tahiti was imagined in its image as a "nouvelle Cythere," an exotic garden of Venus, a fertile Eden where far East became far West.[2] Free from colonization, free from labor, it seemed the antithesis of the sugar islands of the Caribbean.

To give the cultural history of the breadfruit's impact in Europe is to give the history of a symbol—a political symbol of a life of liberty beyond the grasp of empire. It is to give the history of the production and dissemination of a fruit of Enlightenment ideals. The cultural history of the breadfruit reminds us that the Romantic imagination, and the symbols that characterize it, were elaborated as much in the contexts of scientific exploration and commercial colonialism as they were in response to the politics of France. French politics and their fallout, however, came to inflect issues from further afield: the breadfruit became poisonous after the French Revolution led many Britons to associate Enlightenment ideals with rebellion and immorality. Coleridge and Southey, we shall see, found their breadfruit tainted by the changing domestic climate, which altered their view of it, and of the Polynesian liberty for which it stood.

One man was responsible, more than any others, for the breadfruit flourishing in the European imagination. Sir Joseph Banks first encountered the plant when exploring on Cook's first voyage. On Tahiti, Banks and his botanists collected the plant. His artists drew it. Meanwhile, the crew discovered its amazing nutritious properties and experimented with boiling and toasting it. To Banks, it seemed to place Tahitians in Eden before the fall: "these happy people," he wrote, "may almost be said to be exempt from the curse of our forefather; scarcely can it be said that they earn their bread with the sweat of their brow when their chiefest sustenance Bread fruit is procur'd with no more trouble than that of climbing a tree and pulling it down."[3]

It was not only in expedition journals that breadfruit became a symbol of paradise islands that seemed to have escaped Adam's curse. It was through Banks's obsession with representation and classification that it became food for the European imagination. Back in London, Banks's efforts made the breadfruit a sign of plenty, an alluring image of paradise regained, to a public that was never likely to see, still less taste one fresh from the tree. He exhibited specimens of it in his *hortus siccus*. There it could be consulted by botanists from all over Europe, at least in its dried form. He had the drawing of the plant prepared for publication in his *Florilegium*, so that it, along with the other species new to Western science, could be disseminated as an image to scientists unable to examine it in the metropolis.

The breadfruit became the chief delicacy in Banks's Polynesian menu, a rare treat for scientists and public alike. They were fed by Banks's ability to supply an empire of knowledge via his power over the processes by which that empire was sustained—he had, as a wealthy and well-connected baronet, and, after 1778, as the president of Europe's foremost scientific institution—the Royal Society, the resources to maintain a workshop of botanical illustrators and the prestige to shape the printed accounts of the voyages which sold out their editions across Europe. As a friend of ministers and monarch, he also had the influence to ensure that the empire of knowledge remained dependent on him, for he not only shaped the processes of representation, but also controlled the means of distribution. In charge of the botanical gardens at Kew, he had—or rather could get—the fruit, and scientists who wanted to examine it themselves were reliant on his ability to import it in the flesh just as readers were on his ability to disseminate it as a sign. J. F. Blumenbach, the eminent German professor, asked Banks in February 1794 to send him a breadfruit, since being able to exhibit an actual specimen would be "exceedingly interesting for my lectures in Natural History."[4] Banks dispatched some, along with other items from the Pacific, and Blumenbach told him that

> their arrival...excited the universal curiosity of our little town, (remote in the heart of the continent where such exotic Rarities so seldom arrive—) that I may say there was in the first fortnight a kind of pilgrimage to my house, to see them, & above all that fruit so famous since your voyage round the world & so inestimable for the benefit of mankind.[5]

Göttingen, Blumenbach's town, may have been little, but its university was at the forefront of contemporary thought, as Coleridge recognized when he chose to study there in 1799.[6] Blumenbach himself was a pioneer both as a natural historian and an anthropologist. He was not a man given to uncritical raptures: his scientific discourse aims at a detached, objective validity by converting particular objects into component signs/parts in a general classification of nature.[7] Yet here his words show the breadfruit as more than a item in an ordered sign-system. In the flesh, the fruit is a holy grail, or a fetish brought from exotic lands. Possession of it makes Blumenbach's house a sacred site and transfers to him the aura of the man who had brought it back from his quest round the world.

Not everyone treated Banks's plant so piously. If the breadfruit embodied the natural fertility of the Pacific islands, it also symbolized the free love that seemed to flourish there. The narratives of Cook's voyages viewed Tahiti through the neoclassical ideals of the explorers. Tahitian women were "artless nymphs" who were as spontaneously and naturally sexual as the groves in which they disported.[8] And Banks, it was suggested, had indulged himself not only with the island's fruit but also with its women.

Indiscreet phrases included in the voyage narrative compiled by John Hawkesworth encouraged satirists to link botanical with sexual discovery. Hawkesworth not only hinted at Banks's sexual encounters but also featured his comment that the breadfruit almost exempted the Tahitians "from the first general curse."[9] Seizing on this, John Scott had Oberea, a lovelorn Tahitian "queen," carving Banks's name, like an Elizabethan sonneteer, on a breadfruit tree:

> Ah! I remember on the river's side,
> Whose bubbling waters 'twixt the mountains glide,
> A bread-tree stands, on which with sharpen'd stone,
> To thy dear name I deign'd unite my own.
> Grow bread-tree, grow, nor envious hand remove
> The sculptur'd symbols of my constant love.[10]

Here Scott makes the breadfruit tree scurrilously phallic. Oberea seems to be tattooing[11] the "growing" Banks as much as carving her initials on the tree. The tree-like Banks was then imagined back home, spreading his seed over the gardens of Britain's ladies.

The explorers' spreading of their seed rapidly became no laughing matter. What seemed at first to be free love in groves where guilt was unknown soon threatened to destroy the island's reputation as a sensual Eden. Europeans brought not just guilt into Tahiti's sensual bowers, but venereal disease. The voyagers' sexual dalliance corrupted the savage idyll with the infections, physical and moral, of "civilization." George Forster, naturalist on Cook's second Pacific voyage, feared

> that hitherto our intercourse has been wholly disadvantageous to the nations of the South Seas; and that those communities have been the least injured, who have always kept aloof from us, and whose jealous disposition did not suffer our sailors to become too familiar among them, as if they had perceived in their countenances that levity of disposition, and that spirit of debauchery, with which they are generally reproached.[12]

Forster was a political radical, an admirer of the French philosophes whose writings helped precipitate the French Revolution. His critique echoed that of Denis Diderot, who adopted the persona of an islander in his discussion of Tahiti. Diderot's islander called European civilization an infection which blighted his pastoral Polynesian idyll: "Our fields will be soaked with the impure blood that has passed from your veins into ours or our children will be condemned to nourish and perpetuate the sickness that you gave to their fathers and their mothers and then to transmit it in their turn, forever, to their descendants."[13] For Enlightenment radicals, Tahiti's brave new world of noble savagery was already being corrupted by the exploring, and exploiting, Europeans.

Diderot was, of course, bemoaning the destruction of an ideal that was as European as the diseases brought by the explorers. Tahiti, that is to say, served as an imaginary home for social goals which emerged from Europeans' opposition to aspects of their own society. The island became the radical Other of the hierarchical old world and the breadfruit the plant that rooted a utopia of noble savagery into the real soil of Polynesia.

Ironically enough, it was Banks, who had done so much to make that utopia grow in Tahiti, who began its final destruction. He planned to uproot the breadfruit, to turn it to commercial, as well as scientific, use. He did not just export the plant in images and specimens for botanists. He exported it for the benefit of Britain, creating in the process a network of institutions and procedures that linked islands and continents. He joined Tahiti to an economic empire by the transportation of plants that were intended to bring plenty of food, and plenty of profit, to those who grew them. But it was this act that changed the image of the breadfruit, and of Tahiti, irrevocably. For Banks's scheme was to use the fruit, symbol of natural fertility and savage liberty, to feed other islands than those of the Pacific. In his hands, the fruit that sustained peace and love in independent Tahiti was to feed slaves in the colonized West Indies.

Banks, a consummate politician, encouraged a campaign to persuade the government that West Indies' planters, currently in financial difficulty, were clamoring for the fruit. He helped John Ellis to publicize the idea in *A Description of the Mangostan and the Breadfruit.*[14] As president of the Royal Society, he gave the proposals institutional sanction, implying that breadfruit was a miracle cure for the colonies' economic ills: "the benefits arising from the cultivation of this blessed plant might be very sensibly felt by the English inhabitants of the Sugar Islands, as well as the poor negroes, their slaves; especially in times of scarcity."[15] The breadfruit was to be Polynesian manna for Britain's empire.[16]

By 1787 the campaign had succeeded. A correspondent rejoiced that Banks had "prevail'd with the Ministry to send for the Breadfruit. This country will also have Reason to bless you."[17] On Banks's say-so, Captain Bligh was commissioned by the Admiralty to sail to Tahiti, which he had first visited under Cook's command.[18] Bligh was to collect specimens of the breadfruit tree and take them to the West Indies. In 1789 he arrived at Tahiti and collected his trees but found naval discipline collapsing.

The notorious mutiny occurred on 28 April after the *Bounty* had sailed away from the island. One of the mutineers' first acts was to throw the breadfruit plants overboard. They would not take the bountiful fruit of the Pacific to the slave colonies of the Caribbean, and returned instead to Tahiti where, Bligh explained, "they need not labour and where the allurments of dissipation are beyond anything that can be conceived."[19] It was, of course, the plentifulness of the breadfruit that allowed them to live without labor on the island. The mutineers had "gone native," sabotaging the imperialist scheme to make the fruit of Polynesian freedom into cheap nourishment for Britain's slave laborers. The breadfruit, it seemed, would not after all be absorbed into the commodifying empire that turned places and people into profit-producing sugar.

Banks was not a man to let his appetite go unsatisfied, and a second voyage was prepared in 1791. Bligh, having completed his epic escape in an open boat, found himself returning to the scene of the mutiny. This time he commanded the *Providence*, and successfully reached the West Indies in May 1793 with his breadfruit housed in a plant cabin built to Banks's design. Banks's handpicked gardeners James Wiles and Christopher Smith were on board, spearheading Britain's effort to outdo its imperial competitor: Britain wanted to exploit the commercial opportunities offered by transplantation before the French did. But the French had a head start. On 15 July 1788 French St. Domingue received a consignment of plants from Ile de France, including breadfruit. The breadfruit trees were distributed to twelve private and public stations around St. Domingue. The French celebrated the breadfruit's arrival while, back in London, Banks worried but consoled himself that the French consignment was probably from the East Indies "where the good sort is not found."[20]

Banks's botanical network was sophisticated enough to give him a good chance of outdoing the French. He had a backup system in case the *Providence*, like the *Bounty*, went unexpectedly down. On 28 March 1793 Charles Ker, Army Surgeon, wrote from Calicut about a local source of breadfruit trees, of which he enclosed a drawing. Ker suggested that if the export of the trees from Tahiti failed it would be easy to export the plants from Calicut: "and as it is a national object, this might be done by a King's ship on its return from this station."[21] Banks replied with detailed queries about the situation and soil the trees best thrived in; Ker then informed him that the local Commercial Resident meant to send plants to St. Helena to be tried in different soils there. The trading posts and islands of Britain's empire had become research stations, linked by the navy, and dedicated to perfecting the transplantation of crops for commercial and therefore national advantage. Tahiti, like the other remote islands discovered by Britain's navy, could no longer be imagined as innocent and untouched.

The West Indian colonies, on the other hand, did prove independent—in an unexpected way. After all Banks's efforts they remained indifferent to the breadfruit. As a food for empire, it failed, because it fell foul of the complex class and race politics of the slave islands. Alexander Anderson, botanic gardener on St. Vincent, told Banks that "strange to tell, there are some people who undervalue such a valuable acquisition, & say they prefer a plantain or yam: but, however, these are only some self-conceited & prejudiced Creoles."[22] The Creoles wanted to insist on their superiority to black people and to Caribs by disdaining food meant for slaves. And the planters, now less pressed by economic difficulties than in the early 1780s, disdained it for economic reasons:

> The breadfruit, although one of the most valuable productions yet sent them, is neglected and despised, unless by a few persons. They say that negroes do not like it, and will not eat it, if they can get anything else; but this is not really the case, as I know, and can declare from experience, that the very reverse is the fact, when once they are a little accustomed to it. The fact is, that the planters hate giving it a place on their estates, as they regard it as an intruder on their cane land, and they dislike any other object but canes. As to futurity, they think nothing of what may be the wants of themselves or negroes three or four years hence.[23]

Banks's scheme had broken, ironically enough, upon the commodity fetishism it had sought to help. Loving profit, the planters treated everything but sugarcane as an expendable object. Why use land for breadfruit when the slaves it would feed could be replaced by newly imported Africans when they died of overwork and malnutrition?

It was in the British port most strongly linked to the Caribbean and to the sugar planters that Coleridge and Southey emerged into the political arena. They did so via the campaign against the slave trade—and made the planters' indifference to the slaves' welfare central to their protest. Coleridge later explained that cruelty was the inevitable outcome of a system of commodification, which loved a thing (sugar-profit) as if it were a person, and treated people as if they were things: "A Slave is a *Person* perverted into a *Thing*: Slavery, therefore, is not so properly a deviation from Justice, as an absolute subversion of all Morality."[24] Southey agreed, and went so far as to justify rebellion in his sonnets on the slave trade: "No more on Heaven he [the slave] calls with fruitless breath, / But sweetens with revenge, the draught of death."[25] In an act of poetic justice, the slave kills his master with a drink sweetened with poison rather than sugar. The commodity to which he is enslaved destroys him who profits from it.

Not surprisingly, Southey also showed sympathy toward the *Bounty* mutineers who had sabotaged the commodification of the breadfruit and rebelled against a naval discipline almost as severe as that inflicted on slaves.[26] In a letter he declared:

> If the *Bounty* mutineers had not behaved so cruelly to their officers I should have been the last to condemn them. Otaheitia independant of its women had many inducements not only for the sailor but the philosopher. He might cultivate his own ground and trust himself and friends for his defence—he might be truly happy in himself and his happiness would be increased by communicating it to others. He might introduce the advantages and yet avoid the vices of cultivated society.[27]

Here Southey subscribes to the idealized version of Polynesia that positions it as the opposite of hierarchical and imperialist Britain. The mutineers are not solely motivated by lust: they go where the philosopher wishes to go, escaping the dehumanizing discipline of the navy to live in virtue, independence, freedom, and peace. Southey envies the mutineers their ability to slip free of the "vices of cultivated society." He imagines the *Bounty* affair through the ideal of savage liberty. His view was shaped not only by reading Hawkesworth and Forster but also by his own dream of living in liberty abroad, where he might escape the pressure being exerted upon radicals thought sympathetic to the French Revolution. In February 1793 he had imagined a possible location for the commune that he and Coleridge came to term Pantisocracy:

> Why is there not some corner of the world where wealth is useless! . . . Is humanity so very vicious that society cannot exist without so many artificial distinctions linked together as we are in the great chain? Why should the extremity of the chain be neglected? At this moment I could form the most delightful theory of an island peopled by men who should be Xtians not Philosophers and where Vice only should be contemptible. Virtue only honourable where all should be convenient without luxury all satisfied without profusion.[28]

As James C. McKusick argues, here Southey locates his commune on what resembles a Polynesian island as described by Banks, Forster, and Hawkesworth.[29] Such an island would, presumably, be a home for virtue and honor because the abundance of the breadfruit would ensure that all were "satisfied without profusion." To Coleridge, revolted as he was by the "idle gold" whipped by "Bristowa's citizen[s]" from the bodies of Caribbean slaves, the South Sea islands were moral economies, places where human virtue and natural abundance were in harmony.[30] They were the imagined opposites of "civilized" Bristol and of the commodi-fied slave islands on which so much of Bristol's "civilization" was built. Soon the wilds of America, the valleys of Wales and the hills of Somerset were to fulfill the same function. The Romantic idealization of rural life, that is to say, moved from Bristol to the South Pacific and back to the British countryside. Romantic nature first took shape not at home but in the distant tropics of the mind.

The Pantisocrats decided on the Susquehannah as a more practical destination, but Southey and Coleridge continued to imagine Polynesia as a refuge for liberty. In 1809 Southey wrote of Bligh's "unendurable tyranny" and added: "if every man had his due Bligh would have had the halter instead of the poor fellows whom we brought from Taheite. Is not that a sad story of Stewart and the Taheitian Girl?"[31] He told the story in the *Quarterly Review*. The navy had sent Captain Edwards, in the *Pandora*, to arrest the mutineers. Fletcher Christian had disappeared (to Pitcairn island),[32] but Edwards found several and imprisoned them on board. The *Pandora* foundered in a storm en route to Britain, and several of the prisoners drowned:

> A midshipman, by name Stewart, having made himself guilty in the sudden burst of mutiny, took up his abode on the island and lived with the daugh-ter of a Chief, who had borne him a beautiful girl when the *Pandora* arrived, and he was seized and laid in irons. She followed him with her infant to the ship; the officers who witnessed the scene which ensued could scarcely bear to behold it, and Stewart besought them not to let her see him again, So, she was separated from him by force and sent ashore. In the course of two months she pined away, and died,—literally of a broken heart. He, happily for himself, perished in the wreck of the *Pandora*; the orphan has been bred up by missionaries.[33]

Clearly, Southey still regarded the island as an ideal exotic setting for a free love all too often fettered in Britain by issues of property and propriety.

By the mid-1790s, however, free love had a bad reputation in Britain. In the conservative backlash provoked by the French Revolution, radicals were stigmatized as rebels, traitors, and debauchees. Burke portrayed the revolutionary impulse in terms of sexual deviance and monstrosity.[34] Coleridge and Southey saw their friends attacked in similar terms. William

Godwin was branded a pander for advocating the end of marriage; Mary Wollstonecraft was called a whore for living out her ideals of sexual equality. Mary Robinson met the same reaction when she became a radical poet. Coleridge himself was accused in *The Anti-Jacobin* of deserting his wife and children. Radicals were ostracized: Thomas Beddoes, their Bristol scientist friend, had his submissions to the Royal Society turned down by none other than Banks, who had already begun, in the words of a contemporary, "to suppress all *Jacobin innovations*" in science.[35] Soon, Banks was cooperating with an attempt to suppress Polynesian liberty too.

That attempt began with the formation in September 1795 of the Church Missionary Society. The Society recruited missionaries from Evangelicals and dissenters. In sermons and articles in the *Evangelical Magazine*, the chief advocate of the scheme, the Revd. T. Haweis, sought to attract recruits by depicting the sensual delights of Tahiti. Haweis had never been to Tahiti: it was through reading travel narratives that he knew it. He was sure that missionaries would be able to convert it to Christian morality. Ultimately he was right. But first he had to persuade men to go there. And so he presented it in language that tempts its hearers to plunge themselves in exotic delights, only to reform them. He likened it to the "gardens of the Hesperides," spoke of the "fascinations of beauty, and the allurements of the country."[36] But he identified the abundance of food produced by the breadfruit as an opportunity rather than a blessing. For Haweis, the breadfruit was not nature's but God's gift, given to allow the missionaries the chance to convert the islanders: "The natives," he declared, "not harassed by labour for daily bread, or as slaves, worked under the lash of the whip, are always sure to have abundant time for instruction." Natives, in this ideology, had to work. Moral instruction would be a holy labor, an alternative to the work discipline that other Britons imposed on other islanders.

When the first missionaries reached Polynesia, instruction began to operate in the opposite direction, as a number of them abandoned their holy work to live on the fruits of the land with local women. By 1809 the problem was bad enough for the Revd. George Burder to appeal to Banks on the Society's behalf. He requested Sir Joseph to use his transplantation network for the moral purpose of exporting wives for the missionaries who were facing the temptations of Tahiti. Banks had to transport women, as he had done plants, for the benefit of the empire. But that benefit was by now defined differently, in terms of decency and propriety rather than scientific advance or commercial profit. The older, more conservative Banks, living down his Enlightenment enthusiasms, had them shipped. It was late in the day, but he had begun to impose Evangelical control over the Tahiti that, represented in travelers' tales, had become an image of liberty, fraternity, and love. It was a control for which the Tahitians were to pay dearly.

It was also a control that Southey and Coleridge came to support. Having moved from Bristol by the early 1800s, they were no longer looking for a South Sea idyll to oppose to the islands on which the city's prosperity depended. Self-exiled from that political arena, they were no longer Pantisocrats offering Bristolians a radical Other as an alternative to the immoral Other of slavery. And they were influenced by the missionary reports of infanticide, human sacrifice, and prostitution in Polynesia, so that they changed their minds about the islands' supposed harmony and liberty and about the morality of colonization. Evangelical Christianity offered more successful arguments against slavery, and they even came to accept its emphasis that morality and order proceeded from work. Where once they had idealized the culture produced by the breadfruit, they now condemned it. Tahitians were wicked, Southey wrote in 1803, because they failed to conform to the work ethic: "when the Creator decreed that in the sweat of his brow man must eat bread, the punishment became a blessing; a divine ordinance necessary for the health of soul as well as body while man continues to be the imperfect being that we behold him."[37] Coleridge, he added, had a scheme to "mend" the islanders, "by extirpating the breadfruit from their island, and making them live by the sweat of their brows." The two Romantics, having consumed Tahiti and its fruit through travel narratives, having idealized it in opposition to the bloody islands on which sugary Bristol was built, now wished to see its natural fertility disciplined by Christian colonization. This was to replace a radical ideal with an Evangelical one, was to collaborate with the ideology that an increasingly moralistic age used to reform and to justify Britain's spreading empire. The Tahitians, like West Indians after abolition, were to be Christianized and Anglicized rather than enslaved. Southey declared, "I want English knowledge and the English language diffused to the east, and west, and the south." In 1810 Coleridge recommended "Coercion . . . or even compelling" "savages into a form of civilization" through a colonization that made "the moral good & personal Happiness of the Savages part of the End."[38] For both men, savage liberty and tropical nature were now too wild to be trusted. Uprooting the breadfruit from their political imagination, they turned instead to advocating a reformed imperialism of labored righteousness and sweated civilization. Daily bread and not the breadfruit would replace the unholy sacrament of slave-sugar and would symbolize British rule. To be an English writer, for the later Southey and Coleridge, was to accept the task of making the nation, and the world, prefer the communion-wafer of Anglicanism to the fruity flavor of liberty and the sugary taste of profit.[39] By 1833, with the Tahitians Christianized, slavery abolished and missionaries established in India and Africa, they could begin to scent the bland smell of sanctimony successfully spreading across the empire.

What, then, can we conclude about Romanticism, breadfruit, and the South Pacific? Certainly that, in form and content, Romanticism was shaped by—and in turn shaped—issues arising from exploration and the commodities that explorers found and empire exploited. But we can also see that Romanticism's relationship with the cultures that Britain was subjecting to its power was never univocal. Coleridge and Southey emerged as writers through their opposition to slavery and portrayed the sugar islands as shameful dystopias. But this very portrayal was determined by their idealization of the islands of the South Seas, which became utopias by contrast to the British Caribbean—utopias they abandoned only for Byron to revive them.[40] The process at work here was not a "manichean allegory"—not a binary opposition of "good" colonizer to "bad" native, as some theorists have characterized imperialist ideology.[41] Rather, three or more terms are in play, and one indigenous culture is idealized in a rhetorical ploy aimed at making the colonizers' despoliation of another seem shameful. In this process, all the terms are in dynamic redefinition: Britain-the-colonizer becomes oppressive and guilty; the West Indies become sadistic labor camps; Tahiti an idyll of precolonized indigenous life; revolutionary France a place of illicit freedoms that can be symbolized by Polynesia. But the redefinition takes effect first at the imperial center: the tropical islands were shaped by the demands of debate back in Britain.

In the Romantics' hands, redefinition was ostensibly anti-imperialist. And indeed it did enable them to make a vigorous condemnation of Britain—a condemnation that, historically, helped arouse enough guilt to get the slave trade abolished. But, to a degree, it sacrificed the South Seas in the process. Tahiti, that is to say, was appropriated and commodified as a savage idyll, shaped to serve an argument about Britain and the West Indies. And though this appropriation was, by comparison with the appropriation and commodification of Caribbean islands, relatively benign, it nevertheless had dangerous consequences. Because they were subsumed in the breadfruit, real Tahitians figured in European eyes only in Romantic terms. Their lives and culture were buried beneath the tree that supposedly embodied them, so that they could not figure in other ways. Worse still, because Europeans came to believe that Tahiti Romanticized was Tahiti in real life, they began to turn against it. Ironically and tragically, the

Romantic idealization of Polynesia led to its own extirpation, for had the South Sea islands not been pictured by explorers, scientists and poets as sensual Edens, then Evangelical missionaries would not have targeted their culture for "reform." And had the islanders not been seen—as Diderot and Banks saw them—as childlike and pliant in their innocence, then the missionaries might not have dared move in. Yet they were so seen, and the missionaries did move in. Thus an anticolonialist idealization that was effective in opposing Britain's empire of slavery led to a cultural imperialism with pernicious consequences. There were no innocent fantasies in a world in which Britons could increasingly impose their wills, and repress their desires, at native people's expense.

By 1830, the missionaries had, in uprooting the Romantic image of the islands, succeeded in attacking some of the Polynesian customs that they found cruel or immoral. They reduced prostitution and attacked infanticide. But they encouraged and participated in wars and effectively destroyed much of the traditional culture that gave Tahitians their identity. The missionaries introduced European dress; they discouraged communal dwelling. They insisted on labor and enforced a strict moral and legal code where they could.[42] In short, they inculcated the regime that Britain's governing classes increasingly sought to instill in the laboring classes at home: Bible learning, handwork, thrift, and monetary payment. For most islanders, the effects of this were pernicious: by 1835 the population of Tahiti had fallen by three-quarters; the art of making cloth from tree bark was no longer practiced; the great double canoes had been abandoned. A Quaker visitor wrote: "there is scarcely anything so striking or pitiable as their aimless, nerveless mode of spending life." The breadfruit would never again, in fantasy or reality, nourish an indigenous culture unmarked by the desires, fear, and power of Britain. Romantic idylls had, it turned out, a price, and it was the native people of Polynesia, like the Africans enslaved in the West Indies, who would count its cost as their daily bread.

Not all the native people: if some suffered by the missionaries and their introduction of the work ethic, others profited—at least in the short term. One such was the ambitious chief Pomare who, by converting to Christianity, was able to recruit the missionaries, with their armaments and technological expertise, to assist him in wars that were designed to make him paramount over the other chiefs of the island. With the missionaries' guns and tactics, Pomare gained authority while the missionaries, for their part, got new, official, approval of their religion from the most powerful man in Tahiti. They got it too from Britain's Poet Laureate: Southey's supportive reviews of the missionaries' *Transactions* helped to give their actions respectability amongst the Anglican and conservative middle classes. In 1830 he set out to give them authority by another, more traditional, means too—by promoting a would-be imperial epic poetry that glorified their conversion of the islanders. He advised William Ellis, one of the missionaries, on his poem *Mahine*, which dealt with the overthrow of "idolatry" and treated Pomare's wars in epic verse. Southey recommended Herbert and Daniel as poetic models and identified Byron's poems, by contrast, as being "of a kind which carry pollution with them."[43] Ellis's poem, unlike Byron's *The Island*, was patriarchal and monarchical, glorifying a military King and martial God who spread Christianity through holy war. Ellis's islanders sing, taking their text from Zechariah (I. 5):

> The fathers, where are they? No longer among us
> > In front of the battle, these men of renown
> Shall wave the bright banner, where dark legions throng us,
> > Assure us of conquest, and point to the crown.
>
> The fathers, where are they? Securely abiding,
> > From labour they rest in the mansions above,
> Where the Saviour exalted benignly presiding,
> > O'er banquets divine sheds the smile of His love.
>
> The fathers where are they? In glory appearing,
> > In homage they bow at the feet of their King,
> The crown and the white robe of victory wearing,
> > His throne they surround, and His triumph they sing.[44]

Ellis's Tahiti is a Tory vision of chivalric medieval England relocated to the Pacific, an island where ideals that seemed to be crumbling at home could be imagined to flourish. Ellis left the poem in manuscript, but he did publish a prose account of the South Sea islands, *Polynesian Researches*, which portrays Pomare's war against the "idolater" chiefs as a kind of crusade. Southey then reviewed the book with admiration in the *Quarterly*. It was, according to Ellis's biographer, the good reception which the *Researches* received that converted many skeptics to support the missions. Southey's own Church and King nationalism had effectively influenced the development of the muscular Christianity that became a vital force in Victorian imperialism. And if such an outcome seems both unlikely and ironic considering Southey's earlier idealizations of South Sea liberty, then it should remind us that Tahiti had, by 1830, been for many years one of the issues that led the once-radical writers of the 1790s to eat the words in which they had first formulated Romanticism.

Notes

1. For a discussion of the various accounts of the voyages to the South Seas in the period see Philip Edwards, *The Story of the Voyage: Sea-Narratives in Eighteenth-Century England* (Cambridge: Cambridge UP, 1994) and Neil Rennie, *Far Fetched Facts: The Literature of Travel and The Idea of the South Seas* (Oxford: Clarendon, 1992).

2. See Alan Moorehead, *The Fatal Impact: The Invasion of the South Pacific 1767–1840* (London: Hamish Hamilton, 1966), 51. See also Bernard Smith, *European Vision and the South Pacific 1768–1850* (Oxford: Oxford UP, 1960), 24–5.

3. *The Endeavour Journal of Joseph Banks 1768–1771*, ed. J. C. Beaglehole, 2 vols. (Sydney: Trustees of the Public Library of New South Wales with Angus and Robertson, 1962), 1.341.

4. British Library Add. MS, 8098, 215.

5. British Library Add. MS, 8098, 218.

6. Coleridge, in fact, studied with Blumenbach himself, and viewed some of the specimens that Banks had sent him. See Trevor H. Levere, *Poetry Realized in Nature: Samuel Taylor Coleridge and Early Nineteenth-Century Science* (Cambridge: Cambridge UP, 1981), 210.

7. As, for instance, in J. F. Blumenbach, *A Manual of the Elements of Natural History*, tr. R. T. Gore (London, 1825), 37.

8. George Forster, *A Voyage Round the World in his Britannic Majesty's Sloop Resolution Commanded by Capt. James Cook, during the Years 1772, 3, 4, and 5*, 2 vols. (London, 1777), 1.432.

9. John Hawkesworth, *An Account of the Voyages Undertaken By The Order Of His Present Majesty For Making Discoveries in the Southern Hemisphere*, 3 vols. (London, 1773), 2.80–6, 107.

10. *An Epistle from Oberea, Queen of Otaheite, to Joseph Banks, Esq.* (London, 1774).

11. The Tahitian custom of tattooing, and the news that many of Cook's crew had let themselves be tattooed, also excited much comment after the *Endeavour* voyages were published. See Rod Edmond, *Representing the South Pacific: Colonial Discourse from Cook to Gaugin* (Cambridge: Cambridge UP, 1997), 67–72.

12. Forster, *A Voyage* 1.213.

13. *Supplement to Bougainville's Voyage* (1772) in *Diderot's Selected Writings*, ed. Lester G. Crocker (New York and London: Macmillan, 1966), 228.

14. (London, 1775).

15. From a letter to the Royal Society proposing the scheme, quoted in Captain William Bligh, *The Log of H. M. S. Providence* (Guildford, Surrey: Genesis, 1976), 18.

16. See H. B. Carter, *Sir Joseph Banks 1743–1820* (London: British Museum, 1988), 218.

17. Matthew Wallen, letter of 4 May 1787, British Library Add. MS, 33978, 117.

18. Banks's role in this and subsequent schemes is discussed in D. L. Mackay, "Banks, Bligh and Breadfruit," *New Zealand Journal of History*, 8 (1974), 61–77.
19. William Bligh, *A Narrative of the Mutiny On Board Her Majesty's Ship Bounty and the Subsequent Voyage of Part of the Crew* (London, 1790), 10.
20. Letter of 30 October 1788; Brinkman Collection, transcript in Banks Archive, Natural History Museum, London.
21. Banks's Correspondence held at the Royal Botanic Gardens, Kew, 2.94.
22. Letter of Alexander Anderson, 30 March 1796; Dawson Turner Transcripts of Banks's correspondence, Natural History Museum, London, 10.25–26.
23. Alexander Anderson, report to Society of Arts (of which Banks was a member): quoted in K. W. Spence-Lewis, *Sir Joseph Banks. Royal Botanical Garden St. Vincent 1764–1820* (Seattle, London, St. Vincent: K. W. Spence-Lewis, 1994), 16.
24. From a manuscript essay intended for *The Courier*, September 1811. In S. T. Coleridge, *Essays on his Times*, ed. David V. Erdman, 3 vols. (London and Princeton, N.J.: Routledge Kegan Paul and Princeton UP, 1978), 3.235.
25. Southey, *Poems* (Bristol and London, 1797): Sonnets on the Slave Trade, v, lines 13–14.
26. My discussion of the poets and the *Bounty* is indebted to James C. McKusick, " 'Wisely Forgetful': Coleridge and the Politics of Pantisocracy," in *Romanticism and Colonialism: Writing and Empire 1780–1830*, ed. Tim Fulford and Peter J. Kitson (Cambridge: Cambridge UP, 1998), 107–28.
27. *New Letters of Robert Southey*, ed. Kenneth Curry, 2 vols. (New York and London: Columbia UP, 1965), 1.19.
28. *New Letters of Robert Southey*, 1.19.
29. McKusick, "Wisely Forgetful" 107.
30. "Reflections on Having Left a Place of Retirement" (1795), lines 12–13, *The Poetical Works of S. T. Coleridge*, ed. E. H. Coleridge (London: Oxford UP, 1912), 1.106.
31. *New Letters of Robert Southey*, 1.519.
32. Christian's fate was not discovered until 1808, when an American ship discovered his descendants living there. On public and poetic responses to this see Rennie, *Far-Fetched Facts* 171.
33. *Quarterly Review*, 2 (1809), 24–61 (50).
34. In *A Letter to a Noble Lord*. See *The Writings and Speeches of Edmund Burke*, gen. ed. Paul Langford, 17 vols. (Oxford: Oxford UP, 1981–), 9.156.
35. James Watt, Jr., quoted in Jan Golinski, *Science as Public Culture: Chemistry and Enlightenment in Britain, 1760–1820* (Cambridge: Cambridge UP, 1992), 163.
36. "The Very Probable Success of a Proper Mission to the South Sea Islands," *Evangelical Magazine* (July 1795), 264; *Sermons, Preached in London, At the Formation of the Missionary Society, September 22, 23, 24, 1795* (London, 1795), 170.
37. *The Life and Correspondence of Robert Southey*, ed. Rev Charles Cuthbert Southey, 6 vols. (London, 1849–50), 2.243.

38. *The Notebooks of S. T. Coleridge*, ed. Kathleen Coburn, 5 vols. (London and Princeton, N.J.: Routledge Kegan Paul and Princeton UP, 1957–), 3.3921.

39. Although of course in practice an empire of missionary Christianity often went hand-in-hand with one dedicated to profit.

40. In *The Island* (1823).

41. Said's *Orientalism* gave currency to such a model, and Abdul R. JanMohamed developed it into what he terms the "manichean allegory" of colonialist writing. Edward Said, *Orientalism* (London and Harmondsworth: Penguin, 1985); Abdul R. JanMohamed, "The Economy of Manichean Allegory: The Function of Racial Difference in Colonialist Literature," *Critical Inquiry*, 12.1 (1985), 59–87.

42. Daniel Wheeler, quoted in Moorehead, *The Fatal Impact* 88.

43. John Eimeo Ellis, *Life of William Ellis Missionary to the South Seas and Madagascar* (London, 1873), 206.

44. Quoted in *Life of William Ellis* 207.

Chapter 3 ⁓

THE POLITICS OF THE PLATTER: CHARLOTTE SMITH AND THE "SCIENCE OF EATING"

Penny Bradshaw

Food has many metaphorical associations, most notably perhaps with the sensual and erotic, but during periods of extreme social unrest one of the most important uses of food as signifier is political. During the Romantic period, as recent critics have shown, motifs of food proliferate at a cultural level and this can be closely linked to sociohistorical factors.[1] Defining political moments of the period relate to questions concerning food and consumption, and in particular to the dichotomy between the absence of food and excessive consumption. The French Revolution was engendered by an economic structure in which the people were starving while the aristocracy lived in excessive luxury. In Britain during the 1790s and 1800s this same dichotomy was repeated. There were several crop failures during these two decades and these, combined with heavy taxation and continual wars, generated a starving laboring class who were bitterly aware of the wasteful lifestyle and extreme gluttony of the Prince of Wales. But what also makes images of food and eating significant in the Romantic period is that the middle to late eighteenth century witnessed the rapid expansion of a middle-class consumer society. The historian Paul Langford claims that "by the middle of George III's reign" we have no longer "a nation of gentry but a powerful and extensive middle class,"[2] and so at this point in history, consumption and consumerism begin to develop heterogeneous new meanings.

The poet and novelist Charlotte Smith draws extensively on food imagery in her work with regard to both of these sociopolitical phenomena. This chapter explores Smith's politicized use of the trope of consumption in relation to historical and biographical contexts. It argues that she is influenced by the way in which food begins to be deployed in the graphic satires of the late 1780s and early 1790s, in particular those by James Gillray. In her work Smith draws on the images deployed in the print press, but develops this populist use of food imagery to produce a more complex, and politically challenging reading of the moral economy of diet.

In a recent study of Georgian caricature, Diana Donald suggests that satirical cartoons function almost as a "surveillance camera overlooking the major events of the century" and "were a living part of everyday experience in Georgian Britain."[3] But the cartoons do more than simply record, they also translate history, and in so doing provide a useful and accessible means of examining one of the central figurative and metaphorical treatments of politics during the period. They demonstrate the extent to which food carried a political significance during the revolutionary years and beyond, and functioned as a potent metaphor for economic consumption. We can see this clearly in Gillray's *Substitutes for Bread* (1795), published on Christmas Eve in response to the national wheat shortages of the previous two years. In the picture he ironically depicts the British cabinet responding to the call to reduce wheat consumption, by dining on the most expensive and luxurious foodstuffs. On closer inspection of the foods on the table we can see that they are made up of coins, and oral consumption is thus literally translatable as economic consumption. Cartoons such as this one, in which the metaphorical implications of food are made overt, enable us to read the food imagery in some of the more complex literary texts of the period, with a greater degree of sensitivity to the ways in which meaning is encoded.

Like Wordsworth, both Gillray and Smith are clearly influenced by the social inequalities of the age, but they respond to political events in a very direct way, rather than through a process of Wordsworthian reflection and recollection. They both produce dynamic and astute political texts which have an immediacy about them that seems startlingly modern. Although Gillray has been acknowledged as the father of modern political satire, Smith's work is not usually viewed in terms of its modernity, but the directness and topicality of both of their political responses is signaled by the fact that they begin to draw extensively on food imagery during the revolutionary period. During 1792 alone Gillray produces four cartoons which rely extensively on the metaphor of eating for their political message, and

James Gillray, *Substitutes for Bread* (London, 1795). Copyright the British Museum,

during the same year Smith begins to shift away from sentimental to political discourse, and in so doing, draws on similar motifs in her work. This chapter will begin by looking at Smith's appropriation of the satirical strategies of the visual cartoonist. It then considers how she focuses on the moral value of particular foodstuffs in order to produce a more radical interpretation of diet.

One of the most fascinating aspects of Smith's work is her radical shift from the primarily elegiac autobiographical sonnets and sentimental novels of the 1780s to a committed political radicalism in the early 1790s. This movement from sentimental to political discourse coincides with her residence in Brighton from 1789 to 1793, and Smith's sister, Catherine Dorset, apologetically blames her "paroxysm of political fever" and the consequence of this—her radical novel *Desmond*—on the acquaintance formed in Brighton "with some of the most violent advocates of the French Revolution."[4] Such connections are clearly important and expose Smith to revolutionary discourse and ideas in a particularly exciting and immediate way, but the Brighton of these years is significant in other ways which have a direct bearing on her increasing radicalism.

By the mid-1780s the quaint old fishing town of Brighthelmstone had begun to be transformed by the patronage of the Prince of Wales and his friends into a fashionable seaside resort. The future king had first visited the resort in the early 1780s and under his influence it developed into a cosmopolitan pleasure ground. When Smith moved to Brighton in 1789, work had begun on the Pavilion in the town center, which still dominates the town architecturally today. Although it was not until 1815 that it began to be reconstructed into its final incarnation as a wildly extravagant Oriental dream palace, it was nevertheless a vast and imposing construct which contributed considerably to the Prince's growing debts. In a period of national shortage and social unrest it sounded alarm bells and came to be viewed as a symbol of waste and immorality. Built primarily as a venue for his wild and decadent parties, it is described in *The New Brighton Guide* of 1796 as not only a site of architectural waste, but of excessive oral consumption, in which the Prince and his fellow debauchees "swill'd and reswill'd, and repeated their boozings, / Till their shirts became dy'd with purpureal oozings" (Donald 100). This kind of excess was described by another commentator in 1792 as an explanation of why "the nation at this day presents a picture of luxury, selfishness and general depravity, that was never equalled in the most abandoned age of Charles II" (Donald 100). Smith herself echoes this comparison in an ironic passage from *Desmond*, the novel most influenced by her residence in Brighton:

> [I]f at any remote period it should happen... that the crown should descend to a Prince more profligate than Charles the Second, without his wit; and more careless of the welfare and prosperity of the people than James the Second, without his piety; the English must submit to whatever burthens his vices shall impose...[5]

This view of the Prince as corrupt, decadent, and wasteful, parasitically feeding off Great Britain, was common currency from the late 1780s onward.[6] In 1787 Gillray had published a startling and grotesque drawing entitled *Monstrous Craws, at a New Coalition Feast*, in which he depicts the King and Queen and the Prince of Wales gorging on a bowl of John Bull's blood. The cartoon was a response to the parliamentary decision made in May of that year to pay off the Prince's debts, and literalized the idea of aristocratic vampiricism. In a later print, *A Voluptuary under the Horrors of Digestion* (1792), the consequences of the Prince's excesses are more visibly in evidence (see figure 1 on page xvii). He is depicted as a bloated figure with a massively swollen stomach and obese thighs. The *mise-en-scène* of the picture echoes and supports this bodily image of excessive consumption. His plate is littered with stripped meat bones, empty wine bottles are strewn under the table, and the Prince himself, having just completed his gourmandizing, is in the process of picking his teeth with a fork. Behind him, the chamber pot overflows—a symbol of filth, expulsion, and the waste of over-consumption. The title of the cartoon reiterates this theme of excess. It is taken from plate II of Hogarth's *Marriage à la Mode*, in which we encounter the hungover husband, recovering from a night of debauchery. Eating is the dominant metaphor in Gillray's picture—as Donald notes, even the studs on the chair look like teeth (99)—but what we are presented with here, is consumption not as needful sustenance but extravagant and wasteful excess.

The Prince's dietary excesses function as a symbol of other kinds of excess and depravity, both sexual and economic. The first is suggested by the treatments for venereal disease which are ranged behind him and the second by the pile of unpaid tradesman's bills under the overflowing chamber pot, the set of dice and lists of gaming debts on the floor, and the setting of Carlton House itself—which like the Pavilion was designed and decorated in the most extravagant manner. Although the parasitic or vampiric aspect of the Prince's consumption is not so obvious here as in the *Monstrous Craws* print, the implicit subtext to the wasteful excesses of his debauched and decadent lifestyle is a highly taxed and starving people, desperate for the basic requirements of life.

Just four months after Gillray's *Voluptuary* first appeared, Smith wrote a series of poems based on scenes of hardship witnessed in Brighton, in which she moves away from the heavily autobiographical stance of her sonnets. The consumerist pleasures of the city, instead of distracting her from human suffering, seem to have awakened her social conscience. Surrounded by images of excess, she pens poems to the poor and outcast citizens of Brighton. In none of these does she refer to the Prince of Wales or his aristocratic friends, but given the context of Brighton it is difficult not to see their excesses as the subtext to the poems, just as the starving poor are an implicit presence within Gillray's cartoon. In "The Dead Beggar" she offers an elegy to a "nameless pauper, buried at the expense of the parish in the church-yard at Brighthelmstone."[7] The underlying message of the poem is a political one, and she comments in a footnote that "in a country like ours, where such immense sums are annually raised for the poor, there ought to be some regulation which should prevent any miserable deserted being from perishing through want, as too often happens..." (*Poems* 96). Death functions in the poem as a "leveller" in which the two extremes of excess and absence are finally balanced, as it "vindicates the insulted rights of Man" (20). While Smith is beginning to shift into a more politicized discourse here—employing the radical language of rights—much of the poem draws on her usual range of sentimental reference and appeals to those with a "feeling heart" and "stream[ing] eye" (1). In another poem produced in the same month, however, "Written for the benefit of a distressed player, detained at Brighthelmstone for debt," Smith begins to experiment with a different kind of political discourse through the language of satire. She uses the techniques of comic disjunction and satirical humor to formulate her political critique, in a way that seems to draw on the strategies of Gillray's visual satires.

In this poem she turns to the seedy underside of the seaside resort and describes the fate of one of the numerous traveling players, attracted to Brighton by the entertainment culture built-up around the wealthy visitors, observing that "Hard is *his* fate, whom evil stars have led, / To seek in scenic art precarious bread" (100). Her description of this player and his fellows uses the satirist's technique of ironic disjunction to express their plight, and like Gillray she uses literary allusions in a subversive way. In the group of players there is a "pale, lank Falstaff" (29) who "Much needs... stuffing" (30), a "shivering Edgar, in his blanket roll'd" (34) who "Exclaims—with too much reason, 'Tom's a-cold!'"(35), and a "Hotspur, plucking 'honour from the moon,'" (40) who "Feeds a *sick infant* with a pewter spoon!" (41). These inverted pen portraits of Shakespeare's characters are so Gillrayesque that it is almost possible to picture them as one of his characteristic hand-colored etchings. But more than this, these starving actors are the visual counterparts to Gillray's well-stuffed and bloated Prince. The correlative to his excesses engaged in at the Pavilion is precisely this absence of the basic dietary requirements. This implicit contrast parallels the fundamental dichotomy on which the French Revolution was founded, and it is perhaps Smith's growing awareness of the mutual interdependence of excess and absence, brought home to her through the scenes witnessed at Brighton, which causes her to enter so passionately into radical politics at this time.

In the same year in which these poems and Gillray's *Voluptuary* appeared Smith also published *Desmond*, her most politicized novel, with which she claims the distinction of being "the first to join in the intellectual discussion of the Revolution in France with a novel."[8] Again her connection with radical thinkers in Brighton is significant, but the text can be seen as a product of period and place in other ways. Loraine Fletcher notes that "food" in its many guises is "a major preoccupation"[9] in the novel and the emphasis on consumerism, and consumerist pleasures in the town may help to explain why Smith formulates her political ideas primarily through a discourse of diet, since eating represents the most elementary form of consumption. Moreover, Hiblish comments that one of the scenes presented early in the novel describes a picture that is "quite likely drawn from a library in Brighton," noting that the "characters seem too individualised for creations solely from imagination."[10] This passage appears to be constructed directly out of Smith's experiences in the town, and the influence of Brighton—in particular its radicalism but also its consumer-orientated culture—can be traced in the writing at a number of levels. I want to look closely at this crucial Brighton-based scene and consider its significance in terms of the political message of the novel as a whole. For here Smith draws extensively on the techniques of the satirical cartoonist, relying to a great extent on visual signifiers relating to diet to convey political meaning.

Smith's eponymous hero Lionel Desmond recounts for his friend Erasmus Bethel conversations overheard between the visitors to a lending library. Desmond describes the first of these visitors as a clergyman who is "plump, sleek" and has a "peony-coloured face" (41), all signifiers of over-indulgence and excessive consumption of both food and alcohol. After having perused his daily paper for the latest news from France, this cleric offers a tirade against the Republicans, complaining in particular about their depriving the church of its revenues and the confiscation of all church property, a cause presumably close to his own heart, or rather stomach. He is challenged in this complaint by a "plain looking man" (42) who offers a reasoned argument on the church as property of the state. This second figure also offers an indirect attack on the well-fed appearance of the English clergyman, when he points out that the cleric's vows are "vows of poverty...by which, far from acquiring temporal goods, the means of worldly indulgences, they expressly renounced all terrestrial delights" (42).

Shortly after making this observation the rational speaker leaves and another character enters the discussion, who like the cleric is clearly positioned on the side of excess, since he is depicted as "a fat, bloated figure" (43). During this discussion of the Revolution he had been speaking to a woman about "the price of soals and mackerel that morning at market" (43), a subject that combines questions of economic and dietary consumption. On the removal of the "plain looking man" however, he turns his attention to the clergyman. This second glutton, by the same proportion that he is more greedy than the first ("fat and bloated" rather than merely "plump" and "sleek") is also more reactionary and violent in his attitude to the French Republican cause, and he embodies the national racial distrust of the French. While the clergyman impels "the wrath of heaven" (41) to be brought down on the head of the Republicans, this man talks of throat slitting (44), and goes on to justify his hatred of the French people and his rejection of the Republican cause through a discussion of French cuisine.

He recalls for the clergyman incidents of the previous summer during which he had visited Brighton, the site of many anticipated culinary delights. Once there, however, he mysteriously developed an "ugly feel" in his stomach and experienced a consequent loss of appetite (44). Advised by local physicians to take a sailing trip to France, he became violently sick during the voyage. Vomit signifies disgust and expulsion and also suggests saturation and overabundance—as such, it is deeply suggestive of his attitudes to the French people and their politics, and as with the Prince's chamber pot, serves to remind the reader of the kinds of excessive consumption which in Smith's eyes generated the absence of food in France in the first place. Once in France his appetite is further spoiled by French culinary practices, in which good quality soals are "fried in bad lard" and the partridges are served without sauce (44). He dismisses the French nation and their eating habits in one stroke: "I had had enough of them and their cooking in one day; so, Sir, the next morning I embarked again for old England" (44). During most of this narrative the clergyman is unable to get a word in edgeways about his favorite topic, the Revolution, but he brings the discussion round to the matter of politics because "he seemed heartily to coincide" with his companion "in the notions he entertained on the important science of eating" (45). In *Desmond* then, diet is the site of ethical choices which fan out into wider political allegiances, so that the "science of eating" functions as a complex signifier of moral and political economy.

If the implications of this discussion of excessive eating were not sufficiently clear to the reader, Smith adds a footnote to the story. As the two overweight men leave, still talking of exotic foods—"venison," "delicate fat ducks and pigeons," and "turkey powts"—they encounter a French woman who is on the point of starvation: "a thin, pale figure of a woman, with one infant in her arms and another following her" (47). She accosts the two men and begs for some money, a request which the clergyman answers to appease his conscience by giving her sixpence, while his greedy companion refuses to help at all, knowing that "the turnpike through which he must pass in his tour after good dishes, would demand the small money he had about him" (48). Ironically he suggests that her business in England is to "take the bread out of the mouth of our own people" and supposes that she is going to join the "fish-women . . . who are pulling down the king's palaces" (47). Later in the novel Smith returns to the question of the *poissardes* and openly defends them, arguing that the food shortage in the capital had been caused by a royal conspiracy to starve the people into submission. The encounter between the two men and the woman reminds us that the correlative to the useless and excessive consumption of delicacies is the basic need for sustenance, epitomized in the desperate appeal for bread: "du pain, du pain, pour nous & pour nos enfans" (311).[11] In *Desmond*, we are never allowed to forget the interdependence of absence and excess, and here these physical manifestations of the opposition are placed side by side, forcing us to address the dichotomy not in theoretical but in tangible human terms.

Smith's satirical handling of this scene, her depiction of these two men, and her use of food imagery are all deeply Gillrayesque, however, I want to suggest that her political interventions are more radical than those of Gillray in two ways, firstly with regard to representations of the French Revolution and secondly in relation to British class politics.

Gillray's cartoons are by far the most psychologically complex graphic satires of the period and his political allegiances are often deeply ambiguous. But in his visual treatment of the French Revolution from late 1790 onward, Gillray deployed his satirical techniques in a reactionary way, to condemn French Republican politics. While this could be interpreted as a consequence of growing parliamentary anxiety and censorship, the crucial Reeves Act—which took control of caricature drawings for the establishment—was not passed until December 1792, and as Donald notes, Gillray tapped into British xenophobia and "emphasized the horrors of gratuitous killing at an early stage in the unfolding of events," actually inventing "the main categories of satiric imagery dealing with the French Revolution some time before his services were bought by the government" (144).

During the year in which *Desmond* appeared, Gillray published two other cartoons which use the trope of diet to convey political meaning, and which also address the Revolution, namely: *Un Petit Souper à la Parisienne* and *French Liberty and British Slavery* (1797). In the first of these, he uses the motif of cannibalism to suggest the unnaturalness of the Republican impulse. He shows a baby being roasted over a spit, and the *poissardes*—who are defended by Smith—feasting with sharpened teeth on a man's heart and testicles. In the second cartoon, he uses diet to establish a contrast between the British constitution and French Republican theory. In the bipartite structure of his cartoon he depicts a malnourished Frenchman dining on raw vegetables, contrasted with an obese and red-faced Englishman tucking into a side of roast beef. Here, over-consumption is used not as a criticism of excess, but as a sign of well-being and comfort, a distinction which suggests the versatility of dietary metaphors at the time. This figure is just as obese and swollen as the Voluptuary Prince, but as he is John Bull, the common man, his gourmandizing is indicative of a land of plenty, not aristocratic overindulgence.

These cartoons suggest that Gillray's symbolics of diet function at an abstract and theoretical level, and the meaning attached to his images is therefore shifting and versatile. Obesity and other signifiers of over-consumption can have positive or negative readings depending on the context. For Smith however, food does not function simply as a versatile signifier, rather she thinks through the moral implications of diet and presents us with a much more consistent and carefully considered politics of the platter, with dietary preferences standing synecdochally for the whole ethical system of which they are a part. Viewed in this way, overindulgence and excessive consumption are always problematic, because, as she repeatedly suggests, they are dependent on absence and because they represent an avaricious moral economy. In the context of the revolutionary period what we find in Smith's work is a radical reappropriation of the food imagery which was being deployed to condemn the Republican cause in the reactionary press. She subverts the populist images of the French as cannibals and vegetarians, and uses the British distrust of otherness expressed through anxieties relating to diet, to critique British xenophobia, showing how racial distrust of cultural difference slips unquestioningly into reactionary, anti-Jacobin politics.

In this same passage from *Desmond* we can also, however, trace a class politics which further distinguishes Smith's handling of the dietary trope from that of Gillray. The upshot of the discussion between the two overfed men is that the newcomer invites the clergyman to dinner. The former, as well as being "fat and bloated," is also described as wearing a "brown riding wig, a red waistcoat, and boots" (43), and from his luxurious taste in food and his defense of the game laws, we might suppose him to be a member of the landed gentry. We later learn, however, that he is simply "Mr Sidebottom" who originally kept a tavern in London and who has now retired with a fortune. In other words, he is a member of the burgeoning commercial classes. Whereas Gillray's attacks, particularly during the 1790s, were focused on the aristocracy, with the middle classes being represented as decent and virtuous (Donald 99), Smith shifts her attention away from a decadent aristocracy and toward the expanding middle classes, whose wealth, she argues, is similarly built on economic inequality.

Further clues as to the nature of Smith's criticism emerge from Sidebottom's account of the delicacies they are to consume at dinner. Most promising on the menu is a "chicken-turtle" which he tells his companion he has received from his "West-Indian farm; a little patch of property I purchased, a few years since, in Jamaica" (46). There is some further discussion of this food that reinforces the colonial implications of the turtle; Sidebottom informs the clergyman that the dressing of the turtle will be undertaken by a Negro servant, who is an "excellent hand at it" (46). Turtle meat is profoundly significant for Smith as a symbol of both colonial politics and extravagant consumption and luxury, as opposed to needful sustenance. Although turtle meat also appears among the luxurious foods eaten by the British Cabinet in Gillray's *Substitutes for Bread*, it is symbolically linked by Smith with the mercantile classes, since the meat was brought back by commercial agents from their West Indian plantations, a fact which she lingers over here. Sidebottom's gourmandizing and desire for gourmet cuisine functions not simply as a critique of luxury but as a synecdoche for his colonialist mercantile politics. The popular deployment of excessive eating as a signifier of aristocratic decadence is developed into a much more complex signifier of middle-class consumerism and colonial consumption. Through her satirical representation of Sidebottom, Smith suggests that the consumer-orientated, capitalist value system driving the middle classes has created a group whose morals are every bit as corrupt as their aristocratic counterparts, a link which is reenforced by their shared taste for luxurious foodstuffs and excessive eating.

Smith's critique of the commercial classes here and elsewhere can be closely linked to her own tragic and, by now, well-rehearsed biography.

Smith herself was born to the landed gentry; her father was a wealthy landowner with large estates in Surrey and Sussex, and her childhood home was the impressive Bignor Park in Sussex. At the age of fifteen, she was married off to Benjamin Smith, the second son of Richard Smith, a director of the East India Company and a wealthy London merchant with sugar plantations in Barbados. Smith's marriage into this family catapulted her into the heart of eighteenth-century British commercial life. The East India Company was at the forefront of British commercial and colonial activity, as the main importer of goods like cotton, silk, spices, and tea for the middle-class market. The teenage Charlotte Smith was removed to a flat above her father-in-law's warehouse in Cheapside, where she found her tastes for painting and poetry wholly alien to those around her, and where she was criticized for her lack of knowledge of economic and domestic management.

Smith's attacks on mercantile values in her writing do have a very personal dimension, and this comes across in a poignant poem written shortly before she died, entitled "To my Lyre":

> Far from my native fields removed,
> From all I valued, all I loved;
> By early sorrows soon beset,
> Annoy'd and wearied past endurance,
> With drawbacks, bottomry, insurance,
> With samples drawn, and tare and tret;
>
> With Scrip, and Omnium, and Consols,
> With City Feasts and Lord Mayors' Balls,
> Scenes that to me no joy afforded;
> For all the anxious Sons of Care,
> From Bishopgate to Temple Bar,
> To my young eyes seem'd gross and sordid. (7–18)

The language used in this poem—in particular the description of herself as "of a different species" (24)—and elsewhere in Smith's writing, has caused critics to regard her antipathy toward the commercial classes as "snobbish."[12] However, the poem moves beyond the personal and reminds us of the link between the world of commerce and colonialism, through the use of terms employed in her father-in-law's import business and through references to turtle meat. We are told that the merchants at the city feasts dine upon "calepash and callipee" (29)—West Indian terms for the dorsal and ventral shells of the tortoise, which were reappropriated to describe the prized turtle meat itself.[13] Through her depiction of the middle classes Smith begins to formulate an attack on the economic ideology of the age and in particular on the capitalist, individualist economic philosophy expounded by Adam Smith. She makes an ironic reference to *The Wealth of Nations*, in which he put forward theories sanctioning individual mercantile enterprise and commerce as a generator of national wealth. Smith challenges this argument and identifies an alternative location for national wealth; in another Gillrayesque image she describes the "Proud city dames" (19) who carry " 'The wealth of nations on their backs' " (20). The suggestion is that the colonial pillage of the middle classes is responsible for poverty and suffering on a global scale, and capitalism, far from bringing about universal wealth, instead relocates money among small privileged groups in society.

Smith's growing awareness of the link between colonialism and consumer society can be directly linked to her experiences in her father-in-law's house in Cheapside. According to her most recent biographer, Loraine Fletcher, she witnessed there the realities of commerce and empire, embodied most starkly in the five slaves brought back as house servants by Richard Turner from Barbados. But Smith's marriage brought the values of consumer society home to her in other and perhaps more painful ways. At the age of fifteen she was faced with the realization that she herself was a commodity, an object of exchange in eighteenth-century society. Later in life she described the decision on the part of her father and aunt to marry her off, as having been sold "like a Southdown sheep, to the West India Shambles." The same letter formulates a link between her own condition and that of her father-in-law's slaves, referring her marriage as "worse than African bondage" (Blank and Todd 1997 xi). For Smith then, at an early age, the politics of consumerism and colonialism were connected to gender, and she links her own plight as a woman in eighteenth-century society with the treatment of animals and slaves.

Smith's final poems, published either shortly before her death or posthumously, continue to offer a marked critique of colonialism and commercial enterprise. At the beginning of her last major poem, "Beachy Head," she figures a "ship of commerce" heading out to "orient climates" in search of spice and cotton as, "a dubious spot / . . . hanging in the horizon" (40–1), and describes the pillaging of the empire for "gaudes and baubles" (58) as an act of sacrilege in which man "violate[s] / The sacred freedom of his fellow man" (58–9). On the whole though, there is a tendency in Smith's later works, to extend the critique of middle-class values into a more general critique of contemporary economic ideology. We can trace her rejection of this ideology in her representation of an alternative lifestyle, which draws extensively on Rousseau's writings and which is again defined through the signifier of diet. In "Beachy Head," set against the images of colonial pillage enacted by Britain and earlier races of colonizers like the Danes and Romans, are lone figures living peacefully on the margins of society, refusing to participate in its economic structures. These reclusive figures exist on a "rustic meal" (511) made up of "wild fruits / And bread" (561), and the ethical values encoded in this meatless diet are emphasized by the fact that the hermit who dwells in a cave near the sea watches for shipwrecks and "hazarding" (701) his life, snatches drowning sailors "From the wild billows" (708), finally sacrificing his own life in this way. This gesture of humanitarian sacrifice is fundamentally opposed to Adam Smith's individualist, self-interested doctrine. Here, at the other end of the moral spectrum, one's own life is deemed "valueless" (701) in comparison with that of another.

In *Conversations Introducing Poetry* (1804), Smith uses a female narrator to educate children about the politics of diet and to promote an ethical dietary agenda, which is again marked by a refusal to steal or kill food. In "The wheat-ear" she addresses the bird so sought after by Mr. Sidebottom in *Desmond* and laments the fact that it has become a culinary delicacy, so that "luxury's toils for you are laid" (18) and the "shepherd boys prepare / The hollow turf, the wiry snare" (25–6). While this might function merely an extension of Smith's critique of gourmet cuisine, other poems in the collection go on to reject more simple animal fare as well. In "A walk by the water" Smith describes the fish swimming in a river, noting how they swim away in fear at the approach of humans. She teaches children through an address to the fish themselves:

> Do not dread us, timid fishes,
> We have neither net nor hook;
> Wanderers we, whose only wishes
> Are to read in nature's book. (17–20)

For Smith all violent acquisition of food which causes the suffering of other animals has become an extension of colonial politics in which property, countries, people, and raw materials are taken by force by the stronger party. Her most extreme extension of the application of this logic in the collection is her poem, "Invitation to the Bee," in which she invites the bee to build a hive in her garden and to produce its honey there. As the poem progresses, she makes clear that this invitation is not made so that that she can take the honey for herself. Rather she claims that it will be used to feed the bees themselves throughout the winter months. For Smith what is most immoral about such acts of theft is that they are not committed in order to sustain life, but to indulge extravagant desires. Throughout this collection she echoes Rousseau in pointing out that life can be sustained at a much more basic level, and proposes a simpler and more humane diet.

In several of these poems diet is also used to address the cultural differences between nations in a way that challenges Gillray's reactionary satire of Continental eating habits. In "Ode to the Olive Tree" Smith gives the tree overt political significance by connecting it to "Peace" (40) and "Liberty" (42), and in a footnote to the poem she goes on to advocate, almost prophetically, the "pure and fine oil" as a morally, healthier alternative to that "indispensable article of English luxury, butter" (*Poems* 202). In "The heath" she uses another footnote both to offer an alternative food to that represented by the diet of "luxury" and to challenge national antagonisms embedded in the ideology surrounding food. She writes that "the Italians, French, and . . . Russians consider as very excellent food many Fungus's which we think unwholesome, and turn from with disgust" (199). Smith had spent some time in France, both before and after her separation from Benjamin Smith, and here she makes a case for the healthier properties of the Continental diet as a means of offering a subtle challenge to British Francophobia.

Smith's ideas here are clearly influenced by Rousseau's "new ethical principle" of vegetarianism,[14] and as such participate in the debates on vegetarian diet which developed in the radical context of the Romantic era, but they also contributed to what Carol Adams has termed a "feminist-vegetarian literary and historical tradition," in which female-authored texts explore the connections between male dominance and a meat diet (168). Adams argues that meat functions as a symbol of patriarchy, and that a rejection of meat in female-authored texts can be read as a rejection of male power. Adams's classic Romantic example of this feminist use of vegetarianism is Mary Shelley's *Frankenstein*, but in her discussion of this text she links the Creature's vegetarianism more successfully to radical politics in a general sense that to feminist politics *per se*. Adams in fact sees the connection between feminism and vegetarianism in literature of the Romantic period as functioning only at a subconscious level, since she claims that those "who reviled the meat diet of the day failed to see that they were covertly criticising a masculine symbol" (117). Smith can be placed within the same radical and feminist tradition as Shelley, but Smith's rejection of meat is more consciously tied to gender politics—in particular her lived awareness that women, like animals and slaves, were positioned as objects of consumption in eighteenth-century society.

As a coda to this discussion, I want to consider the feminist implications of Smith's later works, by drawing attention to a link between her growing interest in botany and in a vegetarian diet. These topics are connected insofar as they allow her to rethink Romantic constructions of nature and eighteenth-century perceptions of natural boundaries between animal/ human, black/white, and woman/man. Adams claims that a vegetable diet has throughout history been primarily associated with women and a meat diet with men, for very negative reasons, since meat is valued in society and given to those in power. This gendered division has led to a reversal in the meaning of the word vegetable, which originally meant to "*be lively, active*," but which has come to mean passive and unresponsive (36). In the 1790s a vegetable diet was already coming to have pacifist connotations, but Smith draws on the original meaning of the word "vegetable," and develops its more dynamic and transgressive implications.

One of the ways in which Smith begins to imagine a way out of the current sociopolitical framework in these late works, is by depicting the decay of architectural symbols of male power and the reinstatement of nature's potent vegetative power. Smith replaces the more passive images of nature in literature of the period with a powerful force, represented through Flora, the Goddess of Botany, whom she describes in the poem "Flora" as the "Queen of ideal pleasure" (8). This goddess is a potent figure who brings about exciting transformations on the landscape, including an obliteration of castles, fortresses, and abbeys.

This process is shown most clearly in "Saint Monica," one of the best poems from Smith's last collection, which connects nature with female power and at the same time draws on the original meaning of vegetable as active. The poem describes nature's process of reclamation, so that every image of decay is accompanied by a natural image of recovery. It moves from the fairly standard descriptions of a "falling archway overgrown / With briars" (10) and "matted tods" of ivy binding the "arch and buttress" (50), to a detailed botanicized description of particular trees and plants all "creep[ing]" (33) and "trail[ing]" (40) across walls, pavements, and tombs. The poem shifts into the present tense and describes this process so vividly that we can almost sense it taking place as we read:

> From the mapped lichen, to the plumed weed,
> From thready mosses to the veined flower,
> The silent, slow, but ever active power
> Of Vegetative Life, that o'er Decay
> Weaves her green mantle . . . (88–92)

This subtly transgressive image suggests that vegetable life is ultimately more powerful than male power, which is ephemeral and subject to the laws of time. With a linguistic gendering that allows Smith to subtly link women with this active botanicized force, "Nature" is shown to be "ever lovely, ever new" (94), while "Man, and the works of man" (98) are condemned to "dark Forgetfulness" (97). Although in her late poems she validates a peaceful and humane vegetarian ethic, she also seems to take delight in depicting this process of natural reclamation, in which an apparently passive and female vegetative life slowly and surely effaces the symbols of male power.

Smith's personal experiences, though producing an early tendency toward melancholy introspection, later cause her to engage with the wider political and economic framework of the Romantic period with an incisive awareness of the human cost of its dominant economic ideology. Through an interrogation of the complex relationship between consumerism, colonialism, and patriarchy, she formulates a radical critique of the middle-class politics of consumption. Studying these late poems through the trope of diet allows us to rethink the charge of snobbery which has been leveled at Smith in relation to her treatment of the commercial classes. For her, diet is the site of the ethical choices that broaden out into wider political values and allegiances. In the light of Smith's complex treatment of the politics of the platter, her recognition that she is "of a different species" can be reread in moral and ethical terms. For Smith the avaricious colonialism at the heart of the mercantile enterprise situates it at the core of national moral breakdown, and in her writing she formulates a persuasive challenge to a consumer-oriented value system that turns slaves, women, and animals into commodities to be bought and sold for profit.

Notes

1. See for example Timothy Morton, *Shelley and the Revolution in Taste: The Body and the Natural World* (Cambridge: Cambridge UP, 1994).
2. Paul Langford, *A Polite and Commercial People: England, 1727–1783* (Oxford: Oxford UP, 1992), 68.
3. Diana Donald, *The Age of Caricature: Satirical Prints in the Reign of George III* (New Haven and London: Yale UP, 1996), vii and 22.
4. Mrs. [Catherine] Dorset, "Charlotte Smith," in *The Lives of the Novelists*, by Sir Walter Scott (London: Dent, n.d.), 322.
5. Charlotte Smith, *Desmond*, ed. Antje Blank and Janet Todd (London: Pickering and Chatto, 1997), 157.
6. The image is most infamously deployed in Shelley's sonnet "England in 1819," in which he describes "Rulers" who "leech-like to their fainting country cling / Till

they drop, blind in blood, without a blow." *Shelley: Poetical Works*, ed. Thomas Hutchinson (Oxford: Oxford UP, 1970), 575.

7. *The Poems of Charlotte Smith*, ed. Stuart Curran (Oxford: Oxford UP, 1993), 96. All subsequent quotations from Smith's poems are taken from this edition and line numbers are given in parenthesis in the text. References to Smith's footnotes will continue to be given in endnotes, but the text will hereafter be abbreviated to *Poems*.

8. Janet Todd and Antje Blank, introduction to *Desmond* by Charlotte Smith (London: Pickering and Chatto, 1997), xxiii.

9. Loraine Fletcher, *Charlotte Smith: A Critical Biography* (Houndmills: Palgrave, 1998, 2001), 149.

10. Florence Hiblish, *Charlotte Smith: Poet and Novelist* (Philadelphia: University of Pennsylvania Press, 1941), 144–5.

11. Translated by Smith as "Bread, bread, for us and our children" (311).

12. In her study of Smith's novels, Janet Todd notes that "there is much snobbishness" in her expressions of distaste for the world of commerce (*The Sign of Angelica: Women, Writing, and Fiction, 1600–1800* [London: Virago, 1989]), 203, and Loraine Fletcher claims in her biography that Smith "was of course a snob" (Fletcher, 2001 29).

13. See Curran, notes in *Poems* 312.

14. Henry Salt cited in Carol Adams, *The Sexual Politics of Meat: A Feminist-Vegetarian Critical Theory* (Oxford: Polity Press, 1990), 111.

Chapter 4 ∽

SUSTAINING THE ROMANTIC AND RACIAL SELF: EATING PEOPLE IN THE "SOUTH SEAS"

Peter J. Kitson

"The South Seas" and the Romantic Self

This chapter focuses on the place of the body in cultural discourses of the Romantic era, particularly the meanings and symbolism of human bodies eating other human bodies in the area called the "the South Seas." It attempts to show how this practice distinguished between varieties, then races, of humans who inhabited this region. Enlightenment empirical observation was never neutral and the highly charged and richly symbolic discussion of Southern and Central Pacific diet reveals much about the ideological desires and anxieties of the West.

The "South Seas" has been the subject of much intellectual exploration in recent criticism. Most of this has stressed how the South Seas figured as a construction of Western desires and fears. Neil Rennie has explored the construction of the South Sea Islands as Paradise and Paradise Lost.[1] Jonathan Lamb has argued that rather than exporting confident colonial subjects to the Pacific the Europeans "spread ignorance before they spread trade routes and disease" and that the "uncertainties" which assailed the Romantic self were "intensified in the Pacific" at the same time as the "Polynesian self" was being forced out of its own tribal identity (5). Nicholas Thomas has maintained that this colonial encounter is marked by ambiguities and exchanges and not a simple matter of the fatal impact of the West on a victimized and tragic native people.[2] Such new perspectives, combining anthropological, cultural, and literary approaches, are very conducive to a sustained analysis of diet, appetite and difference in the Southern and Central Pacific. Combined with a substantial body of postcolonial or sceptical anthropological discussions of cannibalism, they reappraise the colonial encounter and its most notorious, enigmatic, and fearsome subject, the cannibal.[3] In this chapter I concentrate on the division of the South Seas into racialized groupings of Polynesia, Melanesia, and later Micronesia. The figure of the cannibal becomes key to effecting a racist division between fair- and dark-skinned inhabitants. Concentrating on the distinction between Tahiti and the Maori tribes in Romantic-period ethnological and travel texts, I claim that the "imaginative" literature of the period was partially complicit in ossifying an arbitrary Enlightenment classification into a politics of the body, which justified the exploitation, conversion, and terrorization of native peoples. Focusing on the function of the symbolism and meaning of diet in the process I show how empirical observation of taste and appetite, and the symbolism inscribed in such representations, was central in this psycho-political creation of difference.

Exploring and Classifying: Polynesia and Melanesia

In some of the most poignant and haunting lines in English literature, Coleridge's Ancient Mariner strikes the note of the "colonial uncanny": "We were the first that ever burst / Into that silent sea."[4] When those lines were penned, the Western maritime penetration of the Central and Southern Pacific (what we might more properly call "Oceania") was well under way. In the late eighteenth century, however, vast areas were still unexplored by the European powers; peoples, cultures, flora, and fauna remained unknown to the West. The last quarter of the century witnessed the systematic European attempt to explore, chart, describe, classify, and eventually exploit the Southern and Central Pacific. The area became the locus of stereotypes of travel writing: the dusky maiden, the noble savage, and the fearsome cannibal. As Mary Louise Pratt has argued, this moment in colonial history marked a shift in the public motivation for exploration from the earlier goals of conquest, plunder, and exploitation to those of scientific exploration, devoid of any explicit program for the conquest of territory or the terrorization of native peoples: we see the growth of a "planetary consciousness" driven by Enlightenment imperatives to classify and arrange the various peoples and products of the natural world.[5] James Cook's three great voyages of discovery in the Southern hemisphere included natural philosophers, botanists, astronomers, and mathematicians, such as Joseph Banks, Carl Solander, George [Georg] and John [Johann] Reinhold Forster, Anders Sparrman, William Wales, William Anderson, and others. These explorers took with them the theoretical equipment of Enlightenment classifiers, including Linnaeus, Buffon, and Blumenbach, and used them to arrange this new and extraordinary world in a grand narrative of progress and civilization.

Between say 1750 and 1830 something happened to the cannibal. As Roxanne Wheeler and Frank Lestringant have argued the cannibal changed from being a figure of cultural difference, establishing the differential between savagery and civilization, or paganism and Christianity, to a sign of racial and moral degeneracy.[6] In the process cannibalism became less of a social and customary activity, a matter of culture, or, as in the theories of Voltaire and Malthus, a response to protein deficiency, than a bestial and lustful business governed by the desire for human flesh.[7] The cannibal's skin got darker and his or her hair seemed to be, in the parlance of the time, "crinkly or woolly." Cannibalism became a key sign of racial inferiority, as specific a marker for a nineteenth-century readership as the physical features of skin, skull, and hair. The practice was to be understood as a somatic and innate aptitude, a justification for empire and for the civilization of the dark places of the earth.

Cannibalism thus became a marker of difference in the nascent Enlightenment and Romantic science of human variety and race. Eating people was understood to be the speciality of dark-skinned humans from Africa or the South Pacific. In *The Philosophy of History* Hegel wrote that "the eating of human flesh is quite compatible with the African principle; to the sensuous Negro, human flesh is purely an object of the senses, like all other flesh."[8] Cannibalism as sign of racial degeneration was the view applied by the young Charles Darwin to the natives of Tierra del Fuego in 1846 (Sanborn 38–9). By the mid-nineteenth century, as Thomas has shown, the classification of the peoples of the Central and Southern Pacific into the racial groupings of Polynesia (Eastern Pacific), Melanesia (Western Pacific), and later Micronesia (North Western) had been accomplished.[9] Taking the central dichotomy of Melanesian and Polynesian, the Melanesians (Solomon Islands, New Hebrides, New Caledonia) were dark-skinned, had crinkly hair, and were susceptible to cannibalism. The Polynesians (Tahiti, the Marquesas, Samoa, Tonga, the Society Islands) were fair-skinned with flowing hair and, if they were cannibals it was long ago in the past or, evidence of an uncharacteristic backsliding. Gary Hogg, in his popular study, reflected this equation between Melanesian culture and cannibalism: "It is in Melanesia that cannibalism was longest in dying... [its inhabitants] like the vastly larger island to the west of them, New Guinea, just to north of Australia, are peopled by inhabitants who clung obstinately to their ancient tradition of devouring human flesh long after the tradition had begun to fade, or had even been wholly stamped out, elsewhere."[10] The ambiguous position of the Fiji Islands (not properly known until the 1830s) in this racial divide is solved for Hogg by the substantial number of missionary accounts describing the Fijians as fierce and unregenerate cannibals. Hogg accepts that the Fijian are Melanesians because they are cannibals, and because they enjoy eating human flesh, as do other members of their racial grouping in New Guinea.

Although the practice may have occurred in Polynesia "it certainly began to die out amongst those islands long before the process began in Melanesia" (Hogg 157). Where it exists it is due to Melanesian influence. Hogg presents a populist and unthinking absorption of an anthropological distinction that originated in the late eighteenth century. Behind this belief is the racist axiom that one approaches humanity more closely as one's skin approaches whiteness. Late eighteenth-century Pacific explorers were puzzled by the difference between the fairer-skinned Tahitians and their darker-skinned neighbors. Louis de Bougainville in his voyage of 1766–1769 noted that "Nothing distinguishes" the Tahitians "features from those of the Europeans." If they were "less exposed to the sun at noon, they would be as white as ourselves." The darker-skinned habitants of the New Hebrides he found to be "short, ugly, ill-proportioned," adding that he observed that "the black men are much more ill natured than those whose colour comes near to white."[11] Bougainville's distinction was not racialized. Yet as early as 1799 the evangelical preacher Thomas Haweis implied a racial dimension in his contrast of the lighter-skinned Pacific peoples with a "darker race" occupying Australia, New Guinea, New Caledonia, the Solomons, Vanuatu, and Fiji. These people, he hypothesized, were the original inhabitants of the islands who had been conquered by the Tahitians. For Haweis, "The stature of the Fijians is superior, their complexions are darker, and their hair approaches to wool." They also "retain their practice of eating the bodies of their enemies whom they have killed, which is now abhorred by all the lighter race, except the individuals of New Zealand."[12] In 1831, the missionary William Ellis dogmatically expounded the view that "the islands of the Pacific are inhabited by two tribes of men totally distinct, and in some respects entirely different from each other." One of these tribes is composed of "Oceanic negroes" and the other "belong to the physical character of the Malayan and aboriginal American tribes." The latter "tribe" or "race" has a "facial angle frequently as perpendicular as in the European structure."[13] Such a distinction had become normative by the 1840s when, in the Rev. Michael Russell's *Polynesia*, we are told that the Fijians properly "belong to the black tribes of Melanesia and New Guinea" as with "strong indications of Negro ferocity, they combine some of the worst habits which disgrace the whole population of the Southern Pacific, especially the horrible practice of eating their enemies, now abhorred by all the fairer-skinned families of the windward clusters."[14] In Thomas Williams's *Fiji and the Fijians*, the Fijian is distinguished by his "cruelty" which is "relentless and bloody." The islanders suffer from and "inner depravity" marked by their cannibalism which they practice from motives of lust and revenge, even to the extent of "the most fiendish cruelty... of cutting off parts and even limbs of the victim while still living, and cooking and eating them before his eyes."[15] The Rev. Josiah Priest observes that the "horrid and heart-appalling practice of cannibalism has, in all ages, attached more to the African race than to any other people of the earth." The dark-skinned denizens of the Western Pacific or Africa "have been irrespective of civilization, actually more or less in the practice of the dreadful crime of eating human flesh, as an article of food, the same as dogs or any other carnivorous animal."[16] The Fijians, as even a cursory look over missionary accounts in the era makes clear, were alleged to be cannibals because they enjoyed eating human flesh and because they were addicted to cruelty: this confirms them as Melanesian. As Geoffrey Sanbourn puts it, "Through its association with race, the fixed desire for human flesh had been made visible; through its association with addictiveness, the visible sign of cannibalism—the dark skin—was fixed" (29). The cannibal has come a long way from the honorable and noble warriors of the Tupinamba Indians that Montaigne idealized in his essay "Of the Cannibales" (1580), and the friendly, tractable man Friday, who despite his hankering after human flesh was eminently capable of being civilized to be Crusoe's servant.

The distinction between Melanesians and Polynesians was a result of Enlightenment science, an arbitrary mapping of cultures in terms of physical type, customs, and language. The term "Melanesia" lumps together populations with very different backgrounds, such as Papuans and Austronesians; ethnologists now note that "Polynesia" is best understood as a subgroup of Austronesian "Melanesia." These categories have been sustained though "reiteration and redefinition, rather than on the basis of self-evident human differences" (Thomas, *In Oceania* 133–55). Even when racial distinction is not based on narrow physical traits, Melanesians are most often considered inferior. The missionary George Brown could argue in 1910 that though descended from "one common stock," nevertheless, "the Melanesian is the oldest representative at the present time" and that the "brown Polynesians" "represent a later and greater admixture caused by successive immigration of Caucasian peoples."[17] The distinction is often repeated uncritically in accounts of the exploration of the area. In 1965 John Dunmore commented on Bougainville's encounters: "The dark Melanesians were obviously more warlike and of a less happy disposition than the 'Indian' of Tahiti."[18]

One of several key figures in establishing this distinction was the natural philosopher Johann (or John) Reinhold Forster.[19] Forster and his son George sailed as naturalists on Cook's second voyage in search of the disputed great southern continent, *Terra Australis Incognita* (1772–75). This voyage encountered a vast diversity of peoples over a wide area of the globe. This variety and its possible origins puzzled Cook's natural historians who attempted to find a way of explaining it in terms of the migration of Asiatic peoples. Forster's *Observations Made during a Voyage Round the World* was the most systematic of a number of attempts to map the Pacific:

> We chiefly observed two great varieties of people in the South Seas; the one more fair, well-limbed, athletic, of a fine size, and a kind benevolent temper; the other blacker, the hair just beginning to become crisp, the body more slender and low, and their temper, if possible more brisk, though somewhat mistrustful. The first race inhabits O-Taheitee, and the Society Isles, the Marquesas, the Friendly Isles [Tonga], Easter-Island, and New Zealand. The second race peoples New-Caledonia, Tanna and the New Hebrides, especially Mallicollo.[20]

Forster's movement from the term "variety" to that of "race" is significant. "Race" is synonymous in Forster with variety implying arbitrary change, yet it also implies the biological and morphologically fixed type in the sciences of human classification, closer to the term "species." Forster's distinction between the two great "races" is not made simply on the basis of physical characteristics and temperaments, but on a whole series of cultural phenomena, including language, customs, and diet. He speculates that these two races are descended from different ancestors, though how this happened is a mystery. Within the "Polynesian" or Eastern Pacific group, Forster arranged the islanders he observed on a graded scale with the Tahitians at the apex down through New Zealanders, New Caledonians, New Hebrideans, with the peoples of Tanna and Malekula as the most debased. Forster, however, is not the physical or evolutionary anthropologist we might expect. He attempts to classify the peoples of the Pacific in terms of their approach toward civilization, in the manner of Enlightenment writers such as Montesquieu, Lord Kames, and Adam Ferguson, distinguishing between a childlike state of savagery and an adolescent state of barbarism. His theory of humanity was basically evolutionary rather than biologically racist, unlike his successors.

Cook, Forster, and the Cannibals

Forster had difficulties classifying what he called the "New Zealander," for us the Maori peoples. These were clearly a Polynesian (a term not used by Forster) or Eastern Pacific people, yet, as eighteenth-century explorers discovered to their cost, they were fiercer and less manageable that the Tahitians. Cook's visits recorded a people who seemed to practice cannibalism. During the second voyage two incidents confirmed a sceptical and doubting crew of the Maori's cannibalism.[21] On 23 November 1773 at Totaranui (renamed Queen Charlotte's Sound) some of the crew of the *Resolution* who had gone to trade with the natives came across the severed head of a young man of about sixteen or so.[22] The intestines, liver, and lungs were lying around; the natives gave the party to understand that they had eaten the rest of the body (Barber 251). One of the ship's lieutenants, Richard Pickersgill, purchased the head for two iron nails and returned with it to the *Resolution*. There, as a cultural experiment, a different group of Maori, who showed a desire to eat the head, were allowed to devour a piece of flesh from it. It is reported that the flesh was devoured "most ravenously, by a man who suck'd his fingers... in raptures."[23] Cook, who returned shortly after, recounts what happened:

> The sight of the head and the relation of the circumstances filled my mind with indignation against these Cannibals, but when I considered that any resentment I could shew would avail but little and being desireous of being an eye wittness to a fact which many people had their doubts about, I concealed my indignation and ordered a piece of the flesh to be broiled and brought on the quarter deck where one of these Canibals eat it with a seeming good relish before the whole ships Company which had such an effect on some of them as to cause them to vomit. [Oediddee, one of the islanders aboard the ship] was [so] struck with horror at the sight that [he] wept and scolded by turns, before this happened he was very intimate with these people but now he neither would come near them or suffer them to touch him.[24]

The Europeans' humanity and their distinction from the savagery of the Maori are defined in this recoil from the cannibal scene. "Odiddy" (the

Raiatean Islander, Hitihiti) shows a racial kinship with the European in that he reacts with horror, more violently than Cook and the rest. His distress is a feminized response (he wept and scolded) to the events that places himself apart from the Maori, but close to the European, although lacking the European's clinical reason and anthropological balance. When confronted by cannibalism the European either speculates, or vomits, rejecting (or abjecting) the spectacle.

Readings of this cannibal scene were various. William Wales, the astronomer and the future mathematics tutor of Coleridge and Lamb, believed that it was motivated by the simple lust for flesh and thus implied degeneration and savagery. George Forster reported that the flesh was eaten "with the greatest avidity"; John Elliott remembered that it was eaten "with all the avidity of a Beef Steak, to the utmost horror of the Whole Quarter deck" (Forster 1.512)[25] Elliot's discomfiting equation of the "Beef Steak" greedily consumed by the English sailor with the human flesh devoured by the cannibal focuses, perhaps unwittingly, the reader's mind on the kinds of meat acceptable for eating and the ways in which difference is created. The issue of whether Maori cannibalism was a matter of appetite or taste, custom or necessity was thus left open. Neither Cook nor the Forsters believed that the cannibalism was a matter of hunger. Through interrogation Cook discovered that the youth had been an enemy of the tribe and that the incident had its origins in revenge or warfare, though Wales for one believed it was explicable only as bestial desire.

Sadly, the New Zealanders were not the only group to exploit that poor young man's remains. Pickersgill, who had purchased the head, presumably with a desire to sell it in Britain as a sought-after curiosity, had it preserved in alcohol. Daniel Carl Solander, writing to Joseph Banks on the *Resolution's* return in 1775, reports how Pickersgill "made the Ladies sick by shewing them the New Zealand head of which 2 or 3 slices were broiled and eaten on board of the Ship."[26] Solander states that the surgeon, anatomist, and collector of skulls, John Hunter, was to travel to Deptford with him the next day with a view to obtaining this grisly "curiosity" for his own private collection and as an object for racial study. The final destination of the remains of the head of that unfortunate victim of Maori violence and British anthropological tomb robbing has not yet been traced.[27]

The meaning of cannibalism was further impressed upon Cook's crew by a more intense and urgent encounter that was to indelibly color their recollections of earlier visits. On the second visit to New Zealand Cook's *Resolution* had lost its sister ship, *Adventure*, which arrived on 23 November 1773, four days after Cook left. On the morning of

18 December, Captain Tobias Furneaux sent a long boat in search of the ship's cutter, which had not returned from the previous evening's task. On a small beach close to Grass Cove (Wharehunga Bay) the party found some fresh meat which they assumed to be dog. The commanding officer, Lieutenant James Burney, then recorded how they found about twenty baskets, some "full of roasted flesh & some of fern root which serves them for bread." A severed hand was discovered with the tattooed initials of "T.H.," identifying its owner as the crewmember, Thomas Hill.[28] Proceeding further into Grass Cove the party came across further evidence of cannibalism. Burney's account of this was published in the official narrative of the voyage:

> We found no boat, but instead of her, such a shocking scene of carnage and barbarity as can never be mentioned or thought of but with horror; for the heads, hearts, and lungs of several of our people were seen lying on the beach, and, at a little distance, the dogs gnawing their intrails.[29]

The party returned with two hands, one belonging to Hill and the other to the master's mate who commanded the expedition, John Rowe. They also found the severed head of Captain Furneaux's black servant. These and other remains were wrapped up in a hammock and thrown into the sea, not preserved and transported back to Britain as cannibal curiosities. Most interested parties, including Cook, Furneaux, and the Forsters presumed that this was an act of revenge resulting from a misunderstanding between the two groups in which the aggressive Rowe may well have been culpable. Certainly, as Anne Salmond has shown, the similar killing and possible eating of the French explorer Marion Du Fresne and some of his crew in 1772, resulted from the Frenchmen's ignorance and violation of Maori *tapu*.[30] On his third voyage Cook satisfied himself that the blame for this attack lay as much with the British as the natives and that the cannibalism that followed had to be understood in the context of revenge.[31]

The desire hypothesis, however, though not the consensus view, was still held by some. William Wales remained convinced that the practice occurred not through scarcity or custom but "from Choice, and the liking which they have for this kind of food" (Beaglehole, *Journals III* 819).[32] Though a minority view at the time, Wales's opinion would become the leading nineteenth-century consensus in racialized scientific discourse. Nevertheless, this encounter remains ambiguous. The Europeans were, after all, a third term in the cannibal occurrence and had already shown that they were obsessed, perplexed, and frightened by the possibility of cannibalism (255). The Europeans themselves were avidly collecting partially eaten native human body parts. Gananath Obeyesekere has argued that the European's anthropophagic preoccupations resulted from *their* not uncommon practice of survival cannibalism at sea ("British Cannibals"). Thus the Maori's cannibalism might also be understood in terms of their desire to terrorize the Europeans or demonstrate their manhood.

How then did Forster, who also witnessed this scene, account for cannibalism among the New Zealanders and how did this custom become almost exclusively associated with the Western Pacific Melanesians? Forster rejected explanations that cannibalism first developed as a response to scarcity, arguing that its origin lay in the "strong passion" for revenge. The New Zealanders "never eat their adversaries, unless they are killed in battle; they never kill relations for the purpose of eating them; they do not even eat them if they die a natural death and they take no prisoners with a view to fatten them for their repast" (1.514–18). J. R. Forster's treatment of the subject is the most philosophical and ethnologically developed in the period. He argues that the New Zealanders are of the same racial grouping as the Tahitians, but occupy a lower rung on the ladder of progress. The Tahitians with their physique and their developed government have passed through the childhood state of savagery and are now progressing from the adolescent state of barbarism, as a prelude to attaining the civilization of the Europeans. The Tahitians are not cannibal; their diet is typified by its reliance on the breadfruit, a freely growing staple that does not need cultivation.[33] But they were also carnivores who ate hogs, their varied diet a sign for Forster of their social complexity.

The Maoris, however, are defined as "bold and intrepid warriors; implacable and cruel enemies, carrying even their thirst of revenge to such a degree of inhumanity, as to feast upon their unfortunate prisoners, the wretched victims to a ferocious and uncultured disposition" (J. Forster, *Observations* 238). Thus the Maori are cannibals for reasons of revenge, not desire or lust, and are therefore reclaimable (as Montaigne's noble savages, the Tupinamba), whereas the Fijians will be declared cannibals because they enjoy eating human flesh and are thus racially inferior. For Forster the key sign of New Zealand savagery is cannibalism. Human difference is created by the powerful influences of "climate, food, and peculiar customs upon the colour, size habit, and form of the body." The New Zealand diet is not so various as the Tahitian. Forster and others report that they "absolutely feed on fish" which is plentiful. This staple "by no means contributes to the increase of numbers in a nation" necessary to the development and progress of a people from animality, savagery, barbarism, and civilization (J. Forster, *Observations* 315). Forster thus refutes the argument that Maori cannibalism is occasioned by a shortage of protein by citing the plentiful supply of fish. Cannibalism may have been a custom practiced by all the South Sea islanders in the past, but which they have now outgrown, apart from in New Zealand. Indeed, Forster argued that cannibalism is one of the steps by which a "debased humanity" is prepared for a better happiness, as it demonstrates a passion and vigor that leads a people away from the indolence of animality (J. Forster, *Observations* 330–2).

Forster's Enlightenment anthropology hypothesized a movement to civilization from animality and savagery; progress was determined by climate, mode of living, and diet. All peoples may have been cannibals in the state of savagery and barbarism. His distinction between the Western and Eastern Pacific peoples was couched in the discourse of Enlightenment universalism, which regarded all humanity as essentially one and the same, differentiated by processes of degeneration occasioned by environment. This distinction was, however, to ossify into a strict and clear racial dichotomy by the 1830s. Thomas has demonstrated how this process occurred, citing accounts of their Pacific voyages by the French explorers Labillardière, Jules-Sébastien-César Dumont D' Urville, and the American Horatio Hale (*Oceania* 139–51).

This nexus of diet, politics, and food was seductive to a number of nineteenth-century surgeons, anatomists, and natural philosophers. William Lambe, for instance, had pondered the Tahitian diet and its implications for racial classification. Lambe, influenced by Enlightenment anthropologists such as Blumenbach and Forster, found in the Tahitian the ideal kind of physical beauty that was defined in the classical aesthetics of the Medici Venus and the Apollo Belvedere. The Tahitian physical and racial superiority derives, according to Lambe, from their having a diet mainly consisting of vegetarian food. Lambe notes how an inhabitant of Nukuhiva was measured and the measurements later compared to the Apollo Belvedere by Blumenbach in Göttingen: "The latter compared the proportions with the Apollo of Belvedere, and found that those of that master piece of the finest stages of Grecian art, in which is combined every possible integer of manly beauty, corresponded exactly with our Mafau."[34] Again diet and race are seen as constituent parts in a cultural mindset that brings the Polynesian closer to the European, at the cost of degrading those peoples whose features do not correspond to European neoclassical ideals.

If cannibalism came to be associated with Melanesian dark-skins, then what was to be made of the blatant cannibalism of the Polynesian New Zealanders whose fairer skins precluded them from being classed with their cannibal brethren in the Pacific and elsewhere? Forster had argued that the

New Zealander was a Polynesian at an earlier stage of development. Yet to argue this was to bring the dark-skinned and neo-classically ugly Melanesian closer to the European. As the nineteenth century progressed a process of elision and blaming began: where cannibalism existed it was a recent importation from Melanesia and not a well-practiced Polynesian custom. Anthropologists of the nineteenth and early twentieth centuries thus resorted to the "The Great New Zealand Myth" whereby Melanesian people from a "lower plane of culture" had originally settled in New Zealand and that cannibalism in the area resulted from an earlier connection with Melanesian peoples, reinforcing the great racial and cultural distinction (Barber 267–8).

Byron's **The Island**

Although there exists a substantial body of missionary and travel writing about New Zealand in the period, poets, novelists, and dramatists were attracted to the more Edenic aspects of Polynesian cultures. Literary representations of Melanesian peoples are also very few outside travel and exploration accounts. When such representations occur, as in Southey's "Botany Bay Eclogues," they are thinly-drawn characters in a scarcely imagined topographical backdrop for explicitly European issues. Imaginative writers were captivated by the paradisial themes and the possibilities for excitement and romance. For Anna Seward Tahiti is "the smiling Eden of the Southern Wave"; for Helen Maria Williams "Otaheite's isle" is "Where Spring... Lives in blossoms ever new."[35] Male poets such as the young Coleridge and Byron stressed the sexual freedoms of Tahiti and figured the island as a place of retreat and escape, as Tim Fulford's chapter in this volume demonstrates. James C. McKusick has convincingly argued for the importance of South Sea narratives as a source of the Pantisocratic scheme of Coleridge and Southey, a place where there might be no personal property and no arbitrary government.[36]

Coleridge's sympathetic identification with a South Sea islander appears in "To a Young Lady" where he mourns the death of Lee Boo, the Pellew Prince, who came to England and died of small pox, as told in George Keate's literary account: "My soul... Mourn'd with the breeze, O LEE BOO! o'er thy tomb" (Beer, *Poems* 41). In William Lisle Bowles's dramatic monologue "Abba Thule's Lament for His Son Prince Le Boo," Abba Thulle ("Ibedul") is a vehicle for the dignified and touching expression of sensibility: "I linger on the desert rock alone / Heartless, and cry for thee, my son, my son," close in treatment to the forsaken or bereaved parents of *Lyrical Ballads*, such as the Cumbrian shepherd, Michael.[37] In these accounts the sympathetic attraction to the South Sea Islander is premised on a racial assumption that the Polynesian is close to the European. Indeed this is an absorption or cannibalizing of the Polynesian by the European, effacing cultural difference. No such effusion was possible for the cannibal New Zealander or the darker-skinned Melanesian peoples.[38] This, at best an elision and at worst a demonization, was complicit with the anthropological racial project underway in Oceania.

Byron's fictionalized account of the *Bounty* Mutiny, *The Island* exemplifies how this process was reflected in imaginative literature.[39] Heavily influenced by Byron's enthusiasm for John Martin's rendition of William Mariner's *Account of the Tonga Islands* of 1817, the poem sums up the variety of the Southern Pacific in terms of the Polynesian paradise of Toobonai (Tubuai). Byron's Enlightenment anthropological assumptions allow him, in the tradition of Montaigne, to use the native islander as a rebuke to European civilization. In so doing, he attempts to efface the difference between Polynesian and European, presenting such physical differences as having no moral significance, functioning mainly as a spur to desire and passion:

> True, they had vices—such are nature's growth—
> But only the Barbarian's—we have both:
> The sordor of civilization, mixed
> With all the savage which man's fall hath fixed.
> Who hath not seen Dissimulation reign,
> The prayers of Abel linked to deeds of Cain?
> Who such would see, may from his lattice view
> The Old World more degraded than the New. (2.67–74)[40]

Byron thus constructs a fable of the tensions between Northern duty and Southern pleasure. Toobanai and its metonymic dusky maiden, the "soft savage" (1.32), Neuha, is defined as a place of desire and freedom when mankind has no master "save his mood." It is a place of plenty stocked by "the gushing fruits that Nature gave untilled" and "promiscuous plenty" (1.33, 35):

> Where all partake the earth without dispute,
> And bread itself is gathered as a fruit;
> Where none contests the fields, the woods, the streams:-
> The Goldless Age, where Gold disturbs no dreams,

Inhabits or inhabited the shore,
Till Europe taught them better than before,
Bestowed her customs, and amended theirs
But left her vices to their heirs. (1.213–20)

Neuha, the "gentle savage of the wild" (2.123), the "infant of an infant world" (2.127), indulges in an adolescent romance with Torquil, the Northern Scottish boy, ultimately rescuing him from the retribution of the British naval establishment by hiding him in a womb-like hidden cave on an inaccessible island. Neuha is depicted as not racially distinct from the European but as a voluptuous savage whose "wild and warm yet faithful bosom knew/no joy like what it gave" (2.146–7). Both Neuha and Torquil are offspring of island races, one northern (the Scottish Hebrides), with fair hair and blue eyes, and one southern, with brown eyes. Byron breaks down the traditional binary of European civilization and native savagery. Torquil, "the blue-eyed northern child," is "scarce less wild" than Neuha (2.163–5). The "mutual beauty" of the two lovers unites "the half savage and the whole" (2.303–4). Christian himself is described as "Silent, and sad, and savage" (3.141). Similarly, the face and limbs of Ben Bunting, Byron's comic tar, are so sunburnt they might "suit alike with either race" (2.485). For Byron difference is eroticized and priority is accorded to races on aesthetic and not moral criteria. The Polynesians are closer to us because they may be as beautiful as we ideally could be, evincing a physical perfection and beauty that serves as a reminder of a lost neoclassical ideal. Europeans are thus as savage as them, more degraded by their hypocritical, corrupt, and greedy civilized values.

Byron minimizes cultural and physical difference in assimilating Polynesian and European peoples. But this risks widening the gap between fair-skinned, European-Polynesian peoples and the dark-skinned, Melanesian peoples who are presented only at the fringes of the poem. Byron's islanders are not cannibals. The fertility of the island "flings off famine from its fertile breast" (2.264) preventing scarcity. Nor are its inhabitants ritual or lustful cannibals. But cannibalism does exist at the fringes of the poem as an absent presence. The poem's chief source, John Martin, blames the cannibalism that Mariner actually witnessed on Tonga upon the Fijians (soon to be assimilated into nineteenth-century Melanesia). It was this group who imported the practice. Cannibalism was not a Tongan practice, Martin tells us, it was the "younger chiefs" who indulged, and they "have contracted the Feejee habits." William Mariner says that he did not partake of this "kind of diet," despite his hunger and despite the fact that the human flesh when cooked "was exceedingly delicious." Martin writes that when Cook had first visited the island cannibalism was "scarcely thought of amongst them" but "the Feejee people soon taught them this, as well as the art of war; and a famine, which happened some time afterward, rendered the expedient for a time almost necessary."[41] Byron uses this passage to account for the Toobuaians' practice of war but he fails to mention the issue of cannibalism at all, though the Fijians were famous for the practice by 1823, when the poem was published:

> ... we too recall
> The memory bright with many a festival,
> Ere Fiji blew the shell of war, when foes
> For the first time were wafted in canoes.
> Alas! for them the flower of manhood bleeds;
> Alas! for them our fields are rank with weeds:
> ...
> But be it so:—*they* taught us how to wield
> The club, and rain our arrows o'er the field;
> Now let them reap the harvest of their art! (2.33–43)

Byron's poem avoids depicting the Polynesian Tongan customs of infanticide, human sacrifice, and cannibalism, which were in his chief source. These would muddy the distinctions he is attempting to make between corrupt, hypocritical European civilization and the paradise of desire and freedom that drew Christian and his followers to mutiny. Byron's poem glosses over his sources' refractory material. The result is that, although the Polynesian self is assimilated into the European category on the grounds that both are beautiful and objects of desire, the Fijian or Melanesian cannibal self is alienated further from the European. The cannibalism of Tonga is abjected onto the Fijian.

Not unsurprisingly, Robert Southey's view of Tahiti and its neighbors is less generous and idealized than Byron's; both writers are nevertheless complicit with a process that produces the same effect. Southey's Protestant imperial comments on Tahiti appeared in a series of reviews he wrote for the *Annual* and *Quarterly* Reviews during the first quarter of the nineteenth century. In his review of the *Transactions of the Missionary Society* Southey, ridiculed the earlier Rousseauistic views of noble savagery as mediated to the South Seas by Bougainville and others:

> The philosophists who placed happiness in the indulgence of sensual appetite, and freedom in the absence of legal and moral restraints, were loud in their praise of this "New Cythera;" and even men of healthier intellect

and sounder principles, regarded these islanders as singularly favoured by Providence, because their food was produced spontaneously, and they had no other business in their life but to enjoy existence. But now they are better known, it appears indisputably that their iniquities exceed those of other people ancient or modern, civilised or savage; and that human nature has never been exhibited in such utter depravity as by the inhabitants of these terrestrial Paradises!... Crimes not to be named are habitually committed without shame; and as if to show to us what loathsomeness of pollution a depraved imagination will have recourse when palled with ordinary abominations, a society was formed both in Taheite and Eimeo, who in their meetings were to eat human ordure, as the seal and sacrament of their association!... When the Creator decreed that in the sweat of his brow man must eat bread, the punishment became a blessing; a divine ordinance necessary for the health of soul as well as body while man continues to be the imperfect being that we behold him.[42]

Southey wants to banish the Polynesian as well as the Melanesian to the ranks of the unregenerate and base. He does this by discoursing upon diet. He moves from the profuse breadfruit which is now a sign of sin, removing the islanders from the Christian imperative to labor, the saving curse of Adam, to the eating of human flesh (in the conventional locution of "Crimes not to be named") to the eating of human excrement. Breadfruit is no longer the sign of Eden but of forbidden fruit and ensuing damnation. So much so that Southey commends "Coleridge's scheme to mend" the Tahitians "by extirpating the bread-fruit from their island, and making them live by the sweat of their brows."[43] Southey's lumping together, however, of the Pacific islanders as equally depraved without the unifying bond of Protestant Christianity is less pernicious than Byron's Enlightenment division of Oceania. In Southey's familial scheme all could be saved; in Byron's only the racially beautiful achieve paradise of a kind.

Whether through Byron's inauthentic, imagined paradise, Southey's Protestant imperial thundering, or Forster's Enlightenment grand narrative of civilization, false and arbitrary patterns were imposed on the peoples of the geopolitical area of Oceania. In the process the cannibal was transformed from the soul of honor, to the adolescent barbarian, to the degenerate racial other whose very existence can only point to an unredeemable alterity, the true inhabitant of the heart of darkness of that "silent sea."

Notes

1. Philip Edwards, *The Story of the Voyage: Sea-Narratives in Eighteenth-Century England* (Cambridge: Cambridge UP, 1994); Neil Rennie, *Far-Fetched Facts; Literature*

and the Idea of the South Seas (Oxford: Oxford UP, 1995); Rod Edmond, *Representing the South Pacific: Colonial Discourse from Cook to Gaugin* (Cambridge: Cambridge UP, 1997); Nicholas Thomas, *In Oceania; Visions, Artifacts, Histories* (Durham and London: Duke UP, 1997); Vanessa Smith, *Literary Culture and the Pacific* (Cambridge: Cambridge UP, 1998); Jonathan Lamb, Vanessa Smith, and Nicholas Thomas, eds. *Exploration & Exchange: a South Seas Anthology 1680–1900* (Chicago: University of Chicago Press, 2000); and Jonathan Lamb, *Preserving the Self in the South Seas 1680–1840* (Chicago: University of Chicago Press, 2001).

2. Nicholas Thomas, *Entangled Objects: Exchange, Material Culture, and Colonialism in the Pacific* (Cambridge, Mass.: Harvard UP, 1991); *Colonialism's Culture: Anthropology, Travel, and Government* (London: Polity Press, 1994); *In Oceania* 1–20.

3. See Peter J. Kitson, "Romantic Displacements: Representing Cannibalism," in *Placing and Displacing Romanticism*, ed. Peter J. Kitson (London: Ashgate, 2001), 204–25. See also: William Arens, *The Man-Eating Myth: Anthropology & Anthropophagy* (Oxford and New York: Oxford UP, 1979); Peter Hulme, *Colonial Encounters: Europe and the Native Caribbean 1492–1797* (London, and New York: Routledge, 1986); Francis Barker, Peter Hulme, and Margaret Iversen, eds., *Cannibalism and the Colonial World* (Cambridge: Cambridge UP, 1998); Gananath Obeyesekere," 'British Cannibals': Contemplation of an Event in the Death and Resurrection of James Cook, Explorer," *Critical Inquiry* 18 (1992), 630–54. Frank Lestringnant, *Cannibals: The Discovery and Representation of the Cannibal from Columbus to Jules Verne*, tr. Rosemary Morris (London: Polity Press, 1997); Geoffrey Sanborn, *The Sign of the Cannibal: Melville and the Making of a Postcolonial Reader* (Durham and London: Duke UP, 1998). For an informed review of the debate see C. Richard King, "The (Mis) Uses of Cannibalism in Contemporary Cultural Critique," *Diacritics* 30.1 (2000), 106–23.

4. John Beer, *S. T. Coleridge. Poems* (London: Dent, 1998), 220. Further references to this edition will be contained in the text and cited by line number.

5. Mary Louise Pratt, *Imperial Eyes: Travel Writing and Transculturation* (New York and London, 1992), 15–37, 39.

6. Roxanne Wheeler, *The Complexion of Race: Categories of Difference in Eighteenth-Century British Culture* (University of Pennsylvania Press, 1999); Lestringnant, *Cannibals*.

7. For the motivations for cannibalism see Sanbourn, *Sign* 21–73; and Kitson, "Romantic Displacements," 218–20.

8. Quoted in Emmanuel Chukwudi Eze, ed., *Race and the Enlightenment: A Reader* (Oxford: Blackwell, 1997), 38–64, 134. See Sanborn, *Sign* 38–9.

9. Thomas, *In Oceania* 133–55 and "The Force of Ethnology: Origins and Significance of the Melanesia/Polynesia Division," *Cultural Anthropology*, 30 (1989), 27–34.

10. Gary Hogg, *Cannibalism and Human Sacrifice* (London: Robert Hales Ltd, 1958), 23.

11. Louis de Bougainville, *A Voyage Round the World*, tr. Johann Reinhold Forster (London: J. Nourse, 1772), 249, 291, 320.

94   ✦   *Peter J. Kitson*

12. Thomas Haweis, "Preliminary Discourse," in *A Missionary Voyage to the Southern Pacific Ocean*, ed. William Wilson (London: T. Chapman, 1799), lxxi, lxxxvi. See Thomas, *Oceania* 142–3. See also Rennie, *Far-Fetched Facts* 159–61, 164.

13. William Ellis, *Polynesian Researches in the South Seas Islands*, 2 vols. (London: Fisher and Jackson, 1829); 2nd ed., 4 vols. (1832), 1.78–9. For the concept of the facial angle, see Peter J. Kitson, ed. *Theories of Race*, vol. 8 of *Slavery, Abolition and Emancipation*, ed. Peter J. Kitson and Debbie Lee, 8 vols. (London: Pickering Chatto, 1999), ix–xii.

14. Michael Russell, *Polynesia; or, An historical account of the principal islands in the South of the Cannibal* 27.

15. Thomas Williams, *Fiji and the Fijians: Volume 1. The Islands and Their Inhabitants* (London: Alexander Heylin, 1858), 112, 212, 205–14.

16. Josiah Priest, *Slavery, as It Relates to the Negro, or African Race Examined in the Light of Circumstances, History and Holy Scriptures* (Albany: C. Van Benthuysen and co, 1843), 191, 199. Quoted in Sanbourn, *Sign* 27.

17. George Brown, *Melanesians and Polynesians: Their Life-Histories Described and Compared* (Macmillan: London, 1910), 15–17.

18. John Dunmore, *French Explorers in the Pacific*, 2 vols. (Oxford: Clarendon, 1965), 1, 101.

19. For Forster, see Michael E. Hoare, *The Tactless Philosopher: Johann Reinhold Forster (1729–98)* (Melbourne: The Hawthorne Press, 1976).

20. John Reinhold Forster, *Observations Made During a Voyage Round the World, on Physical Geography, Natural History, and Ethic Philosophy* (London: G. Robinson, 1778), 153.

21. The most authoritative discussion of Maori cannibalism in this period is Ian Barber, "Archaeology, Ethnology, and the Record of Maori Cannibalism before 1815: A Critical Review," *Journal of Polynesian Society*, 101.3 (1992), 241–92. See also Claude Rawson, "Savages Noble and Ignoble: Natives, Cannibals and Others in South-Pacific Narratives by Gulliver, Bougainville, and Diderot, with Notes of the Encyclopaedia and on Voltaire," *Eighteenth-Century Life*, 18 (1994), 168–97.

22. George Forster, *A Voyage Round the World*, 2 vols. (London: White Robson, Elmsly and Robinson, 1777), 1.511.

23. Anonymous [J. Marra], *Journal of the Resolution's Voyage, in 1772, 1773, 1774, and 1775* (London: F. Newberry, 1775), 103.

24. J. C. Beaglehole, ed., *The Journals of Captain Cook on his Voyages of Discovery. II: The Voyage of the Resolution and Adventure 1772–1775* (Cambridge: Hakluyt Society and Cambridge UP, 1961), 293.

25. C. Holmes, ed., *Captain Cook's Second Voyage: the Journals of Lieutenants Elliot and Pickersgill* (London: Caliban Books, 1984), 22.

26. Carl Solander to Joseph Banks, 14 August 1775; Mitchell Library, Banks Papers, MS As 24; Quoted in J. C. Beaglehole, *The Life of Captain James Cook* (Stanford: Stanford UP, 1974), 444–5.

27. The Hunterian Museum at the Royal College of Surgeons contains three crania described as "Maori," all mutilated and the probable subject of violent death in warfare. One is female and the dentition of the other two reveal an older age than that of twenty. All three are complete with mandibles, unlike Pickersgill's head which lacked this part of the skull. The crews of Cook's three voyages were often in search of curiosities, especially human remains that were in great demand by the new proponents of comparative anatomy. The anatomist J. F. Blumenbach frequently requested crania from Joseph Banks. In a letter of 20 June 1787, Blumenbach requested one of Banks's South Sea skulls but on this occasion was unsuccessful as Banks had already given away both the skulls he then had, one to Peter Camper and the other to John Hunter. British Museum Add. MS. 8096. 383–4. For this aspect of Banks's career as a collector and disseminator of exotic skulls, see Tim Fulford, "Theorizing Golgotha: Coleridge, Race Theory, and the Skull Beneath the Skin," in *Coleridge and the Science of Life*, ed. Nicholas Roe (Oxford: Clarendon, 2001), 117–33. See also John Gascoigne, *Joseph Banks and the English Enlightenment* (Cambridge: Cambridge UP, 1994), 119–83.

28. B. Hooper ed., *With Captain James Cook in the Antarctic and Pacific: the Private Journal of James Burney Second Lieutenant of the Adventure on Cook's Second Voyage* (Canberra: National Library of Australia), 96–7.

29. James Cook, *A Voyage towards the South Pole and Round the World*, 2 vols. (London: W. Strahan and T. Cadell, 1777), 2.258.

30. Anne Salmond, *Two Worlds: First Meetings between Maori and Europeans, 1642–1772* (Auckland: Viking, 1991), 359–430.

31. J. C. Beaglehole, ed., *The Journals of Captain James Cook on his Voyages of Discovery. III: The Voyage of the Resolution and Discovery 1776–1780*, 2 vols. (Cambridge: Hakluyt Society and Cambridge UP, 1967) 815.

32. See Barber, "Archaeology," 256–7.

33. For the symbolism of breadfruit see Fulford's chapter in this volume (41–58). Voltaire argued that the profusion of the breadfruit saved the Tahitians from becoming cannibals; see Rennie, *Far-Fetched Facts* 123.

34. William Lambe, *Additional Reports of the Effects of a Peculiar Regimen on Scirrhous Tumours and Cancerous Ulcers* (London: 1809), quoted in Morton, *Shelley* 166. I am grateful to Timothy Morton for bringing this to my attention. See also his general discussion of Lambe (160–8) and his discussion of Joseph Ritson's argument that cannibalism belongs to an earlier phase of human development (150–7).

35. Helen Maria Williams, *Poems on Various Subjects* (London: G. and W. B. Whittaker, 1823).

36. James McKusick, " 'That Silent Sea': Coleridge, Pantisocracy, and the Exploration of the South Pacific," *The Wordsworth Circle*, 24 (1993), 102–6; "Coleridge and the Politics of Pantisocracy," in *Romanticism and Colonialism: Writing and Empire, 1780–1830*, ed. Tim Fulford and Peter J. Kitson (Cambridge: Cambridge UP, 1998), 107–28.

37. *The Poetical Works of William Lisle Bowles*, ed. George Gilfillan (Edinburgh: James Nichol, 1855), 1.51.

38. See Rennie, *Far-Fetched Facts* 168–80.

39. See Catherine Addison, "Elysian and Effeminate" Byron's *The Island SEL*, 35 (1995), 687–706; James C. McKusick, "The Politics of Language in Byron's *The Island*," *ELH*, 59 (1992), 839–56; Nigel Leask, *British Romantic Writers and the East: Anxieties of Empire* (Cambridge: Cambridge UP, 1992), 63–7; Christine Kenyon-Jones, *Kindred Brutes* 132–4; Edmond, *Representing* 63–97.

40. Lord Byron, *The Complete Poetical Works*, ed. Jerome J. McGann, 7 vols. (Oxford: Clarendon Press, 1980–93), 2. 67–74.

41. John Martin, *An Account of the Natives of the Tonga Islands in the South Pacific Ocean With an original Grammar and Vocabulary of their Language . . .*, 2 vols. (London, 1817), 1.115–17.

42. Robert Southey, "Review of *Transactions of the Missionary Society in the South Seas*," in *Quarterly Review*, 2 (1809), 24–61 (45); Southey's review of the *Transactions* in the *Annual Review*, 2 (1803) made a similar point in stronger language. See also Southey's "Review of William Ellis's *Polynesian Researches*," in *Quarterly Review*, 43 (1830), 1–54.

43. Robert Southey to Rev. Charles Cuthbert Southey, in *The Life and Correspondence of Robert Southey*, 6 vols., Charles Cuthbert Southery, ed., (London, 1849–50), 2.243. I am grateful to Tim Fulford for drawing my attention to this letter.

Chapter 5 ⮑

EATING ROMANTIC ENGLAND: THE FOOT AND MOUTH EPIDEMIC AND ITS CONSEQUENCES

Nicholas Roe

> When the green field comes off like a lid
> Revealing what was much better hid...
> —W. H. Auden, "The Witnesses"[1]

England in 2001. The "Foot and Mouth" epidemic leads to the slaughter of millions of animals. The farming community is in crisis, and disruption extends throughout the country. National Parks and National Trust properties are no-go areas. In Devonshire, "all moorland, public footpaths and bridleways" are closed to the public; in Cumbria, tourists are cautioned that they "should not...go onto farmland (including the high fells)."[2] The tourist industry has slumped, and the Wordsworth Trust issues a circular, warning that "if footpaths on the hills are still closed [the annual Wordsworth Summer Conference] will have to do without the walks on the fells that were so much a part of the Wordsworths' lives and have become so much a part of ours."

Which was perhaps an odd thing to announce. Although walks and fells had been part of the Wordsworths' lives at Grasmere, the "public footpaths" so prominently mentioned were not. Paths, tracks, roads, OK. The "public way" and "upright path" in *Michael*. But not "footpaths"—a word used only once by William Wordsworth's poetry, in an unfrequented corner of

Book 8 of *The Excursion*. "Footpath" dates from the sixteenth century, but it was not until the nineteenth century that the word gathered its modern association with "public right of access." The *OED* notices, between "public domain" and "public nursery," "some fields near Manchester... through which runs a public footpath to a little village some two miles distant." The quotation comes from Elizabeth Gaskell's *Mary Barton* (1848), and the location "near Manchester" is significant. Footpaths are features of the new suburbanized landscape of nineteenth- and twentieth-century England, and increasingly, in the age of the motor car, a way of time-traveling away from the present into an idealised rural past, "so much a part of the Wordsworths' lives and... so much a part of ours." It was not a coincidence that Wordsworth's only use of the word "foot path" was in a passage that deplores an "inventive Age" of "potent enginery... / Industrious to destroy" supplanting a scene of "romantic interest" in which "The foot-path faintly marked, the horse-track wild... / Have vanished" (*The Excursion* 8.85–111). Wordsworth, author of a Guide to the Lakes, shows us the footpath as a route into landscape as Romantic "heritage": the National Footpath Preservation Society was founded in 1892, less than twelve months after Dove Cottage first opened to the public.

In April 2001 the Cumbria Tourist Board Web site proclaimed that although the "high fells" were closed, "the Lake District is not shut." Visitors were reassured that they might go to towns, villages, seaside resorts, and join "heritage walks" on footpaths around towns like Whitehaven; visitors may "drive, walk, run, ride horses [and] cycle on or beside tarmacked roads," and they can "travel by public transport of all types." The "markets, museums and visitor attractions" like Dove Cottage are accessible, as are "shops, pubs, restaurants."[3] Forget about Wordsworth and the "Lakers," John Ruskin at Brantwood, and Norman Nicholson at Millom. The poet of the Lake District in our time is John Betjeman, the Milton of Metroland who was delighted to discover that one could ascend Snaefell, on the Isle of Man, by electric train. Indeed, Philip Larkin remarked that his poetry was a Wordsworthian "spontaneous overflow of natural feeling."[4] In his poem "Lake District" we find him at a restaurant table in Grasmere:

> I pass the cruet and I see the lake
>   Running with light, beyond the garden pine,
>   That lake whose waters make me dream her mine.
> Up to the top board mounting for my sake,
> For me she breathes, for me each soft intake,
>   For me the plunge, the lake and limbs combine...

Reeluctant to plunge too, the poet reaches for a "soft intake" more readily
to hand:

> I pledge her in non-alcoholic wine
> And give the H.P. Sauce another shake.[5]

John Betjeman gives us the Lake District as it is now—a suburban prospect
from a footpath or restaurant window, where the Wordsworthian take-in of
"something far more deeply interfused" has been transformed into the
secular eucharist of comfort eating. Anyone for Gingerbread?

The Foot and Mouth crisis has uncovered the extent to which
consumer industries like tourism and agriculture are entwined with
a Romantic idea of England and English landscape: "Wordsworth's Lake
District." The crisis has also brought into the open the ruthless methods of
modern farming, the so-called "industrial production of meat" in "factory
farms" (where the intensive rearing of animals was largely responsible for
the rapid spread of this disease). And, by the way, the Foot and Mouth epidemic followed the BSE scandal in England, in which it emerged that
instead of grazing on grass, cows had been fed high protein meal manufac-
tured from the remains of sheep and cows. The huge pyres and pits which
defaced the landscape were needed not merely to dispose of carcasses but
to reassure the public that all of this infected meat would not get into food
for human consumption. This scandal revealed in turn how the large super-
markets control and manipulate the so-called "food chain": what is produced and where; how much the farmer earns; the price the consumer will
pay in the stores. What we eat is intricately and immediately linked with
production processes alien to but dependent upon Romantic ideas of the
English landscape as a pastoral idyll. The chicken raised with millions of
others in a stinking broiler-house reaches the supermarket in a packet
depicting pastoral meadows. Sunshine. Fresh grass. You've eaten it.

This chapter is in some respects an experiment, a foray into newspapers
and across the internet in quest of England at the start of the twenty-first
century. I want to explore responses to the Foot and Mouth crisis, and to
show how ideas of eating and the consumption of the English landscape
may be related to Romantic perceptions at another time when England,
and the rural way of life, had seemed threatened. Romantic and present-
day responses alike conform to deep-rooted, even archetypal, patterns in
which the "pleasant pastures" of William Blake's England have always
been a paradise lost, and a utopian "new age" yet to come. In our own time
the suburbanization of the countryside—overwhelmingly apparent in the

Cumbria Tourist Board's list of things one can "still do," while "doing without," has continued and, ironically, actually reinforced the idea of an idyllic scene which can be "taken in" and consumed. Anyone visiting the Lake District from Penrith will have noticed the bizarre attraction, "Rheged...the village in the hill," which promisingly announces itself: "The land as never seen." Too right. Situated inside a man-made, turf covered hummock, described as "Europe's largest grass-covered building," "Rheged offers an all-weather world of legends and myths, family fun and excitement, shopping and restaurants—all in the village in the hill." Inside are "waterfalls, limestone crags, a babbling brook and lakes...shops with the finest local food, restaurants where you can combine local dishes with panoramic views" and take a cinematic flight "over the lakes and mountains...The Lake District—all from the edge of your cinema seat." The blurb quoted from the local newspaper "News & Star" is "Eat your heart out, Hollywood."[6]

The "Foot and Mouth Panic" was above all an urban response to a picturesque idea perceived to be under threat, and it was fomented not by farmers or other immediately interested and suffering groups, but by the London-based Ministry of Agriculture, Food and Fisheries (MAFF) and the media. "Where did it go," Neal Ascherson asked in the *Observer*, "Where did it go, that rosy vision of the farmer and his virtues, of the farmyard and its wholesome produce?"[7] The answer, presumably, must be over the hill— or under it—for this is "the land as never seen." He might better have asked, "where did [that rosy vision] come from?" One would expect an article about Foot and Mouth to deal with "the farmer and the farmyard" but, as this article indicates, Foot and Mouth has involved much more than an illness of cloven-hoofed animals. As we know, the disease is mild in its effects on livestock. Animals will recover from it given time. It is rarely passed on to humans. The disease is endemic in many parts of the world, and it was so in Britain until the 1920s when no one thought of postponing a General Election (as in 2001) because of an outbreak. Michael's sheepfold would have encircled a sick flock. A. E. Housman's "blue remembered hills," Edward Thomas's fields of "willows, willow-herb, and grass, / And meadowsweet, and haycocks dry" were stocked with diseased cattle and sheep. Rupert Brooke's country of "gentleness, / In hearts at peace, under an English heaven" was a plague zone. Millions of sheep and cattle have been killed (or "culled" as the euphemism goes) in the hope of preserving the disease-free status required by European Community marketing policies. The "culling" was intended to eradicate the disease, and, by the same token, to retrieve an England that never was—a "far country" of "lost content" to which Housman, Thomas, and Brooke look back in their poems, and which newspapers in 2001 represented by photographs of pet lambs and references to Romantic poets. What was at stake in all of this was an idea of England fit for human consumption—an "all-weather world," "that rosy vision of the farmer and his virtues, of the farmyard and its wholesome produce." Healthy hens in the yard. Free Range.

The outbreak of the disease has highlighted competing interests in agriculture, and it has done so in a way that raises questions about "vision" and "virtues"—cultural ideas of the English landscape inheriting the aesthetics of the Romantic period, including the picturesque. An article in the *Observer* newspaper warned that Foot and Mouth would finally deliver control of the landscape from the farmer (who by implication is "virtuous") into the hands of "big business." In a significant realignment of the political and biological landscape, "big businesses" are the new "Levellers":

> the transnational, commercialised world of the East Anglian "barley barons" with their quasi-prairies, enemies of bio-diversity; the folks who brought you BSE through their industrial cultivation of meat. These are the men who have long dominated the national council of the National Farmers' Union, and through it, wielded overwhelming influence in Maff.[8]

Under threat here is the new picturesque of biological—one might say genetic—particularity and diversity. England is confronted with a faceless "transnational" threat. An ancient landscape of varied scenery is at risk of reduction to the "quasi-prairies" of grain producers. The multiplicity of inhabitants, animal and human, is besieged by the "enemies of bio-diversity" advocating the dangerous and inhumane "industrial cultivation of meat."

In *Rural Rides* William Cobbett had reflected in similar terms, albeit from a different political perspective, on the rural depredations of "tax-eaters and monopolisers":

> All these mansions, all these parsonages, aye, and their goods and furniture, together with the clocks, the brass-kettles, the brewing vessels, the good bedding and good clothes and good furniture, and the stock in pigs, or in money, of the inferior classes, in this series of once gay villages and hamlets; all these have been by the accursed system of taxing and funding and paper-money, by the well-known exactions of the state, and by the not less real, though less generally understood, extortions of the *monopolies* arising out of paper-money; all these have been, by these accursed means, conveyed away, out of this Valley, to the haunts of the tax-eaters and the monopolizers.[9]

Cobbett's monopolizers devouring the rural community are thriving today among "the men who have long dominated" in agribusiness. In Cobbett's time as in the twenty-first century in England, agri-monopolizers are responsible for rural depopulation and for the transformation of the English landscape into a chemically fed monoculture to supply a voracious urban market:

> The mansions are all down now [Cobbett continues] and it is curious enough to see the former *walled gardens* become *orchards*, together with other changes, all tending to prove the gradual decay in all except what appertains merely to *the land* as a thing of production for the distant market.[10]

To put that in slightly different terms, in the modern "transnational, commercialised world" the English landscape is literally being eaten away by "the distant market" of consumers and by the encroachments of "property developers."

Cobbett's England of "changes" and "gradual decay" survives into John Betjeman's "Middlesex," "Where a few surviving hedges / Keep alive our lost Elysium,"[11] and it is dwindling, still, in Philip Larkin's poem "Going, Going":

> I thought it would last my time—
> The sense that, beyond the town,
> There would always be fields and farms,
> Where the village louts could climb
> Such trees as were not cut down;
> I knew there'd be false alarms
>
> In the papers about old streets
> And split-level shopping, but some
> Have always been left so far;
> And when the old part retreats
> As the bleak high-risers come
> We can always escape in the car.
>
> Things are tougher than we are, just
> As earth will always respond
> However we mess it about;
> Chuck filth in the sea, if you must:
> The tides will be clean beyond.
> —But what do I feel now? Doubt?
>
> Or age, simply? The crowd
> Is young in the M1 café;

Their kids are screaming for more—
More houses, more parking allowed,
More caravan sites, more pay.
On the Business Page, a score

Of spectacled grins approve
Some takeover bid that entails
Five per cent profit (and ten
Per cent more in the estuaries): move
Your works to the unspoilt dales

(Grey area grants)! And when
You try to get near the sea
In summer...
            It seems, just now,
To be happening so very fast;
Despite all the land left free
For the first time I feel somehow
That it isn't going to last,

That before I snuff it, the whole
Boiling will be bricked in
Except for the tourist parts—
First slum of Europe: a role
It won't be so hard to win,
With a cast of crooks and tarts.

And that will be England gone,
The shadows, the meadows, the lanes,
The guildhalls, the carved choirs.
There'll be books; it will linger on
In galleries, but all that remains
For us will be concrete and tyres.

Most things are never meant.
This won't be, most likely: but greeds
And garbage are too thick-strewn
To be swept up now, or invent
Excuses that make them all needs.
I just think it will happen, soon.[12]

At the center of this dreadful vista of "greeds / And garbage" is a scene of perpetual, unassuagable consumption—"The crowd / Is young in the M1 café; / Their kids are screaming for more." And more, and more. Demand for food extends outward until all that remains of the landscape is the detritus of "concrete and tyres"—and the "tourist parts."

"And that *will be* England gone." England has always been going, going, and has lingered on in books, stirring feelings of uneasiness. Here is Leigh Hunt, unsettled, like Larkin, at the demise of "Merry Old England."

> [England] is very bustling, very talkative, and, as the phrase is, very successful in the world; but, somehow or other, she is not happy. Nor has she been so, from her birth; though, to hear her talk, one would suppose that all her griefs began with the French Revolution. She was very rich and melancholy before that... Merry Old England died in the country a great while ago; and the sport, the pastimes, the holidays, the Christmas greens and gambols, the archeries, the may-mornings, the May-poles, the country-dances, the masks, the harvest-homes, the new-year's-gifts, the gallantries, the golden means, the poetries, the pleasures, the leisures, the real treasures,—were all buried with her.[13]

In Hunt's wonderful essay from *The Examiner*, Merry Old England has been "buried"—and yet, again, "bustling" and "talkative" continues prosperous yet melancholy and aware of another country, "a great while ago." Haunting Cobbett's landscape of "changes" and "the gradual decay of all," Betjeman's "rural Middlesex," Larkin's "England gone," and the death of Merry Old England "a great while ago" is the memory of a land of lost content: the English paradise, a land of equality and justice where "Adam delved, and Eve span," the "green and pleasant land" which for William Blake was lost and also an imminent utopian prospect.

The song from the era of the Peasants' Revolt in the fourteenth century reminds us that England has always been idealized in response to perceived threats: "tax-eaters and monopolizers," the "Business Page," the French Revolution, Wars, environmental crisis, the French, the EU, even asylum-seekers. Presently the enemy is the commercialized agribusiness that has brought upon us the plagues of BSE and Foot and Mouth. As in Cobbett, Larkin, and Hunt, another idea of England has emerged to set against industrial farming. This is the England of smallness and variety, now, according to the *Observer*, threatened with destruction: "The consequences of small farming's collapse [will be] visible and keenly felt—not just by farmers, but by everyone who uses the countryside: as tourists and providers of tourism; as ramblers, climbers and picnickers, those of us who love the land of Wordsworth, Ruskin, and Constable."[14] Within this materialist discourse of "providers" and "users," small farms are explicitly paralleled with a Romantic England of writers and painters, and William Gilpin's picturesque. The small scale inherits Burkean ideas of the beautiful;

and ranged against it is a shadowy manifestation of the Burkean sublime, the powerful oppressors, agribusiness, and the "barley barons."

On 19 March 2001, the Guardian newspaper reported that the Foot and Mouth disease outbreak was costing the English tourist industry £250 m a week and farmers £60 m a week in lost agricultural production. Drawing attention to the disparity between these figures, the article went on to question the British government's focus on "minimising the impact on agriculture," pointing out that the cost to other businesses ("pubs, shops, hotels and restaurants") far exceeded the damage to livestock farming. But, according to the *Guardian*, the "power to move" released by the crisis had less to do with the balance sheets of profits and losses on the Business Page than with violation of the English "sense of identity [being] invested in the pastoral landscape":

> The grazing of animals has acquired symbolic meaning. The English landscape is a tamed and cultivated one, shaped over centuries by men and animals, medieval drove roads, by generations of ploughing and hill farming and the enclosures. Despite being one of the most industrialised and urbanised countries in the world, we cling to agricultural rituals because they give us our sense of place and season.[15]

This is on the right path, except that I want to suggest that "we cling to agricultural rituals [for] our sense of place and season" because England has become one of the most industrialized countries. Or, to put that the other way round, heightened sense of "place and season" is itself a condition of industrial and urban blight, much as the wish that "the walks on the fells that were ... part of the Wordsworths' lives [might be] part of ours" is a symptom of national crisis. Compare Edward Thomas's poem "Lob," for example, where the sense of the elusive is actually about living in a time of war:

> The man you saw,—Lob-lie-by-the-fire, Jack Cade,
> Jack Smith, Jack Moon, poor Jack of every trade,
> Young Jack, or old Jack, or Jack What d'ye-call,
> Jack-in-the-hedge, or Robin-run-by-the-wall,
> Robin Hood, Ragged Robin, lazy Bob,
> One of the lords of No Man's land, good Lob,—
> Although he was seen dying at Waterloo,
> Hastings, Agincourt, and Sedgemoor too,—
> Lives yet. He never will admit he is dead ... [16]

Foot and Mouth has disrupted the "sense of place and season," leaving "empty fields in a silent spring" and, as the *Guardian* called it, a "Green,

Unpleasant Land."[17] Broad swathes of the countryside were transformed into battlegrounds, and the border country north of the English Lake District was renamed "the killing fields." At the end of March 2001, this area was hazy with the smoke of dozens of pyres of burning carcases. Screened from public view on an abandoned wartime airfield (the location is significant) gigantic burial pits were excavated at Great Orton just to the west of Carlisle. The *Guardian* article goes on:

> Tourists, accustomed to a Gainsborough vision of the English countryside in which all is pastoral peace, have had their view shattered. The order turns out to have been an illusion; with the arrival of foot and mouth, a hellish scene of fire and slaughter has erupted instead, more Hieronymus Bosch than 18th-century landscape portrait.

"The green field comes off like a lid / Revealing what was much better hid." Not "the village under the hill," but cranes and grabs feeding carcases into the flames, shattering the pastoral scene in which, according to William Gilpin's picturesque aesthetic, deformities must be overlooked and decorously concealed. The juxtaposition of "pastoral peace" and "order" with a terrifying "eruption" of "fire and slaughter" also takes us back to the Burkean contrast between the beautiful and the sublime. I want now to investigate this Romantic aesthetic dimension in a little more detail.

For Burke beauty was associated with smallness—remember those "small farms" about to be consumed by agribusiness—with "smooth slopes of earth in gardens," with "gradual ascents and declivities," and variation and change which is only a "very insensible deviation."[18] These are the forms of the English landscape which, during the traumatic years following the French Revolution, Wordsworth sensed might provide "food for future years." We might think that Wordsworth had in mind the "forms perennial of the ancient hills" at the Wye valley and in the English Lake District, but gentler pastoral landscapes—akin to Housman's and Thomas's—also provided spiritual and national sustenance during the alarm of an invasion:

> here we are once more.
> The Cock that crows, the Smoke that curls, that sound
> Of Bells, those Boys that in yon meadow-ground
> In white sleeved shirts are playing by the score,
> And even this little River's gentle roar,
> All, all are English. Oft have I looked round
> With joy in Kent's green vales; but never found

Myself so satisfied in heart before.
Europe is yet in Bonds; but let that pass...[19]

It's important that this is a revisit poem, that the scene is familiar. This land-scape "satisfies" now, more than it did before, inasmuch as it is created by, and is about, the idea of a Napoleonic threat.

This danger, as yet obscure and "[t]hought for another moment," as Wordsworth says, takes us back to the "hellish scene of fire and slaughter" and to Burke on the sublime in *Paradise Lost*—the exemplary instance of which is the portrait of Death in Book 2 line 666:

> The other shape,
> If shape it might be called that shape had none
> Distinguishable, in member, joint, or limb:
> Or substance might be called that shadow seemed,
> For each seemed either; black he stood as night;
> Fierce as ten furies; terrible as hell;
> And shook a deadly dart. (2.666–72)[20]

"In this description," Burke remarks, "all is dark, uncertain, confused, terrible, and sublime to the last degree." The sense of a hidden menace was conveyed powerfully in reports (harking back to the Cold War) presenting Foot and Mouth as an insidious pestilence borne "through the air" and, under the ground, infecting the water supply.[21] This kind of panic gained further impetus after the events of 11 September 2001, when fears about the water supply became acute in the United Kingdom and in the United States. In the *Guardian*, Milton's "Death" reappeared "Under the dark shadow of the slaughterman," armed now with a state of the art deadly dart: "a captive bolt-gun."[22] I've already suggested how depictions of the "deeper struggle" between agribusiness and the "small farmer" replicated Burke's sublime and the beautiful: compare, for another instance, this report in which a picturesque Devonshire scene is placed against a baleful backdrop:

> The pink-washed farm sits on a small rise to the west of the town. In better days the views would be stunning. In these altered times the scene is marred by smoke from giant pyres, like preparations for some monstrous feast... behind...the line of fire on the horizon is coming closer. The time for killing is almost here.[23]

Perhaps most appropriate of all to the "hellish scene of fire and slaughter" is Burke's observation that the "cries of ANIMALS" can often have sublime effects. The "natural inarticulate voices of men, or any animals in pain or danger" are "capable of causing a great and aweful sensation" and are "productive of the sublime."[24] These are "altered times" indeed. The idea of a "pink-washed" pastoral becomes more alluring because the actuality formerly overlaid, or displaced, has been disclosed with apocalyptic force: the mass production of animals and crops. Accordingly, the "monstrous feast" prepared on the pyres of dead cattle and sheep appears as a grotesque suburban barbecue, such as might take place in the garden of Hieronymous Bosch.

Week after week, doom-laden reports filled the newspapers: "Why farming will never be the Same Again"; "Fear grows in plague village"; "there is an anticipation of doom."[25] All of this was reminiscent of millenarian and apocalyptic Romantic period verse which interpreted such terrifying upheavals as retribution visited on a corrupt state. Coleridge's "Fire, Famine, and Slaughter," for example (the unspoken prospect of "famine" lurks in the newspaper report quoted above), or "Fears in Solitude":

> Like a cloud that travels on,
> Steamed up from Cairo's swamps of pestilence,
> Even so, my countrymen! have we gone forth
> And borne to distant tribes slavery and pangs,
> And deadlier far, our vices . . . /
> Therefore, evil days
> Are coming on us, O my countrymen! (47–51, 123–4)[26]

The same ominous note is sounded in Lord Byron's *Darkness*, Anna Barbauld's *Eighteen Hundred and Eleven*, and in Mary Shelley's plague-ridden epic, *The Last Man*. By seeing plague, famine and death as a judgement on England, Romantic writers were invoking the bigger picture of Biblical retribution which James Thomson had also used to sublime effect in the torrid zone of "Summer" in his poem *The Seasons*. For Thomson, such disasters had emerged from "Ethiopia's poisoned woods, / From stifled Cairo's filth and fetid fields"—breeding "inclement skies" and accompanying "plague" ("Summer" 1055–6).[27] The winter of 2000–01 was the wettest on record in England, with widespread flooding. Journalists were not slow to follow Thomson in linking the weather and the onset of plague with paranoid fears about aliens, illegal immigrants, asylum seekers, the East, and poisonous food. So, the outbreak of Foot and Mouth was blamed on "infected meat, probably smuggled from the Middle East or East

Asia" which "went to a restaurant in north east England and the waste ended up in swill fed to pigs at a British farm, where the disease was first detected." A Professor Wallace Lim, from Hong Kong University's Department of Zoology, gave the theory scientific credibility by pointing out that the Foot and Mouth virus was a "Type O," which is found "mainly in Asia and . . . persists in meat products for a long time."[28] The message was that the unsightly "filth and fetid fields" of the East have infected the green fields of England, and adulterated and poisoned the food. In 2003 think SARS, think China.

Against the invisible, global hazard of plague, Thomson articulated the sensibility of a nation of so-called animal lovers when he presented livestock as dumb victims:

> In rueful gaze
> The cattle stand, and on the scowling heavens
> Cast a deploring eye . . . ("Summer" 1123–5)

A tempest "rolls its awful burden on the wind," and the scene is transformed:

> A lifeless group the blasted cattle lie:
> Here the soft flocks, with that same harmless look
> They wore alive, and ruminating still
> In fancy's eye, and there the frowning bull
> And ox half-raised. ("Summer" 1152–6)

Just as Thomson's plague arrived like "Nemesis," Easter in 2001 in England brought comparisons—admittedly, garbled ones—with the Passover in Egypt. Neil Ascherson quoted this from a "farmer's wife" sitting at the kitchen table:

> "The first week after it started was like Passover in Egypt. The angel moving at nights from door to door, smearing some with blood. I lay awake listening." She laughed grimly, and she and her husband knocked on the table for luck.[29]

This fearful picture is, however, contained at the end of Thomson's "Summer" which closes with a hymn to "Happy Britannia" and her (uninfected) "Power of Cultivation." For Thomson, "the stretching land-scape into smoke decays" as the epitome of Italian pictureseque composure, the smoke in this case being the blue haze of a Claude landscape and not a pyre of burning pigs.

All of this represents what might be thought of as the "gothic" strand of Foot and Mouth reporting. At another extreme we find pictures of Phoenix the calf, the white heifer reprieved from the cull and rising again, as it were, from the griddle. The *Observer* offered an image of a muddy and bedraggled lamb, confined to a single field since birth because of restrictions on animal movements, but added the happy news that the lamb "has now been saved by the farmer's son, four-year-old William." Both instances epitomize the Burkean beautiful—weak, tottering, soft, feminine—drawing the eyes of at least some of the New Labour cabinet, prompting a change in policy and encouraging Tony Blair, like a Burkean patriarch, to take personal charge of the crisis.

So the Foot and Mouth episode revived Romantic ideas of the countryside; it has mobilized some key aspects of picturesque aesthetics; and it has stirred deeper ideas of English landscape encapsulated and projected by William Blake's "green and pleasant land." The idea of English landscape as a haven, a blessed sanctuary, is particularly strong—and even a condition of—times of stress, according to Jeremy Paxman in his book *The English*.[30] One of his examples cites John Major's description of an England in fifty years' time which "will still be the country of long shadows on county grounds, warm beer, invincible green suburbs, dog lovers and pool fillers and—as George Orwell said—'old maids cycling to holy communion through the morning mist.'" To which Paxman comments: "Where on earth did all this stuff come from?" (142).

It came, he argues, from Major's need to offer the Tory electorate an image of England's security against takeover by Brussels. As if a pint of warm beer and holy communion will always keep out Jacques Delors. Foot and Mouth has provoked a comparable resurgence of "the country of long shadows," pubs, pink cottages, and pastoral peace. In twenty-first-century suburban England, the England of "dog-lovers and pool fillers," the idea of an idyllic countryside has become, if anything, even more necessary than in Larkin's day, an elegy for elegy. Except that now England is packaged and marketed by the National Trust and English Heritage, purveyors of the national identity associated with the mansion houses and park landscapes whose going was regretted 200 years ago by William Cobbett. The English idyll, England's "green and pleasant land," has become a commodity to be consumed by tourists in cars and coaches, latest descendants of the picturesque travelers of the Romantic period. Which is why the Foot and Mouth panic was never anything to do with the disease or its effects on livestock. This was a suburban nightmare, projected by the media, revealing to the "invincible green suburbs" their own rampant consumption of

England. Hence the Cumbria Tourist Board's urgent reassurance that the "Lake District is still open for business," a "thing of production," as Cobbett put it, "for the distant market." Or, in John Betjeman's bleak summary:

Long stony lanes and back at six to tea
And Heinz's ketchup on the tablecloth. (13–14)

Notes

1. W. H. Auden, "The Witnesses," *The English Auden: Poems, Essays, & Dramatic Writings, 1927–1939*, ed. Edward Mendelson (London and New York: Random House, 1977), 130.
2. *Sunday Telegraph* (15 April 2001); Cumbria Tourist Board Web site, 13 April 2001.
3. Cumbria Tourist Board Web site, 13 April 2001.
4. Philip Larkin, review of John Betjeman, *The Collected Poems of John Betjeman* (London: John Murray, 1958), *Guardian*, 19 November 1959.
5. "Lake District," from John Betjeman, *Collected Poems* (London: John Murray, 1958, 1979), 73.
6. "RHEGED: Discover the village in the hill," publicity leaflet (Penrith, 2001).
7. *Observer* (25 March 2001).
8. *Observer* (15 April 2001).
9. William Cobbett, "The Valley of the Avon" in *Rural Rides*, ed. George Woodcock (1830; Harmondsworth: Penguin, 1967), 313.
10. *Rural Rides* 321.
11. *Collected Poems* 163.
12. "Going, Going," *Philip Larkin: Collected Poems*, ed. Anthony Thwaite (London: Faber and Faber, 1988).
13. "Christmas and other old National Merry-makings," *The Examiner* (21 December 1817).
14. *Observer* (15 April 2001).
15. *Guardian* (19 March 2001).
16. Edward Thomas, *Collected Poems* (London: Faber and Faber, 1979).
17. *Guardian* (19 and 24 March 2001).
18. See *A Philosophical Enquiry into the Origin of our Ideas of the Sublime and Beautiful*, ed. Adam Phillips (Oxford and New York: Oxford UP, 1990), 103–4, 141, 140.
19. "Composed in the Valley, near Dover, On the Day of landing."
20. *Paradise Lost*, ed. Alastair Fowler, Longman Annotated English Poets Series (London: Longman, 1968).
21. MAFF web site, 7 April 2001.
22. *Guardian* (24 March 2001).
23. *Guardian* (24 March 2001).

24. *A Philosophical Enquiry* 55, 77. The passage from *Paradise Lost* is also quoted from this edition of Burke's treatise.
25. *Observer* (15 April 2001); *Observer* (4 March 2001).
26. Quoted from S. T. Coleridge, *Poems*, ed. John Beer (London: Dent, 1999 (1963)).
27. James Thomson, *"The Seasons" and "The Castle of Indolence,"* ed. James Sambrook (Oxford and New York: Oxford University Press, 1984).
28. CNN web site, 27 March 2001, paraphrasing an article from the London *Times*.
29. Neal Ascherson, "Scorned Cultivators of a Fool's Paradise," *Observer* (25 March 2001).
30. Jeremy Paxman, *The English: A Portrait of a People* (London: M. Joseph, 1998), 145.

Part II ∾

WAITER, THERE'S
A TROPE IN MY SOUP:
CLOSE READINGS

Chapter 6 ∾

HEGEL, EATING: SCHELLING AND THE CARNIVOROUS VIRILITY OF PHILOSOPHY

David L. Clark

Emmanuel Levinas criticizes "the Hegelian enterprise" for ignoring the ethical significance of the "residue" that is not "reducible" to the work of "the Concept" [*der Begriff*], and for configuring that labor as an expression of the subject's sovereign potency.[1] Of the *Encyclopaedia Logic's* pretensions to totality Levinas writes: "[I]f philosophizing consists in assuring oneself of an absolute origin, the philosopher will have to efface the trace of his own footsteps and unendingly efface the traces of the effacing of the traces, in an interminable methodological movement of staying where it is" (*OB* 20). The heroic virility of this Sisyphean task blinds the philosopher to the ungraspable remnant haunting speculative idealism's claim to absolute self-sufficiency as its interior limit. Philosophy faces there its radical opening toward an alterity that Levinas identifies with the subject's defenselessness before the hunger of the other. Yet Hegel denies any such liability with a brawny rhetoric of self-possession: "In fact one cannot think for someone else, any more than one can eat or drink for him."[2] Levinas insists that far from validating the project's presence of mind, Hegel's claim to eat and think for himself renders him infinitely vulnerable to the other's vulnerability. "Only a subject that eats can be for-the-other," Levinas argues, comparing this dietary self-unraveling to "snatching the bread from another's mouth" (*OB* 74). Levinas is offended that Hegel proceeds as if he could eat alone and leave no traces, not even of their erasure; he fails to recognize that in his "mouth there remains the word or the morsel of bread that it is impossible for me not to give to...my neighbour."[3]

Levinas's characterization of Hegel as a gluttonous, selfish eater, a supreme instance of what Jacques Derrida calls "carno-phallogocentrism,"[4] derives from Hegel's most complicated critic, F. W. J. von Schelling. In his 1809 masterwork on human freedom Schelling had introduced into speculative idealism the troublesome notion of "the indivisible remainder" [*der nie aufgehende Rest*], the indigestible morsel resisting even the greatest application of reason.[5] Schelling had tried to no avail to share this remnant with his most important philosophical "neighbor" whose company he had enjoyed in Tübingen and Jena. But were there not analogous leavings in Hegel already? For Schelling, as for Levinas, the question is more ethical than merely epistemological or ontological: "we still do not believe... that someone can be virtuous, or a hero, or a great man at all, by means of pure reason" (*PI* 282). In refusing the remainder, Hegel represents not only the apogee of speculative thought but also the greatest threat to the project first delineated in *Of Human Freedom*: to reduce virtue to the calculations and history of reason is to nullify virtue because it annihilates the abyss of freedom "to do Good or Evil" (*PI* 256). As Slavoj Žižek proposes, "Hegel reduces Evil to the subordinated moment in the self-mediation of Idea qua supreme Good"; but for Schelling evil "remains a permanent possibility which can never be fully sublated in and by the Good."[6] Schelling responds to this crisis of consumption by parsing Hegel for the absent presence of the unsublated and unsublatable, to show that the *Logic*'s principles are not only in error, but also unjust. In their ferociously reiterated claim to self-grounding autonomy (or what Schelling calls the "hunger of selfishness" and the "desirous, hungry, and poisonous" (*PI* 263) need for remainderless independence), they are paradigmatic of "evil." Since Schelling, however, must also think and eat ("in this life," Schelling notes, "it is...necessary to interiorize everything"),[7] the question is how to think and to "eat well": how to think eating *otherwise*?[8] How to teach Hegel some table manners? This is the difficult lesson that Schelling undertakes, mimicking Hegel's own gustatory fascinations so as to turn the carnivorous language of the master against himself.

First delivered in the five years following Hegel's death in 1831, *On the History of Modern Philosophy* represents the most passionate battle Schelling fought against the academic celebrity whom he had once called friend. Significant portions were later repeated almost "verbatim" in talks at the University of Berlin,[9] where, in 1841, Schelling was installed by the King of Prussia as Hegel's successor and charged with slaying the great man's intellectual progeny.[10] A more torturously overdetermined philosophical *habitus* would be hard to imagine. Hegel had once asserted that art was a thing of the past,[11] but to make a similar claim about Hegel could only have seemed a monumentally imposing problem. What could taking Hegel's place mean when, as Schelling himself earlier conceded, to reject his work was tantamount to abandoning philosophy itself?[12] More: what did it mean to labor in the void of speculative philosophy's putative conclusion of itself in Hegel? Under these convoluted psychic, professional, and intellectual conditions it is no wonder Schelling lasted in Berlin but a few years. Still, Schelling strenuously renounced the presence of Hegel's ideas both in himself and in others, perhaps no more vividly than in his ardent claim that Hegel's *Science of Logic* "completely eats up being" (*L* 153). The unearthly meal at which Schelling places Hegel is as grim as it is vigorous, a scene of incomparable appetite and predation (who or what could devour this peerless devourer?) culminating in nothing less than the destruction of everything that is. What are we to make of this *holocaust* of being? What is "eating," and what must "being" be if Hegel's philosophy absorbs it without remainder?

What's Eating Schelling?

Schelling's lectures concentrate many of his later themes, but it is Hegel's ghost with which they are most animated; like all histories, they are at some level a work of mourning. Hardly a sentence could be said not to tremble in the awful presence of the *Logic*: all major contributions to modern philosophy—including Schelling's—swirled around the dense gravitational well of its relentlessly capacious dialectic. The Hegelian Absolute Spirit, Schelling remarks, "has the function of taking up all the preceding moments into itself as that which brings *everything* to an end" (*L* 156). But he responds to this hyperbolically strong thought with his own virile pronouncements, unabashedly figuring it not as philosophy's culmination but as the "monstrous" triumph of its "negative" mode. Violently translating actuality into form and idea, Hegel "negates all having-happened, everything historical" (*L* 159). But for Schelling the world is more than its rational intelligibility; it is an open-ended "question of existence" (*L* 159) and the "ecstatic" confrontation with the enigma of the particular, the contingent, the other.

Almost thirty years earlier Schelling had made a similar case:

> [N]owhere does it appear as though order and form were original, but rather
> as if something initially ruleless had been brought to order. This is the

incomprehensible basis of reality in things, the indivisible remainder, that
which with the greatest of exertion cannot be resolved in the understanding
but remains eternally in the ground. (*PI* 239)

From Hegel, however, we learn that the "Absolute Idea" is "the unity of
thinking and being," the pinnacle of a self-generated but "subjectless"
(*L* 155) dialectical process whose conceptual determinations is the task of
the *Logic* to enact. Ostensibly no "indivisible remainder" haunts Hegel's
system; "nothing is left behind" (*L* 141). Schelling himself sought a version
of the "unity of thinking and being"—all German idealists did. But his
perennial fascination with the question of why there is thinking and being
at all enabled him to refuse the destruction of the latter by the former. The
extraordinary fact that there *are* thoughts and that there *is* being (including
the *that* of thought) prevents their straightforward unity and in particular
the unproblematical—remainderless—absorption of being into thought. In
Hegel this unity is the crowning achievement of speculative idealism. For
Schelling it remains "the unruly" problem at its origin, the founding
difficulty toward which he spent a lifetime making more or less convincing
forays.

How does Hegel's system claim to incorporate "reality" [*Wirklichkeit*]
(*L* 145; *SW* 10.141), and to "present itself as the absolute philosophy, as the
philosophy which leaves nothing outside of itself" (*L* 133)? At the source
of Hegel's self-declared "success" is his radical reconception of "the
Concept." Hegel claims to have negated all traces of the negativity attending conventional notions of the Concept. Rather than the abstracting idea
of a thing (and thus *not* the thing of which it is the idea), Hegel's
de-negated Concept is what a thing *is* in its essence—what it incrementally reveals itself to be through the clarifying "concretion" of mediation
and reflection. Nothing lies outside mediation, only entities that have "forgotten" themselves to be mediations, and are therefore imagined as "real."
The Concept is all. But as Schelling remarks in *Foundations for Positive
Philosophy*, "Nothing is more conceivable than the concept.... Nothing is
easier to transportation into pure thought" (cited in White, *Absolute
Knowledge*, 97). Schelling flinches at the *Logic*'s "denigration of nature"
(*L* 154), its illegitimate incursion into the ontological. The *Logic*'s conceptual map, whose explanatory power Schelling is quick to concede, had
become so ambitious as to overtake the world. "Concepts as such do in fact
exist nowhere but in consciousness," Schelling insists, attempting to undo
Hegel's perverse reversal of thought and being: "they are, therefore, taken
objectively, after nature, not before it" (*L* 145).

By "withdrawing completely into pure thinking," Hegel "has splendidly expressed the essence of the truly negative or purely rational philosophy" (*L* 145). A "truly" negative system of "complete" withdrawal—note Schelling's absolutizing adjectives—must negate its negation, so that no trace of its mediation with that from which it withdraws remains. Hegel's system eats up being, and in that self-involved act of total incorporation it consumes and refuses the radical loss that is its founding contingency. What is left is "a science in which there is no question of existence, of that which really exists" (*L* 133). Of that unthought loss, Schelling laconically notes: "philosophy should have grasped this," but instead "it put itself beyond all contradiction" (*L* 133). With nothing but logical thoughts to think, the system's universe is infinitely pliable, a docile territory suffering the strange indignity of having always already been colonized. For once one limits thinking to the thought of the Concept, nothing "real" remains to withstand the maw of the mind. In this self-sealed empire there is only the self-outstretching but finally empty "movement" of the Concept "in pure, i.e. unresisting ether" (*L* 146). What offends is not only the *Logic*'s ambitiousness but also its feigned humility, its concealment of the violence that enables it. For Schelling the Owl of Minerva is not the benign afterthought to actuality but a voracious bird of prey intent on devouring everything in its path.

Hegel will always be more complicated than Schelling makes him out to be, in part because the thinkers were bound together in ways neither fully wished to acknowledge. Xavier Tilliette characterized the relationship as "star-crossed," naming the bonds of rivalry and love with which they were betrothed.[13] In this homosocial mise-en-scène Hegel is not merely Schelling's adversary, but a figure for a certain Hegelianism in Schelling's work and memory: a "Hegel" whose work was itself haunted by recollections of an early significant encounter with Schelling (*Pinkard* 110). This messily interiorized "Hegel" is caught in Schelling's work of mourning, with all the heightened acts of identification and (dis)avowal that such work invariably implies—a process made more convoluted and competitive because of Hegel's claim to have consumed "Schelling" as part of speculative idealism's incorporation of all previous systems.[14]

This anthropophagic clash suspiciously resembles Immanuel Kant's image of desirous coupling as cannibalism,[15] and would partly explain the showily affective contradictions characterizing Schelling's negotiations— his impatience with Hegel for saying too much and too little, for derailing the course of philosophy and making its succession as "positive" philosophy inevitable, for being weak-minded and "monstrously" powerful. It would explain too why Schelling wishes both to anticipate as well as to

succeed Hegel, accusing him of plagiarizing methods he had originally
invented while characterizing the master's work as entirely antithetical to his
own. Even this last claim is contradictory, for in identifying his position as
the "positive" contrary of Hegel's "negative" philosophy, Schelling's coarsely
polarizing language paradoxically fastens him to his opponent even more
closely. Playing the role of the determinate negation of the master's system,
Schelling proves Werner Hamacher's observation that the reach of Hegel's
Logic is so capacious that it hungrily anticipates every dissenting reading.[16]

All You Can Eat

Hegel once remarked that *Aufhebung* was at root a grasping gesture, and in
a commentary on Kant he ironically suggested that concepts have "teeth."[17]
Schelling picks up on these desublimations, as if needing us to feel the
clasping and tearing that underwrites the *Logic*, the the desirous will of the
philosopher behind the philosophy:

> [he] wants the Absolute as the result of a science, and this science is precisely
> the *Logic*. Therefore the Idea continually develops throughout this whole sci-
> ence. By "Idea" Hegel also means what is to be realized, what develops, and
> what is wanted in the whole process; it is the Idea which at the beginning is
> excluded from pure being, which, as it were, *eats up being*, which happens via
> the determinations of the concepts which are put into being; after it has
> completely eaten up being and transformed it into itself, it is itself, of course,
> the *realised* Idea. (*L* 153)

Schelling reconfigures as ingestion the rigorous, vigorous path of the
Concept. From the radical emptiness, indeterminacy and abstraction of
"Being, pure Being" with which the text famously begins, *to* the "fulfilled
being" whose content is identical with its thought and therefore the paradigm of "the Concept that grasps itself,"[18] the *Logic* tracks the unstoppable
progress of a fantastic meal. The end "result" of this gluttony is a state of plenitude, "the concrete and also absolutely intensive totality." For the philosopher
of "the indivisible remainder" the fact that nothing remains, not even "nothing," is as troublesome as it is astonishing. Hence Schelling's amplifying
incredulity: Hegel's system not only "eats being," it "*completely* eats being."
And again: the self-mediation of the "Idea" can only mean that it "has completely eaten up being" [*das Sehn ganz aufgezehrt hat*] (*L* 155; *SW* 10.154).
 What truly last supper are we here being asked to condemn? That
Schelling will proceed to chastize the lifelessness of this infinitely voracious
system only confirms its most ghastly resonances. Death would be among the

closest analogues to Hegel's system, to whom Milton's Satan grimly promises: "ye shall be fed and fill'd / Immeasurably, all things shall be your prey."[19] Like Death, the *Logic* consumes but is never itself the object of consumption. Not so much at the top of an imaginary food chain as over the top, Hegel's system encapsulates what John D. Caputo calls "a site of a metaphysical metaphorics that transports eating to the sphere of absolute eating, of absolutely carnivorous virility."[20] Kant had once playfully warned against eating and thinking simultaneously, the great philosopher of "taste" comprehending how the two acts are not so much antithetical as competing metonymies of introjection. In Hegel, Schelling sees that a thinking that thinks only "concepts" is indistinguishable from a kind of eating, a highly idealized consumption that predigests what it ingests, allowing only "ether" to pass its lips: in theory, the *Logic* takes up only concepts and leaves behind the same in the form of the text's argument, ingestion and expression functioning as virtually identical expressions of the same ruminating impulse. Nothing is therefore said here about Hegel's Concept *digesting* being, about the coils and recoils of its assimilation into the phantasmatic body of the *Logic*, much less about the dregs or remainders that might naturally be assumed to result. The eating body that Schelling's trope evokes possesses an impossible morphology: it is as if the system of the *Logic* were a mouth and nothing else. Hegel's text functions in a suspiciously "angelic" manner, as if eating were magically a matter only of tasting the world.[21] In addition to eating being it has therefore eaten eating itself, an extraordinary instance of what Derrida calls "exemplorality," the phantasmatic process that "assimilates everything to itself by idealizing it with interiority, masters everything by mourning its passing, refusing to touch it, to digest it naturally, but digests it ideally, consumes what it does not consume and vice versa."[22]

Every Breath You Take

Although Žižek contends that there is an "abundance of 'anal,' excremental innuendo in Schelling" (*Indivisible Remainder* 36), the predominant figure in his lectures is oral. The abjected and excreted are significant primarily for their absence, having seceded to modes and metonymies of emission and expression, breathing and eating—all part of an elaborate topology of the mouth. Alongside the immoderate spectacle of the *Logic*'s appetite other oral fixations animate Schelling's lecture. For example, "the meagre diet of pure being" (*L* 138) to which Hegel's system subjects itself proves more than a mouthful, a rich source of critique that the philosopher chose only to disseminate in the form of the spoken word, his voice filling the lecture halls with this talk about Hegel before and after Hegel's own voice had fallen silent. Hegel's speculative idealism dreamt of ending philosophy by assimilating all previous systems, but the mere existence of Schelling's *Lectures on the History of Modern Philosophy* puts to us that reports of that death had been greatly exaggerated. Schelling survives Hegel, complexly embodying the indivisible remainder. Indeed, in specifically creating a history, Schelling seeks to locate Hegel's work in a larger framework as one moment in an epoch whose future is uncertain rather than foreclosed. The ironic "laughter" (*L* 154) that Schelling hears in response to the carnivorous claims of Hegel's system forms the unabashed opposite to the system's "conspicuous narrow-chestedness," the ways in which its fussy restraint about certain modes of representation (i.e. tropes borrowed from nature and natural processes) "means that it cannot speak openly and express itself and it is though breath and voice have been taken from it, so that it can murmur incomprehensible words" (*L* 162). To compare the *Logic*'s self-unfolding "Idea" to "eating" is therefore to desublimate it, to choke off its desires for "subjectless" disembodiment.

Of course, Hegel can only simulate this philosophical reticence and modesty. Schelling observes that even and especially at the beginning of the *Logic*, where Hegel claims to be saying the very least one can say so as not to contaminate the dialectic's inauguration with any unthought presupposition, massively consequential premises are already at work—enumeration and succession, for example. Contemplating the initial move from "Being" to "Nothing" to "Becoming," Schelling asks: "How do I end up, here at the farthest edge of philosophy, where it hardly dare open its mouth yet, where it finds word and expression only with great effort, using the concept of number?" (*L* 148). The *Logic* is from the start overtaken by an other logic, that of the supplement: the body of philosophy cannot *not* resort to "word and expression," including numbers and numbering. Hardly opening its mouth, it is already talking expansively and is thus caught in the network of differentiated signs for which numbers are a kind of pure instance. The system says little, but this quietness belies how much it has already consumed at the instant that the Concept gets underway. The *Logic* cannot eat and talk at the same time; but for Schelling the less it says the more it actually consumes. To suggest that Hegel's *Logic* eats is thus not only to satirize its pretensions to totalization but also to activate what remains alive but unvoiced within it. Part of the permanent complexity of coming *after* Hegel is evident in Schelling's compulsion to speak both against as well as for Hegel, putting words in the mouth of his adversary who, believing that the Concept articulates itself, would rather not speak at all.

Perhaps the most striking instance of this forced ventriloquism comes late in the lecture. Schelling puzzles out what he considers the point of maximum incoherence: how one gets from the world of the Concept to that of living creatures, the passage "into the unlogical world, indeed, into the world which is opposed to what is logical" (*L* 153). Hegel is hypocritically fastidious and evasive in characterizing the transition from Absolute Idea to Nature as a "releasing" ["*entlassen*"] (*L* 155; *SW* 10.153). "Releasing" tolls Schelling back to his sole self, condensing into one term the "common mistake of every philosophy that has existed up until now"—their coy inability to confront the enigma of creation (Bowie, "Introduction" 30). Schelling balks especially at the diction's palliative defensiveness: "The expression 'release'—the Idea releases nature—," he says with mock incredulity, turning the word over as if hearing it for the first time, "is one of the strangest, most ambiguous and thus also timid expressions behind which this philosophy retreats at difficult points" (*L* 155). Schelling responds with deliberate coarseness and schematism, like a child driven to vulgarity in the face of too much refinement. Out of the mouths of babes, then: "Jacob Boehme says: divine freedom vomits [*erbricht*] itself into nature. Hegel says: divine freedom releases nature. What is one to think in this notion of releasing?" (*L* 155; *SW* 10.153). Schelling finds Hegel's tasteful avoidance of the indivisible matter at hand unpalatable, making his insistence on "vomit"—the very figure of distastefulness—as inevitable as it is shocking. "Releasing" hides the foundational crisis of thought and being that the *Logic* should acknowledge and explore: How was it that "something initially ruleless had been brought to order?" (*PI* 238) Why is there anything? As Schelling well knew these questions unsettlingly lack answers. They model for speculative idealism what Derrida describes as the "object" of radical disgust, the disturbing remainder that "does not allow itself to be digested, or represented, or stated—does not allow itself to be transformed into auto-affection by exemplorality." "It is an irreducible heterogeneity which cannot be eaten either sensibly or ideally," Derrida argues, "and which . . . by never letting itself be swallowed must therefore cause itself to be vomited" (Derrida, "Economimesis" 21). Schelling is disgusted by Hegel's refusal to think and to speak about disgust, to confront the aporia about the origin to which philosophy is most deeply summoned.

Schelling had once spoken of God's agonistic self-creation in precisely these theosophical terms: as an originary purgation, a contracting expulsion whose "motivation" may be self-purification but whose uncanny effect is ambivalently and interminably to attach the Absolute both to the abject and to the process of abjection (*Stuttgart Seminars* 208). Without necessarily recommitting himself to the terms of that genesis story, Schelling contrasts Hegel's "releasing" with Boehme's "vomit" because the latter reembodies the conditions of creation whose difficulties and resistances to thought Hegel's negative philosophy has spirited away into the neutral and neutralizing language of relaxation. Whatever accounts positively for creation, it is not primly about "releasement" but raucously about unthought urges, forced losses, unconsciousness abysses, and the sheer messiness of being mortal. "Vomit" succinctly captures this perdurable knot of problems, while also feeding into the chain of oral tropes with which the lecture is quickened in its tensing against Hegel's maw. Schelling doubtless assumes that Hegel would have found its anachronistic theosophical connotations and anthropomorphizing naïveté to be precisely what demanded its expulsion from the body of philosophy.

Let Them Eat Flesh

If philosophy were as ascetic as Hegel seems to wish, if it were truly to disavow all presuppositions, conceptual borrowings and rhetorical supplements, vomiting from itself even and especially "vomit," it would be dumb, the silent night in which all cows are mute. To that enforced stiltedness, to that comical image of Hegel swallowing his own words to accommodate the quietness of thought thinking itself, we might contrast the myriad ways in which Hegel's project draws on alimentary and oral tropes. Schelling's figure of eating embarrasses Hegel to confirm and vivify what he can also baldly command: "Hegel must come to reality" (*L* 154). But Schelling's gustatory tropes also recall the degree to which Hegel elsewhere dwells thoughtfully upon that elusive question: "What is eating?" More than perhaps any other modern European philosopher, Hegel grasped how "eating" is inevitably a "metonymy of introjection," a figure for a range of psychic processes of interiorization and idealization. As Hamacher argues, "the metaphorics of consuming, of sucking, of digesting structure the entire corpus of Hegel's texts just as much as the metaphorics of grasping and generating does" (*Pleroma* 234).[23] Tropes of incorporation seem most readily to hand when Hegel renounces competing philosophical positions as a way of securing his own virile preeminence. Consider the moment in the *Phenomenology* when Hegel demarcates his project from all forms of intuitionism. Schelling would have known this point only too well: it leads directly into Hegel's infamous slur about the weakened philosophy that tries "to palm off its Absolute as the night in which . . . all cows are black."

"This is cognition naively reduced to vacuity," Hegel says, implying that plenitude (non-vacuity) is a sunlit pasture where the philosopher can plainly see what he wants to eat.[24] But who is calling the cows black? Isn't the attempt to think the empty abstraction of being so anorexically bereft of substance that it reduces cognition to vacuity? Had Hegel not told Schelling that he had completed the draft of the *Phenomenology* in the dead of night (Pinkard 256)? A significant portion of Hegel's lecture consists in Schelling's spirited defense of his interest in intuition as a form of cognition that is not merely conceptual. An "intellectual" form of intuition remained an important possibility, whereas for Hegel the term meant but one thing, the soft-headed blurring of "the differentiations of the concept." In dissolving, diffusing, and dissipating the Absolute, intuitionists seek to restore

> the feeling of essential being: in short, by providing edification rather than insight. The "beautiful," the "holy," the "eternal," "religion," and "love" are the bait required to arouse the desire to bite; not the concept, but ecstasy, not the cold march of necessity in the thing itself, but the ferment of enthusiasm, these are supposed to be what sustains and continually extends the wealth of substance. (*P* 5)

Intuitionism salivates at the ringing sound of these wonderful but empty words, "abstract form[s] ready-made" (*P* 19). Introducing them as if they were so alien to his sensibilities that they can only be exhibited as generalities devoid of real content, Hegel notes that philosophical modernity is especially susceptible to their lure. These baiting words only offer the lucidity of intoxication—the intellectual equivalent of empty calories. But philosophy must be more thoughtful than a crude stimulus–response, and more discriminating in its tastes. As with Kant's long-standing critique of the intoxicated *Schwärmerei*, the question is one of nonproductivity and ill-gotten pleasure, of a certain illegality and simulation, when what is called for is a clear head and hard work. Hegel seeks to mortify the intuitionists, with all of their lofty talk and edifying objectives, by rendering them lowly and animalistic; teeth bared, cravings aroused, they reveal themselves to be too vulnerable to the charm of the pharmakon to be included in the manly company of the scientists of absolute knowledge.

The philosophers of feeling are not the only ones at Hegel's dinnertable to feel his scorn. So too are the empiricists, "who assert the certainty of the reality of sense-objects" (*P* 65). Hegel asks: if I say "now" that "here is a tree," where is "here" and when is "now"? These deictics always point to some palpable thing that simply is not there. How to explain this vanishing? What has taken the place of this nothingness? Those who fail to ask these questions and continue to have faith in sense-certainty have yet "to learn the secret meaning of the eating of bread and the drinking of wine," Hegel muses:

> For he who is initiated into these Mysteries not only comes to doubt the being of sensuous things, but to despair of it; in part he brings out the nothingness of such things himself in his dealings with them, and in part he sees them reduce themselves to nothingness. Even the animals are not shut out from this wisdom, but on the contrary, show themselves to be most profoundly initiated into it; for they do not just stand idly in front of sensuous things as if these possesses intrinsic being, but, despairing of their reality, and completely assured of their nothingness, they fall to without ceremony and eat them up. And all Nature, like the animals, celebrates these open Mysteries which teach the truth about sensuous things. (*P* 65)

That the empiricists are superceded by the beasts in their knowledge about the being of sensuously apprehended objects relegates them to the lowest rungs of the great chain of knowing. But Hegel risks identifying his argument about sense-certainty with animals, even under the cloak of irony, reminding us of the unique privilege that he accords to eating—even animalistic *fressen* rather than *essen*—as a way of thinking about thinking.

What is the "truth about sensuous things" that animals "teach" as well as any Hegelian philosopher? Strictly speaking, it does not concern things as such: it is the "as such" of things that is under interrogation. What animals and scientists of knowledge teach comes in the form of what they do to things, or rather what they have summarily already done with them at the moment of translating them into "food." "Things" mean nothing to them. Whether as squirming and fearful prey, or as the fleeting points of the "Here" and "Now," sensuous being is only *apparently* certain and substantial, its particularity always already en route to being transmuted into what it properly is—an "other" that belongs wholly to the devourer's universe. So destined to be eaten are they that Hegel imagines for a moment that they willingly forfeit their lives; they partly "reduce themselves to nothingness."

Without ceremony they fall into the claws of the carnivore and are consumed, in a scene reminiscent of the idylls in early modern texts in which fish gladly jump into the nets of fishermen. Breugel the Elder's hallucinatory canvas *The Land of Cockaigne* (1567), also comes to mind, even if the birds that he represents as willingly lying down on dinner plates serve his condemnation of the sins of gluttony and sloth. As if to remember these improbable scenes of preying and of capture, and to speak for the about-to-be-eaten, Schelling asks: "The whole world lies . . . in the nets of the understanding or of reason, but the question is how exactly it got into those nets, since there is obviously something other and something more than mere reason in the world, indeed there is something which strives beyond these barriers" (*L* 147). Schelling's query recalls an avaricious metaphor Hegel once used for the assimilative reach of thinking—"the diamond-nets of the understanding"—but shifts the purpose of these webs from scooping booty out of the bowels of the earth to capturing animals for slaughter and consumption.[25]

The scene in the *Phenomenology* is no peaceable kingdom but a fantasti-cally carnivorous prospect, as glimpsed through the eyes of a predator whose monochromatic vision allows it to experience the universe in only two shadings—either as itself or as a more or less ready-to-hand extension of itself. Whatever otherness sensuous, particular things might possess, their alterity is translated and nullified at the moment they are worlded and brought within the hungry creature's ken. Completely assured of the non-being and non-exteriority of their prey-objects, the animals "fall without ceremony and eat them up." Scientists of knowing, like animals, do not stand idly by the world of things, either concerned about their solidity as "sceptics," or assured of their certainty and externality as empiricists. Hegelian philosophers swallow the universe whole: what is real is not sen-suous being but "Reality," the matrix of universals that makes the individ-ual parts meaningful, and thus food *for* thought. "[T]o give actuality to the universal, and impart to it spiritual life" (*P* 20): this is the ambivalently gen-erous task of the phenomenologists, who turns things over to universality by taking away their sensuous being. We could call it eating reduced to its ideal form. Consumption would then be the "open Mystery" not of nature but of spirit whose logic nature advances and rehearses, reproducing in the world of "free contingent happening" what is already happening in the world of *Geist* (*P* 492). Is the *Phenomenology* not a history of that spiritual inges-tion, an account of the incrementally achieved coherence by which all things attain a substantial place within an overarching rationality?

Hegel uses animal eating to say something counter-intuitive about con-sciousness: its content is rooted not in the false certainty of sense but in the true certainty of universals. But the metaphor only functions because he is also saying something counter-intuitive about eating. For the animals' rela-tionship with food is not a brute confrontation with an "unwilling" other, but a process of incorporation that has predigested its food at the instant it is deemed to *be* food. And from the point of view of Absolute Knowledge *everything* is food. Animals, like philosophers, exist in a world not experienced as over and against themselves but in fact and from the beginning as an annexation of themselves, always already eaten. Actual eating, like consciousness, is therefore a kind of afterthought, made possible because of an always anterior scene of violent sacrifice. A truly resistant other would not excite the slightest desire to bite since it would not be imagined or experienced as food or even, Hegel seems to suggest, as part of the world of things. Without having been incorporated as food, this world could not be eaten; without having been conceived by and in the Concept, there would be no thought, no consciousness. The carnivorousness, the tearing of flesh and gnawing on bones, the lip-smacking pleasures of taste and texture, all the mortal ferocity of hunting and eating is thus also elided. It is as if for eating to happen at all it must first consume itself, spirit its literal referent away into something less messy, more hygienically proper—closer to "thinking." So idealized is this scene that the animals get caught up in a curious switch. The hungry lives of creatures are mobilized to figure forth the psychic life of the philosopher. Yet the animals devour their prey with ease, soaking up the world of wiggling sensuous things rather than tearing them limb from limb, moving without resistance through an ethereal realm where things are not things at all but mere nothings. Under Hegel's ironic gaze they seem not to be eating others so much as *thinking thoughts.*

You Are What You Eat or, Those Were Pearls That Were His Eyes

For Hegel consumption and digestion are not merely illustrations of consciousness improperly borrowed from the naturalistic realm, but part of the underlying incorporative logic that is clarified and renewed in Hegel's discussion of "Assimilation" midway through the "Organics" section of the 1830 *Encyclopaedia.* So closely matched are these discussions that the latter reads as an extended gloss on the former, testifying to the continuity of Hegel's thinking about eating.[26] Here Hegel makes explicit and unironic what was implicit and ironic in earlier text. Animal life's relationship with externality is explained not positively as the confrontation of two discrete entities but negatively as the forcefully posited outside of the organism: "This basic division, or expulsion of the Sun and everything else, constitutes the precise standpoint of animation" (*Philosophy of Nature* 3.136).[27] There is no extra-organism, no other of the organism except the *organism's* outside, that which it has posited as its exteriority or determinate negation. Externalization is in reality a negative form of *Er-Innerung* or "inwardizing," as Hegel had argued in the *Phenomenology.* And that outside realm is impressively without limit, extending to "the Sun and everything else," a phrase whose disconcerting perfunctoriness mimics animal consciousness in its indifference to the differends comprising the universe of sensuous beings.

The figure of animals eating is itself a trope for their maximally colonial mode of being-in-the-world. As if surprised by what is in truth its own possession, the world in its entirety, the organism shudders, contracts, and in a sustained reiteration of itself in opposition to the world, seeks hungrily through its senses to augment its reach, to forge an "immediate unity of the being of the organism and that belonging to it" (*PN* 138). Therein begins a lifetime of assimilation and its discontents: "This system of living movement is the system opposed to the external organism; it is the *power* of digestion—the power of overcoming the outer organism" (*PN* 120; *W* 9.448). Such conquering is crucial to the organism's ability to replicate itself, to posit itself *as* itself and thus return to itself. To effect this self-possession, the organism's difference from externality comes to be recognized as a repetition of a difference within itself: the process by which the organism consolidates itself begins via its relationship with externality, in which digestion names the means by which the organism relates to itself as an object, as other to itself. But this is only one step in a logical sequence that concludes—or rather, since life is for Hegel processive and so interminably assimilative, is *always* concluding—at the moment when that relationship is itself subject to mediation, and deemed to be an expression of a more profound kinship, the organism's relation to itself.

In positing itself as itself and for itself, retreating to the sanctity of itself as pure self-relation, "as real being-for-self" [*reales Fürsichsein*] (*PN* 163; *W* 9.491), the organism must negate its negation, consume its originating link with its outside. What is most troublesomely *other* is not the outside of the organism but the organism's *relationship* to the outside. The living creature must maintain a certain (biological) confidence and virility against the shaming threat of vulnerability, exposure, and dependence. Disgusted with itself for not exhibiting more self-confidence, Hegel suggests, the organism is filled with "loathing." But the living creature seeks a way to relieve itself of its "lack of self-reliance" in the proud accomplishment of excretion (*PN* 164). As Hegel suggests, "the significance of the excrements is merely that through them the organism acknowledges its error, and rids itself of its entanglement with external things" (*PN* 164). Excretion is therefore not the expulsion of materials that escape the masterful logic of digestion but, quite to the contrary, evidence of the organism's competence in throwing off involvement with anything but itself. Like a criminal covering his or her tracks, no trace can remain of the organism's devouring dependence on another, especially the objectifying otherness generated within itself by virtue of having to eat in the first place. In Hamacher's fine phrasing, "Thus it is not the objective thing, the food itself, which is digested, but rather the external relationship to it. What the organism digests is the process of digestion itself" (*Pleroma* 248). For Schelling this is too weirdly coprophagous by half; what makes the remainder indivisible is precisely its radical resistance to being coopted by the logic of digestion. Proof of the inviolability of the remnant abounds in the living world. In the *Lectures on the History of Modern Philosophy* Schelling consequently turns to that teeming universe, too easily generalized by Hegel as "the Sun and everything else," where even in the lowliest of animate creatures he glimpses the impervious presence of what can only "unwillingly accept the concept": the "shell and casing" of molluscs demonstrate that "matter always seeks to maintain its independence" from assimilation. What for Hegel is self-evidently "excretion" is for Schelling more complicated, neither inside nor outside the organism but both simultaneously, the scene not of annihilating sacrifice but of an open-ended struggle between life and non-life: "the inorganic, matter that lays claim to a being-itself has here already entered the service of the organism, but without being completely conquered by it" (*L* 123). What the living creature eliminates is its negation, as is the case in Hegel's *Encyclopaedia* argument about assimilation, but for Schelling this is only partly successful. In that failure lies a deeper accomplishment. The grittily inedible exterior of shellfish is to some extent its exterior, its determinate negation, yet Schelling's main point is that it is uncanny and inexplicable as well, the product of the conquering work of the negative... and something irreducibly in excess of it.

Without So Much as a Crumb

Hegel's scenes of assimilation exemplify the perfect crime, whose evidence confirms its invisibility rather than remembering its occurrence. To the thinker of "the indivisible remainder," that the logic of digestion can claim to annihilate even its own dregs, emptying them of their embarrassing excess by putting them into its service, seemed extremely improbable. For Hegel this process constitutes life as such, enabling the living creature to ward off the inorganic. But Schelling wonders what life could be if it truly left nothing behind. For Schelling life is saturated with personality, will, longing, and mourning, and thus self-difference, incompletion, and loss. If the discussion of creaturely "assimilation" in the *Encyclopaedia* glosses the passage from the *Phenomenology*, it also encapsulates why for Schelling the *Logic* is deeply lifeless, closer to a machine—"a machine for spinning flax" (*L* 162)—than to any mortal thing that lived and breathed on earth. The *Logic* is dead in the way that life in Hegel is dead, closer to a perfectly efficient motor than existents whose dwelling place is the unlogical world.

We see now why, when Hegel, as Schelling says, tries "to breathe a life, an inner compulsion to the progression" into the dialectic, he does so "in vain" (*L* 144). At best the *Logic* is a mimicry of life, secretly borrowing its self-quickening properties to account for the unfolding of the Concept, but without thereby importing anything unseemly into the dialectic—the very excesses that make life interestingly alive for Schelling. If there is evidence of life in the *Logic* it lies in the traces of the mortal man who created it. For Heidegger, this is where Hegel fails his project's most radical ontological possibilities. In the name of sanctity of being, he complains that the *Logic* is not rigorously impersonal enough, that it remains trapped within the metaphysics of subjectivity.[28] Schelling, by contrast, insists that the problem is that its claim to "subjectless" anonymity is insincere, and in particular that its effort to purge itself of the life of the philosopher is misguided and duplicitous. He sees his task as returning the remainders to Hegel's *Logic*, haunting its pristine architecture with the remnants—the "shell and casing"—of what it has incompletely disavowed.

Evidence of this excess lies in the ruses underwriting the *Logic*, which Schelling treats as the vestiges of the " 'creative' author" (with a "personality and spirit," the very sources of malignancy in Schelling's universe) haunting the "reasonable" thinker as its spectral other (*L* 148). Nothing less than a "double deception" is at work in Hegel's argument: "(1) by the thought being substituted for by the *concept*, and by the *latter* being conceived of as something which moves itself, when the concept for its own part would lie completely immobile if it were not for the concept of a thinking subject.... (2) by pretending that the thought is driven forward only by a necessity which lies in itself, although it obviously has a goal that it is striving toward, and this goal, however much the person philosophizing seeks to hide consciousness thereof from himself, for reason unconsciously affects the course of philosophizing all the more decisively" (*L* 138–9). In both its means and its ends, the *Logic* remains a great deal more than it appears or understands itself to be. Schelling's uncannily psychoanalytic assessment characterizes Hegel's magisterial text as riven by conceptual errors and rhetorical tricks as well as by conflicting levels of awareness. In the face of the *Logic*'s implacably necessitarian self-representation, Schelling invites a symptomatic reading of the desires and self-differences by which Hegel's text is enlivened and troubled but to which it appears confidently blind. Hegel cannot have completely eaten up being, not when his own being-in-the-text is so fraught, layered by conscious and unconscious inclinations and deceptions. In its lucidity Hegel's system seems to possess no unconscious; but for Schelling it is precisely because it *has* an unconscious that its moments of forgetfulness are not simple lapses in conscious apprehension but active modes of remembering beyond conscious control which materially shape the argument. The "hiding" of desires is not the opposite of their frank revelation but their disclosure through negation, all the more decisive for being secreted. Schelling functions as an amanuensis not so much for what the *Logic* has forgotten but for what it remembers, in excess of itself, in the mode of forgetting.

All this talk of *Er-Innerung*, the work of interiorizing remembrances within a text that, in theory, should be a depthless surface of logical determinations and thus possess no interior life, inevitably brings Schelling around to eating and other metonymies of introjection. Why doesn't being, "the most abstract and most empty thing of all" (*L* 138), remain inert? Hegel claims that out of "necessity" being logically demands "to be more full of content." But this account strikes Schelling as less about thinking logically and more about behaving like a creature who "cannot be satisfied with that meagre diet of pure being" (*L* 138). And who could that famished creature be but Hegel, or at least his phenomenological remnant in the text? Schelling's phrasing is curious: the *Logic* displays "not a necessity which lies in the concept itself, but rather a necessity which lies in the philosopher and which *is imposed upon him by his memory*" (*L* 138). The *Logic*'s underlying desirousness remembers the life of the author that its logical "restraint" would rather suppress and forget: where the *Logic* is, there Hegel shall be. But who, "Hegel"? Schelling now evokes an additional memory on the near side of the *Logic*, making its presence felt "inside" Hegel. The diction suggests that the philosopher is himself enlivened by an internal other, feeling the force of his own memory as if it were a kind of intrusion just as the Concept's progress in the *Logic* is irrepressibly vivified from a distance by the philosopher. Neither "Hegel" nor his text can claim magisterial authority over themselves, since they each appear to be informed from elsewhere.

Both psychic and textual memories, then, are scenes of the same unforgettable hunger. The *Logic* remembers a memory that has always already inflicted itself upon Hegel; the latter memory, "Hegel"'s memory, imposes itself upon the *Logic* via the philosopher; the former memory, the *Logic*'s symptomatic traces, imposes itself upon Hegel via the *Logic*. Together they render "Hegel" into a virtualized switch-point across which the unconscious force of recollection flows at will. Hauntingly, Hegel's imposing "memory" survives the death of the author, stimulating the Concept with ferocious appetites that strictly speaking it cannot have and yet does, albeit in a figurative manner not easily described as living or dead. Finally, however, it is the circularly consumptive nature of the system that is most memorable: "the meagre diet of pure being" with which the *Logic* begins its omnivorous if borrowed "life" is born out of a lack it is responsible for having created. For Schelling this is perhaps the final and most devious twist in Hegel's logic of digestion. In its desire to account fully for its own conditions, Hegel's system also invents the lack whose filling up spectrally mimics the ravenous life of the body that Schelling discerns and uses to read Hegel against the grain.

Hegel will not admit to the lived experiences upon which the quickness of the system secretly depends, and, as if shielding himself from this recognition, he ensures that the lack with which the system begins its rigorous journey is not a negative absence against which the system might be imagined to tense itself, but a positive emptiness that the system has imposed upon itself as evidence of its greatest rigor and highest reflective power. A logical lack, being purged of all determinate content, sublates a phenomenological absence, at once holding it away and relying upon it as the source of the system's repressed hunger to fill itself with "the realized Idea." Thus the exiguity with which the system begins is not a sign hiding a lack but a sign of lack that hides Hegel's reliance on what Alan White calls "modes of experience . . . whose differences from conceptual thinking he refuses to acknowledge" (*L* 156). "Meagreness" is for Schelling not another name for the nothingness of pure being but the price the system has paid for withdrawing into thought. The emptiness of the system's beginning can then be said to hide in the open the disavowals that are for Schelling its truest meaning. The initial "meager-ness" is the sign both of the system's inability to rid itself of its phenome-nological remainder, and of its unwillingness to give up trying to do so.

Indian Food

The "meagreness" of Hegel's "diet" triggers in Schelling an unexpected moment of lavishness and exorbitance. Schelling has been refuting Hegelian philosophy for "pretending at the beginning to be asking for very little, which is, as it were, not worth mentioning, as devoid of content as being itself, so that one cannot, as it were, help allowing it." Then his argument blends into the following conceit:

> The Hegelian concept is the Indian God Vishnu in his third incarnation, who opposes himself to Mahabala, the giant prince of darkness (as if to the

spirit of ignorance), who has gained supreme power in all three worlds. He first appears to Mahabala in the form of a small, dwarflike Brahmin and asks him for only three feet of land (the three concepts of "being," "nothing," and "becoming"); hardly has the giant granted them than the dwarf swells up into a massive form, seizes the earth with one step, the sky with the other, and is just in the course of encompassing hell as well as the third, when the giant throws himself at his feet and humbly recognizes the power of the highest God, who for his part generously leaves to him the power in the realm of darkness (under His supreme power, of course). (*L* 148)

What to make of this staging of the icon of modern Western philosophy in the midst of a premodern hallucinated East? The story of Vishnu and Mahabala concentrates Schelling's objections, illustrating the nexus of manliness, incorporation, mealymouthedness, knowledge, and power animating his grievance from the start. Chief among the offences Schelling charges Hegel with is philosophical modesty, the *Logic's* insistence that its ever-widening dialectic is not an aggressively appropriative process directed by human desires but a "subjectless" sequence of determinations to which the thinker must humbly submit himself. The dialectic demands a certain "restraint," "a refusal to intrude into the immanent rhythm of the Concept" (*P* 36), to which Schelling reacts with a digression that is the opposite of "restraint" in form and content: a tale of gluttony told in the "exotic" form of a myth that feels extravagant even in the midst of passionate argumentation. The tale is a spectacular instance of what Schelling finds absent from Hegel's prose, "the bold metaphor" (*L* 143). Let us then call it an hors-d'oeuvre, a morsel imported from outside philosophy for the Hegelians to choke on. Poaching materials from the considerable archive he was developing about the significance of Indian mythologies, Schelling notes that while appearing to practice such selflessness and ascesis, Hegel's system is all about a rationalized violence no less violent for being rationalized. The progressive derivation of the logical categories is not an immanent, self-moving, and self-contained process, but, like Vishnu in the form of the "dwarflike Brahmin," secretly driven by the colonialist desires of the philosopher. There is thus no point at which Hegel's alien hand is not in this process, and this is never more forcefully so that when he is claiming the least, at the inauspicious start of the *Logic*. The apparently unassuming Brahmin vegetarian turns out to have the most voracious appetite of all, and in an instant tricks the meat-eating Mahabala (otherwise known as Bali or "the strong one" in Hindu mythology) into surrendering his world.

This displaced memory of India suggests that Hegel's *Philosophy of History* looms in the background. A text more deeply invested in the carnivorous virility of philosophy, and the European worldhood for which that philosophy can function as an alibi, would be difficult to imagine. As Balachandra Rajan has argued, India is for Hegel nothing but "the home of mixed genres, hybridization, and . . . monstrosity," offering "to the European gaze the sterile yet edifying spectacle of a civilization profoundly unable to analyze itself."[29] Negatively exemplary in its feminized excess, lack of reflective powers, and, above all, deceitfulness, "India" forms only the raw beginning of the Occident's grand march of intellect. "India" is to be explained away, confirming the masterful superiority of Germanic thinking. If there is anything positive to be said about India's moment in world history it is that it isn't Africa, which for Hegel lies on the far side of humanity and history. For the philosopher Africa is hardly worth the effort of abjection, but he savors India, an imagined realm evoking a revealing combination of repulsion and fascination. As Bahti suggests, Hegel distinguishes "India" and "Asia" from "Africa" because they are "historical, comprehensible—and digestible" (*Allegories of History* 304 n. 5). If Hegel's science of logic eats Being, it cannot be unrelated to his science of history, which devours beings, the histories and cultures of entire peoples, in a process that Bahti describes as cannibalistic in nature (80).

Could ontophageous and anthropophageous feeding be rigorously distinguished from each other? In treating himself to one of the founding stories of the Great Puranas, Schelling cites the very Sanskrit texts that Hegel describes as the epitome of the "Orient's" fancifulness and unproductive promiscuity. In using the story of Vishnu to lay bare the willfulness and cunning of the Hegelian system he demonstrates that "India" is *not* entirely digestible, and that there remains in the supposed wastefulness and decadence of its mythologies enough critical power to best the man who claimed imperiously to have bested it. An ancient Eastern tale of mendacious conquest speaks to an analogously assimilative violence underwriting a contemporary Western one. The fact that the ostensibly "primitive" story embarrasses the "cultured" one emanating from Berlin only reproduces the Orientalist condescension that Schelling and Hegel shared. If "India" is for Schelling not a figure for falsehood, it remains the source of a story about lying. The point is hardly to raise ancient Indian mythology to the status of a truth but to denigrate modern European philosophy, in a way roughly analogous to Hegel using the Eleusian Mysteries to condemn contemporary empiricism. This little bit of comparative anthropology is possible not only because it offers a vivid point of ironic purchase on Hegel's argument but also because of the profound failings that he saw characterizing both worlds. As Wilhelm Halbfass has argued, "according to Schelling, neither

the Indians nor Hegel were able to grasp the truly 'positive,' i.e., existence
in its concreteness, the 'factuality' of the one God and of revelation."[30]

What is striking is the aplomb with which this Hindu allegory is folded
into the argument. Schelling does nothing to prepare the listener or reader
for the comparison, and, indeed, with the exception of a brief parenthetical gloss, hardly allows it to be one at all: "The Hegelian concept" is not
like "the Indian God Vishnu"; it *is* this very unlikely thing. What better way
to shock the Hegelians than to spring an "exotic" analogy on them, and
then heighten the disorientation by proceeding as if reaching for an ancient
tale from the Puranas were the most natural thing in the world for a historian of modern philosophy? And perhaps in a way it was. Schelling's long-
standing interest in India appears in an early letter to A. W. Schlegel, praising
their "sacred texts" as greater in critical power even than the holy scriptures.[31] This is precisely the opposite of the position he maintains in the
more than one hundred pages devoted to Indian and related Eastern traditions in his *Philosophy of Revelation*, where he asserts the supremacy of
revealed Christian truth over all its shadowy types—including both "Asian"
religious texts and Hegel's philosophy of reflection. Still, the fact that
Schelling hybridizes his own text, freely mixing "philosophy" with
"mythology," suggests that part of what he is seeking to achieve, narratively
speaking, is a kind of "India" effect—this, as an affront to the supposed
purism of Hegel's *Logic*.

According to one historical model, before he became an apologist for
the Prussian court Schelling inaugurated post–Hegelian philosophies of
finitude. We can characterize these philosophies as struggling with the
question of eating well, dwelling with the knowledge that the interiorizing memory of the other is faithful to the precise extent that it is faithless,
and that at the point one begins to eat being one has already been given
over to that which is otherwise than being. Schelling's focus on the
metonymies of introjection, his fascination with the rhetoric of carnivorous
assimilation belongs to a more extensive visceral philosophical vocabulary
that responds passionally and cognitively to the limits of reflection. This
rhetoric, invested with certain powers of horror, evokes affective phenomena (selfish hunger, addictive longing, lacerating mutilation, unappeasable
melancholy, demonic possession, incombustible waste, malignant fury,
unconscious desire) that unsettle the distinctions (body and spirit, ethics
and ontology, life and non-life, ground and non-ground, freedom and
necessity, negative and positive philosophy, West and East) upon which the
intelligibility and ideological investments of the thetic world rest.[32] As early
as 1809 Schelling had called for speculative idealism to abandon its

enervating obsession purely with matters of the spirit, to cease its ferocious "war against being" (*Stuttgart Seminars*, 232). Speaking as the upright opponent of philosophers who had only managed to "emasculate" themselves during the prosecution of this war, he calls for more potent thinkers to join him in taking on "flesh and blood" (*PI* 236). In the lectures *On the History of Modern Philosophy*, that labor of reincarnation haunts Hegelianism with the specter of its carnivorous virility.

Notes

1. I thank Timothy Morton for his unfailing generosity, both intellectual and personal. An ongoing conversation with Tilottama Rajan, Rebecca Gagan, and Denise Gigante has significantly enriched my understanding about the question of negation and incorporation.
   Emmanuel Levinas, *Otherwise Than Being; Or Beyond Essence*, tr. Alphonso Lingis (Pittsburgh: Duquesne UP, 1998), 18. Hereafter *OB*.

2. G. W. F. Hegel, *The Encyclopaedia Logic*, tr. T. F. Geraets et al. (Indianapolis: Hackett, 1991), 55.

3. John Llewelyn, *Emmanuel Levinas: The Genealogy of Ethics* (London and New York: Routledge, 1995), 143–4.

4. Jacques Derrida, "Force of Law: The Mystical Foundation of Authority," tr. Mary Quaintance, *Cordoza Law Review* 11.5–6 (July/August 1990), 953.

5. F. W. J. Schelling, *Philosophical Investigations into the Essence of Human Freedom and Related Matters*, tr. Priscilla Hayden-Roy, in *Philosophy of German Idealism*, ed. Ernst Behler (New York: Continuum, 1987), 239. *Philosophische Untersuchungen über das Wesen der menschlichen Freiheit* (1809), *Sämtliche Werke*, ed. K. F. A. Schelling (Stuttgart: Cotta, 1860), vol. 7, 360. Hereafter *PI*; the German is cited as *SW*.

6. Slavoj Žižek, *The Indivisible Remainder: An Essay on Schelling and Related Matters* (Verso: London and New York, 1996), 6.

7. F. W. J. Schelling *Stuttgart Seminars*, in *Idealism and the Endgame of Theory: Three Essays by F. W. J. Schelling*, tr. ed. Thomas Pfau (Albany: State University of New York Press, 1994), 239.

8. Jacques Derrida, " 'Eating Well,' or the Calculation of the Subject," tr. Avital Ronell, in *Points: Interviews, 1974–1994*, ed. Elisabeth Weber (Stanford: Stanford UP, 1995):

   > The question is no longer one of knowing if it is "good" to eat the other or if the other is "good" to eat, nor of knowing which other. One eats him regardless and lets oneself be eaten by him . . . The moral question is thus not, nor has it ever been: should one eat or not eat, eat this and not that . . . man or animal, but since one must eat in any case and since it is and tastes good to eat, and since there is no definition of the good [*du bien*], how for goodness' sake should one eat well [*bien manger*]? And what does this imply? What is eating? How is this metonymy of introjection to be regulated? (282)

9. Andrew Bowie, "Translator's Introduction," F. W. J. von Schelling, *On the History of Modern Philosophy* (Cambridge: Cambridge UP, 1994), 1.

10. Terry Pinkard, *Hegel: A Biography* (Cambridge: Cambridge UP, 2000), 662.

11. G. W. F. Hegel, *Aesthetics: Lectures on Fine Arts*, tr. T. M. Knox, Vol. 1 (Oxford: Clarendon Press, 1975), 11.

12. Alan White, *Absolute Knowledge: Hegel and the Problem of Metaphysics* (Athens, Ohio: Ohio UP, 1983), 94.

13. Cited by David Farrell Krell in *Contagion: Sexuality, Disease, and Death in German Idealism and Romanticism* (Indianapolis: Indiana UP, 1998), 198, n.10. Tilliette's Shakespearean image of pathetic misrecognitions and bad timing masks the business of the evil meal at its heart, the scene of poisoning whose tragic consequences consume the couple in death.

14. Franz Xaver von Baader wrote to Hegel that Schelling's "early philosophy of nature was a generous, tasty steak but now he just cooks up a ragout with Christian spices." Cited in Thomas F. O'Meara, *Romantic Idealism and Roman Catholicism: Schelling and the Theologians* (Notre Dame: University of Notre Dame Press, 1982), 89.

15. Immanuel Kant, *The Metaphysics of Morals*, tr. Mary Gregor (Cambridge: Cambridge UP, 1991), 166.

16. Werner Hamacher, *Pleroma-Reading in Hegel*, tr. Nicholas Walker and Simon Jarvis (Stanford: Stanford UP, 1998), 3.

17. G. W. F. Hegel, *Aesthetics* 511; *Hegel's Lectures on the Philosophy of Religion*, tr. ed. E. B. Speirs and J. Burdon Sanderson, 3 vols. (London: Routledge, 1962), 3.341.

18. G. W. F. Hegel, *The Encyclopaedia Logic* (with the Zusätze): Part 1 of the *Encyclopaedia of Philosophical Sciences* with the Zusätze, tr. T. F. Geraets, W. A. Suchting, and H. S. Harris, (Indianapolis: Hackett, 1991), 307.

19. John Milton, *Paradise Lost* II.843–5. *John Milton: Complete Poems and Major Prose*, ed. Merritt Y. Hughes (Indianapolis: Bobbs-Merrill, 1957), 252.

20. John D. Caputo, *Against Ethics: Contributions to a Poetics of Obligation with Constant Reference to Deconstruction* (Bloomington and Indianapolis: Indiana UP, 1993), 199.

21. See Denise Gigante's remarks about this "angelic" form of (non)consumption in Milton in "Milton's Aesthetics of Eating," *Diacritics*, 30.2 (Summer 2000), 88–112.

22. Jacques Derrida, "Economimesis," tr. Richard Klein, *Diacritics*, 11.1 (1982), 20.

23. See also Timothy Bahti, *Allegories of History* 110.

24. G. W. F. Hegel, *Phenomenology of Spirit*, tr. A. V. Miller (Oxford: Oxford UP, 1977), 9. Hereafter *P*.

25. G. W. F. Hegel, *Hegel's Philosophy of Nature*, tr. ed. M. J. Petrey, 3 vols. (London: George Allen and Unwin, Ltd. 1970), 1.202.

26. See Mark C. E. Peterson, "Animals Eating Empiricists: Assimilation and Subjectivity in Hegel's *Philosophy of Nature*," *The Owl of Minerva*, 23.1 (Fall 1991), 49–50. See also Tilottama Rajan's important work on incorporation in

Hegel in "Framing the Corpus: Godwin's 'Editing' of Wollstonecraft in 1798," *Studies in Romanticism*, 39 (2000), 511–31, and "(In)digestible Material: Illness and Dialectic in Hegel's *Philosophy of Nature*" (collected in this volume, chapter 11).

27. *Ezyklopädie der philosophischen Wissenschaften im Grundrisse* (1830), *Zweiter Teil: Die Naturphilosophie, Mit den münlichen Zusätzen*, in *Werke*, Vol. 9. The English translation hereafter *PN*, the German *W*.

28. Andrzej Warminski, *Readings in Interpretation: Hölderlin, Hegel, and Heidegger* (Minneapolis: University of Minnesota Press, 1987), 113–62.

29. Balachandra Rajan, *Under Western Eyes: India from Milton to Macaulay* (Durham: Duke UP, 1999), 140, 108.

30. Wilhelm Halbfass, *India and Europe: An Essay in Understanding* (Albany: State University of New York Press, 1988), 105.

31. Cited in Jean W. Sedlar, *India in the Mind of Germany: Schelling, Schopenhauer, and Their Times* (Washington: UP of America, 1982), 42.

32. I discuss this rhetoric in "'The Necessary Heritage of Darkness': Tropics of Negativity in Schelling, Derrida, and de Man," *Intersections: Nineteenth-Century Philosophy and Contemporary Theory*, ed. Tilottama Rajan and David L. Clark, 79–146, "Heidegger's Craving: Being-on-Schelling," Diacritics, 27.3 (1997), 8–33, and "Mourning Becomes Theory: Schelling and the Absent Body of Philosophy," "Schelling and Romanticism," *Romantic Circles Praxis* Series, ed. David Ferris (June 2000); http://www.rc.umd.edu/praxis/schelling/clark/clark.html.

Chapter 7 ✎

BYRON'S WORLD OF ZEST

Jane Stabler

Byron's attention to food anticipates the new formalist criticism of recent years by impelling the reader into pleasure in formal texture and applying the brakes of a historicist critique. While these two ways of reading are embedded in Byron's poetry, the possibilities of an invigorated formalism have been considerably extended by critics such as Susan Wolfson and Richard Cronin.[1] To a certain extent, I also follow Barbara Gelpi's work on Shelley and her conviction that the conflicting ideologies which governed the Romantic period can only be addressed by a mixture of critical perspectives.[2] Gelpi concentrates on various manifestations of maternity in Shelley's writing, and the significance of the nursing mother for Byron is one of the topics of this essay although it will also consider other forms of feasting.

Byron was famously greedy and fastidious. Among the well-known biographical anecdotes of his dining on potatoes and vinegar or decreeing that women ought not to eat in public unless they could feed on lobster salad, there is the following entry in the Ravenna Journal for Friday, 26 January 1821:

> On dismounting, found Lieutenant E. just arrived from Faenza. Invited him to dine with me to-morrow. Did *not* invite him for to-day, because there was a small *turbot*, (Friday, fast regularly and religiously,) which I wanted to eat all myself. Ate it.[3]

The underscored name of the fish almost constitutes a first slice of it while the parenthetical note about the Catholic tradition of fasting Byron has adopted simultaneously excuses and exaggerates his self-centredness. The prospect of the "*turbot*" distances Byron from Lieutenant E., while it brings us closer to Byron's desire: "I wanted to eat all myself" suggests self-consumption and narcissistic self-delight. The statement of accomplishment— "Ate it"—encapsulates both satisfaction and loss: anticipated pleasure is converted into interior bulk with the intermixture of guilt and delight that accompanies the indulgence of Byron's appetite.

Eating in Byron's poetry ranges from the overwhelming bodily need of the famished ship wreck survivors in the first volume of *Don Juan* to the refinement of the connoisseur in the last instalments of the same poem. Having enjoyed the privilege of extensive travel and very little of its privation, Byron is fascinated by the ways in which eating involves the consumer in complex negotiations of social manners and mores. Food, as Sara Delamont has observed, "carries the history of the country or region"; as Sidney Mintz argues, "foods . . . have histories associated with the pasts of those who eat them . . . consumption is always conditioned by meaning."[4] When Byron tucked into his turbot, he was enjoying something considered a delicacy by both Italians and British consumers because only small numbers are caught in the Mediterranean and the North Sea. Byron's tasting of the word is, therefore, a reminder of the cultural, economic, and geographic frames which shape the pleasure of luxury.

Pleasure has been spread quite thinly in the last decades of Romantic criticism, partly because the study of English Literature has always been beset with guilt about its own methodological rigor: the shameful possibility that it was a subject to be enjoyed was held at bay from the end of the nineteenth century by a predominantly Christian morality and from the end of the twentieth by predominantly Marxist ethics.[5] A deep distrust of pleasure emanated from both American and British Academies: I. A. Richards's approach to literature declared that "the orientation of attention is wrong if we put pleasure in the forefront."[6] This critical severity was matched by T. S. Eliot's ascetic distaste for the body and for food. His puritanical aversion to Byron's "pudgy face suggesting a tendency to corpulence," and "that weakly sensuous mouth" found its expression in poetry which, like Prufrock, was nervous about eating a peach and criticism which shrank from the smell of cooking unless it could be sealed hygienically in the symbol.[7] At the other end of the twentieth century, Paul de Man's deconstruction was famously suspicious of the "seductive notion that appeals to the pleasure principle," while Frederic Jameson's Marxism warned that pleasure could not avoid being dependent on "the great suprapersonal *system* of a late capitalist 'technology.' "[8] Byron's relatively low critical reputation throughout the twentieth century is not unrelated to the dominance of these approaches.

French feminisms of the 1960s did pioneer a way of talking about the pleasure of the text, but using poetic French prose translated into English prose to accompany English poetry is always a bit like trying to follow a recipe without all the proper ingredients. There was also the embarrassing (for some) discovery that the best exponents of feminine *jouissance* seemed to be male writers. I sidestep this problem by returning to the work of a French post-structuralist whose datedness allows us to historicise formal pleasure in another way. In an interview in *Le Nouvel Observateur* on 10 January 1977 Roland Barthes spoke about food as an aspect of culture:

> As a cultural object, food means at least three things to me. First the aura of the maternal model, nourishment as it is considered and prepared by the mother: that is the food I like. Second, from that home base, I enjoy excursions, digressions toward the new and unusual: I can never resist the temptation of a dish endowed with the prestige of novelty. And finally, I'm particularly sensitive to conviviality, to the companionship of eating together, but only if this conviviality is on a small scale: when the company becomes too numerous, the meal becomes tiresome, and I lose interest in the food, or else I over eat from boredom.[9]

Barthes's three categories find startling resonances in Byron's work. I shall consider them in turn, mixing historicised close reading with a post-structuralist interest in the effects of Byronic *jouissance* or *mobilité*. The first area of enquiry is Barthes' emphasis on feminine nurture.

"Myriads of One Breast": Byron and Mother's Milk

> in the thick of all this fashionable Foucaulteanism, there has been strikingly little concern with the physical stuff of which bodies are composed, as opposed to an excited interest in their genitalia. The human body is generally agreed to be "constructed," but what starts off that construction for all of us— milk—has been curiously passed over. Terry Eagleton, "Edible Ecriture"[10]

Byron's poetry was concerned with the figure of the nursing mother, particularly after 1816, since it conditioned his limited memories of his daughter, Ada: "The child of love,—though born in bitterness, / And nurtured in convulsion" (*CHP* 3118).[11] More matter-of-factly, Byron had reported to Thomas Moore in January 1816 that Ada was "very flourishing and fat, and reckoned very large for her days—squalls and sucks incessantly"

(*BLJ* 4.14). The cultural significance of breast feeding changed considerably in the eighteenth century; during the 1740s and 1750s in England breast feeding began to be accepted as a sign of natural motherhood and by the 1790s it was advocated by both conservatives and radicals such as Mary Wollstonecraft.[12] Linked both with the culture of sensibility and an economy of national self-sufficiency, the breast-feeding mother was an icon of feminine tenderness and a sturdy example of virtuous independence. The image of the mother by the hearth with an infant at her breast was beginning to define the ideal of the English home which would dominate Victorian England. Byron gives this ideal cursory treatment in *Don Juan*:

> Yet a fine family is a fine thing
>   (Provided they don't come in after dinner);
> 'Tis beautiful to see a matron bring
>   Her children up (if nursing them don't thin her);
> Like cherubs round an altar-piece they cling
>   To the fire-side (a sight to touch a sinner). (3.60)

The dreamy post-prandial repose of aesthetic pleasure and moral satisfaction is interrupted as the children threaten to emerge from the parenthesis. It is typical of Byron's poetry that the parentheses juxtapose material fact with sentimental idealism: however wholesome a mother's milk is, nursing does tend to shrink the maternal breasts. The interests of the father and the husband are, to some degree, at odds and it is this "at oddness" which Byron's textual feasts so often produce. Byron follows the conduct guides of his day in using the breast-feeding mother as an image of all that is wholesome and mild. But these scenes also highlight the awkward gap between mores and morals and indicate the breaking of taboos that similarly disconcert the reader. At such moments of "bliss" (as Barthes would name them), the pleasure of the text sharpens into crisis and leads to an acute reexamination of the relationship between reader and text, between formal pleasure and contextual cultural issues.

The complex effects of playing with different cultural frames are foregrounded in Byron's most famous depiction of a nursing mother, that of the Caritas Romana in *Childe Harold's Pilgrimage* (Canto 4). These stanzas visit Byzantine debtors' dungeon in Rome where an elderly male prisoner was kept alive by being secretly suckled by his daughter. In some versions of the story the daughter was pregnant and in others she brought her baby to the prison with her. The story was a popular artistic theme: Caravaggio's baroque treatment heightened the eroticism of intimate contact between a father and daughter while Rubens's best known depiction offered a more restrained Nativity scene with an infant child sleeping peacefully on the prison floor as, in shadows behind, its mother tends to its grandfather.

In Roman guides in Byron's time, this episode was part hallowed and part hidden, referred to as an "act of filial piety."[13] John Cam Hobhouse's *Historical Illustrations of the Fourth Canto of Childe Harold* carefully screens any mention of breasts by referring to "a woman [. . .] who had nourished her father in prison with her own milk" and then diverting into a studious study of sources and variants: "It is a pity that so fine a tale should be liable to such contradictions."[14] Writing a little later than Hobhouse and Byron (and with a desire to correct precursor guides), Charlotte Eaton addresses the "beautiful and affecting trait of filial piety" more directly: "the daughter [. . .] saved the life of her father when condemned to perish from hunger, by nursing him from her bosom."[15] Eaton describes the physical difficulty of visiting the site:

> you are made to look down, through an aperture in the pavement at one end of [the church of S. Nicola], into a dungeon, in which you indistinctly descry, by the light of torches, three different columns, in three different places [. . .] Of course they shew you which column was the Temple of Piety; but if you ask how they knew it, they will marvel much at your inquisitiveness.
>
> I could have wished to have lent myself to the delusion; to have believed that I stood upon the spot, and saw the vestiges of the building consecrated to Filial Piety; but it would not do. (2.1–2)

Byron uses this "indistinctness" of historical location to emphasize the confusing welter of aesthetic and moral responses which the scene of nourishment evinces.[16] The problems of discerning the outlines of the site transfer into the problems of what to make of it:

> There is a dungeon, in whose dim, drear light
> What do I gaze on? Nothing: Look again!
> Two forms are slowly shadowed on my sight—
> Two insulated phantoms of the brain:
> It is not so; I see them full and plain—
> An old man, and a female young and fair,
> Fresh as a nursing mother, in whose vein
> The blood is nectar:—but what doth she there,
> With her unmantled neck, and bosom white and bare? (4.148)

The initial sense that the scene is "nothing" captures the discomforted self-censorship of the viewer who almost reluctantly discovers two forms. They are described as "insulated Phantoms of the brain" because imagination holds them in a special cultural category. Only by presenting the act as an isolated one of "filial piety" could Roman and nineteenth-century society come to terms with it. The question, "what doth she there?" cannot be answered directly, but having brought the concrete forms into focus with the "unmantled neck, and bosom white and bare," Byron heads straight for the confluence of the sacred and the erotic with the "swelling" of the "deep pure fountain." The hesitant end-stopped lines of the first stanza roll into enjambment with the words "vein" and "blood." This liquid movement between lines follows the mysterious connectedness between a mother feeding her child, a connectedness in which the ideas of "inside" and "outside" are almost as confused as at the moment of birth. Byron's controversial enjambement within and between Spenserian stanzas is about as close as his poetry comes to the semiotic ethos of Kristevan prose. His attention to maternal overflow invites comparison with the language of "Stabat Mater" and its "weavings of abstractions to be torn."[17] Byron's poetic texture, however, recreates the difficulty of rather than absorption in maternal continuity; this is subtly different from Kristeva's psychoanalytic interest in the mother as "a continuous separation" or a "being of folds."[18]

> Full swells the deep pure fountain of young life,
> Where *on* the heart and *from* the heart we took
> Our first and sweetest nurture, when the wife,
> Blest into mother, in the innocent look,
> Or even the piping cry of lips that brook
> No pain and small suspense, a joy perceives
> Man knows not, when from out its cradled nook
> She sees her little bud put forth its leaves—
> What may the fruit be yet?—I know not—Cain was Eve's. (4.149)

Mother's milk is "Our first and sweetest nurture," but Byron makes it perilously close to blood both with the idea that this is "*from* the heart," and with the proximity of milk and blood in the previous stanza: "Fresh as a nursing mother, in whose vein / The blood is nectar."

The mixture of blood and milk is prohibited by Jewish law and several other ancient cultures, but the two substances are also regarded as opposites in contemporary secular society. Lady Macbeth's ability to imagine "dash[ing] the brains out" of the "babe that milks [her]" (I.7.55–8) still provokes a shudder of revulsion in modern audiences and its horrifying violence is highlighted by bringing milk into that most bloody of Shakespeare's plays.[19] Barthes considered the sanguine properties of foodstuff regarded as "mutilating" and "surgical" in which "blood is visible, natural, dense" as opposed to the morphology of milk: "creamy, and therefore soothing [...] it joins, covers, restores."[20] Such a taboo mixture of nutriments frequently recurs in Byron's poetry at moments of crisis in the narrative (whether the hero's story or the history of the poet's relationship with his English readers). These references become homogenized when critics see persistent returns to the needs of the human body as a satire on transcendental aspirations. They do challenge Romantic idealism; but Byron also uses dangerous or difficult meals to point to his readers' arbitrary reliance on predetermined customs and codes of behavior.

The metaphoric interchangeability of bodily fluids in literature is well-known and breast feeding and vampirism are in the Caritas Romana passage just a breath apart from each other as, indeed, they are in the maternal "hunger" described in Julia Kristeva's "Stabat Mater":

> A spasm that spreads, runs through the blood
> vessels to the tips of the breasts, to the tips of
> the fingers. It throbs, pierces the void, erases it,
> and gradually settles in it. My heart: a
> tremendous pounding wound. A thirst.[21]

Yet, even as Byron's readers are harrowed with the specter of two taboos, incest and cannibalism, they are fed with the more conventionally sentimental images of the "piping cry of lips" and the mother who sees "her little bud put forth its leaves." The potentially cloying diminutive of the "little bud" is, however, held at bay by the separation of the image from what "Man knows" and by the scepticism of the last line: "What may the fruit be yet?—I know not— Cain was Eve's." With this allusion, Byron steps toward more sinister associations of incest and bloodshed before returning to "health and holy feeling":

> But here youth offers to old age the food,
> The milk of his own gift:—it is her sire
> To whom she renders back the debt of blood
> Born with her birth. No; he shall not expire
> While in those warm and lovely veins the fire
> Of health and holy feeling can provide
> Great Nature's Nile, whose deep stream rises higher
> Than Egypt's river:—from that gentle side
> Drink, drink and live, old man! Heaven's realm holds no such tide. (4.150)

The two human figures stand generalized as "Youth" and "Old Age," and the food becomes "Great Nature's Nile," displacing female particularity on to distant geographical terrain; instead of the swollen breast, the woman offers a "gentle side." But again the last line startles us with actuality: "Drink, drink, and live, old man!," a line which is as shocking in its imperative form as Lizzie's instruction to Laura in Christina Rossetti's "The Goblin Market: 'Hug me, kiss me, suck my juices / [...] / Eat me, drink me, love me' " (467; 470). Just as Rossetti oscillates between moral fable and erotic fantasy, Byron's stanzas fold metaphysical conceits and intimate human urgency together.[22]

The narrator insists on the frame of the poem as moral but then invites readers to contemplate physical proximity. This mixture confronts readers with different sorts of pleasure or "sweetness" from the disinterested aesthetic to the sensuous and immediate. By invoking the myth of the Milky Way formed by milk the goddess Hera spilled as she pulled her breast away from the infant Hercules, Byron heightens the physical closeness of the daughter holding her father's head against her: "No drop of that clear stream its way shall miss / To thy sire's heart":

> The starry fable of the milky way
> Has not thy story's purity; it is
> A constellation of a sweeter ray,
> And sacred Nature triumphs more in this
> Reverse of her decree, than in the abyss
> Where sparkle distant worlds:—Oh, holiest nurse!
> No drop of that clear stream its way shall miss
> To thy sire's heart, replenishing its source
> With life, as our freed souls rejoin the universe. (4.151)

By the end of the stanza, however, Byron's register has shifted again from the particular to the general and from the opaque tenderness of the body to the "clear" abstract concept of a bodiless soul merging with an unfathomable cosmic system. He played sporadically with this loss of self in nature: *Childe Harold's* conviction that the poet becomes "Portion of that around me" (3.72) or Manfred's pondering on the brink about the possibility of scattering his "atoms" (I.2.109). The single part of the Byronic hero alters the whole rather than being lost within it, but despite the massive popularity of this hero, the distinct particle is not always a lone male individual and in his later poems, Byron passes the power to stir up trouble over to his readers.

In *Don Juan* Byron juxtaposes the classically trained audience's expectations for meaty epic poetry "so rare and rich," with the "Pharisaic" prohibitions of a bourgeois reading public "with all their pretty milk-and-water ways" (8.90). Likewise, the apostrophe to "Milk and Water" in *Beppo* runs into "sin and slaughter" (80).[23] Self-reflexiveness is enhanced by its presentation of diverse contextual frames and competing cultural codes. Sensuous descriptions or lists of food are always complicated by social issues: the poem teaches us that the aesthetic is contingent on undeniably material aspects of production. It is worth emphasizing the cultural relativity of Byron's scenes of eating because recent criticism has tended to concentrate on the universalism of Byron's depiction of appetite.

In *Don Juan* Canto 3. Lambro is "the mildest manner'd man / That ever [. . .] cut a throat" (3.41), and the destruction of his love for his daughter "wean[s] / His feelings from all milk of human kindness" (3.57). An unsettling proximity between eating and bloodshed continues throughout the digressive stanzas which precede Lambro's discovery of his daughter and Juan together. Much critical attention has been devoted to the decadence of Haidée's feast and entertainments where, as Timothy Morton eloquently observes, "arabesqued pleasure becomes its own warning."[24] Peter Graham developed more anthropological lines of criticism when he suggested that Haidée might be seen as an early anorexia victim.[25] Some of the most disturbing poetic effects in the Haidée episode, however, come from Byron's juxtaposition of intimate scenes of feeding with casual slaughter. Juan is disturbingly "Pillow'd on her o'erflowing heart" (2.195) where the picture of Haidée's full breasts mingles images of blood and milk. Bryon shifts from Juan helpless in the charge of Lambro's men "With the blood running like a little brook" (4.49) to the unexpected account of Haidée's mother's country, "Where all is Eden, or a wilderness":

> There the large olive rains its amber store
>   In marble fonts; there grain, and flower, and fruit,
> Gush from the earth until the land runs o'er. (4.55)

The contrasting images of liquid overflow recall Haidée's maternal tenderness with Juan and anticipate her death in pregnancy: "A vein had burst, and her sweet lips' pure dyes / Were dabbled with the deep blood which ran o'er" (4.59).[26] The release of nutritious fluids is traditionally the prelude to greater connection with the community. In the brief portrait of the biblical plenitude of Fez, however, Byron shows how sources of natural pleasure are tapped by the "the heart of man" (4.55), often with the result that blood is set "running" (4.58).

A strand of imagery in the poem, then, rather than critical reading against the grain alerts us to the distasteful power nexus of Byron's banquets. In the case of Lambro's island, we know that Haidée's feast is underwritten by the economy of her father's mercantile activities including human cargo, "Pieced out for different marts" (3.17). The narrative delays the revelation of these material circumstances, but once they are introduced, Juan's morning "coffee and Haidée" (2.171) on the beach is no longer simply a pleasurable confluence of sound and sense; instead, the coffee threatens to become (as it is today) one of the most commercially exploitative drinks on the market. As Barthes points out in relation to ornamental cookery, "the real problem [concerning food] is not to have the idea of sticking cherries into a partridge, it is to have the partridge, that is to say, to pay for it."[27] It is only possible to regard the Juan/Haidée episode as a pastoral idyll if we isolate the aesthetic from its context. This sleight of hand is fostered by the large-scale artifice of genre, but denied by accumulating small-scale particularities of stanza form. The narrator emphasizes the limited range of aesthetic response, acknowledging that he is moved more by "green tea" than by Juan's and Haidée's plight:

> For if my pure libations exceed three,
> I feel my heart become so sympathetic,
> That I must have recourse to black Bohea:
> 'Tis pity wine should be so deleterious,
> For tea and coffee leave us much more serious. (4.52)

Just as the reader acquiesces in the comic rhyme at the end of this stanza, Byron intimates that we fall into acceptance of a particular moral outlook. As routine and as subjective as a choice of beverage, he implies, our selection of ethical perspective excludes other possibilities. The poem undoes that exclusion.

After the scandal which separated him from his wife and daughter, Byron imagined himself an outcast not just from his family and London society (the "Great World"), but from human society as a whole. Writing to Lady Byron he complained bitterly that

> the World has been with you throughout—the contest has been as unequal to me as it was undesired—and my name has been as completely blasted as if it were branded on my forehead. (*BLJ* 5.54)

By linking himself with Cain and including in his poetry references to his failed marriage, Byron confronted cultural norms of "good taste."[28]

His response to England's arbitrary moral proscription was to write poetry that involved its readers in close encounters with ethical relativity. Byron's fascination with the figure of Cain continued throughout his self-imposed exile in Italy. An acute apprehension of the social and cultural orthodoxy which rejected him boiled over in the sceptical drama *Cain*, which Murray feared would lead to prosecution for blasphemy. One of the taboos that Byron worked away at through the drama was incest: Lucifer points out to a bemused Cain that the divinely approved union between him and his sister, Adah, will become a source of divine wrath for future generations. The trickiness of God's rules is realized through images of nurture and feeding which go beyond the universalism of the human appetite for knowledge inherited from "her who snatch'd the apple" (II.2.409).

Cain's worries over the nature of a God who seems to enjoy destruction are expressed as anxieties about the food chain:

CAIN.   I lately saw
A lamb stung by a reptile: the poor suckling
Lay foaming on the earth, beneath the vain
And piteous bleating of its restless dam;
My father pluck'd some herbs, and laid them to
The wound; and by degrees the helpless wretch
Resumed its careless life, and rose to drain
The mother's milk, who o'er it tremulous
Stood licking its reviving limbs with joy.
Behold, my son! said Adam, how from evil
Springs good!
LUCIFER.   What didst thou answer?
CAIN.   Nothing; for
He is my father: but I thought, that 'twere
A better portion for the animal
Never to have been *stung at all*, than to
Purchase renewal of its little life
With agonies unutterable, though
Dispell'd by antidotes.
LUCIFER.   But as thou saidst
Of all beloved things thou lovest her
Who shared thy mother's milk, and giveth hers
Unto thy children. (II.2.289–308)

Lucifer moves adroitly from the helpless rapture of the mother sheep to Adah. Her blood relationship with Cain is established through the sharing of breast milk, and her innocent raising of the children of an incestuous union is likewise realized through the same pressingly physical image of nurture. This metaphoric linkage helps to make Abel's sacrifice in Act II distasteful both to Cain and to the reader. Cain offers a vegetarian "shrine without victim, / And altar without gore" (III.1.266–7), but he is taught that God "lov'st blood" and prefers offerings which have "Suffer'd in limb or life [. . .] lambs and kids, / Which fed on milk, to be destroyed in blood" (III.1.255; 264; 292–3).

Cain's rebellion is precipitated by his recognition of a Divinity which violates humane standards of taste (a scepticism consistent with the tone of many dissenting pamphlets of the day as, for example, in his friend Hobhouse's controversial publication of "The Essay Upon Entrails").[29] Reversing the usual effect of Christian symbolism, images of milk-white lambs invite readers to consider the Paschal sacrifice of Christ as an act of sadistic infanticide. Cain's self-control snaps when he is urged by Abel to respect "the immortal pleasure of Jehovah," an abstract idea which Cain finds repugnant when contrasted with maternal joy and pain:

> CAIN. *His pleasure*! what was his high pleasure in
> The fumes of scorching flesh and smoking blood,
> To the pain of the bleating mothers, which
> Still yearn for their dead offspring? or the pangs
> Of the sad ignorant victims underneath
> Thy pious knife? Give way! this bloody record
> Shall not stand in the sun, to shame creation! (III.1.298–304)

The slaughter of Abel brings into the world the fear which had "empoison'd" his brother's thoughts. The irony of Cain committing the very act which he abhorred is underlined when the Angel of God asks him "Did not the milk of Eve give nutriment / To him thou now see'st so besmear'd with blood?" (III.1.490–1). The curse called down upon him by Eve as a vengeful, bleating mother is that all human activities such as sleeping and eating will be contaminated for Cain and by him. She wishes that:

> Earth's fruits be ashes in his mouth [. . .]
> May the clear rivers turn to blood as he
> Stoops down to stain them with his raging lip!
> May every element shun or change to him! (III. 1. 427–34)

This curse turns her son into an agent of malign transformation: his punishment is to lose pleasure in the act of eating; his very presence will spoil food. He is the extreme example of scandal for an author who likened scandal to the pleasurable effect of seasoning: "scandal has something so

piquant,—it is a sort of cayenne to the mind."[30] As well as the mythologi-
cal dimension of Cain's homelessness, this holds a local, cultural application.
It might be said that Cain is embittered by his opposition to the Sunday
roast and that by criticising the menu of his homeland, he is condemned and
exiled as an alien body. In short, the outcast Cain becomes the manifestation
of all that the English feared and loathed about nasty foreign food.

"This Conundrum of a Dish": Byron, Dining, and Digression

Stephen Mennell has discussed the aesthetic and social patterning of food
in France and England. Although wary of imposing rigid dichotomies
between the two cultures, he suggests that in the eighteenth and nineteenth
centuries English cooking still tended to be arranged around the preparation of the whole joint of meat whereas the French specialized in "made
dishes," the delicate concoctions and mixtures caricatured by the English as
"kickshaws" (or "quelquechose"). Diversity was associated with French
court culture and plain English country food with the solidity of the
English country house.[31] When the English used sauces or spice, it was often
with the stoical intention of masking unpalatable meat or other foreign
ingredients—hence Byron's instruction in *Beppo* to English travelers to
bring supplies of "Ketchup, Soy, Chili-vinegar, and Harvey, / Or, by the
Lord! a Lent will well nigh starve ye" (8). Byron plays throughout his career
with the opposition of home and abroad, reveling in the role of the aristocratic cosmopolitan as against the grumblings of his homesick man-servant,
Fletcher. Byron, like Barthes, "enjoy[ed] excursions, digressions toward the
new and unusual." In particular, Byron relished the piquancy of foreign
mixture, the pleasure of parts modifying the whole.

Byron's most splendid cosmopolitan mixture of mixed dishes appears at
the Amundeville banquet in *Don Juan* (Canto 15). Like many aristocratic
Whigs in Byron's time, Lord Henry's household enjoys French cuisine and,
as E. H. Coleridge pointed out, Byron's list of "fish, flesh, and fowl, / And
vegetables, all in masquerade" (15.74) is taken from Louis Eustache Ude's
The French Cook. Byron highlights the reader's responsibility for selecting
conceptual frames of reference when he draws attention to the different
ways of pronouncing *gout*:

> *Taste* or the *gout*,—pronounce it as inclines
>   Your stomach! Ere you dine, the French will do;
> But *after*, there are sometimes certain signs
>   Which prove plain English truer of the two. (15.72)

Carol Shiner Wilson discusses this stanza: "Byron's warning appears unambiguous and direct. Fancy French cuisine is like poetry whose seductive and untruthful decoration [...] was eagerly bought and consumed by the public with poor taste," but she also suggests that "Byron subverts the very French–English dichotomy that he sets up."[32] This disruption of perspectives is also accomplished when Byron invokes the food / slaughter juxtaposition in his footnote to "Lucullus' *Robe triumphal*" (15.66):

> A dish "à la Lucullus." This hero, who conquered the East has left his more extended celebrity to the transplantation of cherries (which he first brought to Europe) and the nomenclature of some very good dishes;—and I am not sure that (barring indigestion) he has not done more service to mankind by his cookery than by his conquests. A cherry-tree may weigh against a bloody quarrel: besides, he has contrived to earn celebrity from both.

Weighing a cherry-tree against "a bloody quarrel," Byron reminds his readers (as he does throughout *Don Juan*) that they construct the value which determines celebrity. In this way, the poem's exquisite pleasures in culinary art remain in touch with the social contexts which have shaped them. Jerome McGann argues that "much of the English cantos is grounded in Byron's nostalgia for a world he had left behind with equal bitterness and regret" and Wilson goes a step further, suggesting that "Byron, away from England since mid-1816, did not understand the increasing conservatism of English society, in part a middle-class reaction to the profligacy of regency society."[33] But historicist readings which place Byron is a Regency time-warp neglect the ways in which Byron remained in close contact with English society.[34] Banquets such as the one given by Lord Henry were reported as a matter of course in *Galignani's Messenger*, the newspaper Byron took while he lived in Italy. When Byron celebrates "nutbrown Partridges" and "brilliant Pheasants" (13.75), he takes care to include mention of the poachers and the game laws, a very contemporary topic in Leigh Hunt's journalism.[35]

Pleasure and politics are, therefore, inextricably related in the mixed texture of Byron's poetry while digressive asides to the reader direct attention to the formation of laws of taste and morals. By the time we reach Canto 15, the diversity of the banquet has become an image for the poem itself. Playing with generic expectations, the narrator had informed his readers at the end of Canto 6 that he left them "to arrange / Another part of History, for the dishes / Of this our banquet we must sometimes change" (6.120). In 1820, Byron had revised his verse translation of the

Ars poetica, Hints from Horace, with its dictum against mixture:

> As if at table some discordant dish
> Should shock our optics, such as frogs for fish,
> As oil instead of butter men decry,
> And poppies please not in a modern pie,
> If all such mixtures then be half a crime,
> We must have excellence to relish rhyme. (587–92)

Nevertheless, Byron digressed from Horatian law and despite the classical dis-relish of mixture inherited by conservative British critics, his work displays a fascination with novel or illicit combinations. The menu in Canto 15 is a *tour de force* in which the art of the chef is matched by the skill of the poet in artfully arranging the different clusters of language: we taste the words as much as the idea of the food as we move through the stanzas and work our tongues around the challenge of how to "get this gourmand stanza through?" (15.63). Wilson's reading of the banquet palls when she sees it as an exercise in "joyless excess."[36] The image of "Champagne with foaming whirls, / As white as Cleopatra's melted pearls" (15.65) is for many readers an image of pleasure, complicated by its association with Adeline's "sparkle" and "spirit" and the later image of the "evaporation" of the day, "like the last glass of champagne, without / The foam which made its virgin bumper gay" (16.9). The poem demonstrates that metaphoric connection is a social art, haunted by the possibility of boredom with the company.

"The Company is 'Mixed' ": Byron and the Poet as Host

The issue of "conviviality" and "the companionship of eating together" was the third and final aspect of food with which I linked Barthes and Byron as Romantic consumers (to borrow Colin Campbell's term) and it is, obviously, the point at which the sensuous pleasures of eating and sexual flirtation coincide. The exquisite artifice of both activities is combined in Byron's allusion to Lady Mary Wortley Montagu's "The Lover" in his prose defense of Pope:

> "And when the long hours of the Public are past
> And we meet with Champaigne and a Chicken at last,
> May every fond pleasure that moment endear!
> Be banished afar both discretion and fear! . . ."

There—Mr. Bowles—what say you to Supper with such a woman? And her
own description too?—Is not her "*Champagne and Chicken*" worth a forest or
two?—Is it not poetry?[37]

Having mocked English women in *Beppo* with their "smell of bread and
butter" (39), the later cantos of *Don Juan* concede that, like Lady Mary,
English women might exude greater attraction, style, and complexity: "they
are like virtuous mermaids, whose / Beginnings are fair faces, ends mere
fishes" (13.73). This is, of course, the image of Horace's grotesque mixture,
desinat in piscem mulier formosa superne, the failed work of art which Byron
applied to his own poetry.[38] Its recurrence in *Don Juan* suggests a connection between feminine artifice and the art of the poem. Byron's personal
scandal, the scandal of Cain, and the scandal of his poetry after 1816
become imaginatively aligned with feminine "adulteration."

Don Juan invites its readers to enjoy the aural and visual pleasure of a list
of exotic dishes, and then shifts attention to the social manoeuvrings making
up the dinner party where the women hardly eat at all, but (like the poet)
plot various forms of indiscretion. This makes an enjoyable narrative, but it is
also a political game with part of the poem's audience in the Holland House
circle and supporters of the Congress system who continued to exercise arbitrary power through sumptuous dinner party politics. When Byron compares
an "à l'Espagnole" dish and a damsel, he draws out the particular ability of
the female characters to alter the texture of the poem:

> Don Juan sat next an "à l'Espagnole"—
>   No damsel, but a dish, as hath been said;
> But so far like a lady, that 'twas drest
> Superbly, and contained a world of zest. (15.74)

The piquancy of "zest" allows a small particle to alter the quality of the
whole to which it is added. Adeline is more than eye candy for connois-
seurs of female beauty; she controls "the consumers of fish, fowl and game"
with consummate aesthetic success:

>   blending,
>   As all must blend whose part it is to aim
>   (Especially as the sixth year is ending)
>   At their lord's, son's or similar connection's
>   Safe conduct through the rocks of re-elections. (16.95)

Adeline imparts flavor to these large-scale (boring) electioneering dinners
and therefore plays no small part in the establishment of political power,

a possibility which Byron underlines with his allusion to Jane Shore (16.76). By insisting on the reader's ability to cooperate (or not) in the construction of frames of reference which determine the aesthetic success or moral worth of individual moments in the poem and by emphasizing the power of readerly "taste," Byron's reader becomes part of the small-scale conviviality enjoyed by Barthes. Byron's foodiness is less to do with large-scale oppositions between mind and body or philosophy and history ("History can only take things in the gross" 8.3), than it is with minute adjustments of seasoning. Assuming responsibility for our pleasure in Byron's poetry at different historical moments, we become the particle that changes the whole, the agent of enraptured zest or the spice that prolongs decay.

Notes

1. See Richard Cronin, *The Politics of Romantic Poetry: In Search of the Pure Commonwealth* (Basingstoke and London: Macmillan, 2000) and Susan J. Wolfson, *Formal Charges: The Shaping of Poetry in British Romanticism* (Stanford: Stanford UP, 1997). I would also like to thank Tim Morton for his generous advice and suggestions during work on this essay.

2. See, for example, Barbara Gelpi, "The Nursery Cave: Shelley and the Maternal," in *The New Shelley: Later Twentieth-Century Views*, ed. G. Kim Blank (New York: St. Martin's Press, 1991), 42–63; "Keeping Faith with Desire: A Reading of *Epipsychidion*," in *Evaluating Shelley*, ed. Timothy Clark and Jerrold E. Hogle (Edinburgh: Edinburgh UP, 1996), 180–95; *Shelley's Maternal Goddess: Maternity, Language, Subjectivity* (New York: Oxford UP, 1992).

3. Leslie A. Marchand, ed., *Byron's Letters and Journals*, 13 vols. (London: John Murray, 1973–94; hereafter *BLJ*), 8. 36. According to Marchand, Byron's visitor is Giovanni Battista Elisei, a riding companion.

4. Sara Delamont: *Appetites and Identities: An Introduction to the Social Anthropology of Western Europe* (London and New York: Routledge, 1995), 25; Sidney W. Mintz, *Tasting Food, Tasting Freedom: Excursions into Eating, Culture, and the Past* (Boston: Beacon Press, 1996), 7.

5. These questions have been discussed recently in Stephen Regan, ed., *The Politics of Pleasure: Aesthetics and Cultural Theory* (Buckingham: Open UP, 1992) and Wendy Steiner, *The Scandal of Pleasure: Art in an Age of Fundamentalism* (Chicago: University of Chicago Press, 1995).

6. I. A. Richards, *Principles of Literary Criticism* (London: Routledge, 1924; repr. 1955), 80.

7. T. S. Eliot, "Byron" in *On Poetry and Poets* (London: Faber and Faber, 1957; repr. 1971), 193–4.

8. Paul de Man, *Resistance to Theory* (Minneapolis: Minnesota UP, 1986), 64; Frederic Jameson, "Pleasure: A Political Issue" in *Formations of Pleasure*, ed. Tony Bennett et al. (London: Routledge and Kegan Paul, 1983), 13.

9. Roland Barthes, *The Grain of the Voice: Interviews 1962–1980*, tr. Linda Coverdale. (Berkeley and Los Angeles: University of California Press, 1991), 265–6.

10. Terry Eagleton, "Edible Ecriture," in *Consuming Passions*, ed. Sian Griffiths and Jennifer Wallace (Manchester: Manchester UP, 1998), 207.

11. All references to Byron's poetry are to Lord Byron, *The Complete Poetical Works*, ed. Jerome J. McGann, 7 vols. (Oxford: Clarendon Press, 1980–93; hereafter *CPW*). References to Spenserian and *ottava rima* poems are by canto and stanza number.

12. See Carol Barash and Susan Greenfield, eds., *Inventing Maternity: Politics, Science, and Literature. 1650–1865* (Lexington, Ky.: UP of Kentucky, 1999); Toni Bowers, *The Politics of Motherhood: British Writing and Culture 1680–1760* (Cambridge: Cambridge UP, 1996). For the literary inheritance of Rousseau's theories of nurture, see Timothy Morton, "The Pulses of the Body: Romantic Vegetarian Rhetoric and its Cultural Contexts," in *1650–1850: Ideas, Aesthetics, and Inquiries in the Early Modern Era*, vol. 4, ed. Kevin Cope (New York: AMS Press, 1998), 53–88.

13. See e.g., Madame de Staël, *Corinne*, tr. Sylvia Raphael (Oxford and New York: Oxford UP, 1998), 70.

14. John Cam Hobhouse, *Historical Illustrations of the Fourth Canto of Childe Harold* (London: John Murray, 1818), 295–6.

15. Charlotte A. Eaton, *Rome in the Nineteenth Century*, 3 vols. (Edinburgh: James Ballantyne, 1820), II, 1.

16. In other versions of the tale, it is a mother who is saved by her daughter. This would fit Byron's sense of the "Reverse" of Nature's decree more accurately, but would also involve more troubling associations of lesbian eroticism which, Nicholas Roe has suggested to me, are implicit in the echoes of Coleridge's "Christabel."

17. Julia Kristeva, *Tales of Love*, tr. Leon S. Roudiez (New York: Columbia UP, 1987), 246–7, 235.

18. Kristeva, "Stabat Mater" 254, 260.

19. A trail of milk imagery in the play is evident in I.5.17 and I.5.47–8. Alan Richardson discusses Wordsworth's use of the "milk of human kindness" allusion in *British Romanticism and the Science of the Mind* (Cambridge: Cambridge UP, 2001), 71, suggesting that "the conventionally gendered opposition between (masculine) transcendent reason and (feminine) embodied emotion begins to erode within Romantic-era physiological theories of mind."

20. Roland Barthes, *Mythologies*, tr. Annette Lavers (1957: London: Paladin, 1973), 68–9. Mary Douglas dismisses the possibility that Jewish dietary regulations derive from simple hygienic precautions and argues for reading them as a form of communication in *Purity and Danger: An Analysis of the Concepts of Pollution and Taboo* (1966: London: Routledge, 1999), 30–58. Julia Kristeva sees dietary prohibitions as screening a more radical separation between the fecund mother and the being who speaks to his God. See *Powers of Horror: An Essay on Abjection*, tr. Leon S. Roudiez (New York: Columbia UP, 1982), 65–6, 99–101.

21. Kristeva, "Stabat Mater" 249.

22. As in Rossetti's poem, Byron recalls the sacrament of Eucharist. The linkage of cannibal and Christian is more obvious in the shipwreck episode in *Don Juan* where Pedrillo is sacrificed: "And first a little crucifix he kiss'd, / And then held out his jugular and wrist" (2. 76).

23. A similar discomforting design influences Hunt's satire in *The Liberal* when he points out that "Lord Castlereagh [. . .] had his buttered toast [. . .] served up for breakfast the day he killed himself" (Castlereagh cut his own throat). *The Liberal* (London: John Hunt, 1822–23), 3.64.

24. Timothy Morton, *The Poetics of Spice: Romantic Consumerism and the Exotic* (Cambridge: Cambridge UP, 2000), 21. See also Carol Shiner Wilson, "Stuffing the Verdant Goose: Culinary Esthetics in *Don Juan*," *Mosaic*, 24.3–4 (1991), 33–52; Christine Kenyon Jones, " 'Man is a Carnivorous Production': Byron and the Anthropology of Food," *Prism(s): Essays in Romanticism*, 6 (1998), 41–57 and Christine Kenyon Jones " 'I Wonder If His Appetite Was Good?': Byron, Food and Culture: East, West, North and South" in *Byron: East and West*, ed. Martin Procházka (Prague: Charles UP, 2000), 249–62.

25. Peter W. Graham, "The Order and Disorder of Eating in Byron's *Don Juan*," in *Disorderly Eaters: Texts in Self-Empowerment*, ed. Lilian R. Furst and Peter W. Graham (University Park: Pennsylvania State UP, 1992), 113–23.

26. Peter Manning argues that the womb-like refuge Haidée offers is lethally threatening. See *Byron and His Fictions* (Detroit: Wayne State UP, 1978), 185–6.

27. Barthes, *Mythologies* 86.

28. Byron's identification with Cain predates the failure of his marriage. In the first canto of *Childe Harold's Pilgrimage*, Harold is described as "Pleasure's pall'd victim! life-abhorring gloom / Wrote on his faded brow curst Cain's unresting doom" (I. 83). For further discussion of Byron and taste, see Jocelyne Kolb, *The Ambiguity of Taste: Freedom and Food in European Romanticism* (Ann Arbor: University of Michigan Press, 1995).

29. For further discussion of Byron's attitude to blood sacrifice including Hobhouse's contribution to the debate, see Peter Cochran "Atonement, Suffering and Redemption in Byron's poetry" in Gavin Hopps and Jane Stabler, eds., *Grace Under Pressure: Religion and Romantic Literature* (Aldershot: Ashgate, forthcoming).

30. Ernest J. Lovell, Jr., ed., *Lady Blessington's Conversations of Lord Byron* (Princeton: Princeton UP, 1969), 76.

31. Stephen Mennell, *All Manners of Food: Eating and Taste in England and France from the Middle Ages to the Present* (Oxford: Basil Blackwell, 1985; repr. 1987), 72–125.

32. Wilson, "Stuffing the Verdant Goose" 46–7.

33. *CPW*, 742; Wilson, "Stuffing the Verdant Goose" 48.

34. Peter Graham's discussion of *Don Juan's* England as a "chronotype" that "blends" 1792, 1811–16 and 1822–3 is much more sensitive to the historical complexity of the poem's texture. See *Don Juan and Regency England* (Charlottesville and London: UP of Virginia, 1990), 163.

35. See Hunt's parody of a club-house gentleman in the Preface to the first issue of *The Liberal*: "Wars must be carried on; Malthus has proved that millions must be slaughtered from time to time. The nonsense about that is as stupid as the cry about the game-laws and those infernal villains the poachers, who ought to be strung up like hares" (ix).
36. Wilson, "Stuffing the Verdant Goose" 43.
37. Lord Byron, *The Complete Miscellaneous Prose*, ed. Andrew Nicholson (Oxford: Clarendon Press, 1991), 126.
38. See *BLJ* VI, 46.

Chapter 8 ✍

BEYOND THE INCONSUMABLE: THE CATASTROPHIC SUBLIME AND THE DESTRUCTION OF LITERATURE IN KEATS'S *THE FALL OF HYPERION* AND SHELLEY'S *THE TRIUMPH OF LIFE*

Arkady Plotnitsky

Introduction

This essay examines well-known passages from John Keats's *The Fall of Hyperion* (*FH*) and Percy Bysshe Shelley's *The Triumph of Life* (*TL*), and parallel poetic or allegorical arguments offered by both poems.[1] These arguments concern the possibility of the ultimate destruction of both the sublime and literature, at least of the project of literature as it has been conceived in Western intellectual history. It is possible, following Maurice Blanchot, to take a different view and ask whether we are still capable of literature under these conditions.

Why the sublime? First, the allegories of both poems proceed through the sublime. Second, this passage appears rigorously necessary to reach the limit beyond which neither literature nor the sublime itself are possible. This role, as the sublime is understood here (from Immanuel Kant's *The Critique of Judgment*), is fundamentally linked to the question of "consumption."[2] The problem of consumption is irreducible in the *economy* (including political economy) of the aesthetic and in what Paul de Man sees as "aesthetic

ideology." Both have jointly defined the history of modern aesthetics, beginning with Friedrich Schiller's (mis)reading of Kant and extending throughout modernity and postmodernity.[3] Counterbalancing Schiller's "Kant" and
aesthetic ideology, however, the critique of both aesthetics and aesthetic ideology develops in the wake of, and already in, Kant's work. This critique is
pursued in particular by literary figures associated with Romanticism, such
as Keats and Shelley, Friedrich Hölderlin, Heinrich von Kleist, and William
Wordsworth. It extends throughout subsequent intellectual history, culminating in such thinkers as de Man, Jacques Derrida, and Jean-François
Lyotard. Both poems are among the most extraordinary cases of this
critique. They are also allegories of, first, the irreducibility of the material
and the consumptive; second, with the sublime, of a certain economy of the
inconsumable; and, third, ultimately, of what I shall call here the "beyond-
the-inconsumable," which emerges as each poem reaches an even more
radical stage of this critique and perhaps its limit.

At this limit, the sublime can no longer survive as a viable instrument of
philosophical understanding, even though it appears necessary in order to
reach this limit itself. This rupture from the sublime emerges because it retains
a residual element of consumption, even though it aims to capture a radical
form of experience that appears to defy the possibility of any consumption.
Pleasurable consumption, linked to the beautiful in Kant, is impossible in the
case of the sublime. It would be more accurate to say that the sublime retains
an element of "*quasi*-consumption": that which, while not itself consumption, makes consumption possible and, in certain circumstances (those of the
beautiful, for example), directs experience toward consumption. The workings of quasi-consumption in a given experience may repress those aspects of
experience that would take it, through the sublime, not only beyond
consumption but also to the "beyond-the-inconsumable." The concept of
experience, as it has functioned throughout its history, is grounded in the idea
of consumption or, at least, quasi-consumption. The latter could also involve,
as in the sublime, various opposites of consumption or more interactive
dynamics of pleasure and displeasure, consumption and expenditure.[4]

By contrast, the "beyond-the-inconsumable" cannot be seen as belonging to experience or/as quasi-consumption, even though its role is irreducible in the *efficacity* or (they are always multiple) efficacities of the *effects*
of the consumptive and the quasi-consumptive, or of the experiential. Such
effects are not discarded as a result of this understanding, but are refigured
as those of a very different type of efficacity/ies, which, however, are also
responsible for those experiential effects that disrupt quasi-consumption.
I use the term "efficacity" in the sense of agency producing effects without

ascribing this agency causality. The efficacities in question here cannot be seen as non-consumptive or non–quasi-consumptive either, even though they are mediated through quasi-consumptive and consumptive processes and mechanisms, whether those are of the human body or mind. Hence, I speak of these efficacities as being "beyond-the-inconsumable." Ultimately, while they do have irreducible effects, such efficacities cannot be seen in any conceivable terms, whether those of being, or becoming, or, conversely, nothingness, or those of "beyond" and "efficacity." Both poems unname them in this radical way.

This argument also allows one to reread the unclosed closure of both poems and to rethink their unfinished nature. (In this reading, the term "fragment" becomes unsuitable.) Instead I read their (un)closing interruption as indicating the radical suspension of the possibility of any conceivable conception of what is placed "beyond the inconsumable," including any conceivable form or name of the "beyond" itself, human or divine. It is this possibility that would make poetry, or literature, possible and would define it, in accordance with the idea and ideology (aesthetic ideology?), introduced in Plato's *Ion*, which Shelley in part translated. The "divine madness" of poetry invoked in *Ion* enables a link or glimpse into the (otherwise) inconceivable. This type of possibility appears to have been still entertained in Keats's *Hyperion* and Shelley's *Adonais*, which invoke "the abode where the Eternal are," where Keats or the "Adonais" in Keats is placed (*Adonais* 495), or in "A Defence of Poetry."

By the time we reach *The Fall of Hyperion* and *The Triumph of Life* this possibility or even hope for it is abandoned. Nothing is immortal anymore: neither light nor poetry; neither the body nor spirit; neither gods we can conceive of nor gods whom we can postulate as beyond any conception. At stake, however, is not a nihilistic abandonment of knowledge and meaning, but an affirmative abandonment of the ultimate knowledge of the efficacity of knowledge, as part of the poems' Nietzschean affirmation of life even in its most tragic aspects. By the same token, a certain (en)closure of what can be seen or conceived of is announced. The poems' unending endings are allegories of both this (en)closure and the impossibility of ascribing any "beyond" to what is beyond their (en)closures—their scopes of vision and their ends as works.

Passages

The main vision of Keats's *The Fall of Hyperion*, after an introduction on the nature of dreaming (1–18), opens with a luscious description of a dream of a garden in late summer or early fall, if one speaks in human terms of seasons. It is a kind of paradise, before fall and seasons. The earthly counterpart of the vision, perhaps best read via "To Autumn," is evident, as the mortality/materiality theme pervades the poem. "Ode on Melancholy" may be invoked as well, and "Ode to Psyche" and its famous garden (50–67). *The Fall of Hyperion* holds together Keats's whole oeuvre, giving it, in the language of Shelley's "Ode to the West Wind," "a deep, autumnal tone" (60), only possible for what is material and mortal, for what "dwells with Beauty," but "Beauty that *must* die" ("Ode on Melancholy" 21; emphasis added). There may be no other beauty or sublimity. The mortality/materiality theme is pronounced at the opening, reinforced by the invocation of Proserpine and "the white heifers" (24–38) echoing those of "Ode on A Grecian Urn" (32–3). Moneta, "the sole priestess of [Saturn's] desolation" (366), addresses Keats as "Mortal," the persistent signifier giving a sense of material mortality rather than simply the opposition of the human and the divine. The sense of the mortal as incommensurable with the divine remains significant, especially in Moneta's "Mortal, that thou may'st understand aright, / I humanize my saying to thine ear, / Making comparison of earthly things" (2.1–3), echoing Book 5 of Milton's *Paradise Lost*, where Raphael confronts a similar problem in conveying events in heaven to Adam and Eve. The passage "beyond the inconsumable" and "beyond of the beyond" is beyond everything conceivably human; and in that task the divine helps only to a point, since this passage also gestures toward something other than the divine. The divine is only logical, theological, and hence only human. Or, in Heidegger's and Derrida's terms, both the human and the divine are ontotheological, that which may not be strictly theological but is modeled on theology. In Keats and Shelley alike, this nonhuman also entails a very different concept of the human and of the (human/inhuman) body, and of everything bodily, for example consumption, here by Keats's description of the consummate workings of all five senses (19–39), echoing the famous passage in *The Eve of St. Agnes* (263–74). Then he moves to "delicious" eating itself:

> Before its [the arbor's] wreathed doorway, on a mound
> Of moss, was spread a feast of summer fruits,
> Which, nearer seen, seem'd refuse of a meal
> By angel tasted, or our mother Eve;
> For empty shells were scattered on the grass,
> And grape stalks by half bare, and *remnants* more,
> Sweet smelling, whose pure kinds I could not know,
> Still was more plenty than the fabled horn

Thrice emptied could pour forth, at banqueting
For Proserpine return'd to her own fields,
Where the white heifers low. And appetite
More yearning than on earth I ever felt
Growing within, I ate deliciously; . . . (1.28–40; emphasis added)

It is worth pausing at this peculiarly Keatsian juncture of the all-you-can-eat meal and the menu-degustation meal, which is allegorically that of all-you-can-eat literature and menu-degustation literature, or indeed all-you-can-eat Romanticism and menu-degustation Romanticism. Aeschylus once said that "his tragedies are merely remnants [leftovers] of the great banquets of Homer."[5] Aeschylus's remark, however, and Keats's allegory also reciprocally suggest that, in consequence of the inexhaustible poetic "food supply," there are always remnants of such great feasts. Or there are or have been at some time remnants of still greater divine feasts of exquisite, gourmet treats of which Homer and whoever feasted on them before him were already partaking. This supply assures both the possibility and the eternal, or in any event long enough, life of literature. This economy of poetic distribution is questioned and ultimately abandoned by Keats in the poem, as it is by Shelley in *The Triumph of Life*. In their economy of poetic production-transformation one no longer can depend on such supply that also places the poetic vision beyond consumption and ultimately quasi-consumption, beyond the inconsumable, and beyond itself. This is where Keats's allegory is about to lead us. The consumption economy continues to guide Keats, as his thirst comes after his meal:

And, after not long, thirsted, for thereby
Stood a cool vessel of transparent juice,
Sipp'd by the wander'd bee, the which I took,
And, pledging all the mortals of the world,
And all the dead whose names are in our lips,
Drank. That full draught is parent of my theme.
No Asian poppy, no elixir fine
Of the soon fading jealous caliphat;
No poison gender'd in close monkish cell
Could so have rapt unwilling life away.
Among the fragrant husks and berries crush'd,
Upon the grass I struggled hard against
The domineering potion; but in vain:
The cloudy swoon came on, and down I sunk
Like a Silenus on an antique vase. (1.41–56)

I move to Shelley, leaving Keats at an appropriate point of his swoon—"How long I slumber'd 'tis a chance to guess"—before his "sense of life return[s]" and he "start[s] up/ As if with wings" (1.57–9). Shelley's passage is even more commented upon.[6] The vision parallel to Keats's is that of Rousseau within that of Shelley, beginning with ". . . In the April prime / When all the forest tops began to burn / 'With kindling green, touched by the azure clime / Of the young year, I found myself asleep . . ." (*The Triumph of Life* 307–11). I omit Rousseau's description of the landscape of his dream, parallel to Keats's vision (before he falls asleep), and move to Rousseau's awakening vision:

> . . . there stood
> "Amidst the sun, as he amidst the blaze
>   Of his own glory, on the vibrating
> Floor of the fountain, paved with flashing rays,
>   "A shape all light, which with one hand did fling
> Dew on the earth, as if she were the Dawn
>   Whose invisible rain forever seemed to sing
> "A silver music on the mossy lawn,
>   And still before her on the dusky grass
> Iris [rainbow] her many coloured scarf had drawn.—
>   "In her right hand she bore a crystal glass
> Mantling with bright Nepenthe; . . . (*TL* 348–59)

"Nepenthes" is the drug erasing pain and sorrow that Helen of Troy gives to Telemachus in Homer's *Odyssey*. The vision so far might best be associated with the sublime: it teases us with but ultimately defeats the possibility of visual and, more generally, phenomenal consumption. Shelley continues:

> ". . . as one between desire and shame
> Suspended, I said—'If, as it doth seem,
>   Thou comest from the realm without a name,
> " 'Into this valley of perpetual dream,
>   Shew whence I came, and where I am, and why —
> Pass not away upon the passing stream.'
>   " 'Arise and quench thy thirst,' was her reply.
> And as a shut lily, stricken by the wand
>   Of dewy morning's vital alchemy,
> "I rose; and, bending at her sweet command,
>   Touched with faint lips the cup she raised,
> And suddenly my brain became as sand
>   "Where the first wave had more than half erased

> The track of deer on desert Labrador,
> > Whilst the fierce wolf from which they fled amazed
> "Leaves his stamp visibly upon the shore,
> > Until the second bursts—so on my sight
> Burst a new Vision never seen before. (*TL* 394–411)

If the previous vision could be seen as the sublime, this "new Vision," like that at the end of Keats's poem, takes us beyond the sublime and beyond the inconsumable, and beyond the possibility of the visionary (or all phenomenality) and of literature.

Keats's and Shelley's passages have parallel structures and offer parallel allegories (using this term in de Man's sense, explained below). One is presented with a sequence of dream visions in which each vision, already extraordinary, is from within itself erased and replaced by a yet more extraordinary one. This sequence culminates in a vision entailing the impossibility of the visionary in any sense—from the impossibility of phenomenological visualization to that of developing any conception of what is beyond that vision. At the same time, that un-envisionable and inconceivable "beyond" produce effects upon what we can envision, conceive of, experience, and so forth. Accordingly, we can only confront these efficacities through their effects. Such efficacities may, thus, be mysterious without being mystical: one cannot postulate a single independent agency, in the way, say, mystical or negative theology would.[7]

Each poem enacts this structure differently. In Keats, drinking from the vessel initiates a gradual, continuous process, first of sleep and then "awakening," preceded by yet another (preparation) process, allegorized in terms of the taste and eating allegory. This process eventually leads to a sudden shift into a new vision, that of "the bright Hyperion" (*FH* 49–61). In Shelley, Rousseau's drinking from the cup given him by the Shape leads to the sudden transformation of vision: "And suddenly my brain became as sand" (*TL* 405). Ultimately, however, in both cases the sun and the sunrise—light—are rendered, as de Man observes of Shelley, as a sudden event, quantum-like, rather than continuous.[8] If one is permitted a metaphor from physics, we find ourselves, together with both Rousseau, or Shelley, and Keats, inside black holes, all-consuming artifacts of nature filled with light inside. Light can never escape from them and so they are dark, black, on the outside. Similarly neither Rousseau nor Keats can escape from their new vision. One is also reminded of Dante's fall through the body of Satan, including its digestive tract, at the end of *Inferno*, before he can "see—once more—the stars [a riveder le stelle]," in the last line (*Inferno* 34.139). This purgatorial vision, extended by Dante to *Purgatorio* and then to

Paradiso and recast by Shelley in *Adonais*, in part via *Hyperion*, is no longer possible in *The Triumph of Life* or in *The Fall of Hyperion*. Poetic or philosophical light and all enlightenment die within this region, which consumes and destroys them.[9] It is the death of light and of enlightenment through light, through "light's severe excess" (*TL* 424).

Both poems become allegories of a radical transformation of our cognitive machinery, ultimately reaching beyond the inconceivable and, correlatively, the inconsumable, beyond the sublime and literature, or beyond the beyond of the sublime and of literature. They are also allegories determined by (quasi-)consumption and, reciprocally, determining consumption. Reaching beyond the inconceivable and/as beyond the inconsumable is the most crucial event of both poems, defining the resulting allegories. As the same epistemology defines allegory according to de Man, both poems also becomes allegories and allegories of allegory in de Man's sense. The inconceivability itself defines "the beyond" in question, the beyond of the sublime within the sublime and the beyond of the inconsumable within the inconsumable, and the ultimately inaccessible nature of the process by which we reach this stage. The process erases not only the final vision, perhaps the ultimate possible vision, that the protagonists encounter but also the very possibility of the visionary, in particular as the literary, via the mediating destruction of the sublime, allegorized by the destruction of life. This is why these final visions entail, at the limit and as its limit, a form of un-vision. We are forced to confront that which is invisible and un-visualizable, and ultimately inconceivable by any means that are or will ever be available to us. Ultimately this "invisible" is un-visible even as anything that would be beyond our reach but exist somewhere in and by itself, available, say, to divine apprehension. The conception of the divine or of poetry as that which can partake in or capture something of the divine—by way of the divine madness of Plato's *Ion* or "[catching it] from the Penetralium of mystery" with the help of Keats's "negative capability"—is grounded in this possibility.[10] This view may be seen as Platonism in its greatest formality, the possibility of the original object of possible imitation, or of something that exists as impossible to imitate.[11] The poems bring us to the limits where this possibility is no longer available, destroyed by the poems' analytics.

Decompositions

This machinery of destruction arises in the poems' passage through the sublime and from the nature of the sublime itself—the catastrophic sublime, a rigorous passage beyond and radical rupture with the sublime, but in the sense that this "beyond" does not remain within or returns to what is outside or precedes the sublime. This limit is also the limit of the literary, and it could thus again be correlated with the limit of Platonism. Beyond this limit literature may no longer reach, although literature may be (re)defined as a (possibly interminable) approach to and exploration of this limit.[12]

To argue this case I shall first discuss a particular dimension of the sublime that de Man locates in Kant's third *Critique*. De Man speaks of "the material vision," which may be seen as the condition of the possibility of the sublime and the way to "find" it. This material vision also reveals the quasi-consumptive elements that the sublime retains, even though it resists consumption in all circumstances. According to Kant, we (must) "*find*" the sublime, if we regard the ocean, "as poets do, merely by what the appearance to the eye shows [or points to] [*was der Augenschein zeigt*]" (130). A stable translation of Kant's passage may not be possible. It is this possibility of a mere appearance to the eye of the poets' vision that defines quasi-consumption as the possibility of presence, including Derrida's sense of the metaphysics of presence. One might say that quasi-consumption is presence, although not pleasure. Given Kant's definition of the sublime as an interplay of pleasure [*Lust*] and displeasure or non-pleasure [*Unlust*], the sublime cannot be seen in terms of pleasurable consumption or, again, ultimately consumed, even with disgust, distaste, which appears as the limit of pleasure and which at least shadows the sublime. Nor can it be simply unconsumed, vomited, an uncritical reversal that would ground the economy of the sublime in something that is merely a metaphysical equivalent of consumption.[13] Quasi-consumption occupies a precarious intermediate and mediating position in the overall economy of the sublime as presence. As presence, quasi-consumption is the condition of the possibility of both consumption and the opposite of consumption, or their interactions, for example in the beautiful or in the sublime, but is itself none of these. If any experience corresponds to quasi-consumption, it may be something like the material vision of poets: "Kant's [phenomenal?] architectonic world is," according to de Man, "not a metamorphosis of a fluid [material?] world into the solidity of stone, nor is his building a trope or a symbol that substitutes for the actual entities."[14] One might (mis)read it in this way, as a form of aesthetic ideology, as one might also misread similar moments in Shelley's and Keats's texts, which contain strong sculptural imagery. As de Man's explains, it is difficult to define the phenomenality of this vision in any phenomenal terms (81–2). "The only word that comes to mind," de Man says, "is that of a *material* vision" (82).

The nature of this materiality and its accompanying formalism is complex. First of all,

> the sea is called [by Kant] a mirror, not because it is supposed to reflect anything, but to stress a flatness devoid of any suggestion of depth. In the same way and to the same extent that this vision is purely material, devoid of any reflexive and individual complication, it is also purely formal, devoid of any semantic depth and reducible to the formal mathematization or geometrization of pure optics. . . . The critique of the aesthetic ends up, in Kant, in a formal materialism that runs counter to all values and characteristics associated with aesthetic experience, including the aesthetic experience of the beautiful and the sublime as described by Kant and Hegel themselves. (83)

The sublime itself now appears in its material form, which is also its ultimate and defining form: the sublimity of the sublime. This materialization of the sublime is only a part of its catastrophe: even this materialism or formalism does not reach far enough, at least not yet. One must take the Kantian sublime further—to the point where a yet more radical stage of reading Kant, and of formalization and materiality, is reached and where how "[the] materiality in question is understood in linguistic terms" becomes more "clearly intelligible" (82). This "linguistic" understanding will bring with it further complications of the sublime and a more radical dislocation of aesthetic ideology than those entailed by the material vision, qua *vision*, as described by Kant and de Man—or, at least, *as* this vision has been described so far. For, this vision may in fact imply a more radical limit, "beyond-the-inconsumable." At this point we encounter the catastrophic sublime, the catastrophe that destroys the sublime and, along with it, literature.

This destruction *arises* from an extraordinary "vision" of the material constitution of the sublime and, with respect to the viewpoint of mathematization and especially geometrization of pure optics invoked by de Man, *de*-constitution and, as it were, formal de-formalization of this vision. This vision entails a suspension of any possible "geometrical" or spatial configurativity. It becomes the first stage of the process that brings us to the threshold of what is beyond this, or any, vision; we can reach no further. This stage appears necessary if we indeed can, phenomenally, and especially geometrically or spatially, "see" anything in this radically disjointed way. For it may not be humanly possible to do so in view of our phenomenological propensity to connect individual elements, even though in contrast to the beyond-the-inconsumable to which this vision ultimately leads, each such element is available to our phenomenological apprehension. This propensity defines both the beautiful and even the sublime, although the sublime defies any ultimate cohesion into a coherent form. It does, however, retain certain geometrical opticality. By contrast, the disfigurative phenomenology of the vision in question must divest the elements of this vision of any opticality or any other configurativity, leading, in de Man's phrase, "the material . . . disarticulation of nature" or the disarticulation of the materiality of matter, as well as of the phenomenality of mind.

This epistemology emerges in or is allegorized by both Keats's and Shelley's poems, in especially graphic terms in the passage of *The Triumph of Life*:

> And suddenly my brain became as sand
>> "Where the first wave had more than half erased
> The track of deer on desert Labrador,
>> Whilst the fierce wolf from which they fled amazed
> "Leaves his stamp visibly upon the shore,
>> Until the second bursts—so on my sight
> Burst a new Vision never seen before.— (*TL* 405–11)

This complex catachresis entails an irreducible multiplicity of readings. They may proceed from considering the violence in the change from one vision to another, to the nature of "reading" half-erased tracks and traces of images within a vision in which dream and awakening, perception and conception, material and phenomenal, reality (if any) and interpretation (or interpretation of interpretation), and so forth, are all irreducibly entangled. But, to begin with, how does one read such traces, which invite the engagement with Derrida's concept of trace?[15] Shelley's allegory makes Rousseau's vision/reading divest these traces of all conceivable configurativity, even that of the sublime. If so, however, the question re-imposes itself: How does one "read" such disfigured traces? And what, then, does the poem or both poems ultimately allegorize in their allegories of such as a reading, perhaps ultimate "allegories of reading" in de Man's sense?

Until the very last lines of both poems, at least a possibility of a certain theological or ontotheological efficacity of these traces appears to be entertained, which would enable a certain opticality or figurativity, perceptual or conceptual. It might also be seen as suggested by Rousseau's attempt to give a particular meaning to the procession—the triumph—of life–death, or by the narrator's attempt to read Rousseau's or his own vision as an ontotheological or indeed theological allegory. This possibility also transpires in Moneta's "visage":

> . . . Then I saw a wan face
> Not pinned by human sorrow, but bright blanch'd

By an immortal sickness which kills not;
It works a constant change, which happy death
Can put no end to; deathwards progressing
To no death was that visage; it has pass'd
The lily and the snow; and beyond these
I must not think now, though I saw that face—
But for her eyes I should have fled away. (*FH* 1.255–64)

Here one still "sees" and has a vision. This possibility of vision is suspended, narratively and epistemologically, only by the abrupt interruption ending the poem itself, as an allegory of a destruction of any vision, still deemed possible, even if not undertaken, here. Keats indeed ends or exits the poem "beyond these," but now in the sense of the impossibility of anything visionary or en-visionable. This final "beyond/not-beyond" is irreducibly materialist, as "death" is deployed as a very different type of allegory, invoked by de Man in "Shelley Disfigured": *The Triumph of Life* warns us that *nothing*, whether deed, word, thought or text, ever happens in relation, positive or negative, to anything that preceded, follows, or exists elsewhere, but only as a random event whose power, like the power of death, is due to the randomness of its occurrence" (*The Rhetoric of Romanticism* 122; emphasis added). Everything, ultimately, but only ultimately (at certain levels a more classical epistemology must be retained), becomes an effect of a material, beyond-the-inconsumable, efficacity that can never be causal. Everything ultimately begins or ends in this irreducibly random and disfigurative way. Thereby this machinery is not theological, even in the sense of negative or mystical theology, which makes impossible an attribution to the divine of any conceivable properties, but assumes the divine. Nor is it ontotheological. Both Shelley's and Keats's final (in either sense) interruptions enact this epistemology. By the same token, closer to Derrida's concept of the (en)closure of metaphysics, the poems also demarcate what kinds of answer we humans can in principle give, or what kinds of question we can possibly ask.

Then what is life? I ask this question assuming, which appears reasonable, that life is the efficacity (it may be plural) of such a vision, as it is the efficacity of history and/of mind and culture, here allegorized as well. Indeed, both allegories are bound to be irreducibly mixed. I also see life as ultimately material (physical, chemical, biological, and so forth) efficacious dynamics. "What is Life?" is Shelley's final, unanswered and unanswerable, question in the poem:

"Then, what is Life?" I said . . . the cripple cast
His eye upon the car which now had rolled

> Onward, as if that look must be the last,
> And answered . . . ."Happy those for whom the fold
> Of (*TL* 544–7)

The fold of what? Is any question, let alone answer, still possible? Is the last question still possible? Are questions still possible, as Shelley suspends even them? The same may be asked about Keats's (un)closure of *The Fall of Hyperion*, "on he flared/ . . ." (2.61–2).

Through the sequence of visions—from the beautiful to the sublime to the material vision, ultimately of traces, material and mental, divested of any meaningful vision—one arrives to the threshold (one can go no further) of that which is both beyond the inconsumable and beyond the (en)closure of all possible conceptions, where one locates the efficacities of the de-figured effects-traces. These effects appear within our (en)closure. How otherwise would we be able to think rigorously of such efficacities rather than merely imagine them? The nature of these effects, however, and their configurations do not appear to allow for any quasi-consumption–like dynamics of emergence and require the epistemology of the beyond-the-inconsumable and of the beyond-the-beyond; all consumption is suspended earlier in the process.

One might argue that it was life itself—the death of both poets—that brought both poems to this interruption of vision. That may be, especially in the case of *The Triumph of Life*, where the closing lines are likely to have been changed had Shelley lived longer. Certainly, life or life–death entered the scene and the very text of the poem in an especially tragic way, "as a random event whose power . . . is due to the randomness of its occurrence," now indeed the power of actual death. There is, however, enough textual evidence, some already suggested and some to be offered presently, that the present reading may rigorously apply. At the very least, our readings of both poems would, as de Man argues in "Shelley Disfigured," depend on how one reads the dead and decomposed bodies of both poets.

We are now ready to consider de Man's understanding of the material vision, which allows us to see the radical epistemology, the (radicalized) material vision, at the textual level and as enacted by the text, in the way they are in the (un)closure of both poems as just considered, or the titles, as de Man argues in the case of *The Fall of Hyperion*.[16] (The complexities of Shelley's title, beginning with its origin in Petrarch's *Trionfi*, could be considered from this perspective.) In the first stage of this process along with the material disarticulation of nature, one might think of the materiality of language itself, to the smallest material or phenomenological marks seen as disconnected marks, indivisible punctual entities, divested of all possible meaning or form linking them (*Aesthetic Ideology* 88–90).[17]

If a reading proceeds along the lines of aesthetic ideology, even that modeled on the nonconsumptive economy of the material sublime (prior to the linguistic understanding of it), one can *then* reassemble the elements of such texts configuratively. Indeed such a configurative assemblage, or its sheer possibility, defines one's reading or vision. Hence, the above "then" is not an irreducible structural operator; it is in what de Man sees as disfigurative reading. In Keats's and Shelley's allegories, which are also allegories of disfigurative reading, no configurative assemblage of linguistic atoms defines them individually. Such assemblages could only be added "then," after the event or, in de Man's terms, actual act of material occurrence, *nächtraglich* (in Freud's sense) or supplementarily in Derrida's sense, making any such configurativity appear as added to rather than preceding the disfigurativity in question. Ultimately, this disfigurativity is secondary or supplementary with respect to its own ultimate efficacious dynamics, which is no more atomic (disjoint) than configurative (connected). Once made "more intelligible," "linguistic understanding [of the material vision of poets] in linguistic terms" reveals a textual un-architectonic of any architectonic, whether Kant himself offers us this understanding or not. Some poetic works allegorically enact this decomposition, leading to the inaccessible "behind" the material vision. But then, Kant's text acquires this poetic quality too, even if against Kant (87–90, 125–8).

On the one hand there is a certain "collective" shared semantic field within which linguistic atoms function and which they obey. On the other, once rigorously considered individually, or in a certain ultimate decomposition, these elements can no longer be fully subsumed by any coherent configuration of meanings. One may thus speak of a decoherence of figures and tropes, or of all language, in an allegorical text. An analogous decoherence is suggested by de Man's remark, via Montaigne, that we must consider "our limbs," formally, "in themselves, severed from the organic unity of the body." "We must, in other words, disarticulate, mutilate the body in a way that is much closer to Kleist than to Winckelman," and hence enact "the material disarticulation not only of nature but of the body, . . . [which] moment marks the undoing of the aesthetic as a valid category" (88–9). One can construct partial and ultimately inadequate allegories of the materiality of the "body." Indeed the original "parts" or "limbs" are already such allegories, as supplementary as the "body" itself. Accordingly, a more radical dis-articulation, mutilation, disfiguration of the (un)body is at stake, even at the level of manifest effects. The efficacity of these effects is inaccessible in any way, no more by means of disarticulation than by articulation. This dismemberment is linked to the linguistic understanding of materiality and specifically to the disarticulation of tropes, as the trope of "disarticulation" suggests: "to the dismemberment of the body corresponds a dismemberment of language, as meaning-producing tropes are replaced by the fragmentation of sentences and propositions into discrete words, or the fragmentation of words into syllables or finally letters" (89).

One thus encounters radical disarticulating materiality both in the world, specifically the body, and in the text. It would, however, be a mistake to see them as mirroring or mapping each other, as de Man's "corresponds" might suggest, given the complexities of "correspondence" in de Man. Instead, insofar as one can approach the world by way of a text, the dismemberment or "decoherence" of language—the ultimately irreducible, uncontrollable divergence of figures, signifiers, or whatever can carry meaning—manifests the irreducible inaccessibility of the world or life through peculiar configurations of material and phenomenological effects. Keats powerfully enacts this decoherent fragmentation of language in one of his final poetic efforts, his sonnet "I cry your mercy—pity—love!—aye, love." The sonnet is an ever more dramatic illustration of the dis- or de-figurative economy in question, which leaves the efficacity of the whole process—What is Love? What is Life?—beyond any possibility of consumption, or of consummation, or anything. Shelley's "What is Life?" leads us toward the same limit. Indeed "What is Life?," as asked textually and bodily, materially by Shelley, is *The Triumph of Life*, leading us to something beyond which we cannot think.

Corporealities

The efficacious processes in question take place through the mediation of the human body, the corporeality and corpo-reality, the reality of the corporeal, which is consistent with the radical anti-realism of the epistemology in question. This epistemology now applies to the ultimate material constitution of this corporeality itself or any materiality, which by no means prevents the ponderous and palpable, indeed deadly, reality of certain effects of the irreducibly inaccesible; quite the contrary. The body, including the consumption economy—breathing, eating, drinking, and so forth, or the way it manages and disposes of its waste products inside and outside itself—supports and sustains this mediation. It must be seen as the irreducible part of such processes, while representations or conceptions of the body, including those as "body," must be seen in terms of its effects, and becomes subject to de-coherence. This efficacious dynamic is a product of the particular constitution and deconstitution of both the life and death of the human body, including its consumptive and disposing machinery. We could not otherwise *see* or *un-see* the world (nature and mind alike) in this cohering–decohering way. Our conceptions of the physical world according to the key theories of twentieth-century physics, relativity and quantum theory, may be subject to the same epistemology.[18] As such, however, these conceptions may also be tied to the particular nature of our physical constitution as human and animal beings, including the biology and the physiology of our body. To cite Marcel Proust: "the trees, the sun and the sky would not be the same as what we see if they were apprehended by creatures having eyes differently constituted from ours, or else endowed for that purpose with organs other than eyes which would furnish equivalents of trees and sky and sun, though not visual ones." Such "organs" (if the term applies) may not furnish even that much, in any event nothing equivalent.[19]

The question of consumption acquires new dimensions from this perspective of the body as a constitutive part of the efficacity of all our experiential, including perceptual, interpretive, and conceptual, machinery. The preceding argument extends that of Georges Bataille concerning theories of unutilizable and ultimately meaningless consumption and expenditure. He calls such theories "general economies," juxtaposing them to "restricted economies" as theories of meaningful consumption—material (including economic), philosophical, or aesthetic—such as those in Marx's political economy, Hegel's speculative philosophy, and Kant's third *Critique* ("taste"). These theories and related conceptions of Romantic literature and thought introduce subtle relationships between meaningful, especially pleasurable, and meaningless consumption and expenditure, ultimately linked to the efficacity not only beyond all consumption but also beyond the inconsumable. Keats's and Shelley's works considered here do so by a subtle literary philosophical exploration of the idea and practices of "consumption," or the impossibility thereof. Reciprocally, reconceived along the lines of Bataille's general economy, the consumption/expenditure conglomerate offers an effective metaphor for the epistemological and interpretive and creative processes in question in both poems. The very material processes at stake, from the functioning of the human body to political economy, are part of the efficacities of the processes they allegorize, insofar as the constitution (or deconstitution) of our bodies enable or disable any vision or un-vision we might have.

Consider Keats's famous description of his experience of eating a nectarine, although a number of other passages would also work well. Keats lives, lives/dies, pleasurably consuming with one hand, painfully wasting/writing with another: "Talking of pleasure, this moment I was writing with one hand, and with the other holding to my Mouth a Nectarine—good god how fine—It went down soft, pulpy, slushy, oozy—all its delicious embonpoint melted down my throat like a large beatiful [sic] Strawberry" (*Letters* 2.179). We would miss the import of this passage if we saw it in terms of the body as organism, with organs of senses, such as taste, each designed for a particular function. We must instead read it in terms of Deleuze and Guattari's conglomerate, introduced in *Anti-Oedipus*, of "the body without organs" and the economy of "desiring machines," including those of writing, to which the processes in the body without organs give rise from time to time. These desiring machines can sometimes be linked to actual organs of the human body, such as mouth or hand, or to certain parts of various social and political collective organs or bodies, but ultimately cannot be reduced to such organs.[20]

In considering an analogous economy in Kleist, de Man traces the case of the irreducibly divergent German signifier "Fall" (*Rhetoric of Romanticism* 289–90).[21] The English signifier "Fall" is explored by him in his reading of *The Fall of Hyperion* (*Resistance to Theory* 16–18). He also considers the concept of fall in Baudelaire in his analysis of irony in "The Rhetoric of Temporality."[22] "Fall" is a decisive figure in these works, as in Shelley's *The Triumph of Life*, where everything is in a state of catastrophic fall. "Fall" is materiality, both literally (gravity) and (intimately connected to consumption) allegorically, in the irreducible decoherence of language, as it, as it were, falls away from itself. We may, however, only separate them if gravity is anything less than allegory, which it may, ultimately, not be. It would be impossible to consider the relevant physics here, for example, the way gravity bends light itself (which would bring all three figures together in yet another way). In the case of Einstein's general relativity, we deal with a *horizontal* fall, in some ways not unlike Adam centrifugally falling away from God in Michelangelo's "Creation of Adam." The matters of materiality and of falling are irreducible in everything in question here, from the body and consumption, or waste—weight and waste—to the physics of black holes, the ultimate manifestation of consumption, all-consuming consumption, in the physical world; or the question of geometrical representation of physical processes in Einstein's theory, which appears no longer possible, and hence is fundamentally linked to the epistemological problematic of this essay. These connections are beyond my scope. I would like, however, to take advantage, with Blanchot, of relativistic cosmology to close on the question of the possibility or impossibility of literature:

> I ask myself why . . . the whole history of criticism and culture closed and why, with a melancholy serenity, it seemed at the same time to send us off

178 ~ *Arkady Plotnitsky*

and to authorize us to enter a new space. What space? Not to answer such a question, certainly, but to show the difficulty of approaching it, I would like to invoke a metaphor. It is nearly understood that the Universe is curved, and it has often been supposed that this curvature has to be positive: hence the image of a finite and limited sphere. But nothing permits one to exclude the hypothesis of an unfigurable Universe (a term henceforth deceptive); a Universe escaping every optical exigency and also escaping consideration of the whole—essentially non-finite, disunified, discontinuous. What about such a Universe? . . . What about man the day he accepts confronting the idea . . . But will he ever be ready to receive such a thought, a thought that, freeing him from fascination with unity, for the first time risks summoning him to take the measure of an exteriority that is not divine, of a space entirely in question, and even excluding the possibility of an answer, since every response would necessarily fall anew under the jurisdiction of the figure of figures? This amounts perhaps to asking ourselves: is man capable of a radical interrogation? That is, finally, is he capable of literature, if literature turns aside and towards the absence of the book?[23]

With this thought or un-thought, literature turns toward the absence of literature itself, at least since Romanticism, for which literature or/as un-literature became a form of radical interrogation. Blanchot's seemingly incongruous jump from relativistic cosmology to literature is logical. It is much more than merely a metaphor, unless we see it in terms of the epistemological parallel between both fields, relativistic cosmology and literature, which also involves the question of consumption in its greatest generality. A radical interrogation acquires a new sense, which becomes necessary, even though and because it may lead us to the death of literature, the death of reading, the death of writing, the death of interrogation. This end, however, is also the beginning of something else in this unfigurable universe, in the un-universe of the unfigurable, in the un-sublime of the sublime, the un-consumption of consumption and of the un-consumption or the inconsumable, of the beyond-the-inconsumable, in short that beyond which we cannot think. We, our mind and body, must think *of* this something. We must think of that which is beyond what we can think, beyond what thinking can consume and beyond what is the inconsumable for thinking.

Notes

1. All references to Keats's and Shelley's works are from *The Poems of John Keats*, ed. Jack Stillinger (Cambridge, Mass.: Bellknap Press of Harvard UP, 1978), and *Shelley's Poetry and Prose*, ed. Donald. H. Reiman and Sharon B. Powers (New York and London: W. W. Norton, 1977).

2. Immanuel Kant, *Critique of Aesthetic Judgement*, tr. Werner S. Pluhar (Indianapolis: Hackett, 1987).

3. Aesthetic ideology is defined by a broad spectrum of aesthetic, philosophical, and political views; it would be difficult to properly delineate the architecture of de Man's concept here. However, the question of consumption and quasi-consumption is germane to aesthetic ideology; one might indeed view aesthetic ideology as based on "quasi-consumption."

4. In part for this reason Derrida relates consumption to what he calls "the metaphysics of presence," which may be defined in terms of quasi-consumption.

5. See Atheneus, *The Deipnosophists* (*Deipnosophistai*), tr. Charles Burton Gulick (Cambridge, Mass.: Harvard UP, 1930), 96 (vol. 4, Books 8–10, (8.347e)).

6. See Arkady Plotnitsky, "All Shapes of Light: The Quantum Mechanical Shelley," in *Shelley: Poet and Legislator of the World*, ed. Stuart Curran and Betty Bennett (Baltimore: Johns Hopkins UP, 1995), 263–73.

7. This argument in part follows Derrida's analysis (*Margins of Philosophy*, tr. Alan Bass (Chicago and London: University of Chicago Press, 1982), 13–14).

8. Paul de Man, *The Rhetoric of Romanticism* (New York: Columbia UP, 1984), 289–90, 117.

9. A similar epistemology may apply to black holes. We may not be able to extend our customary conceptions of physical processes to what happens in those regions.

10. John Keats, *The Letters of John Keats*, ed. Hyder Edward Rollins, 2 vols. (Cambridge, Mass.: Harvard UP, 1958), 1.193.

11. See Derrida's analysis of Mallarmé in "The Double Session" in *Dissemination*, tr. Barbara Johnson (Chicago: University of Chicago Press, 1981).

12. The situation may also be seen as corresponding to Hegel's epistemology and his argument for "the death of art" in his *Aesthetics*. On consumption in Hegel, I permit myself to refer to *In the Shadow of Hegel: Complementarity, History and the Unconscious* (Gainesville, Fla.: UP of Florida, 1983), and, on Bataille, "The Effects of the Unknowable: Materiality, Epistemology, and the General Economy of the Body in Bataille," *Parallax*, 18 (Winter 2001), 16–28.

13. See Derrida's analysis of Kant in "Economimesis," *Diacritics*, 11.3 (1981), 3–25.

14. Paul de Man, *Aesthetic Ideology* (Minneapolis: University of Minnesota Press, 1996), 82.

15. See Arkady Plotnitsky, "All Shapes of Light."

16. Paul de Man, *The Resistance to Theory* (Minneapolis, Minn.: University of Minnesota Press, 1986), 16–18.

17. See my "Algebra and Allegory: Nonclassical Epistemology, Quantum Theory and the Work of Paul de Man," in *Material Events*, ed. Barbara Cohen, Thomas Cohen, J. Hillis Miller, and Andrzej Warminski (Minneapolis: University of Minnesota Press, 2000), 49–89; and *The Knowable and the Unknowable: Modern Science, Nonclassical Thought and the "Two Cultures"* (Ann Arbor, Mich.: University of Michigan Press, 2002).

18. See *The Knowable and the Unknowable*.

19. Marcel Proust, "The Guermantes Way," *The Remembrance of Things Past*, tr. C. K. Scott Moncrieff and Terence Kilmartin, 3 vols. (New York: Vintage, 1981), 3.64.

20. Gilles Deleuze and Félix Guattari, *Anti-Oedipus: Capitalism and Schizophrenia*, tr. Robert Hurley, Mark Seem, and Helen R. Lane (Minneapolis: University of Minnesota Press, 1987).

21. Paul de Man, *The Rhetoric of Romanticism* (New York: Columbia UP, 1984), 289–90.

22. Paul de Man, *Blindness and Insight: Essays in the Rhetoric of Contemporary Crticism* (London: Methuen, 1983), 213–14.

23. Maurice Blanchot, *The Infinite Conversation*, tr. Susan Hanson (Minneapolis: University of Minnesota Press, 1993), 350.

Part III ∾

DISGUST, DIGESTION, THOUGHT

Chapter 9 ⌁

THE ENDGAME OF TASTE: KEATS, SARTRE, BECKETT

Denise Gigante

. . . life is a thing of beauty, Gaber, and a joy for ever. He brought his face nearer mine. A joy for ever, he said, a thing of beauty, Moran, and a joy for ever.

— Samuel Beckett, *Molloy* 226

Monsieur, at one time I ventured to think that the beautiful was only a question of taste. Are there not different rules for each epoch?

— Jean-Paul Sartre, *Nausea* 108

In deciding what kind of weather suits his taste, Beckett's absurdist quest-hero Molloy decides that he has no taste, that he had lost it long ago.[1] Modernism never wholly let go of the aesthetic legacy of taste, and by 1947 when Beckett was working on the first novel in his trilogy, *Molloy, Malone Dies*, and *The Unnamable*, it had already experienced this legacy in the form of an existentialist nausea. Perhaps nowhere do we see this more clearly than in Keats's late fragmentary epics, *Hyperion* and *The Fall of Hyperion*, where the metaphor of taste gives way to an all-pervasive sickness in the stomach. While the starving speaker of *The Fall of Hyperion* fails to relish the stale banquet he is offered at the outset of the poem, the defeated gods of *Hyperion* suffer an existential queasiness playing itself out in bodies that are "crampt and screw'd."[2] Hyperion experiences a "nauseous feel" from the repulsive smells he is forced to consume. Critics since Walter Jackson Bate have noticed the proleptically existential tone of the *Hyperion* poems: they "anticipate much that we associate with existentialism (no other major nineteenth-century poem does this to the same extent)."[3] Here I pursue the possibility, evinced by Keats, that existentialism itself— and its dominant paradigms of nausea and disgust—constitutes the philosophical aftermath of aesthetic taste.

The gesture is toward an extended literary history of the aesthetic in which the metaphor of taste does serious work in the philosophical field of subjectivity. Because the reach of such a gesture is potentially unbounded, the following pages will limit themselves to a consideration of the Romantic legacy of taste (particularly Keatsian taste) in key moments of Sartre's *Nausea* and Beckett's *Molloy* (1955). In the opening scene of *Nausea*, when Sartre's existential man stands on the shore, feasting his eyes on the traditionally sublime seascape, he suddenly finds himself cloyed and disgusted, unable to stomach the raw existence obtruding upon him in the form of a nauseating stone. Beckett revises this trauma of taste by transforming Sartre's stone (*galet*) into a collection of absurdist "sucking stones" (*pierres a sucer*) that the vagabond Molloy collects from the shore and periodically sucks in a bravado display of connoisseurship. The existential stone takes on figurative significance in a tradition of iconic taste-objects extending back through the Century of Taste to Addison's tea-leaves in *The Spectator* 409 ("On Taste") as testing ground for the so-called Man of Taste to prove his fine palate.[4] In the end, Beckett's absurdist epicure finds that the more he sucks, the more he transforms the idealized subject of taste, turning him inside-out via his digestive tract. According to Beckett's revisionary aesthetic of disgust the subject becomes constituted according to a general economy in which waste and taste lose all distinction. My particular concern in the following pages is how Keats's late epic poetry mediates between the two intellectual fields of taste and existentialist nausea.

I

In his foundational study of Keatsian taste and distaste, Christopher Ricks proposes that Sartre has produced "the best criticism of Keats ever written not about him."[5] When reversed, this trenchant insight also holds true: Keats has produced the best criticism of Sartre ever written not about *him*. This is not to say that Keats's nausea is equivalent to Sartre's fictional portrayal of nausea in his novel by that title, or that Sartre's nausea is equivalent to Molloy's disgust as modernist efforts to digest Romanticism. Rather, I wish to suggest that the nausea Keats describes follows philosophically from taste and hypostatizes certain elements of the existentialist condition. Let us keep in mind the figurative deployment of "taste" and "relish" by the Keatsian poet who "lives in gusto," an oral formulation whereby the poet *tastes* and *relishes* the world: "its relish of the dark side of things . . . its taste for the bright one."[6] This poet is also described as a "camelion poet," a figure of endlessly negative capability who inhabits a world of "gusto"—a term derived from taste (*gustus*) and defined by William Hazlitt as an effect whereby the eye acquires "a taste or appetite for what it sees."[7] As Keats knew from *Hamlet*, chameleons were not only capable of changing colors, but of surviving on airy nothings, "the chameleon's dish . . . the air" (III.2.95–6). The chameleon was thus an ideal figure to enact the ethereal feasting that Keats used to allegorize the process of aesthetic consumption and production. The poet gorges on beauty and gives it back as expression, or "sees Beauty on the wing, pounces upon it and gorges it to the producing his essential verse."[8] Everything in this closed cycle circulates through the mouth as the place of both taste and expression (a more tasteful mode of emission than occurs at the other end of the digestive tract).

In the *Hyperion* poems, the same poet who "lives in gusto" enters a realm where taste devolves into disgust. When he first appears, Hyperion is attempting to taste the sweet smell of incense that drifts up to him from the world below. Yet his pleasure is blocked:

> when he *would taste* the spicy wreaths
> Of incense, breath'd aloft from sacred hills,
> Instead of sweets, his ample palate took
> Savour of poisonous brass and metal sick. (I.186–9; emphasis mine)

In this scene of frustrated pleasure, the "poisonous brass and metal sick" interferes with Hyperion's effort to taste. In fact, as Keats's manuscript of the poem makes clear, the final line of this passage did not originally begin with "Savour," or taste proper. It began instead with "A nausea."[9] As Jonathan Bate narrates this revision, "Keats struggled with the final line in an attempt to convey the sickly sweet smell of incense. 'A nausea,' he begins. 'A nauseous feel,' he then tries, but 'feel' is heavily crossed out."[10] Whether Keats could not bring himself explicitly to admit nausea, or whether he abandoned "Nausea" in favor of "Savour" (albeit sickening), the holograph suggests how closely these concepts were bound together. His lines in fact register a trauma of taste: Hyperion's physiological failure to taste and express beauty by means of his "ample palate."[11]

Technically, Hyperion is attempting to taste the sweet *smell* of incense. In medical discourses of the eighteenth and early nineteenth centuries, these senses were linked as "chemical" as opposed to "mechanical" senses. Smell was however distinguished from taste as more receptive to disgust than to pleasure. Kant ponders the implications of this distinction in *Anthropology from a Pragmatic Point of View*, observing that "when confronted with many dishes and bottles, one can choose that which suits his pleasure without forcing others to participate in that pleasure"; on the other hand, "Smell is, so to speak, taste at a distance, and other people are forced to share a scent whether they want to or not."[12] In its sensual invasiveness smell leaves little room for idealization. This obtrusive quality disturbs Kant again in the *Critique of Aesthetic Judgment*, where he considers the problem of a scented handkerchief. Even the sweet smell of perfume can be a source of disgust, especially in a crowd where it is forced upon us: "the man who pulls out his perfumed handkerchief from his pocket gives a treat to all around whether they like it or not, and compels them, if they want to breathe at all, to be parties to the enjoyment, and so the habit has gone out of fashion."[13] By the same token, he claims that objects "awaken nausea less through what is repulsive to eye and tongue than through the stench associated with it . . . this sense can pick up more objects of aversion than pleasure" (*Anthropology* 45–6). Given the emphasis on smell in Keats's text, when Hyperion consumes incense and "metal sick" through his "ample palate," he finds himself particularly vulnerable to disgust.

Like Hyperion, the narrator of *The Fall of Hyperion* is immediately confronted with the task of attempting to taste. Here too the matter he is offered augurs nausea far more than delight. The picked-over banquet he discovers strikes him as rubbish, "refuse of a meal / By angel tasted, or our mother Eve" (1.130–1). Everything seems parched and stale for this already sickened speaker for whom the grape-stalks appear not half-full but "half bare" (I.133). Far from bursting joy's grape against his palate fine like the speaker of Keats's "Ode on Melancholy," he can hardly stomach the sight of them. Readers such as W. J. Bate, Harold Bloom, and Marjorie Levinson have interpreted this scene as an allegory of poetic belatedness, the difficulty of assimilating literary tradition into original expression.[14] When viewed as a key moment in a literary history of the aesthetic, the unpalatable meal in *The Fall of Hyperion* prefigures the more full-scale souring of taste into nausea that marks existentialism's point of departure. As the speaker digs into the remnants of the potentially nauseating meal, he experiences a "nauseous feel."

While he was working on these poems Keats's physical condition entailed digestive complications from an advanced state of tuberculosis. He complained miserably of his prescribed diet of "pseudo-victuals," and his physician, James Clarke, properly guessed that "The chief part of his disease . . . [was] seated in his Stomach" (*Letters* 2.271).[15] Painfully describing Keats's final days, Joseph Severn exclaimed "his Stomach—not a single thing will digest—the torture he suffers all and every night—and the best part of the day—is dreadful in the extreme—the distended stomach keeps him in perpetual hunger or craving" (Rollins 177). Yet neither hunger nor a fevered condition aided Keats's effort to distinguish himself through taste. On the eve of his *annus mirabilis* (31 December 1818), he declared that he had "not one opinion upon any matter except in matters of taste" (*Letters* 2.19). Hunger was counterproductive to the experience of taste, and when viewed in light of Keats's ongoing efforts at aesthetic self-creation through taste, the queasiness and "nauseous feel" of his late poetry signal more than his own deteriorating physicality. They are symptomatic of the greater philosophical and cultural sickening of the idealist subject of taste.

II

Keats's metaphorical encounters with taste help us to consider the ways in which Sartre's portrayal of nausea, as both a fictional event of high modernism and a phenomenological symptom of subject-making, results from the oral schema defining the idealist subject of taste. In *Nausea*, Antoine Roquentin confronts a world that will no longer be assimilated by the idealist-turned-existentialist self. Sartre associated digestive imagery with Kantian apperception, which he applied to the vogue for neo-Kantianism in France at the time: "We have all read Brunschvicg, Lalande and Meyerson, we have all believed that the [Kantian] Mind-Spider drew things into its web, covered them with white goo and slowly swallowed them, reducing them to its own substance."[16] In *Nausea* this all-consuming idealist selfhood, which readily assimilates the world of objective reality, comes in for fictional critique. Such critique is part of Sartre's more overarching challenge to Romantic idealism in the years leading up to the novel in *La Transcendence de l' ego*, where Sartre disputed Kant's notion of a "transcendent ego," and *L' Imagination*, in which he separated perception from imagination as modes of consciousness-consumption. His novelistic depiction of nausea, in turn, is an explicit response to idealist taste.

Derrida has shown how in Kant's third critique the aesthetic subject is organized around the *Os*, or all-consuming mouth. According to the restricted cycle of consumption that defines aesthetic taste, everything passes through the mouth: the socially acceptable end of the digestive tract and the gateway to aesthetic subjectivity.[17] A classic example of the consuming orality that characterizes the post-Kantian subject of taste is the Wordsworthian mind that feeds upon infinity in the final book of *The Prelude*. Romantic scholars recognize the philosophical correlative of this scene to be the all-devouring Hegelian subject from the *Phenomenology of Spirit*. In his *Philosophy of Nature*, Hegel describes this subject in physiological terms as an organism that relates to the external world through the medium of its assimilating skin. This interface with objective reality is conceived as an expanded orifice, which when it "turns back on itself towards the organism's interior in addition to being a general orifice, it is now a single orifice, the mouth, and organic nature is seized and ingested as an individual thing."[18] Werner Hamacher has shown that Hegel's "sucking mouth, enjoys more than one specific location in the system of spirit, for this . . . is what systematizes body and spirit, what joins them together and articulates their unity."[19] As body and spirit are unified through the circular economy of the "sucking mouth," the resulting totality becomes an idealist culmination of the Kantian subject of taste. Molloy's "sucking stones" demonstrate the absurdity of the aesthetically sucking mouth, but their existentialist progenitor is the Sartrean stone from *Nausea*, the modernist taste-object *tout court*.

Groping to express the feeling provoked by the touch (etymologically, taste) of the stone in the opening scene, Sartre's existentialist man describes it as a "sweetish sickness" (*d'écoeurement douceâtre*). "Now I see," he observes, "I recall better what I felt the other day at the seashore when I held the pebble. It was a sort of sweetish sickness. How unpleasant it was! It came from the stone, I'm sure of it, it passed from the stone to my hand. Yes, that's it, that's just it—a sort of nausea in the hands" (*N* 10). A similar sickly sweet sensation keeps Hyperion from experiencing pleasure, and there too the "sweetish sickness" is akin to "A nausea." Sartre's existential man explicitly recognizes this "sweetish sickness" as "the disgust of existing . . . My saliva is sugary, my body warm: I feel neutral" (*N* 100). The stone that prompts Roquentin's initial wave of nausea presents itself as an unconsumable lump of external reality. As he gags on the unpalatable taste-object, he becomes uncomfortably aware of the salivary interface between self and world and his organ of taste turns literal.

Roquentin becomes a self-conscious literalization of the aesthetic organism tasting and relishing the world, and he begins to perceive the mouths of others (an increasing obsession) as not only a means of expression, but an opening to a disgusting, even monstrous reality. In one typical nightmare vision, he imagines himself as he "goes to the mirror, opens his mouth: and his tongue is an enormous, live centipede, rubbing its legs together and scraping his palate. He'd like to spit it out, but the centipede is part of him and he will have to tear it out with his own hands" (*N* 159). In place of a proper self-effacement in tasting and expressing (for which the tongue achieves privileged status in the idealist subject of taste), the tongue of Sartre's existential man obtrudes itself as an unwelcome reality. Everywhere he looks he sees smiles revealing the horror of rotting teeth, mouths opening as dark passages into a digestive tract, which traditionally leads in the opposite direction from taste. Simultaneously, the eyes, which since classical times have represented the ideal mode of aesthetic intake, become occluded with their own materiality: "His eyes are glassy, I see a dark pink mass rolling in his mouth" (*N* 116). For Sartre's existential quest-hero seeking a way out of contingent existence the eyes are no longer the window to the soul. Nor is the tongue a path to aesthetic existence. Rather, as his bodily "white goo"—saliva as an analogue for semen (another appetitive discharge)—intrudes upon the act of aesthetic perception, the one sure route left to freedom, it sickens the subject of taste.

In *Nausea* the organ of taste itself is slimy. When Ricks cites Sartre as the final word on Keatsian taste, he quotes Sartre's extended meditation upon *le visqueux*—both slime and the slimy—in *Being and Nothingness*. For Sartre the slimy resists standard categorizations of solidity and liquidity in a disgusting physical condition between the two: "Slime is the agony of water. It presents itself as a phenomenon in the process of becoming; it does not have the permanence within change that water has but on the contrary represents an accomplished break in a change of state. This fixed instability in the slimy discourages possession."[20] The slimy presents an existence that cannot be perceived as object. It will not circulate through the restricted economy of aesthetic perception, to be converted into expression, and the inevitable result is nausea. As a mucous substance that collects in the mouth, *le visqueux* enters the metaphorical world of *Nausea* where disgusted by his own slimy tongue, Roquentin struggles to maintain the consistency necessary to exist as a subject in a world of things. When he finds himself devolving into a gelatinous pool of fat, he struggles to pull himself together, to feel his "body harden and the nausea vanish."[21] Yet as the act of aesthetic perception yields to the aftertaste of existence, the existential man is blocked from tasting his way into a higher ideal of selfhood.

Roquentin's name relates him to the stone (French *roc*) and just as *le visqueux* coats his organ of taste, it coats the untasteable stone. According to the *Oxford English Dictionary*, the original meaning of slime is "Alluvial ooze; viscous matter deposited on stones, etc." Stones are thought of as smooth and round, but Roquentin focuses on its slimy underside: "I saw something which disgusted me, but I no longer know whether it was the sea or the stone. The stone was flat and dry, especially on one side, damp and muddy on the other. I held it by the edges with my fingers wide apart so as not to get them dirty" (*N* 2). This metaphysically disturbing underside of the stone is damp and muddy (*humide et boueux*) or, in a vocabulary more significant for Sartre, slimy.[22] Roquentin holds it gingerly in order to avoid contact with its repulsive coating.

His paramount fear is of "being sucked into the body of the slimy substance," and despite his best efforts to avoid contagion, the slimy stone (*roc*) sticks to Sartre's existential man. Sartre writes in *Being and Nothingness*: "I cannot *slide* on the slime, all its suction cups hold me back; it can not slide over me, it clings to me like a leech" (*Being and Nothingness* 776). Roquentin finds it impossible to let go of the slimy stone throughout the novel. As he reflects upon his experience, what stands out is his inability to throw, or otherwise detach the stone from himself: "I was going to throw that pebble, I looked at it and then it all began: I felt that it existed. Then after that there were other Nauseas; from time to time objects start existing in your hand."[23] Sartre's latter-day Man of Taste becomes acutely aware of the stone's mucous touch in a novel founded on an oral schema whereby everything passes through the mouth and all perception is metaphorized as consumption.

After his initial, nauseating contact with the stone, Roquentin's orifices of aesthetic perception become blocked. Everywhere he looks, existence rises up to choke him: "I'm suffocating: existence penetrates me everywhere, through the eyes, the nose, the mouth" (*N* 126). In a clean cycle of consumption whereby the subject tastes and expresses, nausea inevitably occurs when an external object refuses to pass smoothly from substance into expression, obtruding itself. Such objects, stubbornly resisting being broken down and assimilated into a subjective system of meaning, get stuck and disrupt the circular economy of taste. In *Nausea* the encounter with the stone recurs in the form of other stuck taste-objects. The climax occurs when Sartre's existential man finds himself gagging on the sight of an immense black chestnut-tree root: "the black stump did not move, it stayed there, in my eyes, as a lump of food sticks in the windpipe. I could neither accept nor refuse it" (*N* 131). The root gets stuck in his "eyes," just as food gets stuck in the windpipe, causing one to gag or spit it out it. Dominick LaCapra refers to this scene as "one of the more lapidary philosophical interludes in the text," punningly associating it with the opening scene.[24] Roquentin's experience with the root registers on a grand scale the existential sickness prompted by the stone. His nausea is a phenomenological reminder of his own existence—his saliva, a physiological barrier between himself and aesthetically consumable reality.

III

Like Keats's nauseated epic hero and Sartre's protagonist, Molloy experiences an existential sickness hinging on an anxious relation to taste. Early critical responses to the novel intuited that his bodily activities entailed powerful metaphysical statements. Maurice Blanchot argues that Molloy brings about the death of the author through a brutal self-deconstruction, while Bataille extends this eschatological vision to encompass the end of subjectivity itself. Molloy is misunderstood if his appetites and aversions are read as merely contingent, mired in the body, stripped of philosophical import. Beckett's use of the term "taste" suggests that Molloy's pleasures and perversions (experienced via *his* ample palate) remain accountable to the civilizing project of taste.[25] At the point that he would declare his independence from taste ("I had neither taste nor humour, I lost them early on"), his narrative perspective pulls back, in a rare moment abandoning the first person, to portray himself not as tasteless, or free from the imperative to exercise taste, but as an inside-out version of the chameleon poet: "Chameleon in spite of himself, there you have Molloy, viewed from a certain angle" (*M* 39). As descended from Keats's idealized creature of taste, Beckett's "Chameleon in spite of himself" would also live in gusto. Yet Molloy is not capable of feeding on the ethereal food of beauty and turning all substance into expression. He is obsessed not with the "relish of the dark side of things" but the dark side of relish—the physiological realities of ingestion, digestion, and excretion, and his gusto is ultimately in the service of disgust.

Should a relation between these two seemingly antithetical chameleons, Keats's ethereal poet and Beckett's rudely appetitive, even scatological, antihero seem hard to swallow, one need only recall the climactic line from *Molloy*, "life is a thing of beauty . . . and a joy for ever" (*M* 226). This line, derived from Keats, occurs at the point in the novel when Molloy's alterego, Moran, finally learns the nonsensical reason for his nonsensical quest.[26] In reaction to his stunned disbelief, the line is again repeated: "A joy for ever, he said, a thing of beauty, Moran, and a joy for ever" (*M* 226). Keats himself set the terms for the reception of this maxim in his preface to *Endymion* where he offered up the poem as more cloying than tasteful, productive of disgust rather than pleasure. As a result, the poem whose opening line is "A thing of beauty is a joy for ever" became associated with what Keats had called that "mawkishness, and all the thousand bitters" that readers "must necessarily taste" in going over the romance. For nineteenth-century readers, the poem came to represent, as Keats's friend John Woodhouse put it, "that sugar & butter sentiment, that cloys & disgusts" (*Letters* 2.161). Moran is unable to swallow Keats's line on beauty, which in addition to being ridiculously out of place, is freighted with the same nauseous associations as its Romantic prototype.

Beauty and its aesthetic pleasures fail both Molloy and Moran while they continue to hold themselves accountable to the paradigm of tasteful subjectivity. At the beginning Molloy defensively remarks,

> if I have always behaved like a pig, the fault lies not with me but with my superiors, who corrected me only on points of detail instead of showing me the essence of the system, after the manner of the great English schools, and the guiding principles of good manners, and how to proceed, without going wrong, from the former to the latter, and how to trace back to its ultimate source a given comportment. (*M* 32)

Molloy recognizes that he is a product of a cultural system whose principles elude him (as they in fact eluded all the philosophers of taste). Yet, unlike Enlightenment taste theorists who recognized the difficulty of establishing rules for what was supposed to be an inherent faculty, while proceeding to pin down its slippery principles nonetheless, Molloy responds to the inaccessibility of the system by turning his back upon it. He disclaims all responsibility to the ideal of tasteful selfhood, plunging headlong into the antithetical realm of the appetitive. His bold and randomly directed desires, whether physical or psychological, are such that he claims to "swallow everything, greedily" (*M* 15). Yet his excessive appetite is overdetermined by the modernist nature of the text, and his desire constitutes more than a merely physical desire directed at food. Molloy postdates the extended worrying over human identity that generated the various paradigms of sensibility, sentiment, and taste deployed throughout the eighteenth century: his appetites are necessarily directed *against* all his efforts to taste.

Not only is Molloy separated from the Century of Taste by Romanticism, but he is further removed from the early modern vision of the human being as a creature driven by appetite. Hobbes's materialist vision of appetitive man had helped to motivate the Enlightenment culture of taste and its favorite fiction of selfhood, the Man of Taste. For Hobbes, human beings are organized around the stomach not the mouth (the site of both taste and expression); they are spurred by a drive that "when it is toward something which causes it, is called APPETITE, or DESIRE; the later, being the generall name; and the other, often-times restrayned to signifie the Desire of Food, namely *Hunger* and *Thirst*. And when the Endeavour is fromward something, it is generally called AVERSION."[27] This pre-Enlightenment creature of "APPETITE" and "AVERSION" does not confront the same cultural and metaphysical anxieties of the palate that Beckett inherited from Romanticism. As a result, when Molloy describes his eating habits, they are revealed as contradictory. They confound the distinctions between taste and appetite, aesthetic pleasure and bodily enjoyment, which grew out of the discourse of taste.

Molloy eats little and casually, as if guided more by distinction than appetite; yet he describes this toothless eating (a version of sucking) as uncontrolled:

> I ate like a thrush. But the little I did eat I devoured with a voracity usually attributed to heavy eaters, and wrongly, for heavy eaters as a rule eat ponderously and with method, that follows from the very notion of heavy eating. Whereas I flung myself at the mess, gulped down the half or the quarter of it in two mouthfuls without chewing (with what would I have chewed?), then pushed it from me with loathing. (*M* 72)

Impossibly vacillating between two oppositional modes, hunger and aesthetic disinterestedness, Molloy at once gives in to his appetite and maintains the disinterestedness necessary to taste. As Kant makes plain, hunger disqualifies a person from taste: "Hunger is the best sauce; and people with a healthy appetite relish everything, so long as it is something they can eat. Such delight, consequently, gives no indication of taste having anything to say to the choice. Only when men have got all they want can we tell who among the crowd has taste or not" (*Critique of Judgement* 49–50). Since Molloy is perpetually hungry, he maintains an uneasy relationship to his own self-identification as connoisseur. His paradoxical displays of appetite always entail a touch of indifference. According to the same logic Malone, who is likewise toothless and who has also struggled all his life against the menace of starvation, exercises a decided indifference (or discrimination, the distinction again unclear) toward the institutional soup he is offered: "I eat it one time out of two, out of three, on an average. When my chamber-pot is full I put it on the table, beside the dish."[28] The chamber pot beside the dish suggests the general-economic confusion in which Beckett's modernist aesthetic implicates taste, a coprophagic scenario replacing the connoisseur's taste-test.

Yet like Sartre's existential quest-hero, randomly seeking a way out of a nauseous existence, Beckett's vagabond protagonist is compelled to imagine himself as something *more* than a creature of appetite. His desire not to eat in part can be seen as a frantic reaction to the hunger that disqualifies him from taste. Shortly after his bravado display of culinary disinterestedness, Molloy describes himself "bent double over a heap of muck, in the hope of finding something to disgust me for ever with eating" (*M* 77). In this light, any description of Beckett's protagonist as Rabelaisian is insufficient. Rabelais's giant who "shat, pissed, vomited, belched, farted, yawned, spat, coughed, sighed, sneezed, and blew his nose abundantly" experiences a far greater freedom than Beckett's antihero from the cultural constraints of taste.[29] The former has been described by Mikhail Bakhtin as a porous creature whose orifices, clotted with waste, represent unregulated exchange between self and world. If this exchange can be considered triumphant, as Bakhtin argues, productive both of sociality and commensality, it is because it occurs prior to the Enlightenment's lasting distinction between bodily enjoyment and aesthetic pleasure.[30] Insofar as the physiological pleasures described by Rabelais had not yet been conscripted into the sociopolitical project of taste, in other words, they cannot be compared to Molloy's. Molloy himself is aware of this distinction, and his displays of greedy gorging, absurdly mixed up with his finicky preferences, suggest the dialectic relation to taste in which his appetites are always involved.

Despite a driving appetite, Molloy cultivates a refined palate through his habit of sucking stones. Much like Sartre's indigestible stone, these "sucking-stones" are absurdist taste-objects that bring the tension between taste and appetite into relief. Molloy acknowledges that his habit of sucking stones is a defense against driving hunger: "I thought of the food I had refused. I took a pebble from my pocket and sucked it. It was smooth, from having been sucked so long, by me, and beaten by the storm. A little pebble in your mouth, round and smooth, appeases, soothes, makes you forget your hunger, forget your thirst" (33). These stones first introduced as pebbles (*caillou*), and later renamed "sucking-stones" (*pierres a sucer*), divert Molloy from a hunger that would disqualify him from taste. Stones would seem a poor substitute for food, yet Molloy is extremely picky about them, preferring to suck nothing than an unsatisfactory stone. When he loses his original sucking-stone, he refuses to allow a servant to fetch him another from the garden: "I deemed it wiser to say nothing about it, all the more so as he would have been capable, after an hour's argument, of going and fetching me from the garden a completely unsuckable stone" (59–60). Molloy is a connoisseur of stones, and to be a connoisseur one must maintain a disinterested attitude. Even though he does achieve or perform (one never knows quite which) the disinterestedness necessary to exercise taste, Molloy boasts of his lack of distinction: "And now I come to think of it, my attempts at taste were scarcely more fortunate, I smelt and tasted without knowing exactly what, nor whether it was good, nor whether it was bad, and seldom twice running the same thing" (67). Where there is no taste, there is only taste for Molloy, who not only fails to distinguish between tastes and smells that do exist, but who makes fine distinctions among stones that he admits have no taste.

Shortly after his haughty dismissal of the unsuckable stone, Molloy embarks on an extended meditation on his sucking-stones. This episode, in part a critique of an Enlightenment faith in ratiocination, establishes the sucking-stones as a specific conundrum of taste. The question that preoccupies him is how to suck sixteen stones, which he carries in his pockets, in such a way as never to suck the same stone twice in a row. Any possibility that he might suck his stones out of order threatens to destroy all aesthetic delight. He proceeds to devise a complicated system of circulating the stones throughout his four pockets, which as one of Beckett's permutation games serves as an allegory for the restricted circulation of taste. He decides, "as I sucked a given stone, to move on the fifteen others, each to the next pocket, a delicate business admittedly, but within my power, and to call always on the same pocket when I felt like a suck. This would have freed me from all anxiety" (99). The "anxiety" Molloy speaks of here is the *Angst* of a connoisseur devoted to a pleasure that theoretically does not exist. From his perspective, taste winds up in a place its own principles would never allow: the scene of a hunger that is no hunger, the paradoxical pleasure of sucking tasteless stones.

A radical contingency governs Molloy's most exacting discrimination, and at the height of the crisis he is forced to admit: "deep down it was all the same to me whether I sucked a different stone each time or always the same stone, until the end of time. For they all tasted exactly the same" (100). Just as he had formerly abandoned the "guiding principles of good manners," Molloy concludes his experiment of taste with sudden indifference: "And the solution to which I rallied in the end was to throw away all the stones but one, which I kept now in one pocket, now in another, and which of course I soon lost, or threw away, or gave away, or swallowed" (100). The only solution to the futile attempt to taste is, in the end, to break the habit, to swallow. Consuming that which he prefers only to process according to the restricted economy of taste, Molloy sucks taste back into the body, returning this iconic existentialist taste-object back to the unconscious realm of enjoyment.

Eventually, the wider economy in which Molloy's sucking involves him turns the mouth, as portal to aesthetic subjectivity, into the other physiological end of the digestive tract. Whereas aesthetic taste (in Derrida's words) "prohibits the substitution of any non-oral *analogue*," such substitution is precisely what *Molloy*'s absurdist, inside-out mode of consumption manages to do.[31] When Moran sees a face that "vaguely resembled" his own, he focuses on the "thin red mouth that looked as if it was raw from trying to shit its tongue" (206). Such physiognomy stands as an embodied critique of the all-consuming idealist subject, which gives priority to the mouth in the role of philosophical becoming. Novalis sums up this oral, self-constituting model of selfhood when he writes, "If an organ serves another then it is, as it were, its tongue—its throat, its mouth. The instrument that serves spirit most willingly and is most readily capable of manifold modifications, is above all its linguistic instrument."[32] Against this idealist model, Molloy drags the organ of taste through the dark channels of the digestive tract and out the other end, turning the aesthetic subject of taste upside-down and inside-out. Simultaneously, he invests the one orifice that traditionally has nothing to do with taste with a subjective (and subject-making) capacity: "We underestimate this little hole, it seems to me, we call it the arse-hole and affect to despise it. But is it not rather the true portal of our being and the celebrated mouth no more than the kitchen-door" (107). Demoting the "celebrated mouth" to a kitchen door (an escape route, as well as means of ingress, for servants, raw meat, trash, and other distasteful elements), Molloy refigures the "arse-hole" as "the true portal of our being." He finds it no paradox to speak—both literally and metaphorically—of his "First taste of the shit" (20). And rather than expressing himself into spirit, Beckett's "Chameleon in spite of himself" speaks of excreting (or "shitting out") his organ of speech. His perverse physiognomy seems adapted to the absurdist subject who no longer "lives in gusto," but inhabits a world of disgust.

Like their Romantic prototype in *The Fall of Hyperion*, Molloy and Moran are both sickened, rapidly decomposing creatures involved in senseless quests. Moran's description of his counterpart Molloy could apply equally well to the Keatsian poet: "He hastened incessantly on, as if in despair, towards extremely close objectives" (154). Yet whereas in Keats's poem the speaker wastes away after several frustrated efforts to taste, Moran finds himself "succumbing to other affections, that is not the word, intestinal for the most part," and vows: "I would get there on all fours shitting out my entrails and chanting maledictions" (228). As he gropes his way forward in despair, he ends up trailing not clouds of glory but entrails, and the rest of his physical interiority. We increasingly become privy to the details of his digestive problems as his exterior becomes caked with his own physiological excess, his breeches having "rotted, from constant contact with my incontinences" (234). And whereas Keats's speaker is propelled forward in order not to starve or have his flesh "parch for lack of nutriment" (*Fall* I.110), both Molloy and Moran treat their hunger with indifference. Moran recognizes his hunger to result from an inability to digest: "For several days I had eaten nothing. I could probably have found blackberries and mushrooms, but I had no wish for them . . . And though suffering a little from wind and cramps in the stomach I felt extraordinarily content, content with myself, almost elated, enchanted with my performance" (223). Moran is rotting, falling apart like the chameleon-poet of *The Fall of Hyperion*, but he remakes himself according to a general-economic schema that (to borrow Raphael's pun from *Paradise Lost*) turns all nourishment to wind. His performance is a perverse form of expression on the part of his absurd, reformulated *Os*.

In reimagining the idealist subject of taste, a creature capable of turning everything into ideality or expression rather than excretion, Beckett goes further than Sartre in transforming taste as a modernist aesthetic. Sartre reorients the subject in a world of nausea, but he is deeply invested in idealism and has often been accused of returning to the same idealism his novel had seemed to oppose. At the end of *Nausea*, his existentialist man seeks "to drive existence out of [himself], to rid the passing moments of their fat, to twist them, dry them, purify myself, harden myself, to give back at last the sharp, precise sound of a saxophone note" (*N* 175). His existentialist quest (really nothing more than a senseless wandering around the provincial French town of Bouville) ends on the distinct possibility of finding a way out of the contingent existence that was choking him through all his orifices of aesthetic perception. Allan Stoekl speaks for those who find themselves dissatisfied with the conclusion when he claims, "Roquentin, then, may be not only a jerk, but the final savior of neo-Kantianism" (14). For many readers, Roquentin's status as existential man is compromised by this final urge to raise himself out of his own existence into a higher subjectivity. At the height of his nausea, he declares, "If you existed, you had to exist all the way, as far as mouldiness, bloatedness, obscenity were concerned" (*N* 128). But whereas Roquentin finally turns back from the obscenity of full-blown existence, Molloy goes all the way, winding up in the ditch of his own excreted materiality.

In the end, Beckett's eponymous quest-hero attains an identity as the expelled. From the beginning of his senseless wanderings, he had been preoccupied with his mother, or "her who brought me into the world, through the hole in her arse if my memory is correct" (20). We are never told where he set out from, and he himself does not know where he is going, but if he has any goal at all it is to find his way back to this ur-site, the maternal arse-hole. Similarly, the first-person narrator of *The Unnameable*, presumably a deteriorated version of Molloy, delights in imagining himself as an excrementum: "I like to fancy, even if it is not true, that it was in mother's entrails I spent the last days of my long voyage, and set out on the next" (50). Like the narrator of Beckett's "The Expelled," Molloy is a scatological creature self-identified through the "other" end of the digestive tract. Both are products of creation-via-purgation, and like Molloy after his formative expulsion, the title character of "The Expelled" claims to have "dragged on with burning and stinking between my little thighs, or sticking to my bottom, the result of my incontinence."[33] Rather than seeking his way back through the usual channels to the proverbial womb, he directs himself toward the site of his original expulsion. The "Expelled" refers to this expulsion as a "fall," drawing upon the esoteric notion of creation as a fall into materiality. I would submit that Molloy's expulsion from his mother can also be understood as a metaphysical fall into matter. Just as the Expelled winds up in the gutter (a place of refuse, drainage, and waste), Molloy winds up in a ditch. Malone perhaps puts it best of all when he says: "In any case here I am back in the shit" (98).

One strain of Beckett criticism locates him in a tradition of Irish satire extending back to Jonathan Swift, and the ditch at the end of *Molloy* bears too close a resemblance to the metaphysical ditch at the end of Swift's *A Discourse Concerning the Mechanical Operation of the Spirit* to go unremarked in conclusion here. Swift's scatological satire was directed against the developing Enlightenment culture of taste, and the volume that contained it also contained *A Tale of a Tub*. In the preface to both Swift explicitly distances himself from Anthony Ashley Cooper, third earl of Shaftesbury, the prototype for the eighteenth-century Man of Taste.[34] The premise of his intentionally distasteful *Discourse* is that all subjective pretensions to spirit can be reduced to the mechanical operations of the body, whose various expressions and emissions have a material basis. In the final paragraph, Swift's narrator remarks: "Too intense a contemplation is not the business of flesh and blood; it must by the necessary course of things, in a little time let go its hold and *fall into matter* . . . a perfect moral to the story of that philosopher who, while his thoughts and eyes were fixed upon the *constellations*, found himself seduced by his *lower parts* into a *ditch*" (141; initial emphasis mine). When Molloy falls into a ditch, he falls metaphorically out of the world of spirit (for the sucking Molloy, aesthetic subjectivity) and into an excremental place where the "*lower parts*" find relief. As he relates: "The forest ended in a ditch, I don't know why, and it was in this ditch that I became aware of what had happened to me. I suppose it was the fall into the ditch that opened my eyes, for why would they have opened otherwise?" (122–3). Molloy is Beckett's remade creature of taste, and his fall is also out of himself into his own excreted materiality, or the absurdity of general-economic existence. The orifice that orients this space is no longer the Kantian *Os*, but what Derrida would call its unthinkable analogue. Ironically, it is Molloy's self-expression through this *Os*—an absurdist inversion of the ideally sucking mouth—that opens his eyes.

Notes

1. "I had neither taste nor humour, I lost them early on." Samuel Beckett, *Molloy*, tr. Patrick Bowles in collaboration with the author (New York: Grove Weidenfeld, 1955), 39; hereafter *M*. Beckett's translation of *Molloy* (1951), begun in collaboration and completed on his own, will here be treated as an original.
2. John Keats, *Hyperion*, II.25, in *Complete Poems*, ed. Jack Stillinger (Cambridge, MA: Harvard UP, 1978); all references to Keats's poetry are to this edition.
3. Walter Jackson Bate, *John Keats* (Cambridge: Harvard UP, 1963), 591.
4. I borrow the phrase from George Dickie, *The Century of Taste: The Philosophical Odyssey of Taste in the Eighteenth Century* (New York: Oxford UP, 1996).
5. Christopher Ricks, *Keats and Embarrassment* (Oxford: Clarendon P, 1974), 139.
6. *The Letters of John Keats*, ed. Hyder Edward Rollins, 2 vols. (Cambridge: Harvard UP, 1958), 1.387.
7. William Hazlitt, "On Gusto," in *The Complete Works of William Hazlitt*, ed. P. P. Howe, 21 vols. (London: J. M. Dent, 1930), 4.78.
8. Quoted in Beth Lau, *Keats's Paradise Lost* (Gainseville, UP of Florida, 1998), 142.
9. John Keats, *Manuscript Poems in the British Library: Facsimiles of the Hyperion Holograph and George Keats's Notebook of Holographs and Transcripts*, ed. Jack Stillinger (New York: Garland Publishing, 1988), 13.
10. Jonathan Bate, "Keats's Two *Hyperions* and the Problem of Milton," *Romantic Revisions*, ed. Robert and Keith Hanley (Cambridge: Cambridge UP, 1992), 321–38 (328).
11. I offer a fuller account of this episode in "Keats's Nausea," *Studies in Romanticism*, 40 (Winter 2001), 481–510.
12. Immanuel Kant, *Anthropology from a Pragmatic Point of View*, tr. Victor Lyle Dowdell (Carbondale: Southern Illinois UP, 1978), 45.

13. Immanuel Kant, *The Critique of Judgement*, tr. James Creed Meredith (Oxford: Clarendon Press, 1952), 196.

14. All these readings take their cue from Keats, who stood his guard against Milton (*Letters* 2.167, 212).

15. Hyder Edward Rollins, ed., *The Keats Circle*, 2nd ed., 2 vols. (Cambridge: Harvard UP, 1965), 1.172.

16. Quoted in Allan Stoekl, "The Performance of *Nausea*," *Yale Journal of Criticism*, 1.2 (Spring 1988), 1–22 (7).

17. Jacques Derrida, "Economimesis," tr. R. Klein, *Diacritics*, 11.2 (1981), 3–25, developed further in *The Truth in Painting*, tr. Geoff Bennington and Ian McLeod (Chicago: U of Chicago P, 1987).

18. Georg Wilhelm Friedrich Hegel, *Philosophy of Nature; Being Part Two of the Encyclopaedia of the Philosophical Sciences* (1830), tr. A. V. Miller (Oxford: Clarendon P, 1970), 2.372.

19. Werner Hamacher, *Pleroma: Reading in Hegel*, tr. Nicholas Walker and Simon Jarvis (Stanford: Stanford UP, 1998), 241; Tilottama Rajan shows how metaphors of digestion are used in Hegel's system in her essay (chapter 11) in this volume.

20. Jean-Paul Sartre, *Being and Nothingness: A Phenomenological Essay on Ontology*, tr. Hazel E. Barnes (New York: Washington Square P, 1973), 774.

21. Jean-Paul Sartre, *Nausea*, tr. Lloyd Alexander (New York: New Directions, 1964), 22; hereafter cited as *N*.

22. Cf. Sartre, *La nausée* (Paris: Gallimard, 1938), 10.

23. *N* 123. Cf. Sartre, *La nausée* 174.

24. Dominick LaCapra, *Rethinking Intellectual History: Texts, Contexts, Language* (Ithaca: Cornell UP, 1983), 207.

25. The term "taste" occurs nine times in Beckett's trilogy, each time as an instance of what the eighteenth century called "mental taste." Michèle Aina Barale and Rubin Rabinovitz, *A KWIC Concordance to Samuel Beckett's Trilogy: Molloy, Malone Dies, and The Unnameable*, 2 vols. (New York: Garland, 1988), 2.919.

26. I do not wish to oversimplify the relation between Molloy and Moran, but some shorthand is necessary here and the term "alter-ego" seems justified within the series *Molloy, Malone Dies*, and *The Unnameable*. The "me" behind all three novels manifests itself narratologically in a series of characters whose names start with "M." The voice of *The Unnameable* remarks: "All those Murphys, Molloys, and Malones do not fool me. They have made me waste my time, suffer for nothing, speak of them when, in order to stop speaking, I should have spoken of me and of me alone." Samuel Beckett, *The Unnameable*, tr. Samuel Beckett (New York: Grove P, 1958), 21.

27. Thomas Hobbes, *Leviathan*, ed. Richard E. Flathman and David Johnston (New York: W. W. Norton, 1997), 31.

28. Samuel Beckett, *Malone Dies*, tr. Samuel Beckett (New York: Grove P, 1956), 7.

29. Francois Rabelais, *Gargantua and Pantagruel*, tr. Burton Raffel (New York: W. W. Norton, 1990), 50.

30. Bakhtin's optimistic reading of Rabelaisian orality has invited substantial critique: Leah Marcus, *The Politics of Mirth: Jonson, Herrick, Milton, Marvell and the Defense of the Old Holiday Pastimes* (Chicago: University of Chicago Press, 1986) and Peter Stallybrass and Allon White, *The Politics and Poetics of Transgression* (Ithaca, N.Y.: Cornell UP, 1986).

31. Derrida, "Economimesis" 25. Derrida argues that "the mouth may have analogues in the body at each of the orifices, higher or lower than itself, but is not simply exchangeable with them," since it organizes the system around itself (19).

32. David Farrell Krell, *Contagion: Sexuality, Disease, and Death in German Idealism and Romanticism* (Bloomington: Indiana UP, 1998), 38.

33. Samuel Beckett, *Stories and Texts for Nothing* (New York: Grove Weidenfeld, 1967), 14.

34. Jonathan Swift, *A Tale of a Tub and Other Works*, ed. Angus Ross and David Woolley (Oxford: Oxford UP, 1986), 3.

Chapter 10 ⁓

A "FRIENDSHIP OF TASTE": THE AESTHETICS OF EATING WELL IN KANT'S *ANTHROPOLOGY FROM A PRAGMATIC POINT OF VIEW*

Peter Melville

In his *Anthropology from a Pragmatic Point of View [Anthropologie in Pragmatischer Hinsicht]* (1798), Kant poses a curious question concerning the origin of the metaphor of taste: "How might it have happened that the modern languages particularly have chosen to name the aesthetic faculty of judgement with an expression (*gustus, sapor*) which merely refers to a certain sense-organ (the inside of the mouth), and that the discrimination as well as the choice of palatable things is determined by it?"[1] Despite its ancillary position, the question plays a significant role in establishing the conditions for one of the text's most elaborate and (for Kant) most pleasurable sketches of enlightened anthropological life, the cosmopolitan dinner party. In answer to the question why transcendental matters of taste linguistically resemble empirical or sensuous ones, Kant happily answers: "There is no situation in which sensibility and understanding, united in enjoyment, can be as long continued and as often repeated with satisfaction as a good meal in good company" (*AP* 145). For Kant, taste is a faculty of "social judgement" [*gesellschaftlichen Beurteilung*] manifesting itself most admirably in the ability of a host to make an "acceptable selection" of dishes for his guests (*AP* 143, 145). The last of Kant's works published in his lifetime, the *Anthropology* presumes that matters of taste are metaphorically tied to the tongue because the tasting of food, seasoned with a disciplinary mixture of table etiquette, provides the optimal conditions for that partly sensuous, partly ethical, partly aesthetic feeling of "civilized bliss" (*AP* 186). Promising pleasures that ground the faculty of aesthetic judgment, the dinner table confidently reclaims its position in the *Anthropology* as a privileged site for the *tasteful* advancement of sociality.

The *Anthropology*, however, is not the first of Kant's works to signal an interest in the social meal.[2] *Critique of Judgement* also draws on the dinner party as bridging the gap between the merely agreeable sense of physical taste and the subjective universality of aesthetic judgment. In the *Critique* Kant stresses that the dinner party is a considerably limited metaphor for the aesthetic: the rules or manners of the dinner table are only "*general* (as all empirical rules are), not *universal*, as are the rules that a judgement about the beautiful presupposes."[3] For the pragmatically minded Kant of the *Anthropology*, however, there is something powerfully attractive about the dinner party. His enthusiasm emerges in the exclamatory refrains garnishing his instructions for the "full dinner," where "the multitude of courses is only intended to keep the guests together for a long time" (*AP* 189). The charm of Kant's dinner party lies in its embodying the conflicted movement from the transcendental project of the third *Critique* toward the *Anthropology*'s more pragmatic and empirically "interested" account of "man."[4] Written for the "general public" (*AP* 6), the *Anthropology* presents its dinner party as a didactic parable for the cultivation of taste, palpably consumable for Kant's cosmopolitan readers.

The party is a moral tale containing a modified version of the anthropological imperative: if man must "make himself a rational animal" (*AP* 238), then he must also make himself something good to eat. He must learn to live with taste. In the *Anthropology*, eating is always a matter of form as well as substance. But for an activity that is literally a matter of life and death (not just for the individual, but for the whole community), form acquires a deeply serious and ethical significance. The aesthetics of eating are forever complicated by a constant negotiation between what is pleasurable and what is good. Kant's aesthetics of eating are thus irreversibly entangled with his *ethics* of eating. The tension inherent in this entanglement reproduces itself in an ultimately irresolvable conflict between the social eater and Kant's solitary feasting philosopher—the one who eats, drinks, and thinks alone. The struggle between these figures affects an odd but necessary process of consumption in which fellow interlocutors are served, as it were, as dishes for table companions; whereas certain dis-gusting others are vomited from the social mechanisms of the meal.

The *Anthropology* introduces its solitary eater before itemizing its detailed instructions for the social meal. A troubling guest that never leaves, this figure lingers, motivating the well-bred, presumably self-regulating guests of Kant's ideal gathering of friends:

> Eating alone (*solipsimus convictorii*) is unhealthy for a philosophizing man of learning; it does not restore his powers but exhausts him (especially when it becomes a solitary feasting); it turns into exhausting work, and not into a refreshing play of thoughts. The indulging person who wastes himself in self-consuming thought during the solitary meal gradually loses vivacity which, on the other hand, he would have gained if a table companion with alternative ideas had offered stimulation through new material which he had not been able to dig up himself. (*AP* 188–9)

What is especially distasteful about the solitary man of learning is the fact that he is a *wasteful* consumer, an insatiable eater without manners, recklessly devouring all things before him, including food, thought, and especially himself. If, as Leon R. Kass argues, the "experience of taste manifests an openness to the world, tinged with wonder and appreciation,"[5] then Kant's lonely philosopher demonstrates that this experience can also be spoiled by an utter lack of ethical responsibility to the self and the other, or even the self *as* other, as the ready-to-taste object of contemplative consumption. In this sketch the process of consumption is increasingly interiorized within the self; the metaphor is of disease. The solitary eater "wastes himself" [*sich selbst zehrt*], wasting away in "self-consuming thought" (*AP* 188). Drawing much needed energy from the stomach in order to think, the philosopher leaves himself vulnerable to a self-squandering disorder of the senses, which, as Kant says elsewhere, potentially leads one to the "madhouse" (*AP* 17). Similarly, *The Conflict of the Faculties* [*Der Streit Der Fakultäten*] (1798) is surprisingly clear on this point: an example of thinking at "Unsuitable Times," the practice of "occupying oneself with reading or reflecting when dining alone provokes pathological feelings."[6] It "brings on hypochondria," with which Kant was personally familiar (*CF* 199).[7] If hypochondria is the desire to observe oneself too closely (*AP* 17), then eating and thinking in isolation induce a similar pathology of self-fixated ingestion.

In the strangely elliptical and hypochondriacal logic of *solipsimus convictorii*, the solitary eater is absorbed by the very food he eats. His private victuals are seasoned by his own obsessive contemplation. Feasting on food and mind alike, this hermetic philosopher practices gluttony. Bloated and stuffed, he is thus dis-eased, the subject and the object of one and the same act of incorporation. As a figure of intemperance, the lonely man of learning turns out to be a kind of anti-*mensch*, a subject who does not know how to care for itself, who allows its own "seed of discord" (*AP* 238) to swell and give birth to itself. Opposed to the ideals of middle-class "sociability (that is, to living with taste)" (*AP* 154), this hungry hermit stands as a warning that to be properly self-managing, the self must not take up this task alone. Isolated from his fellows, the solitary eater abandons himself to self-consumption, losing his vivacity as his pathologically self-reflexive gaze becomes evermore fixed on his own failing health. The more he turns inward, the more he wishes to "play the spy" (*AP* 17) on his own thoughts and feelings, the sicker he gets. As a preventative measure, Kant issues an ultimatum: the self, if is to eat well, must "go on a *diet with regard to thinking*" (*CF* 199). It must learn to control the digestive process of its mind as it does the work of its intestines. In the words of Paul Youngquist, "dinner and company provide the substance of this diet, without which thinking might ravage the stomach."[8] If the self wishes to survive the undiscriminating predatorial instincts deep within its breast, it must remain socially responsive. "It is a duty to oneself as well as to others," says Kant, "not to *isolate* oneself (*sepataristam agere*) but to use one's moral perfections in social intercourse (*officium commercii, sociabilitas*)" (*MM* 588). The self must abandon its most primal and self-destructive urges, and embrace the stern strictures of ethical life.

As Kass rightly contends, however, "the good is not simply given" (*HS* 91). Even more to the point, Derrida asks: "since one must eat, and since it tastes good to eat, and since there's no other definition of the good, *how* for goodness' sake should one *eat well*?"[9] At the heart of Derrida's inquiry lies an uncertainty as to what eating means. Does one consume a plant, a painting, or another person? Everything that happens at the "edge of the orifices," he argues, demands that the metonymy of "eating well" be the rule—above all, that the self must know that it is never entirely on its own ("Eating" 282). The imperative to "eat well" is shared, not only through language but also through "*learning* and *giving* to eat, learning-to-give-to-the-other-to-eat" ("Eating" 282). The self is always already given to the other, though not because it gives itself intentionally. Rather, Derrida's "learning-to-give-to-the-other-to-eat" suggests a process and a knowledge in excess of any self or subject that could be said to learn much less to give. It is a knowledge and an apprehension of knowledge "older" than the subject, since the giving and the gift it evokes "happen" prior to and are the founding condition of a self that then gets troped as doing willful things like "giving" and "learning." As Derrida says, "one eats [the other] regardless and lets oneself be eaten by him" ("Eating" 282). To "eat well," therefore, is always to remain responsible to the others *with* and *on* whom one dines. With its conduct book rhetoric, the *Anthropology*'s dinner party aims to teach the bourgeois subject how to regulate or at least negotiate its necessary and constitutive engagement with its community through the medium of food. The solitary eater will in effect limn the social eater, haunting the dinner table as the absent guest who functions as a counter memory to Kant's idealization of sociability, inadvertently reminding his readers of a hard truth about the being-cosmopolitan of middle-class society.

As Kant understood only too well from his own experience, some food and drink (such as certain mushrooms, wild rosemary, acanthus, Peruvian chicha, South Sea Islander's ava, and opium) weaken one's vitality "as poisons," while others (fermented beverages, wine and beer, or brandy) "strengthen the powers of vitality" (*AP* 59). A certain discipline is required for eating well, which might enable the self to prefer, for example, a wine-party, normally "merry, boisterous, and teeming with wit," over the "beer-drinking bout" that frequently leads to "taciturn fantasies" and "impolite behavior" (*AP* 59). To avoid the dangers of intoxication and excessive eating, the self must choose wisely.

For Kant, the trick is to mediate one's meal through a screen of sociality. As Gulyga explains, company exerts a "beneficial influence," even upon the hypochondriac, whose "spirits and appetite improve by it."[10] To be an ethical eater one must have other table companions to whom one can respond and be responsible. The solitary eater "loses vivacity," lacking a "companion with alternative ideas" as food for thought. In his *Lectures on Ethics*, Kant speaks of a "friendship of taste" through which pleasure is derived from companions whose interests are different than one's own.[11] Oddly enough, this statement restricts one from eating with one's own colleagues. "I am not attracted to another," admits Kant, "because he has what I already possess, but because he can supply some want of mine by supplementing that in which I am lacking" (*LE* 205). Two scholars, to use Kant's example, are *not* to dine together. They will not form a friendship of taste because "their capacities are identical; they cannot entertain or satisfy one another, for what one knows, the other knows too" (*LE* 205). While thinking may be a "scholar's food" (*CF* 199), the thought of another scholar is not. Unable to stomach the other's presence, these scholars dining together resemble the self-consumption of the solitary eater. The scholar is a döppelganger of the self, injurious to mental health. This is a queer fear, perhaps a fear of the queer itself, of the same, or what is imagined to be the same. While Kant's ideal dinner party is properly homosocial in nature (and I will return to this), there are certain homophobic limits to this intimacy. Paying too much attention to the faculties of a companion too similar to oneself is simply in bad taste. The healthy consumer, who eats as well as he thinks, craves diversity with his meal. Heterosociality being perhaps distastefully broad and undiscriminating (not to mention unfamiliar for Kant, veteran bachelor that he was), the good meal in good company finds a more manageable sense of variety in a heterogeneous homosociality.

Kass reminds us of the etymology of "companion," which is composed of the Latin prefix *cum* (together) and *panis* (bread), hence, "Company . . . comes to accompany the bread" (*HS* 131). But if man comes together *with* or *through* bread, he also comes together *as* bread. Susan Shell remarks that Kant would refer to his friends as dishes, likening Moses Mendelssohn, for instance, to a rare and unexpected delicacy: "he honored me," Kant writes in a letter to Marcus Hertz, "by attending two of my lectures, taking potluck [*fortune du pot*], so to speak, since the table was not set for such a distinguished guest."[12] This sharing of the self for consumption is precisely what occurs during the meal that brings together "men of taste" in the *Anthropology*, who "are not only interested in having a meal together but also in enjoying one another" (*AP* 187). The main course of the good meal in good company is the company itself. The dinner party appears "only as a vehicle" for "social enjoyment," says Kant, and as such is essentially anthropophagic or *cannibalistic* in nature (*AP* 187).[13]

The question of eating well constantly returns to "determining the best, most respectful, most grateful, and also the most giving way of relating to the other, and of relating the other to the self" (Derrida, "Eating" 281–2). Eating well is a matter of regulating *how* one eats, of managing these practices of giving to and taking from the other, which even in "nonanthropophagic" cultures organize themselves and their codes of moral conduct around what Derrida calls "symbolic anthropophagy" ("Eating" 282). In the *Anthropology*, an economy of figural cannibalism underwrites the moral code, and specifically, duties concerned with the tasteful consumption of another's secrets:

> There can be no question that whatever is publicly said by an indiscreet table-companion at all dinner parties or even at an inn, to the detriment of someone absent, should not be used outside this company and should not be gossiped about. Even without any special arrangement any such gathering has a certain sanctity and duty of secrecy about it in consideration of what embarrassment fellow members of the dinner party might be caused afterward. Without such confidence the wholesome gratification of enjoying moral culture within society and of enjoying culture itself would be denied. (*AP* 187)

Although these words sound strange coming from the philosopher who would reveal the location of his guest to his likely assassin rather than tell a lie,[14] the pragmatic rule of the dinner party is to digest the other's secrets without regurgitating them. As Kant states elsewhere, to be human is to feel strongly the need to "*reveal*" oneself "candidly" to another.[15] However, great risks accompany this desire. Kant knows that others will "prudently keep back" and "conceal" their thoughts and judgments while taking advantage of the self's personal disclosures (*MM* 587). Warning his readers to exercise care in a mercantile world where the creed is eat or be eaten, he serves up a more palatable solution in which the self strikes a mutual confidence with the other. As courteous as he is cautious, the social eater presents his friends with the most precious gifts—his private self, his thoughts, his secrets.

Within the bounds of "moral friendship" (*MM* 586) the self is at ease with its secrets, sharing them with the other who exchanges them for its own. Dining with friends is like eating with Arabs, says Kant, "with whom a stranger may feel safe as soon as he has been able to obtain a refreshment (a drink of water) in the Arab's tent" (*AP* 188). The analogy, however, inadvertently reveals the darker side of sharing one's food: the refusal to partake of the other, to refuse his hospitality, is the hostile gesture *par excellence*. Denying the other is refusing to give oneself to the other, to offend the other by signaling one's disgust and refusal to digest the other. Kant's social eaters, on the other hand, enter into a "bond of hospitality" (*AP* 188). Mutual ingestion sanctifies mutual respect and leaves a good taste in one's mouth. Reciprocally cannibalistic, one's moral friendships guarantee that one's secrets, including one's indiscretions and *faux pas*, will remain confidential. "Eating together at the same table," writes Kant, "is regarded as formal evidence of such a covenant of security" (*AP* 189). Anything a guest reveals about himself or his companion (be it in good taste or in bad) is the privileged food of the present company. There are no leftovers from Kant's dinner party, nothing to take home or to bring to another gathering of friends. Without this condition prohibiting the consumption of rumors beyond the table there can be no "open exchange" of ideas among men of taste (*AP* 188).

At the social dinner tasting is policed by a taste of a higher kind. The party becomes an aesthetic procession, a performance through which the individual's relation to and consumption of the other is regulated according to aesthetic norms of sociality and table etiquette. The individual learns to present itself tastefully to the other by practicing the protocols of "civilized" conduct. Kant rehearses two ideal descriptions of the aesthetic form of the meal. The first "full dinner" goes through "three stages of (1) narration, (2) reasoning, and (3) jesting" (*AP* 189). In each stage a necessary connection is drawn between the matter consumed and the matter discussed. In the first stage, for example, appetizers are accompanied by news of the day. After the "first appetite is satisfied" (*AP* 189), the main course is served alongside, and is "felt to be beneficial" to, a livelier discussion involving disputes (*AP* 189). Finally, the meal ends in the "mere play of wit" (*AP* 189). Kant elaborates most precisely on this last stage, but in doing so grounds the dinner's aesthetic alliance between the physical and the social in an anatomical correlation between the digestion of food and the laughter of the meal. "Such laughter," he claims, "if it is loud and good-natured, has ultimately been determined by nature to help the digestive process by moving the diaphragm and intestines, consequently contributing to the physical well-being" (*AP* 188). Is this what it means to eat well? To eat, drink, and be merry? Would malicious laughter stimulate the diaphragm in a way that would be harmful to good digestion?

In *The Conflict of the Faculties*, Kant pauses to consider what he calls the "*vermicular*" movement of the intestines: "If they are removed," he says, "still warm from an animal and cut into pieces, they crawl like worms, and one can not only feel but even hear them working" (*CF* 195–6).[16] This recollection endows the intestines with an alien subjectivity all their own, living a separate existence within the self, whose demand for sustenance exceeds or outlives man's own. Imagining himself with a belly full of worms that continue to move and work independently of his mind, Kant confirms his own hypochondriacal suspicion that digestion is a dangerous endeavor. If left unchecked, the vermicular organs threaten to consume the entire life of the organism. There are, however, several ways to master their hunger, such as eating only once a day (in the evening during middle age, or at midday in later years) and not "giving in" to attacks of thirst, which "are, for the most part, only habit" (*CF* 197). The most effective regimen, however, keeps the intestines at bay by bringing them into communion with sociality. For Kant, conversation, like laughter, helps to regulate the movements of the diaphragm. His anxiety over the rapport between eating and speaking is so acute that he appends to his first account of the good meal in good company a second more detailed description, particularly sensitive to the transitions and interruptions between the specific conversational topics and themes of the meal. Kant offers the following rules of decorum: for a "tastefully arranged dinner" that "animates the company" rather than exhausting them,

a) choose topics for conversation which interest everybody, and always give everyone a chance to add something appropriate; b) do not allow deadly silence to fall, but permit only momentary pauses in the conversation; c) do

not change the subject unnecessarily, nor jump from one subject to another
. . . An entertaining subject must nearly be exhausted before one can pass on
to another; and, when conversation stagnates, one must know how to suggest skillfully, as an experiment, another related topic for conversation. In
such a way one individual in the company can direct the conversation, unno-
ticed and unenvied. *d)* Do not tolerate the beginning or continuation of anything dogmatic, neither for yourself nor the companions in the group.
Rather, since this conversation ought not to be business but merely a pas-
time, avoid such seriousness by means of a jest deftly introduced. *e)* In a serious conflict, that cannot be avoided, control yourself and your emotions
carefully so that mutual respect and good faith always prevail. What counts
more is the *tone* (which must neither be ranting, nor arrogant), not the content of the conversation, so that none of the guests should go home from the
company at variance with another. (*AP* 190)

While Kant never liked to "talk shop" in his spare time, he never ceased to
speak at mealtime (*IK* 53). Fearful of long awkward pauses, he preferred to
keep his guests from pausing and inwardly redirecting their hunger for
ideas, and subsequently, consuming themselves in thought. His rules are so
riddled with anxiety, so rigorous and overdetermined in their desire to
keep communication flowing that they expose the precariousness and
fragility of his subject. Nothing specific or exclusionary that might leave
some guests bored, silent, and otherwise vulnerable to introspection; no
lengthy pauses; nothing abrupt or unexpected; nothing dogmatic; nothing
contentious. These are the five commandments designed to limit the
conversation and protect the subject from itself.

Hoping one day to write a *Critique of the Culinary Art*, Kant placed
several limits upon the social eater (*IK* 151). Owing to his concern for
pauses during the meal, he decrees that the company shall not break into
small groups; one should address not only one's neighbor but the entire
company, whose number "must not be fewer than that of the Graces, nor
more than that of the Muses" (*AP* 186). Should the company break into
smaller groups, the conversation might become exclusive, forcing some
into isolation. As the citation suggests, the fewer the number of interlocutors, the more one is likely to loose oneself in heated debate. For a tastefully
arranged dinner that animates the company a jovial tone is best.

What, however, does this privileging of the jest ultimately suggest about
solipsimus convictorii? Without laughter, without conversation, there is only
upset, the agonizing heartburn of an ill-consumed meal. If the self hungers
for friends through the medium of the good meal, then the solitary meal is
an odd feast indeed, a diseased spiral into nothingness and oblivion. Perhaps

this is why the solitary eater is abreacted from Kant's ideal dinner party. If, as Derrida argues, the Kantian scheme of taste "throws up" that which it can incorporate only in the form of a substitution of dis-gust,[17] the solitary eater of the *Anthropology* will be incorporated into the aesthetics of the party precisely by being vomited. He stands in as a regurgitated replacement for the indigestible remainder of a self that has an ethical obligation never to redirect its hunger inwardly. He names a vast array of unspeakable solitary practices, including those of a sexual kind. Midway through his *Lectures on Ethics*, Kant pauses to censure that other autoerotic form of self-incorporation, namely "onanism" (*LE* 170). The onanist exercises the sexual appetite in the "complete absence of any object of sexuality," and in doing so, says Kant, "degrades himself below the level of animals" (*LE* 170). "Contrary to the ends of humanity," this solitary self-predator is too disgusting even for words (*LE* 170).[18]

The solitary eater is also a displaced figure for the exclusion of women from the homosocial atmosphere of the meal. For Kant, the presence of "ladies" is regrettable, "limit[ing] the freedom of the conversation to what is polite" and preempting that "certain sanctity and duty of secrecy" that exists only among "men of taste" (*AP* 187n., 187). Is the woman, then, to eat alone—banished from the brotherhood of taste? Where will she go to eat in peace, to escape the "intentional, but not insulting attacks on her sex" committed by the men of the meal (*AP* 189)? And who is preparing and serving this meal, after all? Perhaps one reason for Kant's refusal of the female consumer can be discerned from his characterization in the *Metaphysics of Morals* of the generative act as being uncomfortably close to *literal* cannibalism (*MM* 495). The "absurd demand" of carnal desire is to gorge on human flesh in "unending gluttony."[19] Sexual exhaustion is "in principle" virtually indistinguishable from death, be it in the form of a fatal pregnancy or as the result of being eaten alive by "mouth and teeth" (*MM* 495). The only difference separating sexual consumption and masticatory ingestion is found "in the manner of enjoyment" (*MM* 495). One eats one's lover as readily as one chews a piece of cod (Kant's favorite dish). Female reproductive organs are, after all, just another set of "consumable thing[s] (*res fungibilis*)" (*MM* 495)—the woman herself a mere *dish* too tasty to be indiscriminately blended with the healthier cosmopolitan platters of the Kantian feast. This confusion between the feminine sex and food is sustained throughout the *Anthropology*, as Kant compares women to everything from ugly black fish (*AP* 150) to succulent ducks skinned, stuffed, and roasted to perfection (*AP* 168n.). While Kant finds a certain humor in the analogy—especially in the idea of that "very rare specimen," an "aunt" [*Tante*] mistaken for a "duck" [*Ente*] and cooked *à l' orange*—there is something sobering about a feminine presence that threatens the replenishing exchange between men of taste (*AP* 168n.). Copulatory desire is simply another form of gross self-consumption. Kant's doctrine of dining and camaraderie continues to operate within what Foucault and Derrida respectively call a "classical" or "androcentric" structure of friendship, a fraternal attachment that necessarily excludes the sexual relation for its asymmetrical and recklessly self-destructive penetration of the other.[20] The proper self, the masculine self, requires a reciprocal relation, lest it consume itself. The self needs the other to eat back, to be afflicted by a hunger as virile as its own. Kant's dinner party sets no place for a feminine self that foregoes eating in favor of being eaten.

The solitary eater is consummately dis-tasteful precisely because he is so attractive. He is a compelling counter-aesthetic figure haunting the homosocial companions of the dinner table. He scares them into talking to one another, spooking them into becoming the formally aesthetic, openly social eaters they ought to be. The forced and overdetermined relation that Kant strikes between the digestive process and the laughter of civilized communication, enables him to ensure that the presentation of the meal will remain both necessary and ethical. For the *Anthropology*, acts of incorporation are cooperative—both aesthetically managed and ethically motivated. One must always think of others, preserve them as food for thought at all times. Known as a recovering hypochondriac, Kant aims to teach what he doubtless tried to teach himself—to look away!—To stop abusing himself![21] The self must be taught to look elsewhere and otherwise. Always the gracious host, Kant distracts his table companions with a tasteful assortment of culinary and conversational treats. In a moment of reflection, he looks around at the feast he has prepared. He looks and laughs, knowing his guests will sleep well because they have eaten well. But how will Kant sleep at night? How will he sleep knowing the truth about the indigestible and irrepressible hunger of the solitary eater, which will always be vomited from the meal, will always return to haunt the social eater? "What do we know about the nightmares of Immanuel Kant?" Paul de Man once asked.[22] They must have been interesting indeed: Kant lying restless in his bed, clutching his aching belly, longing for the digestive laughter of a good meal in good company.

Notes

1. There are two English translations of *Anthropology from a Pragmatic Point of View [Anthropologie in Pragmatischer Hinsicht]* (1798). I have chosen to use the most

recent: Immanuel Kant, *Anthropology from a Pragmatic Point of View*, tr. Victor Lyle Dowdell (Carbondale and Edwardswille: Southern Illinois UP, 1978), 144. Hereafter *AP*. The question that I cite here occurs in a supplementary note following the *Anthropology*'s section "On the Feeling for the Beautiful" (141–6).

2. Kant's devotion to this metaphor of the social meal lasted well into his old age. Arsenij Gulyga explains that, in the final days of his life, Kant had himself brought to the table before his dinner guests even though he was unable to eat (*IK* 256). His guests would eat in silence, honoring the resilience of their accomplished host. As Thomas De Quincey notes, "It disturbed [Kant] to see his . . . dinner companions conversing together whilst he himself sat like a mute on the stage with no part to perform" (154).

3. Kant, *Critique of Judgement*, tr. Werner S. Pluhar (Indianapolis: Hacket Publishing Company, 1987), 56.

4. Late in his career, Kant became increasingly interested in the figure of man, believing that anthropology would prove to be the final resting place for all philosophical inquiry. In his lectures on *Logic*, he famously introduces the question "What is Man?" as a fourth, and ultimately comprehensive, question to the questions of the three *Critiques* (What can I know? What ought I do? What may I hope?). With the subsumption of these three questions into a fourth, Kant aimed to unify "metaphysics," "morality," and "religion" under one anthropological discourse (*Logic* 89). For a close commentary of Kant's institution of a "philosophical anthropology," see Martin Heidegger, *Kant and the Problem of Metaphysics*, tr. James S. Churchill (Bloomington: Indiana UP, 1962). See also Frederick P. Van de Pitte, *Kant as Philosophical Anthropologist* (Netherlands: Martinus Nijhoff, 1971); Peter Melville, "Kant's Dinner Party: *Anthropology* from a Foucauldian Point of View," *Mosaic*, 35.2 (June 2002), 93–109.

5. Kass, *The Hungry Soul: Eating and the Perfection of Our Nature* (Toronto: Maxwell MacMillian Canada, 1994), 90. Hereafter *HS*.

6. Kant, *The Conflict of the Faculties*, tr. Mary J. Gregor (New York: Abaris Books, Inc., 1979), 199. Hereafter *CF*.

7. See Susan Shell, *The Embodiment of Reason: Kant on Spirit, Generation, and Community* (Chicago: University of Chicago Press, 1996). See also Peter Melville, " 'Illuminism and Terrorism': Melancholia and Hypochondria Kant's *Anthropology from a Pragmatic Point of View*," *The Dalhousie Review*, 79.3 (Autumn 1999), 335–54.

8. Paul Youngquist, "De Quincey's Crazy Body" (*PMLA*, vol. 114, May 1999), 349.

9. Jacques Derrida, " 'Eating Well'; or the Calculation of the Subject," *Points . . . Interviews, 1974–1994*, ed. Werner Hamacher and David E. Wellbery, tr. Peter Conor and Avital Ronell (Stanford: Stanford UP, 1995), 282.

10. Gulyga, *Immanuel Kant: His Life and Thought*, tr. Marijan Despalatovi (Boston: Birkhäuser, 1987), 52. Hereafter *IK*.

11. Kant, *Lectures on Ethics*, tr. Louis Infield (New York: Harper & Row, 1963), 205. Hereafter *LE*.

12. Kant, *Correspondence*, tr. Arnulf Zweig (New York: Cambridge UP, 1999), 162.

13. For a discussion of Kant's interest in cannibalism as it relates to war and international relations, see Susan Shell, "Cannibals All: The Grave Wit of Kant's Perpetual Peace," *Violence, Identity, and Self-Determination*, ed. Hent de Vries and Samuel Weber (Stanford: Stanford UP, 1997), 150–61.

14. Kant, "On a Supposed Right to Lie From Altruistic Motives," *Critique of Practical Reason and Other Writings in Moral Philosophy*, tr. Lewis White Beck (New York: Garland, 1976), 348. Kant tells the following tale to test his imperative to tell the truth: "After you have honestly answered the murderer's question as to whether his intended victim is at home, it may be that he has slipped out so that he does not come in the way of the murderer, and thus the murder may not be committed. But if you had lied and said that he was not at home when he had already gone out without your knowing it, and if the murderer had then met him as he went away and murdered him, you might justly be accused as the cause of his death." Evidently, rather than lying to your friend's assassin, it would be better for one to invite him in and to serve him dinner. Might this be infinite hospitality?

15. Kant, *The Metaphysics of Morals*, tr. Mary Gregor (New York: Cambridge UP, 1996), 586. Hereafter *MM*.

16. We can only speculate on Kant's thoughts the first time he witnessed (or learned of) this gory scene, his attention no doubt drifting from the strange intestinal afterlife of a slaughtered carcass to the grumbling of his own gut and what had yet to be digested therein; but the timeliness of its recall confirms, with spectacular clarity, the furthest reaches of the philosopher's hypochondria.

17. Derrida, "Economimesis," *Diacritics*, vol. 11, no. 3 (1981), 25. Derrida maintains that what is vomited is not always the same as what is indigestible. Rather, he argues for "the possibility of a vicariousness of vomit" (25). What this means is that for every agitation, retch, or upheaval, there is always some deeper, unrepresentable disgust for which the vomit can only be a substitute. For example, we might say that what disgusts Kant is not simply the idea of a self-consuming solitary eater (although the idea certainly does upset the philosopher to some degree). Rather, the real repulsion lies in his inability to purge himself of this figure once and for all. And since one cannot throw up an inability to vomit, Kant must repeatedly disavow the solitary eater (in all its various shapes and forms) as he negotiates the demands of eating well.

18. The prudishness of these remarks is interesting indeed coming from one of the loudest champions of the Enlightenment, a man who would elsewhere famously inspire the self precisely to free itself from the dogma of blind irrationalism ("*Aufklärung*" 7). While Kant's motto may be to *know thyself*, examining oneself *too closely* is sheer folly. As the saying goes, it leaves one blind—blind to one's respect for oneself and to one's obligations to the other.

Again, clarity of mind and good health come with a certain distance that only the other can supply.

19. Bernard Edelman, *The House that Kant Built: A Moral Tale*, tr. Graeme Hunter (Toronto: University of Toronto Press, 1987), 16.

20. Foucault, "On the Genealogy of Ethics: An Overview of Work in Progress" (Interview), *Ethics: Subjectivity and Truth*, ed. Paul Rabinow, tr. Robert Hurley (New York: The New Press, 1997), 259. Derrida, *Politics of Friendship*, tr. George Collins (New York: Verso, 1997), 13.

21. For a close reading of Kant's strategy of "*negative attentiveness*" (which is to say, of *turning away*) see David Clark, "Kant's Aliens: The *Anthropology* and Its Others," *The New Centennial Review* 1.2 (Fall 2001): 201–89. I cannot resist citing Clark's most memorable witticism: "For Kant, something like Attention Surplus Disorder is the paradigmatic threat to mental health" (72).

22. Paul de Man, "Kant and Schiller," *Aesthetic Ideology*, ed. Andrzej Warminski (Minneapolis: University of Minnesota Press, 1996), 134.

Chapter 11 ✒

(IN)DIGESTIBLE MATERIAL: ILLNESS AND DIALECTIC IN HEGEL'S *THE PHILOSOPHY OF NATURE*

Tilottama Rajan

> The main point of view from which medicine must be considered is that it is an indigestible substance . . . the medicine . . . . force[s] the organism . . . to come out of its self-absorption and not merely to concentrate itself inwardly but to digest the external substance . . . the organism is thus drawn back again into the general activity of assimilation; a result which is obtained precisely by administering to the organism a substance much more indigestible than its disease, to overcome which the organism must pull itself together.
>
> —Hegel, *The Philosophy of Nature* 436–8[1]

Hegel is often seen as a thinker who assimilates, or more melodramatically, "digests" otherness, including the self's otherness to itself. His philosophies of art, religion, and other subjects exemplify this incorporation of the other into an encyclopedic dialectical system. The redescription of alien domains in the terms of Hegelian philosophy can be seen as cognitive imperialism.[2] Or this subsumption into a philosophical absolute of the process whereby spirit complicates itself may be located in the very structure of the dialectic as self-consciousness. Thus Gasché describes Hegelian self-reflection as the self-constitution of philosophy: even "the reflective mirroring process" is recuperated as an "alienating or metaphoric detour to itself."[3] Indeed Hegel himself parallels self-reflection and digestion. Noting that in chemical interactions each substance "loses its quality," whereas the animal always "preserves" itself by "sublat[ing]" the "object and the negative," Hegel describes reflection as digestion and digestion as the "organism's reflection into itself": its "uniting of itself with itself" (*PN* 395).

Hegel himself characterizes his philosophy as assimilation. At the beginning of the section on "Organics" in *The Philosophy of Nature* where assimilation plays a major role, he writes:

> The perpetual action of life is thus Absolute Idealism; it becomes an other which, however, is always sublated. If life were a realist, it would have respect for the outer world; but it always inhibits the reality of the other and transforms it into its own self. (274)

Hegel's use of digestion is itself an example of such Idealism. Digestion and nutrition are central for Hegel's contemporary Xavier Bichat, who makes them the defining aspect of life as "the totality of those functions which resist death."[4] But Hegel appropriates Bichat's materialism into a philosophy of Spirit that is not content with death. The use of the sublative mechanism of metaphor is crucial to this deployment of the natural sciences as food for philosophy, inasmuch as it spiritualizes biological into cognitive processes such as *Aufhebung* and self-reflection.

Yet *The Philosophy of Nature* does not move from the literal to the figural but the reverse. Whereas Coleridge in his similarly idealistic *Theory of Life* sets Bichat's materialism aside,[5] Hegel describes bodily processes in lurid detail, inflecting scientific description with a pathos that bespeaks his inability to digest nature. Through the impropriety of his anthropomorphisms, Hegel confesses that "the animal . . . is a lasting unrest in its self-relation" (394) and that digestive mastery is the supplement produced by an unhappy consciousness. The "refractory . . . detail" of nature (444) thus pushes Hegel back toward "realism." To be sure he means nature to be the self-revelation of spirit: "Spirit is presaged in Nature" (3), as Schelling also argues in *Philosophical Investigations Into the Nature of Human Freedom*. But nature is an "an alien existence in which Spirit does not find itself"; it is "the Idea in the form of otherness," as "the negative of itself" (3, 13). Self-revelation thus becomes a reflection of mind through body that results in a psychosomatics of Spirit.

Illness is the most troubling of these remainders, produced when Hegel extends Schelling's visionary physics in *Ideas for a Philosophy of Nature* from physical and chemical phenomena to "organics." Schelling's study of magnetism and electricity had allowed nature to be grasped synchronically as the dynamic manifestation of conflicting but balanced energies. But in shifting to the organism Hegel introduces the human as growth, history, and change, yet also as the finitude of life. Life contains, or perhaps is illness, and even when illness is worked through in fever, disease remains in the organism as "the inborn *germ of death*" (441). Hegel thinks illness dialectically so as to digest a dis-ease in the psyche and the body politic. He privileges "acute" over "chronic" illness and assigns a cathartic role to fever. But the transference he sets up between philosophy and nature proves dangerously reversible, as the dialectic confronts its own dis-ease with itself.

Hegel thinks illness through the privileged philosophical term of negativity. Since this valorization and romanticization of illness result in a phenomenology and not just a pathology, he also faces the question of whether negativity is a failure in the system of assimilation and cultural reproduction, rather than the motor of this system for which a better word is "negation." Negation is a form of predication that establishes one position by negating another through what we now see as the "violence" of language or "position": in negation, the subject "preserves itself" by "negat[ing] the specific quality of the other" (394). "Negativity," by contrast, is the "inner process" (357) by which all positions are unworked; it has the structure of what Sartre calls an "internal negation" that cannot be redirected outward so as to separate this from that, or self from other. Digestion is Hegel's figural attempt to contain negativity within negation.[6] But from Hegel onward, negativity has been the scene of a debate over whether non-positive experiences can be made the basis for a progression within the dialectic. Bataille critiques Hegel for thus economizing the negative. But through illness Hegel himself comes up against the very "unusable" negativity he is often accused of foreclosing.

I

Hegel first worked on his philosophy of nature in several incomplete attempts at a system from 1802 to 1806. In these "Jena System Drafts," Hegel followed the Romantic project also elaborated by Schelling of arriving at Spirit only after remembering, repeating, and working through Nature. While at Jena Hegel was a mere Privatdozent, and lacked the professional security he acquired when he took up a Chair at Berlin as a philosopher of (Objective) Spirit publicly represented by the *Encyclopedia*. Yet as if he himself must constitute the growth of his mind as return rather than *Aufhebung*, in Berlin Hegel cannot divest himself of the problems posed for philosophy by nature. Instead the relevant parts of the Jena drafts become the second part of *The Encyclopedia*, which omits chronic illness and death in the shorter 1817 version, only to bring them back in later versions that expand the discussion of nature to an entire volume. This second volume of a project that is ambitiously totalizing in its subsumption of one "sphere" as a mere "level" in another sphere, yet infinitely complicated by the doubling of levels as spheres and the sheer number of these divisions, brings back into the heart of Hegel's philosophy a crisis merely bracketed after his Romantic period. On the one hand, *The Philosophy of Nature* is itself an "encyclopedia" of the natural sciences ascending from matter to form, and from the inorganic sciences to those of life. It subsumes mechanics into physics, physics into organics, and the whole sphere of Nature into Spirit. Within this progression each science is a level within the larger sphere of Natural Science, which itself is only "one circle in the whole" (2). But on the other hand, each level is a sphere in its own right, made up of further levels that also insist on being understood on their own terms. Like the parts of the organism in illness, each part claims an autonomy that at times threatens to derail the very project of encyclopedic totalization.

Thus biology is a "level" within the natural sciences. But as a sphere in its own right, it is further divided into botany and physiology. Physiology contains the sphere of pathology, which cannot clearly be digested as a level of normal physiology. Hence at the precise point when Nature—as the crossing of extended and living matter—stands on the verge of Spirit, the lectures end with illness and the return to the organism's inorganic remainders. The *Encyclopedia*, as an organization of knowledge that tries to control the wanderings of philosophy into the proliferating subdisciplines of non-philosophy, thus proves to be a psychoanalysis of philosophy by its own interdisciplinarity. More specifically *The Philosophy of Nature*, far from exemplifying Hegel's omnivorous interdisciplinarity, exposes philosophy to the remainders that result from its attempt to reflect itself, and reflect on itself, through its disciplinary others.

The "metaphorics of orality" in the *Encyclopedia* have been traced by Werner Hamacher who, like Derrida in *Glas*, allies Hegel with the superego. For Hamacher the surreal extremity of the account of digestion is a "nausea of the organism" breaking open the repressive totalizing to which Hegel remains obscenely committed. Hamacher thus reduces the physiological details of this discussion to a "disgusting object, extruded by the logical organism."[7] My approach differs in seeing them as the scene of the logical organism's rethinking of its subjectivity. I therefore start with digestion as Hegel's traumatized metaphor for philosophy's self-reflection and trace its unworking through a subsequent cluster of figures.

These figures of excretion and illness produce a further reflection on Spirit's goals of productivity and reproduction at odds with digestive self-constitution.

The Philosophy of Nature is divided into three parts (Mechanics, Physics, and Organics), subdivided into three parts, which are subdivided into three further parts, the last of which is again divided. The tripartite logic that projects dialectic as *Aufhebung* thus spirals inward into infinite reflection and self-complication. Focusing on the third part of "Organics," on "The Animal Organism," I emphasize its culminating discussion of illness as a lens through which we can reread the account of digestion in the penultimate section. Hegel wants to see life as anthropogenesis: a "power" that "acquires its form by evolution and its mass by assimilation."[8] But even in the section on digestion there is a curious contiguity between digestion and infection: digestion functions as infection (395).[9] Conversely medicine is an infection that the organism digests to be cured. This proximity makes the section on illness an intensification and opening up of problems already present in the discussion of "assimilation" that earlier articulates self-consciousness as an egotism of Spirit.

Digestion is the means by which the ego takes in the negative or other, through the "conversion" of "externality" into a "self-like unity." Hegel thinks both life and self-consciousness through a schema borrowed from medicine and comprising three stages: sensibility, irritability, and reproduction. His schema reverses that of Schelling, who begins with reproduction and ends with sensibility. Reproduction, Hegel says, is the "infinite negativity of transforming what is outside me into myself, and myself into externality" (358). Given this emphasis on reproduction—sexual, racial, and cultural—digestion underwrites a process of self-reproduction through the incorporation of foreign matter into a self-like unity. Through digestion the negative is put to use, assimilated, and eliminated as other.

There are, however, profound strains in this section, disrupted by anthropomorphisms that describe bodily processes in terms of anger, power, and self-rejection (402, 405). Digestion is predicated on the elimination of the indigestible—a process that anticipates Kristeva's notion of abjection. Thus excretion is the organism's "repulsion of itself by which it makes itself external to itself . . . separating itself from itself" in disgust (402–3). To be sure excretion facilitates digestion, since Absolute Digestion would be constipation. Bichat similarly writes, "life results from two great orders of functions": "digestion, circulation [and] respiration," which "assimilat[e] to the animal those substances which nourish him," and excretion, "exhalation [and] secretions," which "carr[y] off the heterogeneous substances" (119).

In this sense digestion and excretion are linked processes that maintain subjectivity within an economy that separates inside from outside.

Yet Hegel also unsettles this economy when he says that excrement consists "mainly of digested matter, or what the organism itself has added to the ingested material" (405). If excretion is the importation of raw material and its export as a more refined, interiorized product—which Hegel implies in linking sex, art, and excrement as instances of "reproduction"—why must the organism "rid" itself of "what it has itself produced" (396)? But on the other hand, excretion seems a form of (in)digestion: "even in the healthiest animals," the excrement is not "homogeneous" but contains "undecomposed food," because the organism ingests more than it can assimilate (405). Thus excretion is a failure of digestion as much as a part of its enabling machinery. Though Hegel is reluctant to concede this, it is the symptom of an imbalance in the conversion of nature into spirit, and of the other into the self: an "unchanged surplus" resistant to dialectical totalization (405).

Excretion is a pushing of the inside outside, a collapse of "self-confidence" as Hegel curiously puts it in another anthropomorphism (405). But digestion too involves a "turning in" on oneself (403). For it is never clear whether the other is inside or outside. On the one hand, "the organism has its other, not within it, but outside it . . . it is not itself its non-organic nature" which confronts it as an "object" (321). On the other hand, "life has its other within itself," a sign of its superiority to the chemical body (275) but also of its vulnerability. In a continuation of this ambiguity over the location of otherness, what the subject digests is not just "the object" but itself. Higher organisms eat plants. But in Hegel's lurid figuration of nature as spirit and thus of mind as (human) nature or psyche, such organisms also consume themselves. The companions of Aeneas "in Blumauer's *Aeneid*" "consume their [own] stomachs." The very structure of the organism is a perpetual autodigestion in which "nothing . . . endures, but everything is reproduced" including "the bones." After "twenty years" the organism "no longer contains its former substance" because it "converts its own members into a non-organic nature . . . lives on itself and produces its own self" (377–8). Not surprisingly this masochistic *Bildung* risks slipping into illness: when the organism is cut off from the outer world, it no longer "has the power to assimilate its non-organic world but can only digest its own self." "This is the cause of emaciation in disease" (378).

II

In discussing digestion Hegel draws a clear line between disease and health, even if it is logically troubled by a contradictory patho-logic. But his discussion of illness explores rather than disciplines illness. Hegel's account can be placed in an arc that leads from work he knew by the Scottish physiologist John Brown—which can be read against the grain as Krell does, but is empirical and positivist—through its continuation by Claude Bernard and Auguste Comte, to the radical rethinking of the relations between the normal and the pathological by Michel Foucault's mentor Georges Canguilhem. Medicine, as Canguilhem points out, protects the normal from the pathological: either it opposes them, or it approximates them, but by making the pathological a merely quantitative variation on the normal.[10] Brown takes the second route in equating physiological and pathological phenomena, not to make disease a source of vitality—though this is a byproduct of his argument picked up by Schelling—but to see disease as normal, manageable.[11] Brown's radicality lies in seeing illness as produced by the same factors that produce life: diseases arise either from a deficiency or excess of "excitability." But the similarity of health and disease means that medicine must measure the deviation of excitement from the healthy standard in order to bring the body back to normality. Canguilhem, for his part, tries to avoid this technologization of illness by postulating a "continuity" that exposes the normal to the pathological, even as it respects the singularity of the latter (58). For Canguilhem disease is an altered way of being. Diabetes is not localizable as the sickness of a particular organ, but is a revolution in the structure of the organism that entails a whole new way of encountering the world. Illness, as a decentring of the entire structure by this organ, is a deprivation, an "evil," as Canguilhem says using the term as Schelling had used it in the *Freedom* essay. But it is also a "positive, innovative experience in the living being"—not as individual, but as Dasein (58, 88, 104, 186).

To be sure Hegel does not go as far as Canguilhem toward thinking disease within a philosophy of existence. He is closer to the Greek theory of medicine, that of Hippocrates and Galen, which he sees as at least avoiding the positivism of the later nineteenth century. Whereas the germ theory is an optimism that sees disease as external and curable by technology, the Greeks saw it as internal: a discordance in the organism that sought to "effect a new equilibrium in man." Moreover, humoural medicine, which, along with an interest in "constitutional" diseases, was still the dominant theory in Hegel's time, treats disease in the context of the whole organism, whereas the germ theory localizes it in a particular organ.[12] These two notions—that disease is internal and that it involves the whole organism—have significant consequences for Hegel. This is all the more true given that the part–whole logic that informs the theory of constitutional disease is also that which subtends the idea of the *Encyclopedia*.

The notion of constitution (both physiological and political) elaborated by Hegel's British contemporaries including Abernethy, Green, and Coleridge, is the integration of the body's parts within a whole. In constitutional disease, disease is not confined to a single organ but reflects and threatens a sickness in the whole.[13] The integration of part and whole precludes the containment of disease as merely physical. For the German Romantics, who push the limits of this interdisciplinarity, pathology is thus psychology, and science has ramifications for social science. Moreover, Schelling extends the notion of illness as the withdrawal of part from whole into the issue of systems of knowledge, parts of which are at odds with the whole.[14] Hegel's own analysis of disease as the defection of a part from the whole is thus a mise-en-abime of the very system of assimilation at the heart of his *Encyclopedia*.

The holistic consideration of disease has two consequences. First, disease is symptomatic of larger problems. Hegel includes "diseases of the soul" under illness and observes that illnesses may be historical, national, or social (431–2). As for Comte later, and for Kant earlier, the health of the body is uneasily bound up with that of the body politic. The second consequence is a utopian ex-tension of the *Encyclopedia* that Hegel makes possible without achieving it, since he will not finally deregulate the economy of Subjective and Objective Spirit. For Hegel, disease cannot be cured so long as it is confined to a single organ: it must encompass the whole body, at which point its rigidity is released back into the fluidity of the body and recomprehended in a wider frame of reference (432, 436). In the philosophical clinic, this means that the sick member must be allowed to rethink other parts of the corpus of knowledge: pathology has ramifications for society. Illness is, in this sense, a vital part of life as reproduction and of the organism's renewal, its autopoiesis: this may be why Hegel nowhere mentions the physician but sees disease as an event in the organism's self-regulation. Indeed Hegel does allow disease to be a negative value in the life of the *Dasein*, giving it as value a strange kind of productivity. At the same time he seeks to contain its "evil," and his means of doing so is the dialectic, which is why his discussion of disease is so closely and anxiously entwined with his theory of negativity.

Hegel thinks of the body as an organism: a whole where each part is incorporated. Illness is the revolt of subaltern parts against this whole, wherein the sick organ makes itself the sole object of attention. Hegel analyzes illness in three stages: sensibility, irritability, and reproduction. Because these stages are also the stages of self-consciousness, his physiology doubles as a psychopathology, while his analysis of the physical organism is also a psychoanalysis. In sensibility the illness is "*virtually* present, but without any actual morbidity" (*PN* 433). Sensibility is a self-generated excess, but since illnesses can be culturally specific (431), one can also see it as care of the self and its dis-ease with things as they are. In Hegel's second stage the organism is "irritated" into conflict with its "being." Irritability involves a reaction against external stimuli and a "repelling" of what is "other" (358–9), but also a turning of the sick member against the larger body. Irritability, like evil in Schelling, is thus the stage in which the disease "becomes for the self" (433, 429). It is an "active maintenance of self" against the outside (359), but as the "negative" of itself (429). The self reconstitutes itself against itself, as what it cannot digest.

In the larger system, this turning of the subject against its structure through a process that tropologically produces it as its internal torsion, is resolved in reproduction. We shall return to the point that reproduction in illness takes the problematic form of excretion. Suffice it to say that illness reaches a crisis in "fever" as the cathartic working through of morbid matter through "sweat." Through sweat the organism "master[s]" itself: it "attains to an excretion of itself, through which it eliminates its abnormality and rids itself of its morbid activity." The disease is "sublated, digested"; and the organism thereby "produce[s]" or re-produces "itself as a whole" (434–5).

Through reproduction illness acquires a narrative, teleological structure. Yet if fever and crisis return irritability to its part in Hegel's argument, this discussion itself turns away from the larger whole to become "for" itself. One reason is the philosophical and psychological terminology used to discuss irritability as negativity,[15] which distinguishes this analysis from the more purely physiological discussion of the two other stages. Irritability installs itself at the intellectual center of illness, figuring the usurpation of Hegel's larger system by the negativity it cannot digest. As irritability, illness is the separation of one part of the organism from the whole, and its introversion as what Hegel, like Blake, calls a "selfhood" (428). One bodily subsystem "makes itself the centre" and becomes "an isolated, independent activity"; it is then "shut off from the outer world . . . [and] lives on its own resources" (429–30). Hegel employs the common notion of irritability as a principle of change more characteristic of man than other animals.[16] But for him irritability is also closely tied to negativity. Hegel describes it as a turning of the self "against its structure" so that "the negative thing" becomes "the structure itself" (429). Moreover, inasmuch as this torsion becomes the self's structure, negativity is not just a stage in self-consciousness but an alteration in its very being.

Moreover Hegel cannot contain illness and negativity within the merely physiological. "Every disease . . . is a hypochondria of the organism, in which the latter disdains the outer world which sickens it, because, restricted to itself, it possesses within its own self the negative of itself" (438). Kristeva will describe how in "maladies of the soul" such as melancholia, the subject clings to her illness as to a "primitive self—wounded, incomplete, empty."[17] Similarly for Hegel illness is not simply an error of the (social) body to be contrasted with the normality of health. In illness, to be sure, "one side is increased" beyond the organism's "inner resources" and "usurp[s] the self" (429, 433). But this one-sidedness lives from "its own resources," as a new self, "the negative of itself" (429–30). Moreover, illness distinguishes living from inert matter: a stone cannot become ill, since "if it becomes the negative of itself" by becoming fluid, it is "chemically decomposed" (429). As Canguilhem says, "Biological pathology exists but there is no . . . chemical or mechanical pathology" (127). Illness is characteristically organic, and is the ability to survive or subsist in negativity, as what Hegel calls a "*dual life . . . a differentiating movement*" at odds with "the stable universal self" (*PN* 429, 434). Organisms, then, have two characteristics that compromise them as material for Spirit. The first is their tendency to become the negative of themselves in the first place. The second is that they are changed by this negativity. For because Hegel thinks the human as a unity, he also thinks illness "at the level of organic totality" as affecting the entire being (88).

IV

Hegel's sympathy for irritability has consequences for the return to normality in terms of which he narrativizes illness. What are we to make of health if it requires that the subject digest and excrete not a foreign substance, but "itself"? There are gentler ways of describing self-constitution: for instance in terms of memory and selection, as a re-membering or gathering together of the past wherein forgetting is the condition of reproducing the self anew for the future (See Schelling, "On the Nature of Philosophy as Science" 231). But Hegel's "carnivorously virile" figure draws attention, through its very literalization, to the sacrificial structure involved in the reproduction of the subject. Digestion, in other words, names the masochism of a subject founded by what Judith Butler, talking of "stubborn attachments" to the means of one's subjection, calls a "constitutive loss."[18]

Even more problematic is the status of this "reproduction" given that what illness "produces" is an excretion. The curious view of secretions as productive goes back to the discussion of reproduction in the earlier section on "Assimilation." Here Hegel links three disparate forms of reproduction: aesthetic, sexual, and excretive. Although the aesthetic is the highest, the excretive claims an affinity with it through its association with "shape-formation" (*PN* 435). Shape (*Gestalt*) is a term used throughout the *Aesthetics*, as well as in *The Philosophy of Nature* where it connotes the emergence of Spirit from matter. Moreover, reproduction, as the continuation of the race and species, must also be read culturally. Indeed Hegel himself points in this direction when he says that reproduction distinguishes animals from plants. Plants multiply by division in space, whereas reproduction is tied to an evolution in the species: "The animal," as H. S. Harris explains, "is not a standing syllogism but a syllogism moving to the definite conclusion from which a new one can begin."[19]

Given these connotations of reproduction, what does it mean that Hegel literalizes it as sweat? In theory the third stage of illness returns the organism to the destiny of the species and completes the process of self-consciousness as the assimilation of the negative and the excretion of its morbidity. But in terms of the parallels between bodily processes and self-consciousness, the figure works only physiologically and not logically. For it is hard to accept the identification of reproduction, now a prelude to the reproduction of nature as Spirit, with waste. Or put differently, the very figure of reproduction seems irritable, constituted by a turning in which the text reproduces itself through an indigestible figure. The figure of excrement as reproduction (or vice versa) seems a Freudian slip, a catachresis that interrupts the seamless transfer from literal (biological) processes into metaphorical (philosophical) functions. In his own terms, Hegel's joining of reproduction with waste is an abjection of the assimilation forced on the subject by the laws of Objective Spirit. In dis-figuring reproduction as excrement, the philosophical organism engages in a "repulsion of itself by which it makes itself external to itself . . . separating itself from itself in disgust" (402–3), excreting what it forced itself to digest.

In digestion the organism divides itself, "repelling . . . itself from itself" (404). This division means that the text's conclusion too has not achieved a "self-like unity": Hegel's argument has not digested itself. The conclusion thus throws us back to the middle of Hegel's narrative and to the question of why he makes illness so central to higher organisms. The answer may lie in his radicalization of Schelling's *First Projection for a System of Nature-Philosophy*, which also distinguishes animal organisms from plants in terms of a susceptibility to illness that marks their greater sensibility.[20] Begun at Jena when he was still close to Schelling, Hegel's philosophy of nature intensifies an insight into the proximity between illness and life into which Schelling stumbles in the *First Projection*. Here as Krell points out, the system earlier begun in *Ideas for a Philosophy of Nature* becomes unglued in ways that anticipate Schelling's *Freedom* essay. But Schelling confines this section to an appendix, and returns to a visionary physics and chemistry that are still part of the Identity-Philosophy (Krell, *Contagion* 100–14),[21] and thus still part of a transcendental rather than existential idealism.

Hegel, by contrast, gives illness a climactic position in his exploration of "organics"—an aspect of nature to which Schelling never gets in the *Ideas*. Whereas the early Schelling sees the organic and inorganic realms as parallel and postulates a synchronic system in which spirit reveals itself in nature, Hegel proceeds from nature to spirit through a temporal ascent up the Chain of Being from the inorganic (physics and chemistry) to the organic (biology and physiology). Hegel planned this development as an evolution in which the organic sublates the inorganic as spirit digests (its) nature. But it becomes an unworking of the idealism that the early Schelling protects by avoiding a detailed exposition of the organic.[22] For the development from chemistry to biology exposes transcendental principles of polarity and indifference (or in Hegel's case dialectic) to death, change, and finitude—the equivalents, in the natural sphere, of history and existence.

In the *First Projection* Schelling intimates what will also be at issue in Hegel's analysis of illness. Drawing on the physiology of Brown, but not on his positivism, Schelling writes that illness has the same causes as life itself: namely "excitability" as sensibility and irritability. Given this proximity we can no more say that illness is contrary to nature than that life itself is unnatural: life is a "chronic illness," which means that the pathological deserves the same respect as the normal (*Erster Entwurf* 222, 222n.). Hegel wants to contain the dis-ease he has introduced into his system by thinking of illness as the dialectical working through of negative matter through fever. He therefore favors "acute" illness that reaches a crisis, over "chronic" illness in which the negative is not worked through (432). Acute illness has a terminus, as in Freud's distinction of remembering from repetition: it can be remembered as something "belonging to the past," and is worked through, not simply repeated. But in the chronic state the morbid matter is repeated "as a contemporary experience."[23] Yet Hegel cannot deny the existence of chronic illness and thus of an "unusable" negativity at odds with reproduction in any meaningful genetic or cultural sense. Chronic illness is the body's way of holding on to the negative that acute illness digests. Hegel, of course, sees acute illness as a more healthy phenomenon. Yet he too holds on to illness. For even when he has won his rhetorical battle against illness, he insists on its continued latency in the organism. "The organism can recover from disease," but "disease is in its very nature" and death is inevitable (441).[24]

V

Hegel's discussion of illness touches the heart of his theory of negativity, and its place in the economy of the subject and that of history as the life of a metasubject that is organic, not transcendental. Through illness, Hegel makes a place for negative values in life. Given the parallels between the body and the body politic, he also protects a space for the separation of Subjective from Objective Spirit, or for what Schelling in the *Freedom* essay calls "evil"—a term Hegel himself uses (18–19). This separation is what makes Spirit into "life" or "existence"—again terms Hegel uses (273). The reintegration of Subjective and Objective Spirit is of course the goal of the *Encyclopedia*. The Hegelian sociologist Georg Simmel will later describe this reintegration as "culture": culture is "the perfection of individuals achieved as a result of the objectified spirit at work in the history of the species." Culture is produced by "mediation," an activity that Hegel connects with digestion (396–404). But Simmel also acknowledges the "tragedy of culture."[25] For the digestion of the object by the subject is in fact a reversed figure and palliative trope for the formation of the subject by and as "a power that turns on itself," digesting itself into the objective (Butler 6). Illness is Hegel's resistance to this disciplinary goal of the *Encyclopedia*, especially given that he treats illness phenomenologically, universalizing and not just pathologizing it.

Illness is a crisis in Hegel's conception of the relation of Objective Spirit to subjectivity. On the one hand, as a philosopher of the State and its Objective disciplines (law, morality, and ethics) he believes in the subsumption of the subject into the system. The result is a series of assimilations, graphically figured as the process in which the body consumes its own bones. Derrida evokes this carnivorous virility of culture when he asks what "consciousness" is if its "ultimate power is achieved by the family." Derrida then further describes how the family "through marriage, possession, and education, annihilates . . . 'sacrifices' itself" to civil society (*Glas* 108). But as a Romantic thinker Hegel also respects the inhibition of the universal by the individual, which profoundly threatens the return of the organism from its self-separation to the cooperative functioning of the physical and social whole. As Žižek puts it:

> "System," in the precise sense of German Idealism, is a totality that is all-encompassing since it includes/contains its own inversion . . . . what is originally a subordinate moment of the Absolute can posit itself as its own Center. . . . Therein resides what Hegel calls the "infinite right of subjectivity."[26]

Given Hegel's reluctant yet powerful sympathy for the negative, separated selfhood, the last section of *The Philosophy of Nature* raises questions about the relation between illness and dialectic, arising from the profound ambiguity of the links among life, illness, and vitality. Is illness, which sometimes comes from inside the subject as its own decadence (431), productive in the life of the organism? Does it thwart or forward life? And what is "life," if it culminates in death? At times illness seems to be the assertion of an inorganic principle within the organism, as in Freud's death drive: it is an "entanglement [of the system] with its non-organic nature" (433, 440). At other times illness as negativity is a resistance to this inertia of a dead matter within spirit: illness occurs when one of the body's "systems or organs [is] stimulated into conflict with the inorganic power" (428). Illness might then be a form of vitality,[27] a "positive, innovative experience" in the life of the organism, as Canguilhem says. Indeed illness may be a form of desire. For even as Hegel claims that life contains "the inborn *germ of death*," he also describes the organism's "*original disease*" as a disparity between its finitude and its "universality," the removal of which is either the inertia of "habit" or the "repose of death" (441–2).

This carries another disturbing overtone, however. If illness is the body's resistance to stasis, is it not the case that progress occurs only through illness?—a strange conclusion in the century that produced Darwin. But as Krell suggests it is possible to see a utopian potential in the entwinement of disease and health that involves creation in "a more general structure of infection and toxification." In effect Krell describes a negative dialectic in which the dialectic's infinite inhibition by its illness can still be thought in terms of potences and stages: "each individual product of nature must be seen as 'a botched attempt to depict the absolute.' . . . . each species and each stage of development, in turn, is yet another such botching" (93–4, 96–7). Hegel too speaks of nature as "a system of stages," each one "being the proximate truth of the stage from which it results" (20). Lest this sound too optimistic, one should remember the powerfully retrospective form of Hegel's stages, where each recognizes its precursor as the inhibition of the

Idea, and in which the final stage that Hegel can only ambiguously subl(im)ate is illness and death.

Perhaps such a dialectic—an archeology of the psyche as well as a teleology of Spirit—is what Hegel cannot quite articulate when he finally absorbs illness back into the "genus, the procession of spirit" (443). It is a strange "procession" in which death can be re-produced as Spirit. Only a metaphoric jump of the most bizarre kind could produce this subl(im)ation: in this case through a transsubstantiative Christian rhetoric absent from *The Philosophy of Nature* until it erupts in the last paragraphs. Here Hegel speaks of Nature as breaking "through its husk of immediate, sensuous existence, to consume itself like the phoenix" and "come forth . . . rejuvenated as spirit," and most importantly of a "separation" with which "living being ends" (443–4). The rhetoric of spirit as resurrection is a *deus ex machina* that rescues Hegel from the unravelling of life by the death drive, allowing him to say something about this entanglement of life in death for which he has no other words. But it also gives him the wrong words, precipitating him into a life felt as death wherein "living being ends."

The last pages are a missed encounter that confusingly opens up and closes down thought. The rhetoric of resurrection intrudes into an argument that has hitherto been physiological and psychological but not religious. As such the resurrection of Spirit from nature is what de Man calls a catachresis: a figure that gives a face to "a still unnamed entity," in the process giving it the wrong face (as when one speaks of a cabbage, impossibly, as having a head).[28] This rhetoric wants to see something productive in death's unravelling of life. Hegel wants to believe, like Schelling, that the "original ground of existence continues to act even in evil, as health continues to act in sickness." Hegel's teleology thus hyperbolizes a desire that is at issue for the later Schelling who, as Krell allows, also seeks to "reveal the concealed trace of freedom in nature" (74). The last pages of Schelling's *Freedom* essay, speaking of "Love" and a "new covenant" and offering themselves as a prelude to "the ideal portion of philosophy," are no less committed to a philosophy of "Spirit" and no less carried by a promise that is a figural leap. If Hegel completes the system whose beginning Schelling endlessly repeats, that is so only in the sense that Hegel constitutes this system through a contraction that retains what it expels within itself as its ground, its unconscious (as Werner Marx says of "God" in Schelling's work).[29] Thus the discussions of psychic illness excreted from Hegel's philosophy of nature after the Jena period turn up again in the third part of the *Encyclopedia* in the Berlin period as a contingency of the system. Hegel and

Schelling are in this sense counterparts, as Feuerbach says: reversed mirror images, each of whom can and should be used to read the other.[30]

Given this affinity between Hegel and Schelling, health and illness, Idealism and the larger Romanticism in which it is implicated, it is hard to read Hegel's emphasis on reproduction and his curious entanglement of reproduction with waste.[31] Perhaps we should not be too quick to assimilate Hegel: to absorb this remarkable aporia into a notion of dialectic as digestion. Perhaps if each individual product is "a botched attempt" at the absolute, then waste is productive, and perhaps then reproduction is not illegitimate. Perhaps it is not really clear what the term "productive" means to Hegel anyway, nor what wholeness is. For these terms do not so much define an argument as create an environment for thinking things through in which the very values of the orienting terms are in flux.

For instance, "acute" illness can be seen as submitting to the rule of the dialectic the singular pathology that chronic illness protects. But from another perspective, the chronic is a rigidity that holds on to illness, whereas the acute releases illness back into the general "fluidity" of the body so as to work through its value for the larger organism: thus "the organism breaks out from the limitation with which it had become identified" and makes its "limitation" an "object for it[self]" (3.202). This release into a larger conceptuality—which Merleau-Ponty calls "generalization"— is after all at work in any thinking about illness, any psychoanalysis. Thus even contemporary theories that come to rest in some form of unusable, chronic negativity—for instance Kristeva's protection of melancholia from the Freudian mourning that digests it—do still put this negativity to cultural, cognitive use (see *Black Sun* 1–68).[32] Perhaps this is what Hegel intimates when he absorbs illness back into the "proceeding forth" of the individual into the species. And perhaps it is thus appropriate that reproduction consists in excrement. Waste is in its own way productive, in ways Hegel himself cannot yet grasp but allows us to sense, his work itself being part of the proceeding of thought into further thought.

Notes

1. References to *PN* are to G. W. F. Hegel, *The Philosophy of Nature*, tr. A. V. Miller (Oxford: Clarendon, 1970). The text is Volume II of the 1830 *Encyclopedia*, ed. Karl Michelet in 1847. The first version was published in the 1816 *Encyclopedia*.

2. Henry Sussman, "An American History Lesson: Hegel and the Historiography of Superimposition," in *Theorizing American Literature: Hegel, The Sign and History*, ed. Bainard Cowan (Baton Rouge: Lousiana State UP, 1991), 33–42.

3. Rodolphe Gasché, *The Tain of the Mirror: Derrida and the Philosophy of Reflection* (Cambridge: Harvard UP, 1986), 16–17 (emphasis mine). See also Derrida, who says of *PN* that in "freeing itself from the natural limits that were imprisoning it, the spirit returns to itself but without ever having left itself . . . This joint will assure, in the circle of the *Encylopedia*, the circle itself, the return to the philosophy of spirit" (*Glas*, tr. John P. Leavey and Richard Rand (Lincoln: University of Nebraska Press, 1986), 109).

4. Xavier Bichat, *Physiological Researches Upon Life and Death*, tr. Tobias Watkins (Philadelphia: Smith and Maxwell, 1809), 1–3.

5. Samuel Taylor Coleridge, *Shorter Works and Fragments*, ed. H. R. and J. R. de J. Jackson, 2 vols. (Princeton: Princeton UP, 1995), 1.489.

6. Julia Kristeva recapitulates the distinction between negativity and negation (as mastery versus predication) in *Revolution in Poetic Language*, tr. Margaret Waller (New York: Columbia University Press, 1984), 117–25. On "internal negation" as against negation as sorting and separation, see Jean-Paul Sartre, *Being and Nothingness: An Essay on Phenomenological Ontology*, tr. Hazel Barnes (New York: Washington Square, 1956), 43, 243. The dangerous slippage of negation as self-positing into the unhappy consciousness of "internal negation" can be seen in Hegel's description of hunger: "The negation of myself which I suffer . . . in hunger, is . . . present as an other than myself, as something to be consumed" (5).

7. Werner Hamacher, *Pleroma: Reading in Hegel*, tr. Nicholas Walker and Simon Jarvis (Stanford: Stanford UP, 1998), 248, 252, and more generally 230–95.

8. The phrase is Coleridge's (2.1090–1), though in *Theory of Life* he is uncomfortable with this definition.

9. As David Farrell Krell points out, infection had a broader meaning then, implying "infusion or absorption by osmosis or porosity, or perhaps even an affection by means of an *actio in distans*. Nevertheless the proximity to pathology . . . remains a significant overtone" (*Contagion: Sexuality, Disease, and Death in German Idealism and Romanticism* (Bloomington: Indiana UP, 1998), 92).

10. John Brown, *The Elements of Medicine*, 2 vols. (London: J. Johnson, 1788); Krell, *Contagion*, 48–50, 103; Georges Canguilhem, *The Normal and the Pathological* (1966), trans. Carolyn R. Fawcett and Robert S. Cohen (New York: Zone, 1989), 40–5. Canguilhem discusses Bernard, Comte, and René Leriche in detail (33–101).

11. Brown uses the proximity of the normal and pathological to normalize illness. But Schelling uses it to pathologize life, while arguing phenomenologically that illness has a disclosive force in life.

12. There are sporadic explorations in the early nineteenth century of disease as externally caused by airborne or waterborne germs, but the germ theory did not take hold until later.

13. Coleridge, *Shorter Works and Fragments*, 2.1027; John Abernethy, *Introductory Lectures, Exhibiting Some of Mr. Hunter's Opinions Regarding Diseases*

(London: Longman, Hurst and Rees, 1823), 101–2, 269; J. H. Green, *Vital Dynamics: The Hunterian Oration Before the Royal College of Surgeons* . . . (London: Pickering, 1840), 82.

14. F. W. J. Schelling, "On The Nature of Philosophy as Science" (1823), tr. Marcus Weigelt, in *German Idealist Philosophy*, ed. Rüdiger Bubner (Harmondsworth: Penguin, 1997), 212–15.

15. Earlier, just prior to the discussion of digestion, irritability is still described in terms closer to negation and the struggle for mastery: it is "a capacity for being stimulated by an other" and an "active maintenance" of the self against the other, in which the self "is at the mercy of an other" (359).

16. In Blumenbach's earliest theory of generation, the embryo contained in the maternal egg is awakened from its "slumber" by the irritation caused by the sperm. Leaving aside the vexed question of preformation versus epigenesis, the point here is the role of "Irritation." According to Carl Kielmeyer, whereas birds are Sensibilitätstieren, in man irritability increases "its strength and independence from the rest of the organic system" (Timothy Lenoir, *The Strategy of Life: Teleology and Mechanics in Nineteenth-Century German Biology* (Dordrecht: Reidel, 1982), 9, 46, 49. See also Abernethy, *Introductory Lectures*, 28.

17. Julia Kristeva, *Black Sun: Depression and Melancholia*, tr. Leon S. Roudiez (New York: Columbia UP, 1987), 12.

18. Jacques Derrida, "Eating Well," *Points . . . Interviews 1974–1994*, ed. Elisabeth Weber, tr. Peggy Kamuf et al. (Stanford: Stanford UP, 1995), 278–80; Judith Butler, *The Psychic Life of Power: Theories in Subjection* (Stanford: Stanford UP, 1997), 92.

19. H. S. Harris, *Hegel's Development: Night Thoughts (Jena 1801–1806)* (Oxford: Clarendon Press, 1983), 457.

20. Schelling writes that "illness is a fully relative concept." A particular "degree of irritability" that constitutes health in a plant, is illness in a human being. There is thus no absolute "illness"; the sensibilities of different organisms differ, and so can always be thought of as a kind of health (*Erster Entwurf eines Systems der Naturphilosophie*, in *Schriften von 1799–1801, Ausgewählte Werke*, vol. 7 (Darmstadt: Wissenschaftliche Buchgesellschaft, 1967), 221; my translation).

21. While Krell sees the Schelling of the *First Projection* as already the author of the *Freedom* essay, the "tormented idealism" that fascinates Krell and Slavoj Žižek seems largely parenthetical at this point. In 1802 Schelling still wanted to be represented by the *Ideas*, which concentrates on physics and chemistry, and leaves aside the troublesome realm of "organics" which Hegel is more willing to confront. While Schelling was unsatisfied with the 1797 *Ideas*, his 1802 revision simply adds a metacommentary that develops the philosophical implications of the more empirical and scientific analysis (in Schelling's own unique sense) of 1797. In *The Philosophy of Art* (1799–1805) Schelling is still committed to the Identity Philosophy, though here too the synchronicity of unity (a single essence of art) and multiplicity (its many actual forms), and thus of the ideal and the real, is becoming unravelled by a history of actual art forms.

22. By avoiding "organics" Schelling concludes the *Ideas* triumphantly with the synchronicity of the real and the ideal: "In Nature . . . the whole absolute is knowable, although appearing Nature produces only successively, and in (for us) endless development, what in true Nature exists all at once" and eternally (tr. Errol E. Harris and Peter Heath (Cambridge: Cambridge UP, 1988), 272). Though Schelling planned a third book on organics, by 1810 he had still not completed his system of nature and wrote that he would "never continue" his project except through "a scientific physiology, which alone can give it completeness" (quoted in *Ideas*, 272n.).

23. Sigmund Freud, "Beyond the Pleasure Principle," *Metapsychology: The Theory of Psychoanalysis*, tr. and ed. Angela Richards (Harmondsworth: Penguin, 1984), 288.

24. Correspondingly Hegel admits that secretions are not always purgative: "critical secretions" differ "from secretions arising from exhaustion, which are not strictly secretions but a dissolution of the organism" (435).

25. Georg Simmel, "Female Culture" and "The Tragedy of Culture," in *Simmel on Culture*, ed. David Frisby and Mike Featherstone (London: Sage, 1997), 46, 58–9, 72.

26. Slavoj Žižek, "The Abyss of Freedom," in *The Abyss of Freedom / Ages of the World* (Ann Arbor: University of Michigan Press, 1997), 13.

27. As Cathy Caruth argues, for Freud too the life and death drives are closely entwined in trauma as "a theory of the peculiar incomprehensibility of human survival" (*Unclaimed Experience: Trauma, Narrative, and History* (Baltimore: Johns Hopkins UP, 1996), 8, 58).

28. Paul de Man, "Hypogram and Inscription," *The Resistance to Theory* (Minneapolis: U of Minnesota P, 1986), 44.

29. F. W. J. Schelling, "Philosophical Investigations into the Essence of Human Freedom and Related Matters," tr. Priscilla Hayden-Roy, in *Philosophy of German Idealism*, ed. Ernst Behler (New York: Continuum, 1987), 274, 278, 280, 284; Werner Marx, *The Philosophy of F. W. J. Schelling: History, System and Freedom*, tr. Thomas Nenon (Bloomington: Indiana UP, 1984), 69.

30. Ludwig Feuerbach, quoted in Thomas McFarland, *Coleridge and the Pantheist Tradition* (Oxford: Clarendon Press, 1969), 306. Feuerbach casts Hegel as the masculine principle and Schelling as "the feminine principle of receptivity" to other forms of thinking.

31. I use "Idealism" to denote a specifically philosophical movement committed to dialectical totalization, Identity (however agonistically established), and Absolute Knowledge. However, (Jena) "Romanticism" is the larger literary-cum-philosophical context within which Idealism emerges as no more than an "idea" continually put under erasure by the exposure of Spirit to its body. Schelling complains that Idealism, as "the denial and nonacknowledgment" of a resistance at the heart of things, "is the universal system of our times." Humans "show a natural predilection for the affirmative just as they turn away from the negative" (*Ages of the World*, tr. Jason M. Wirth (Albany: SUNY Press, 2000), 6–7).

32. Phenomenological psychoanalysis, even as it questions the subject–object dualism of a clinical gaze that separates doctor from patient (and normality from pathology), nevertheless sees mental illness as a "constriction" and "rigidity" from which it tries to free the patient through Merleau-Ponty's "generalization." See Hubert Dreyfus, "Foreword," to Michel Foucault, *Mental Illness and Psychology* (1962), tr. Alan Sheridan (Berkeley and Los Angeles: University of California Press, 1987), xx–xxii. See also Foucault's own discussion (44–56).

Chapter 12 ∽

ROMANTIC DIETETICS!
OR, EATING YOUR WAY TO
A NEW YOU

Paul Youngquist

> All things entering the mouth, descend to the stomach and leave it.
> —Jesus (Matthew 15:17)

Christ exhorts us to ponder the ends of eating. What enters the mouth leaves by another passage, but only after its descent into that physiological underworld, the stomach. That eating sustains life is obvious. That it does so to specific cultural ends, however, is a circumstance worth closer consideration than it often gets, at least in studies of Romanticism. What are the cultural politics of eating in the age of revolution? We're all familiar with the dietetic promises of today's popular media. A recent issue of *Parade Magazine* touts the wisdom of a book entitled *The Glucose Revolution*, which propounds the truth of something called the "glycemic index," a new system that ranks food by its effect on blood sugar: "according to the system it's not so much whether you're eating sugars or carbohydrates that counts, as how quickly and easily your choices are digested." Digestion is the means to bodied happiness, and food choices are its matter. With a little dietetic care you can eat your way to a new you: "The important thing is for you to find out about how the glycemic index may revolutionize your diet just as soon as possible. For let's face it. You've gone without it long enough."[1] Good digestion turns out to incorporate a new you: it transforms substance (food) into a subject (you) who has made all the right dietetic choices. This Romantic dietetics directs digestion toward socially serviceable ends, producing a proper body and sustaining a private subject.

Vivification

The renowned physiologist John Hunter, member of the Royal Society and surgeon-extraordinary to King George III, discovered in digestion, more even than conception, the impetus of life. Conception begins life but digestion perpetuates it. Hence the honorific status in Hunter's physiology of the stomach. Where other anatomists took the brain to be any animal's chief organ, Hunter chose the stomach instead. The stomach after all is in Hunter's words "the converter of food by hidden powers into part of ourselves, and is what may be called the true animal, no animal being without it; and in many, perhaps in most, it is what constitutes the principal part of an animal."[2] Life happens in the belly, the organ that animates the animal.

Hunter's vitalist ontology traces the destiny of common matter from substance to sustenance and ultimately to subjectivity. In what Hunter calls "vivification," inert matter is endowed with a "living principle" characteristic of all organisms with the power of self-production. This principle is not so much an essence superadded to material substance as the sublimation of that substance through the physiological process of digestion. First common matter gets converted into organic matter compatible with living bodies. "Out of this change," he writes, "life is to arise, digestion being the first step toward vivification" (1.231). Organic matter is assimilated to living bodies, acquiring the principle of life. For Hunter life arises continuously and without supernatural aid. Good digestion is divine to the extent that it, and not some deity, creates life from dead matter.

Such vital effects indicate that digestion is no less intelligent for being a purely physiological process. In a weird discussion of its mechanism, Hunter attributes to digestion a sentience usually reserved for cognition. Assimilation of organic matter to flesh requires consciousness and effects consensus:

> The remote cause of absorption of whole and living parts implies the existence of two conditions, the first of which is a consciousness, in the part to be absorbed, of the unfitness or impossibility of remaining under such circumstances, whatever they be, and therefore they become ready for removal, and submit to it with ease. The second is a consciousness of the absorbents of such a state of the parts. Both of these concurring, they have nothing to do but to fall to work. (1.255)

Hunter materializes consciousness and identifies its operations with physiological process. Digestion involves deliberation between digester and digested and yields agreement about how best to do the work of vivification. The stomach has a politics of its own, complete with inferior and superior constituents. Vivification would be impossible without their accord. Such a stomach literally incorporates a politics of appropriation that works as naturally and as effortlessly as good digestion. Social form follows physiological function, grounded materially in the body's labor. And it is interesting to note what Hunter includes and excludes from this bodied politic. Physiologically considered, the living organism is a laborer, and digestion is virile business. When it works, the body labors like a man whose every movement is free, firm, and fully conscious. Missing from this description is any mention of the role women might play in the process of vivification. Hunter liberates the feminine from its traditional ties to bodily function to advance, however quietly, a phallic physiology. The stomach is a hungry little man who eats, thinks, and acts on behalf of the living organism.

Sinning Against the Stomach

" 'Physic and metaphysic all depend upon the inspiration of roast beef. If you would do well, you must eat and digest like a ploughman; nay if you would walk well, think well, write well, etc.' "[3] So a Lady of some repute advises her sick son. Thomas Beddoes, Bristol physician and friend of Samuel Taylor Coleridge, quotes her sage opinion with approval in *Hygeia*, a medical manual addressed explicitly to the "middling and affluent classes." If, as Michel Foucault suggests, the late eighteenth century saw a transition from a social order bound by relations of blood to one administered through relations of health, then manuals like Beddoes's play a role in creating a body subject to medical management.[4] As the ideal of a unitary body politic yields to a dispersed politics of individual bodies, health comes to function as means of assimilating those bodies to functional and behavioral norms. Beddoes's manual and others like it teach the middling and affluent classes how to achieve and maintain healthy bodily functions and hygienic behaviors. Bodies become health machines whose proper operation requires practical knowledge and perpetual vigilance.

Digestion becomes one of the preferred sites of this medicalized introspection. The seventh chapter of *Hygeia* is entitled "Essay on the Preservation of the Physical Power of Enjoyment with Remarks on Food and Digestion." Where for Hunter digestion produces life, for Beddoes it produces the *good* life. Eating becomes a means of incorporating morals through managing "the physical power of enjoyment." Gaston Bachelard has remarked that for middle-class culture "digestion corresponds in effect to the possession of unequivocal evidence, an unassailable certainty."[5] Whether digestion is good or bad, the bowels produce the true. Food becomes the substance of certainty, the material *a priori* of moral judgment:"among the bourgeoisie, nothing is so rationalized as food. Nothing has such benefits under the sign of the substantial" (171). Beddoes thus makes digestion the site of an introspection whose force is as moral as it is medical: "No process in human life is more common than sinning against the stomach and repenting shortly afterwards" (2.63). To avoid such lapses, to preserve true health, Beddoes recommends a disciplined attention to the ends of eating:

> To pass one's table-transactions in frequent review, as the golden verses ascribed to Phythagoras recommend with regard to our whole conduct; to dwell upon their consequences, particularly their disagreeable ones; to call up in lively colors before the imagination that delightfully and unencumbered state of all the faculties, which accompanies an easy digestion; to compare what is lost and gained by throwing into the stomach materials that puff it up like a balloon, is our best moral preservative against the danger of becoming dyspeptic. (2.60–1)

Digestion may be a natural bodily function, but it becomes the occasion for a moral judgment that equates health with autonomy. A good eater is a careful, calculating, self-disciplining subject.

For Beddoes as for Hunter, the process of digestion is a lot of work. Extending Hunter's description of the stomach as a laborer, Beddoes compares its diverse actions to those of "a very complicated manufactory" (2.20). Just as manufacturers transform raw materials into profitable commodities, the stomach changes food into flesh. Labor makes this change possible, the incorporated labor of an industrialized digestion, building the body that becomes subject to medicalized introspection. Food may be the substance of what is certain for middle-class culture, but thanks to the labor of digestion it literally becomes the body, that near, dear possession that epitomizes all others in liberal political theory. As any eater knows, however, the labor of digestion has its byproducts, whose accumulation can be a pressing matter. Beddoes inventories these byproducts when discussing the transformative effects of digestion: "Some of the elements, after undergoing new combinations, shall be given out in the form of air; some in a liquid state; and the remainder shall be unlike any thing the body contained at first" (2.22). Indeed. To Beddoes the ends of eating are inscrutable compared to the means. The unspoken—and unspeakable—problem for the good eater is how to account for their production. If digestion produces life and incorporates morals, then what is a body to make of its inscrutable, excretable remainder?

Personal Property

This question of ends might not loom so large if liberal political theory didn't make eating the epitome of human agency. However hard to swallow now, the belief that all men are basically the same arose as much from digestive as cognitive reflections. Digestion becomes important to bourgeois culture for normalizing bodily function and behavior because it sustains the one possession that all men as men have in common: a body. In *Two Treatises on Government*, John Locke famously grounds his theory of possessive individualism in the physical body as the archetype of all personal property: "Throughout the Earth, and all inferior Creatures be common to all Men, yet every Man has a *Property* in his own *Person*."[6] To be human is to be propertied, to possess a person as your very own. But to justify this primordial possession it is not enough for Locke simply to declare it. How is it that a body can possess itself as personal property?

The answer is as simple as it is necessary. The body eats its way to property. Locke reasons as follows: "He that is nourished by the Acorns he pickt up under an Oak, or the Apples he gathered from the Trees in the Wood, has certainly appropriated them to himself. No Body can deny but the nourishment is his" (306). Nourishment belongs to a body as its rightful possession. You own what you eat because without it your body wouldn't be. But eating is a complicated process, and Locke examines it closely to determine exactly how acorns and apples become the property of one body and not all: "I ask then, When did they begin to be his? When he digested? Or when he eat? Or when he boiled? Or when he brought them home? Or when he pickt them up? 'Tis plain, if the first gathering made them not his, nothing else could" (306). Acorns and apples become personal property when appropriated to the ends of eating. For Locke digestion is only possible because food has been gathered first. Eating is the epitome of human agency both because it requires work and because that work is transformative. Labor turns acorns and apples into food, which digestion then turns into flesh. The agency of eating transforms common matter into personal property, giving all men a property in their own person. The possessive individual of Locke's liberalism eats his way to ownership.

But Locke's sense of labor involves more than just proprietary eating. If ownership becomes possible through the transformative effects of labor, that can only be because labor is a kind of property, one that appropriates to the individual what might otherwise remain common matter. In Locke's words, "The *Labour* of his Body, and the *Work* of his Hands, we may say, are properly his. Whatsoever then he removes out of the State that Nature hath provided, and left it in, he hath mixed his *Labour* with, and joyned to it something that is his own, and thereby makes it his *Property*" (305–6). Labor produces the property of the body which then produces personal property through its labor. For Locke labor is both cause and effect of embodiment. That may explain why medical writers such as Hunter and Beddoes make digestion the metonymy of labor, locating the physiological foundation for political liberalism in the labor of the guts. Digestion becomes the material process where the cause meets the effect of embodiment, where the labor that produces the body (Hunter's vivification) coincides with its labor of appropriation (Beddoes's manufactory). No wonder eating becomes a means of incorporating morals in middle-class culture, as the labor that sustains the life of the proper body.

But who pays the price for propriety? Locke believes that when it comes to possession, some bodies are better than others. Acorns and apples become the autonomous individual's property when taken for food: "*labour* put a distinction between them and common. That added something to them more than Nature, the common Mother of all, had done; and so they became his private right" (306). Nature may be the mother of humanity, but *labor* fathers the private, proper body. Locke genders the agency of eating in such a way that all proprietary effects become a man's possession. Labor makes it so, and if for Hunter the stomach is a hungry little man, for Locke that little man owns all the property in his own person that constitutes his body. Mothers produce only common matter. Fathers work flesh into personal property. In this sense the proper body is always male and eating well always masculinizes. Women get left out of the logic of personal property. Their bodies remain common matter, the raw material of proper embodiment, associated in the end with the remains of eating well. On the basis of Locke's own inquiry, one might interrogate those remains. If a man's person is his property, what about his most personal bodily products?

"A Dreadful Labor"

The case of Samuel Taylor Coleridge proves instructive in this regard. His digestion was a mess. The phrase "bowels bad" occurs like an alias at the mention of his name in Dorothy Wordsworth's journals. One reason was his fondness for "the Milk of Paradise" (more commonly called laudanum). As Beddoes explains at some length in *Hygeia*, habitual use of opium obstructs the labors of digestion. It seems fair to wonder, given Locke's emphasis on the transformative effects of bodily labor, what becomes of a body whose bowels refuse to move. Coleridge provides painfully frank testimony in his notebooks. His relationship with the physiological workforce of digestion reached an impasse during his passage to Malta in 1804, where he was going in hopes of regaining his health. In his notebook on the evening of May 13, Coleridge describes the malaise that accompanies bad digestion, the "Weight, Langour, & the soul-sickening Necessity of attending to barren bodily sensations, in bowels, in stomach, or organ of Taste. . . . the Obscure, or the disgustful—the dull quasi finger-pressure on the Liver, the endless Flatulence, the frightful constipation when the dead Filth *impales* the lower Gut."[7] When digestion shuts down, the proper body reverts to common matter.

This is not exactly to say that it quits laboring altogether, but that it labors in another way, with effects beneath the dignity of the proper body and its masculinizing agency. Constipation feminizes Coleridge, reducing him physically to the condition of a laboring female. In a harrowing prayer for deliverance from the pains of impaction, Coleridge confesses what it feels like "to weep & sweat & moan & scream for the parturience of an excrement with such pangs & such convulsions as a woman with an Infant heir of Immortality" (2.2092). In the labor of excretion Coleridge becomes the natural mother of political liberalism, delivering a common matter that remains beyond the pale of proper embodiment. Constipation feminizes the proper body. The humiliation involved for the liberal subject becomes obvious when Coleridge summons a ship's physician to assist him in his hour of need:

The Surgeon instantly came, went back for Pipe & Syringe & returned & with extreme difficulty & the exertion of his utmost strength injected the latter. Good God!—What a sensation when the obstruction suddenly *shot* up!—I remained still three-quarters of an hour with hot water in a bottle to my belly (for I was desired to retain it as long as I could) with pains & sore uneasiness, & indescribable desires—at length went/O what a time. . . . (2.2086)

Thank heaven for a safe delivery! In a weird compression of the biology of geneture, penetration and impregnation occur at the moment of parturition, allowing Coleridge to experience the whole beautiful cycle of birth during the course of his contractions. When digestion goes bad laboring men become women in labor. To mothers, then, belongs the common matter of such deliveries. Coleridge's confession identifies women with the unspeakable remainder of digestion, and concludes with the only words that can adequately explain the whole experience: "A Warning."

Coleridge proves equal to the admonition. His ordeal ends in humility as well as humiliation. In a strange if intelligible coincidence of body and soul, the miracle of excretion induces the penance of prayer: "O dear God! give me strength of Soul to make one thorough Trial—if I land at Malta/spite of all horrors to go through one month of unstimulated Nature—yielding to nothing but manifest Danger of Life!—O great God! Grant me grace truly to look into myself, & to begin the serious work of Self-amendment—accounting to Conscience for the Hours of every Day" (2.2092). Constipation becomes an occasion for moral introspection and reform. Coleridge resolves to submit to the imperatives of proper embod-iment, to avoid stimulants and adhere to more healthful norms of bodily function and behavior. That this resolution accompanies a renewed commitment to self-amendment demonstrates the disciplinary effects of Romantic dietetics. God may be Coleridge's witness, but bad digestion is His avenging angel. If constipation is the condition of contrition, then all that remains undigested is matter for moral inspection.

The Subject of Shit

In this Coleridge is not alone. In his *History of Shit*, Dominique Laporte investigates the odd prominence that digestive and excretory functions achieve in bourgeois culture. Human waste provides an occasion for bodily discipline, not merely as Freud would argue because psychic health requires it, but more imperiously because shitting invests individual bodies with social value. Laporte proceeds with care: "To touch, even lightly, on the rela-tionship of a subject to his shit, is to modify not only that subject's relation-ship to the totality of his body, but his very relationship to the world and to those representations that he constructs of his situation in society."[8] The ends of eating seem so inevitable a production as to be beneath the notice of crit-ical inquiry. But Laporte shows how bourgeois culture exploits that neces-sity to reinforce the legitimacy of both a proper body and a private subject overseeing its function and behavior. The liberal subject that superintends property in his own person always does his business by himself.

Laporte's claim is that with the emergence of bourgeois culture there occurs a privatization of human waste and the habits of its production and disposal. On this view you are not so much what you eat as what—and where—you shit. The liberal subject becomes identified with his (always *his*) personal waste: "This little heap is my thing, my badge, a tangible sign that distinguishes me from, or likens me to, my neighbor" (30). That the production of said little heap occurs in the privacy of the home only reinforces Laporte's point that there is something historically specific about bourgeois bathroom habits. Just because privies "in the modern sense have no historical equivalent" does not mean that their proliferation is merely the effect of human progress (44). Laporte reads the introduction of a privy into the private sphere as a domestication of waste that makes the family responsible for waste production and the liberal subject responsible for its disposal. Shitting is for Laporte as sexuality is for Foucault: a biopolitical apparatus of discipline that bourgeois culture assigns to the family and deploys upon the body. The home becomes a space that manages the production of waste, the domestic equivalent of Beddoes's "complicated manufactory" of digestion. At home the proper body takes responsibility for the remainder of digestion and acquires political legitimacy as a subject who behaves in accordance with social norms. "Thus," writes Laporte, "as a 'private' thing—each subject's business, each proprietor's responsibility—shit becomes a political object through its constitution as the dialectical other of the 'public' " (46). The most private matters turn out to have public consequences.

Laporte does not adequately address, however, what Coleridge's intestinal pregnancy makes obvious: the cultural identification between women and waste. Carole Pateman has shown how Locke's theory of possessive individualism legitimates a sense of social contract that not only excludes women from participating in civil society but presumes a prior sexual contract guaranteeing men access to their bodies.[9] Men father children on mother flesh only to discard it as so much waste, unassimilable to the corporate body of civil society. The analogy between women and food in various states of digestion is inescapable. Men consume women in a labor of love that turns the common matter of mother flesh into the proper body of the civil subject. What remains is woman as waste, a *materia mater* inadmissible to the circle of the social contract. The privatization of waste and its introduction into the domestic sphere institutionalizes this exclusion, making space in the home for what civil society ignores but can never be without. As the bourgeois bathroom displaces the toilette of the aristocrat as the place where female bodies receive their fullest treatment, the identification between women and waste becomes fixed. Toilet training may be women's work, but waste is their fate in a bourgeois world. Hence Laporte's description of the private sphere as "the dejected space of domesticity. The place where one 'does one's business' is also the place where waste accumulates" (Laporte 46).

"The Majesty of Human Nature"

This identification of women and waste might explain the anxiety Mary Wollstonecraft, liberalism's first feminist, shows toward female behavior in the privy. Wollstonecraft proves completely aware of the alimentary associations that turn women into waste in British society. An ideology of sexual appetite makes them toothsome dainties to glut the maw of hungry men: "a very considerable number [of women] are, literally speaking, standing dishes to which every glutton may have access."[10] And naturally waste accumulates with every meal. Wollstonecraft's *Vindication of the Rights of Woman* attempts to redress this gynophagic politics. It contests the distinction of sex that makes men eaters and women the eaten: "the first object of laudable ambition is to obtain a character as a human being, regardless of the distinction of sex" (9–10). Wollstonecraft's humanism insists that women as much as men are liberal subjects. Wollstonecraft refuses Locke's identification of the mother with common matter and asserts instead that a man's property in his own person is only possible because a mother conceives and feeds it. Without a matron's labors there would never be a proper body to possess, which is why Wollstonecraft includes the work that women do in "bearing and nursing children" among "the grand ends of their being" (139). One of the reasons Wollstonecraft feels so strongly that mothers must breastfeed their babies is that nursing revalues the alimentary implications of femininity. No longer food to be consumed by men, mothers feed the infant body as it develops property in its own person. They labor to raise the bodies that will labor to possess property. Wollstonecraft insinuates the work of women into proprietary logic of bodily labor in order to vindicate her claim to female reason and autonomy.

It is interesting, then, that Wollstonecraft should be so troubled by the tribulations of digestion. The subject of a stomach ache can inspire imperial disdain: "Some women, particularly French women, have . . . lost a sense of decency in this respect; for they will talk very calmly of an indigestion" (137). The labor of the bowels, apparently, must remain invisible and unspoken. When it becomes obtrusive Wollstonecraft becomes irritable, as when discussing the excessive familiarity that can develop among women in the privy:

> How can *delicate* women obtrude on notice that part of the animal oeconomy, which is so very disgusting? And is it not very rational to conclude, that the women who have not been taught to respect the human nature of their own sex, in these particulars, will not long respect the mere difference of sex in their husbands? After their maidenish bashfulness is once lost, I, in fact, have generally observed, that women fall into old habits; and treat their husbands as they did their sisters or female acquaintance. (128)

Wollstonecraft may earnestly wish to see the distinction of sex confounded in society, but not in the bathroom. The disgusting part of the animal economy is a purely private affair, and when it obtrudes into the company of others it creates a gross familiarity. The ends of eating threaten the propriety of domestic relations.

Wollstonecraft thus urgently recommends that young women be taught to pursue those ends in private: "girls ought to be taught to wash and dress alone, without any distinction of rank; and if custom should make them require some little assistance, let them not require it till that part of the business is over which ought never to be done before a fellow creature; because it is an insult to the majesty of human nature" (127). The proper body and the liberal subject require a policing of digestive production. The majesty of human nature commands it, and the liberal subject complies. Female compliance seems for Wollstonecraft particularly important for participation in the empire of rationality. But Laporte cautions against dissociating any empire from the disciplinary practices that sustain it: "for its subjects to participate in the body of the empire . . . the patrolling and controlling of orifices are sufficient strategies. It is enough to enforce a code of shitting—the master's code, the code of he who knows; namely, he who knows how to hold it in" (Laporte 62). Wollstonecraft's code of that most personal conduct advances in the name of human majesty the privatization of waste that Laporte associates with bourgeois culture. The rationality Wollstonecraft wants for women takes personal waste for its material correlative, the body's most private property. Liberal feminism as Wollstonecraft articulates it has its headquarters (or would that be hindquarters?) in the privy.

Is this preoccupation with toilet training merely a question of personal hygiene? Wollstonecraft indicates that more is at stake that just human health and domestic happiness. There is a counter-knowledge of abjection that Wollstonecraft associates with collective toiletry, a wisdom of common matter to which groups of women are particularly privy. Wollstonecraft abjures the abject wit of women who gather together to conduct their business: "women from necessity, because their minds are not cultivated, have recourse very often to what I familiarly term bodily wit; and their intimacies are of the same kind. . . . In short, with respect to both mind and body, they are too intimate" (128). Excessive intimacy breeds an abject wit that threatens norms of bodily function and behavior: "Why in the name of decency are sisters, female intimates, or ladies and their waiting-women, to be so grossly familiar as to forget the respect which one human creature owes to another?" (127).

Why indeed? Perhaps because that familiarity challenges the politics of privatization that takes waste for a solitary product and the liberal subject for its master. The wisdom of common matter emerges in a feminine familiarity that affirms the carnival of the body through the necessity of its functions. Such familiarity with the common cause and effect of digestion presents a threat to the proper body as the personal possession of a sovereign subject. The counter-knowledge of abjection thus registers the troubled status of that body in the political theory of possessive individualism. After all, in digestion the body labors to produce what is of no value to possess. Julia Kristeva claims that it is "not lack of cleanliness or health that causes abjection but what disturbs identity, system, order. What does not respect borders, positions, rules. The in-between, the ambiguous, the composite."[11] For Wollstonecraft, feminine over-familiarity disturbs a physical and symbolic order grounded in privatized bodily function. These amazons of the powder room follow the movements of digestion toward a beyond of the proper body, disgusting in its carnality and abject in its wit.

In her eagerness to eradicate the distinction of sex among rational subjects Wollstonecraft recapitulates all too traditional associations between women and waste. For her the vindicated woman is the rational and independent mistress of property in her own person. Not for Kristeva. She argues that the real threat to the order of the autonomous subject comes from "the demoniacal potential of the feminine": "the latter, precisely on account of its power, does not succeed in differentiating itself as *other* but threatens one's *own and clean self*, which is the underpinning of any organization constituted by exclusions and hierarchies" (64–5). Wollstonecraft's abject, witty women menace her liberal politics of proper embodiment. That their bodies move in common and that their minds consort with filth disqualifies them from fully realizing the majesty of human nature. Wollstonecraft remains, for all her obvious contribution to the cause of women's rights, a practitioner of Romantic dietetics, materially incorporating an exclusionary politics in the private trials of digestion.

"Food for Future Years"

This dietetic regimen, thoroughly preoccupied with the ends of eating, gains ascendancy in British culture with the emergence of a Romantic movement. Much more than a passing fad, Romantic dietetics circulates a cultural logic of good digestion that legitimates exclusionary politics through an appeal to eating well. The operation of that logic can appear in the most surprising places. In this regard Lord Byron's fond moniker for the legend of the Lake District—"Turdsworth"—might reveal something queasy about Wordsworth's revolutionary verse. The crux of that revolution, as every undergraduate learns, was linguistic: the overthrow of poetic diction and the installation in its place of the language of the people. As with many another political dispute, this one had its culinary implications. In his "Preface" to the second edition of *Lyrical Ballads* Wordsworth describes the practitioners of poetic diction as bad eaters depending upon an artificial diet "to confer honor upon themselves and their art in proportion as they separate themselves from the sympathies of men, and indulge in arbitrary and capricious habits of expression, in order to furnish food for fickle tastes, and fickle appetites, of their own creation."[12]

Writing well boils down to eating well as good digestion becomes the measure of both. Wordsworth wants to purify British poetry so that its readers can feed naturally and digest with ease. The cultural logic of Romantic dietetics makes moral health a correlative of bodily process. Laporte has argued that, in France at least, the literary initiative to purify language corresponds to a social initiative to regulate waste, and that purity of expression and excretion both become the responsibility of the private citizen. When Wordsworth brings the language of poetry "near to the language of men," he purifies it in two ways: by pruning the "inane phraseology" of poetic diction that produces "feelings of disgust," but also by purging dirty vulgarities, leaving it "purified indeed from what appear to be its real defects, from all lasting and rational causes of dislike or disgust" (450, 447). Poetic diction and common vulgarity become the linguistic equivalent of waste, and it falls to the individual poet, that "Man speaking to men," to distinguish between true words and verbal turds (453). Wordsworth's devotion to the purity of language recapitulates the disciplinary practice of Romantic dietetics. Both make the elimination of waste the responsibility of a private subject who is a master of digestion.

Wordsworth is such a responsible eater, at least in his best poetry. "Lines Written a Few Miles above Tintern Abbey" demonstrates how completely he incorporates and digests his experience. Wordsworth's relationship to the abbey that situates but never directly appears in the poem has been the subject of critical interest, the most compelling of which takes the poet to task for ignoring its function of providing shelter for displaced workers.[13] But it was once the site of another function oddly coincident with Wordsworth's project of verbal purification. The monks who inhabited Tintern Abbey devised for their cloacae an ingenious drainage system, living as they did within flushing distance of the tidal basin of the river Wye.[14] Is it mere coincidence that the site of the indigenous origins of the WC should appeal to Wordsworth as the necessary place to undertake a peculiarly personal kind of hygiene? That digestion is one of the constitutive metaphors of "Tintern Abbey" shows the poem to be advancing the operative logic of Romantic dietetics. Wordsworth ruminates his way to consolation for discomfort. The poem becomes a pure, verbal equivalent of eating your way to a new you. Its initial emphasis upon the eye, the sights it sees and forms it feels, should not blind one to the importance of the stomach to the poem's vivifying effects. When Wordsworth turns inward to remember the boy he was in bygone days, the present world acquires a promisingly alimentary character:

> The picture of the mind revives again:
> While here I stand, not only with the sense
> Of present pleasure, but with pleasing thoughts
> That in this moment there is life and food
> For future years. (62–6)

When Wordsworth's relationship with the world becomes that of eater to eaten the possibility emerges of life and sustenance for years to come.

But Wordsworth must digest the world he incorporates. In "Tintern Abbey," memory functions as an organ of digestion, the stomach of cognition that assimilates the bounding boy Wordsworth was to the solitary man he has become in order to sustain the growth of the Poet's Mind. Romantic dietetics makes eating a cognitive matter, which is by no means to suggest that it transcends cultural politics: preparing food for future years turns out to be woman's work. The Poet, that exemplary individual, thrives upon a natural aliment that "the common Mother to all," to quote Locke, serves up with love and timely kindness: "for she can so inform / the mind that is within us, so impress / With quietness and beauty, and so feed / With lofty thoughts . . ." (125–8). Wordsworth eats to achieve autonomy, and female labor feeds him. Nature is "the nurse, / The guide, the guardian of my heart, and soul / Of all my moral being" (109–11). The sublime digestions of memory require a sustenance only women can prepare.

As with Locke, however, so with Wordsworth: female labor gets swallowed up in the proprietary movements of an autonomous man. Digestion is never complete, and perhaps predictably Wordsworth leaves it to a woman to clean up after him. In this regard there is something diarrheic about the way "Tintern Abbey" develops. Just when Wordsworth seems finished, he discovers something more about to be. After the apparently satisfying insight into nature's nursing ways, the urge to ruminate returns. And what emerges is something that remains indigestible to memory. The poem's last movement (112–60) puts the poet into material relation with memories he has already digested. He embodies them in his sister Dorothy, who has been obligingly invisible for 116 lines only to appear suddenly as the young Wordsworth's body double: "Oh! yet a little while / May I behold in thee what I was once, / My dear, dear Sister!" (119–21). This strange materializing of memory is the poem's equivalent of waste, the remainder of digestion unassimilable to the being it sustains. Dorothy incarnates a materiality irreducible to the proper body and incommensurable with a private subject.

Wordsworth's own becoming waste inspires this incarnation: "Nor, perchance, / If I should be, where I no more can hear / Thy voice, nor catch from thy wild eyes these gleams / Of past existence . . ." (146–9). Wordsworth commends to Dorothy the corpse of his material body, an indigestible remainder that memory can never assimilate. Kristeva calls the corpse "the utmost of dejection" and memorably describes the grim attrition of material existence: "wastes drop so that I might live, until, from loss to loss, nothing remains in me and my entire body falls beyond the limit— *cadere*, cadaver. If dung signifies the other side of the border, the place where I am not and which permits me to be, the corpse, the most sickening of wastes, is a border that has encroached upon everything" (4, 3). For Wordsworth, Dorothy becomes the woman of waste who alone can preserve his memory as he passes bodily to the other side of that border. As with Wollstonecraft's vindicated women, managing waste becomes a personal responsibility of the apparently independent female—the wasted woman. In the politics of waste promulgated by Romantic dietetics, the ends of eating devolve to women. There is a chauvinism of digestion that poetry like Wordsworth's reinforces. When Wordsworth hopes for Dorothy that her mind "Shall be a mansion," he must have imagined it with a beautiful bathroom.

Water Music

Perhaps with a water closet. Wordsworth's implied politics of waste has its social correlative in the development and astonishing triumph of the English WC. Historians of the modern toilet frequently wonder why it took so long to catch on. Even though the Romans were masters of the aqueduct and their baths were temples of joy, their toilets were common affairs, often open to whole crowds. The technology of the modern toilet became available, to those who found it compelling and could afford it, as early as the reign of Elizabeth. The great father of the flusher was Sir John Harrington, a kinsman of the queen and author in 1596 of the potentially world-transforming text, *The Metamorphosis of Ajax* ("a jakes" for those who like jokes). There Harrington describes, complete with diagrams and doggerel, "how to reform all unsavoury places, . . . whether they be caused by privies or sinks, or such like (for the annoyance coming all of the like causes, the remedies need not be much unlike)" (in Palmer 29). His diagrams compel. His technology persuades. The queen herself installed his new-fangled privy for her personal use in Richmond Palace.

But in the words of one historian of the WC, "the water music that Sir John started was not to be heard again for nearly two hundred years" (Palmer 26). With only a few eccentric exceptions, the English remained deaf to it until—strange conjunction of politics and plumbing!—an age of revolution dawned and Alexander Cummings applied in 1775 to patent his valve closet, the first successful design to become widely available. Its appeal in the words of its inventor arose from its ability to "far excel any ever made or invented for SWEETNESS, and Ease to be kept in repair," two considerations of prime importance for the domestication of the privy (quoted in Palmer 38). Three years later the indomitable Joseph Bramah, watchmaker and jeweler, patented an improved double-valved closet that instantly became the household standard and maintained that distinction for a hundred years. It could be argued that the British empire sat squarely on Bramah's throne, since its triumph owes so much to the colonization of excretion, as James Joyce's witty disquisition puts it: "The Roman, like the Englishman who follows in his footsteps, brought to every new shore on which he set his foot . . . his cloacal obsession. He gazed about him in his toga and he said: It is meet to be here. Let us construct a water closet."[15]

What distinguished English from Roman imperialism, however, and what explains the sudden proliferation of the water closet, is the cultural imperative emerging by the late eighteenth century to take personal responsibility for one's waste. The water closet privatizes waste disposal and thus the responsible subject in a way no Roman cloaca ever could, making possible both a domestic site of ritualized hygiene and its installation in the single-family home. As mothers and maids come to preside over this space, the water closet institutionalizes the association between women and waste, reinforcing their confinement to the private sphere in bourgeois culture. And the water closet does all this, quite brilliantly, by making shit disappear. With a simple flush the proper body asserts its autonomy over and against the common matter it produces. That an empire can be built on such homely practices is the lesson of nineteenth-century British history. Victoria reigned supreme over a toilet on which the sun never set. The material practice of personal waste disposal and the bodied logics of digestion work to administrate the body and direct the subject in bourgeois culture toward imperial ends. And it all happens so effortlessly. As Laporte points out, and thanks in no small part to the WC, "the disciplinary effects of [empire's] inquisitional gaze are adequately enforced simply by removing excrement from sight" (64).

"The Great Phenomena of Nature"

If Romantic dietetics incorporates an exclusionary politics that the material practices of the water closet reinforce, then what, it seems urgent to ask, constitutes resistance to a cultural regime built upon the ends of eating? Given the identification of women and waste characteristic of political liberalism, what alternatives might exist to a lifetime of latrine patrol? In a cultural context that so effectively appropriates the labors of digestion, the spectacle of Signora Girardelli provides food for reflection. She staged a public ordeal of female embodiment, a trial by fire that proved her impervious to prevailing dietetic imperatives. Billed as "The Great Phenomena of Nature," Signora Josephine Girardelli came to London in 1814 from the Continent, where her phenomenal skills had won her the patronage of royalty, or so she claimed. That her skills *were* phenomenal could be confirmed daily at Mr. Laxton's Rooms, 23 New Bond Street, at 12, 2, 4, and 6 o'clock for a mere three shillings. The crowds came and the Signora's reputation grew, making her England's most incombustible woman, and until the appearance a few years later of "The Fire King" Chabert, its least flammable human being.[16] In full view of all who ponied up their shillings, she performed an astonishing series of fiery feats: she walked barefoot over a red-hot iron plate, she place lighted candles under her arms, she bathed her body in aquafortis, she cooked an egg "fit for eating" in oil bubbling in her cupped hands, she dropped sealing wax onto her tongue, she took boiling oil into her mouth, and she poured boiling lead into it as well, joyfully removing it when cool to display the imprint of her teeth. Contemporary reviews mix skepticism with awe in the manner of the report that appears in the *Wonderful and Eccentric Museum or Magazine of Memorable Characters*: "that the whole is a trick cannot be doubted; but the vulgar gape and stare, and are fully prepossessed that the fair heroine is by nature gifted with this extraordinary repellent" (in Jay 258).

This woman is no "standing dish" to slake a glutton's appetite. She's too hot to handle, too repellent to consume. If she cannot so easily be eaten, she will not succumb to the effects of digestion. Signora Girardelli defies the cultural logic of Romantic dietetics that both incorporates the proper body and identifies women with waste. She becomes the other of digestion, the woman who resists reduction to common matter. She practices an incendiary bulimia that diverts the matter of ingestion away from its fate as waste. Eating and its ends become the most public of practices, a spectacle of incorporation that yields evidence, not of privatized subjectivity, but of social celebrity. Signora Girardelli's bitemarks in the lead affirm her celebrity as the Fire-Proof Lady. Her labor makes her independent rather than another's nurse. Here is a woman without interiors, irreducible to a Romantic dietetics that transforms substance into a subject who has made all the right choices. The Fire-Proof Lady eats to differ, and resists the common effects of digestion.

To paraphrase Wittgenstein, there is no such thing as a private digestion. Privacy as we know it, that liberal privilege of the proper body, is much an effect of digestion as its prerequisite. Romantic dietetics incorporates a responsible eater, one who digests, reflects, and disposes all alone. That these habits of body and mind become pervasive social practices only attest to the expedience, culturally speaking, of taking digestion for a site of bodily discipline. What could be more natural than going alone? What more inevitable than associating women with waste? But if as Laporte attests, "the space of defecation has not always been that of interior monologue," then perhaps the cultural logic of our most private practices is not absolute. A new politics of digestion might occasion new subjetivities, insurgent in a way that troubled Wollstonecraft for being witty, womanist, abject, and carnivalesque. It is worth remembering that the Reformation began in Luther's privy.

Notes

1. *Parade Magazine*, 9 July 2000.
2. John Hunter, *Lectures on the Principles of Surgery*, vol. 1 of *The Works of John Hunter*, ed. James F. Palmer (London, 1837), 247.
3. Thomas Beddoes, *Hygiea or Essays Moral and Medical on the Causes Affecting the Personal State of Our Middling and Affluent Classes*, 4 vols. (Bristol, 1802), 2: 6.
4. See Michel Foucault, *The Birth of the Clinic*, tr. A. M. Sheridan Smith (New York, 1973) and "The Politics of Health in the Eighteenth Century," in *Power/Knowledge*, tr. Colin Gordon et al. (New York: Pantheon, 1980), 166–82.
5. Gaston Bachelard, *La Formation de L'Esprit Scientifique* (Paris: J.Vrin, 1965), 169.
6. John Locke, *Two Treatises of Government*, ed. Peter Laslett, 2nd ed. (Cambridge: Cambridge UP, 1967), 305.
7. Samuel Taylor Coleridge, *The Notebooks of Samuel Taylor Coleridge*, 4 vols., ed. Kathleen Coburn (Princeton: Princeton UP, 1957), 2: 2092.
8. Dominique Laporte, *History of Shit*, tr. Nadia Benabid and Rodolphe el-Khoury (Cambridge: MIT Press, 2000), 29.

9. See Pateman's *The Sexual Contract* (Stanford: Stanford UP, 1988), especially chapters one and three.

10. Mary Wollstonecraft, *A Vindication of the Rights of Woman,* ed. Carol H. Poston, 2nd ed. (New York: Norton, 1988), 138.

11. Julia Kristeva, *Powers of Horror: An Essay on Abjection,* tr. Leon S. Roudiez (New York: Columbia UP, 1982), 4.

12. William Wordsworth, *Selected Poems and Prefaces*, ed. Jack Stillinger (Boston: Houghton Mifflin, 1965), 447.

13. See Marjorie Levinson's *Wordsworth's Great Period Poems* (Cambridge: Cambridge UP, 1986).

14. Roy Palmer, *The Water Closet: A New History* (Newton Abbot: David and Charles, 1973), 20. See also Lawrence Wright's *Clean and Decent: The Fascinating History of the Bathroom and the Water Closet* (New York: Viking, 1960).

15. James Joyce, *Ulysses* (New York: Vintage, 1961), 131.

16. On Signora Girardelli see Richard Altick's *The Shows of London* (Cambridge: Harvard UP, 1978) and Ricky Jay, *Learned Pigs and Fireproof Women* (New York: Villard, 1986).

Afterword ∾

LET THEM EAT ROMANTICISM: MATERIALISM, IDEOLOGY, AND DIET STUDIES

Timothy Morton

Der Mensch ist, was er ißt
—Ludwig Feuerbach[1]

Dis-moi ce que tu manges, je te dirai ce que tu es
—Jean-Antheleme Brillat-Savarin,
The Physiology of Taste, fourth aphorism[2]

Butchery,—a regiment of English militia, at the command of their officers, firing on their countrymen, the unarmed inhabitants of Bristol, when a number of men, women, and children were killed.
—Charles Pigott, *A Political Dictionary*, 8[3]

Reality Bites

The study of food has been necessarily interdisciplinary, as evidenced by journals devoted to it such as *Food and Foodways, Gastronomica,* and the publications of the Oxford Food Symposia. I call this work "diet studies." In its etymology *diet* is close to *culture*. The Greek *diaitia* implied Raymond Williams's idea of culture, "a whole way of life." Diet studies constantly gesture toward ways in which life is lived. Consider David Clark's work on figures of eating in Hegel and Schelling: they delineate a livable orientation—including sexual orientation. Interdisciplinary studies connect things in surprising ways. Paul Youngquist brings Lockean philosophy to bear upon the quotidian subject of using a toilet. Perceived gaps between different areas of human life are always theoretical, compelling us to reflect. Under-theorized or even antitheoretical studies of food and diet risk resembling Gillray's cartoon of the theoretical carrot-eating Frenchman and John Bull, his plumpness the empirical "proof" of English superiority, as Penelope Bradshaw points out. All the essays in *Eating Romanticism*, whether explicitly so or not, are theoretical, opening gaps between food and its cultural places. There's many a slip 'twixt cup and lip.

There is a fruitful conjunction between philosophical-literary scholars and historicists, between the study of what falls out of the movement of thought, and histories of what has been excluded from the grand sweep of history. It is no accident that both forms of marginalization arose in the eighteenth century. The parallel between history and philosophy is that between the Whiggish history that in Britain underpinned the entrepreneurial bourgeoisie, and the nascent new order in Germany, struggling to think itself out of the Middle Ages and become a modern state.[4] Nevertheless, while historicism uses the "real" as a rhetorical supplement that enriches its analytical observations, poststructuralist work in psychoanalysis and deconstruction posits the real as inaccessible, visible as a gap or as an inert presence. Diet studies need what Theodor Adorno meant by negative dialectics: the encounter of thought with what it is not—nonidentity.

Jacques Derrida and Michel Foucault inspired current literary attention to the margins. In very different ways, the work of the Annales School, Pierre Bourdieu, and Michel De Certeau have stimulated the study of "everyday life." Diet studies implies what Derrida himself, in a moment that may surprise those affiliated with a philosophical or historical hardcore, describes as a radical form of empiricism, qualified by a sense of how empiricism, standing for "nonphilosophy," actually implies a philosophical dilemma—should we include it or nor?[5] At the very heart of his delineation of deconstructive method Derrida is claiming that empiricism is not deconstruction's enemy. Elsewhere Derrida called Emmanuel Levinas and Friedrich Schelling radical empricists.[6] These things look rather different depending on which side of the English Channel you are on. It might surprise someone in the lineage of Locke and Hume that empiricism was "nonphilosophy." But here we re-encounter historical determination. Marx observed that empiricism was a progressive philosophy still ideologically affiliated with the bourgeois reality-principle, rather than with reality as such.

The intersection between history and philosophy could be literature. For Sir Philip Sidney, figurative language has all the particularity of history and all the generality of philosophy. Poetry presents philosophical generalities as if they had sensuous historical embodiment, delighting while it instructs. Like other forms of aesthetic artifact, food holds a place between the material and the conceptual. Sidney hesitates between the aesthetic as something that merely supplements the cognitive, and as something more deeply interfused, evoking a metaphor of consumption, "a medicine of cherries," borrowing from the Epicurean theory expounded in Lucretius's *De rerum natura*. Such a hesitation could only come into question during a crisis of legitimation. For Denise Gigante, at the beginning of the reign of the bourgeoisie, which made its paradoxical legitimation from permanent crisis, there emerges the outline of crisis in anxieties about the notion of "taste."[7] At *our* end of the same story, scholars study and generate the very same anxieties.[8]

Diet is particularly suited to this crisis. Everyone eats: food is the great leveler. The construal of identity through eating is thus a massive reduction of human value and potential. As being becomes portable it becomes potable. In consumerism eating can stand for an aesthetic experience of others' lifeworlds. We can "eat Chinese." In the ideological gaze of imperialism, that is pretty much (and increasingly so) that in which *being* Chinese consists. This was already true for Oliver Goldsmith, and as Alan Bewell demonstrated in his study of how local and national identity is constructed through food and eating, it was the case in the Romantic period (135–54). Colonialism and nationalism reproduced the local as the edible: see Gillray's picture of Germans eating sauerkraut. The modern idea of national identity was born, dependent upon meaningless morsels of enjoyment exemplified by reified fictions of the "national dish." Just as news has recently been reduced to soundbites, nationality is reduced to bite-sized pieces. The extreme discrepancy between general and particular, between global and local, between citizens of the world and frogs, is a symptom of the sundering of fact and value.

How to distinguish oneself as belonging to the right sort of people, if the philosophical determinants of one's identity are abstract and universal derivations from the American and French Revolutions? Distinction upon distinction was required in a fluid process of social relations. Identity is performed as *habitus*, regulated improvisation (Bourdieu). For Colin Campbell consumerist diet became a menu of performative acts.[9] Meanwhile the working class was treated as if its members were engines that needed stoking.[10] A dichotomy arose between the undead subjectivity of the bourgeoisie and the morbid objectivity of the working class. For the middle classes it was other people who did not to know how to eat properly: they were cannibals, they did not know how to use a knife and fork, they allowed terrible behavior at table . . . Norbert Elias, whose history of table

James Gillray, *Germans Eating Sour Krout* (*sic*) (London 1803). Copyright the British Museum, London.

manners has inspired scholars such as Margaret Visser and in another key Peter Stallybrass and Allon White, makes a strong case for this view.[11] There are, however, uneven developments in this history. Hannah Glasse's canonical *Art of Cookery*, published in America for the first time while Wordsworth was redrafting *The Prelude*, contains material on proper methods of carving that would not have seemed out of place in the early seventeenth century, with its technical vocabulary of "rearing" geese and "unbracing" mallards, appealing to ancient aristocratic traditions of full-frontal knife-work.[12] Diet studies must pay attention to this unevenness.

Diet studies necessitates both "long history" such as that practiced by Elias and Fernand Braudel and "microhistory." Diet studies possesses both the sweep of generality and the redolence of particularity. The asymmetry here, akin to assymetries in modernism between the local and the global, is subtended by views of history as an emulsion of small details and world-historical tendencies. This is the intellectual equivalent of *nouvelle cuisine*: an enormous ground marked by a tiny, vivid figure. One minute a historian might be chatting about knives and forks; the next, outlining the entire history of bourgeois consciousness. This method simultaneously analyzes and reproduces an ideological form: bourgeois consciousness may indeed be reducible to worrying about how to use a knife and fork.

Taste and Appetite, High and Low

What does it mean, to eat? *Does* it mean, to eat? One could pass too swiftly over these basic questions. My earlier assumption was that the significance of food supplements its necessity for survival. Raymond Williams asserted that the former does not take precedence over the latter.[13] But this is already to install a potent opposition between luxury and necessity shaping the very food we eat during the emergence of commercial capitalism: some kinds of food are central, others marginal. It appears that however far one wishes to travel into the physical, questions of the metaphysical cannot be shirked.

Two philosophies appear in the Romantic period, reducible to the slogans "you are what you eat" (materialism) and "you are how you feed" (idealism). The gourmand Brillat-Savarin and the metaphysical materialist Feuerbach invented the first phrase. Dickens's novels and Percy Shelley's representations of dyspeptic tyrants take seriously the idea that we are what we eat. The second slogan emerges as a theme in German philosophy's meditations upon subjectivity, and also in Romantic poetry. Subjectivity is theorized as a circulation around a fantasy object. Identity becomes the (mental) digestion of digestion. For Jacob Boehme, much loved by Hegel, existence is an eating of God's being. Sartre remarked in 1939 that French philosophy has been "mired" in such language for a century—that is, since the Romantic period:

> "His eyes devoured her." The expression provides one of many hints of the illusion, common to both realism and idealism, that knowing is a sort of eating . . . we've all imagined a spider-Mind drawing things into its web, covering them in white saliva and slowly ingesting them, reducing them to its own substance.[14]

This idea, resonant in phenomenology, has a history in empiricism and materialism. The Romantic-period scientist Pierre-Jean-Georges Cabanis suggested that the brain "digests" impressions as the stomach digests food.[15]

Which slogan is the reason for the request of Frankenstein's creature to live a simple vegetarian life of nonviolence with his mate in South America?[16] How can we account for the ideological slang that was already apparent in the Romantic period, associating the French with frogs, the English with roast beef? Either way: "you are what you eat" (the stupid English are practically made of roast beef); "you are how you feed" (French eating habits are effeminate). Surely each slogan's theory of identity would compromise the other one? But this is precisely how they work, slipping through metonymy from diet to identity: the French eat frogs . . . they *are* frogs. This aporetic choice between inconsistent solutions indicates that we are in the presence of ideology; diet studies need precisely to study ideology. Studying ideology is the corrective for scholarship that, dare one say it, comes *too close* to its subject, missing its target through myopic scrutiny. It may be confusing for epistemophiliacs to hear that they can come too close to an object of knowledge. But this is the import of Alan Liu's essay on historical detail (see the following section).

The collusion between idealism and materialism consists in eliding what one eats with how one feeds. Gillray's representation of "Krauts" (Germans eating sauerkraut) manifests a short circuit: the Germans are the *kind* of people who would eat sauerkraut. The rigid designator "sauerkraut" stands in the place of an ungraspable notion of identity. This is the form of racist ideology: a troubling emulsion of specific details and vague generalities that betrays a "lack [of meaning and consistency] in the other."[17] Englishness seems to consist in a certain embodied thingy, a metastasized enjoyment; but if you have to ask what it is, you are not one of "us." Let us consider this Möbius strip a little further.

Jocelyne Kolb distinguishes between texts that mention food ("low" ones such as the novel) and those that do not ("high" epic and tragedy).[18]

This is true of Thomas Chatterton's deliquescent parody of an epic battle in the food fights of the *Constabiliad* and the *Consuliad*.[19] A "high" form is brought "low" when greasy geese become substitutes for spears. But where does that leave the banquets in Milton's epics—Satan's banquet in *Paradise Regained*, the quasi-vegetarian poetics of *Paradise Lost*?[20] Consider also the vivid ambience created by the imagery of fruit in Andrew Marvell's "Bermudas"—a "high" lyric. A Bakhtinian approach to the "low"—it expresses the body, is visible in novelistic but not high poetic forms—risks reifying the material realm in the same way as invoking "the body."

Kolb concedes that "high" literature does denote foods if they are not artificial, invoking Lévi-Strauss's distinction between the raw and the cooked. Artificial food—anything involving cooking or decorating—is unseemly.[21] Where does that leave one of the most significant figurations of food in the late eighteenth century: the representation of sugar? Thomas Grainger's *The Sugar Cane* is a didactic work, considered by many eighteenth-century writers as an example of the highest form of rhetoric, higher even than epic. The poem is concerned with how to grow and refine sugar cane, which many discourses of the period would have construed not as natural but as artificial. Joseph Litvak has explored the notion of the sophisticated, which involves the consumption of what is considered low or crude or raw in a high manner. Sophistication is caught up in issues of gender and of class. To be sophisticated is to be queer. It is also to be or to imitate, the aristocracy. Stallybrass and White have argued that it is primarily the bourgeoisie that distinguishes between the coarse and the refined. Constantly anxious, having to pull itself up by one's own bootstraps, bourgeois consciousness makes increasingly nice distinctions.

The laddish young Jamie Oliver, the brilliant "naked chef," describes a fish pie as "tacky, but tasty."[22] By the beginning of the twenty-first century working classness itself has become a sign of distinction. "Tacky" is an oddly chosen adjective—surely "old fashioned" or just "lower class" would have been more accurate? But with the kitsch like which it connotes stickiness, greasiness and tactility, the tacky has become a symptom of bourgeois anxiety that one's attempt to beautify or otherwise elevate oneself will be seen as too obvious, not "natural" enough. What is tacky has been tacked on. Physicality is the new fashion, as long as the consumer maintains the appropriate distance toward it, a postmodern strategy of embracing what Jean-Paul Sartre called "the slimy" rather than gliding away from it. The fish pie is tacky not because it is inherently low but because of its role in postmodern distinction. Mashed potato likewise became chic in Britain and America throughout the 1990s. At the very moment at which real working-class cultures, let alone jobs, are threatened, working classsness emerges as a style of middle-class aesthetics.

The long eighteenth century had its own versions of this kind of culinary retro or camp.[23] The phenomenon of "antiqued" food, a fascination for example with medieval banquets, may be discovered in the diverse work of Richard Warner and Thomas Warton.[24] Exotic foods such as spices were given complex poetic treatment though nutmet survives in Glasse. Vegetarianism is an avant-garde version of what became a more pervasive style of bourgeois ideology, the new age or hippie aesthetic of eating crude or natural foods in a highly sophisticated manner. The distinction in Boulder, Colorado, between a tofu and arugula salad and a piece of fried chicken ensues from strong divisions between raw and cooked, crude and refined—but also white and black, and upper and lower class. But even vegetarianism complicates these divisions, which are themselves crude. Staring at his piece of broccoli as if it were "a substantial wing of chicken," Percy Shelley was ahead of his time.[25]

Food already falls into representation prior to its inclusion in aesthetic forms such as poetry. Let us consider the notion of incorporation: the representation of how, or whether, the other becomes the self, is known or grasped by the self; the question of subject and object that so preoccupied Samuel Taylor Coleridge, and Hegel (see Tilottama Rajan's essay, chapter 11). Ingestion appears as an ambiguous metaphor for this process, and sometimes not just as a metaphor. Maggie Kilgour has shown the extent to which such motifs negotiate between the basic metaphysical distinction between inside and outside. Coleridge confused the two, establishing "a fallacious regression to a Golden Age," "in a time which demands that individuals be autonomous, and that authors control the meaning and boundaries of their textual propriety."[26]

Kilgour describes Coleridge as an orouboric, self-swallowing snake (211), a perpetual Romantic motif. Hegel's describes a Hindu statue (he thinks it is an expression of Buddhism), an image of a man with a toe in his mouth, as an incarnated symbol of abstract contemplation: consciousness circling upon itself, consciousness "in itself" in Hegelese.[27] The leading Romantic heroes, subject and object, here play conflicting roles. Only when subject and object are perceived in general (socially) to have been sundered from each other would the issue of their fusion or reconciliation become an anxious topic.

"The body" names a topsy-turvy counter-aesthetics. In those Romantic-derived languages, psychoanalysis and phenomenology, the body is not an empirical object but a screen or experiential envelope.

The more we ponder the idea that the body is neither inside nor outside mind and matter, that it awkwardly straddles these traditionally opposed levels of reality, the more we threaten entirely to undo the opposition between inside and outside, and hence the distinction between subject and object. Where does the body stop—is food part of it? When? In the hand? The mouth? The stomach? The toilet? Acknowledging the existence of what in phenomenology is called the perceptual field is to admit that subject and object cannot properly be distinguished.

You Eat What You Are

Is food a sign or a thing? Food can substantiate empirical reality: the stone against which Dr. Johnson refuted Berkeley might as well have been a bowl of oats. The uses of food in both historicism and philosophical criticism are intimately related, but as two points on the "opposite" sides of a Möbius strip twisted in ideological space. Cultural analysis often appeals to some kind of metaphysical Real beyond the text. To what extent is such an appeal a ruthless desacralization of the "place" reserved in the social symbolic order for the aesthetic? On the other hand, to what extent is it in fact an anxious attempt to reinvent and hold open that very place, much as the role of food and excrement in modern art paradoxically holds open the space of the aesthetic against the commodification of everything, and the aestheticization of the commodity?[28] Does the process of looking in a sidelong way at literary texts, via their material "remainders," actually reinforce rather than undermine the aesthetic dimension—as the sidelong look of the lady in Keats's "La Belle Dame Sans Merci" reinforces the power of her position as sublime object of desire? Might the mechanical insistence on contextualization paradoxically turn context into (aestheticized) text? Instead of running away from poststructuralism a more rigorous materialism should be keen to explore it and apply it all the more intensively.

In a fetishistic manner, transcendence and detail can coexist in historicist literary studies, including normative studies of diet. Liu criticizes texts in which culture appears with an existential punch, "with all the ontological zing of the Real."[29] "Zing" hesitates between a fetishism of detail and a totalizing effect, a sudden illumination: the ring or zing of truth. "Zing" sounds like Kant's *das Ding*, but is also the onomatopoeic equivalent of the sparkling droplets on an image of a can of Coca Cola, that realest of real things. The German pharmaceutical firm Bayer, the eventual marketers of what they named aspirin, gave the brand name "Heroin" to diamorphine, a concentrated extract of morphine (an opium derivative), a name with zing. "Zing"

266 ~ *Timothy Morton*

incarnates the enjoyment of hallucinated accuracy. What is interesting about "the real" is not merely its reality but the open secret of its superficial "zing."

"Zing" expresses enjoyment in the form of fetishized realism, allowing such personifications as Catherine Gallagher's: "the potato threatened to break the bread nexus" (127). A complex of social forces has disappeared from this phrase, making it difficult to recall that a major reason for William Cobbett's and others' conflation of the potato with the brute misery of existence, perhaps the main reason why for them it "represented a shrunken humanity" (135), was that it exemplified social domination enforced by rationality and science. The bugbear image of the Irish reduced to the merely biological "homo appetitus" (130) is itself an ideological product of a powerful social order, not some absolutely irreducible remainder. "Homo appetitus" resembles Giorgio Agamben's recent formulation "homo sacer," the starving and otherwise victimized human subjects of the global humanitarian gaze. Acting on behalf of welfare "reform," it was Thomas Malthus who insisted that the English poor be fed on potatoes, whose consumption would place them, like the Irish, beyond the pale (134). The asymmetries in the study of food are resolved if one brings into view the ideological space in which they are expressed. Diet studies could go beyond academically transgressive "wow."

Given the nature of what Peter Sloterdijk calls cynical reason, the fascination for "zing" in historicizing prose is illusory. One never actually quite believes in "reality-effects." In truth "none of us would actually believe" an advertisement, however resonant its "zing." This would not, however, disqualify advertisements from working. Ideology, never more potent than when one believes one has seen through it, does not operate via convincing reality effects. A certain amount of cynicism is very effective: " 'They know that, in their activity, they are following an illusion, but still, they are doing it' "—in this sense, as Terry Eagleton continues, citing Žižek, " 'falsity' lies on the side of what we *do*, not necessarily of what we say."[30]

We should thicken Eagleton's "do" by observing that ideology resides not only in ideas about McDonalds hamburgers, but in those very burgers themselves. Soft as sofas, they embody the view of comfort and the notion of instant gratification that encompasses, in different shades, the middle and lumpen classes. As Jane Stabler makes clear in her essay on milk and blood in Byron, food embodies fantasies at the root of ideological positions. Louis Althusser's theory of ideology offers a decentered version of Feuerbach's and Brillat-Savarin's "you are what you eat." If ideology is a way of positioning a subject, then it is more strictly true that "you eat what you are." The contemporary pop singer Laurie Anderson wittily derives her identity from a chocolate bar in her father's pocket.[31] Ultimately, then, we obtain

an even more potent formula, altogether different from classical materialism and idealism: "*you are what they eat.*"

For a Marxist, zing is as unsatisfying as chewing gum. In Marx's favorite
Shakespeare play, *Timon of Athens*, Timon expresses his disillusionment with
zing by serving his guests a banquet of lukewarm water. Coke turns flat,
eventually. Moreover, its very zinginess has something flat about it, flat but
not unprofitable, at least for the corporation: it embodies pure flavor, an
utterly nonutilitarian drink that renders the taste of thirst itself.[32] This is the
secret of the secret, the reverse side of the study of excluded things. The
secret connection between historicism and philosophical criticism is detail-
ism, the morcelization of human reality. Ideological criticism recombines
the study of history and philosophy at a higher level. Rather than reproducing the antinomies that are the essence of ideology, such criticism
resolves the ideological cynical distance by tampering with the objectal
kernel of enjoyment. Diet studies could undermine not only dominant
assumptions about reality, but also the pseudo-neutral subjectivity that
guarantees their validity by holding them in fascination.

Here we encounter another form of dialectical criticism well suited to
food studies. Instead of rendering the zing of the real, radical kinds of collage that vividly illuminate a quilting-point of identity (taste and appetite),
could render the social and political "real of zing" via the shock of juxtaposing the categories of food and eating, as in the epigraph to this chapter.

Capital Sucks: Production, Consumption, Ideology

Marx ignores the "polite" tastes of the bourgeoisie, refusing to disengage
physical from psychic satisfaction: neither raising the aesthetic to a height of
ascetic abstraction, nor degrading it to the lowest common denominator. He
dissolves the knot of taste and appetite. Diet studies as they relate to literature
are currently exploring different materialisms. For some, materialism smacks
of the distasteful, the lowbrow. For others materialism is the poststructuralist
"materiality of the signifier." Julia Kristeva and Judith Butler explore issues of
materialism without foregoing the stringencies of post-structuralist theory.[33]
Both direct distaste and as it were "inverted" post-structuralist (dis)taste for
materialism risk disavowing Marx. Ironically those very studies in which the
materiality of food or of the culinary signifier pops up like a receipt resort to
a metaphysical materialism which Marx would dislike.

For Marx capital itself is the ultimate Romantic subject, making more
of itself in a hyperbolic process of self-transcendence encapsulated in the
formula for capitalism, Money–Capital–Money or more precisely M–C–M′

(money begetting even more money; *Capital* 1, chapter 4). But this self-transcendence is secretly based upon a vampiric sucking of labor-power; Franco Moretti and Jennifer Wicke have related vampires to the class structures and history of consumerism in Marx's time.[34]

Abstract homogenized labor is the secret of capital's vampiric form. Capitalism is materialized Hegelianism, chewing up the world without leaving any leftovers. The Young Hegelians perilously ignore the "profane" aspect of history, its "real basis": "the truly historical appears to be separated from ordinary life, something superstitial." Metaphysical distinctions arise between what history includes ("history") and what it excludes ("nature"). History only addressing "the political actions of princes and States"—as opposed, say, to food and eating—is one example; another would be Hegel's idea that the philosophy of history is the history of philosophy. In this brand "it is not a question of real, nor even of political, interests, but of pure thoughts, which consequently must appear . . . as a series of 'thoughts' that devour one another and are finally swallowed up in 'self-consciousness.'"[35]

Marx anticipates Mikhail Bakhtin's preoccupation with profanity, catching authority with its trousers down. Idealist history puts the cart before the horse: "Just as according to the old teleologists plants exist to be eaten by animals and animals by men, history exists to serve as the act of consumption of theoretical eating—proving. Man exists so that history may exist and history exists so that the proof of truths may exist" (139). Idealism is like deriving "the general idea 'Fruit'" from actual fruit such as "apples, pears, strawberries, and almonds":

> if I . . . imagine that my abstract idea "Fruit" . . . is an entity existing outside me, is indeed the true essence of the pear, the apple, etc.: then . . . I am declaring that "Fruit" is the substance of the pear, the almond, etc. I am saying, therefore, that to be a pear is not essential to the pear. (136)

Thus "different profane fruits" become "different manifestations of the life of the one 'Fruit'"—"'Absolute Fruit'" (136, 137). Idealism performs a totalizing function, simultaneously abstracting and essentializing.

What capitalism and idealism construe as essential hollows out actual human beings. By contemplating "profane" fruits Marx makes them stick in the throat rather than be digested into generality. Idealism uses the post-Enlightenment model of digestion: the stomach and intestines as a factory furnace in which the generalized substance of "chyle" is obtained from specific foods—the "crap factory" as Bart Simpson eloquently puts it. This is not just an analogy. For Nicholas Roe industrial food production since the Romantic period sacrificed concrete flavor and good quality to abstract nutrition. The "rendering" of cattle (a word poised between carving and writing),[36] producing both Bovril and food for other cows, spawned bovine spongeiform encepalopathy. Foot and mouth disease, which ravaged British agribusiness and tourism in the late 1990s, is also a product of treating concrete sentient beings as abstract capital investments. For Mark Rowlands "few are willing to realize that the packaged, sanitized supermarket meat that materializes on their dinner tables every day is the result of an industrial process involving unimaginable pain and suffering."[37] Marx enjoys disturbing tables that reduce the needs of the working class to nutrition, seen in bland Victorian terms as a certain ratio of carbon and nitrogen (*Capital* 1.835). The crass utilitarian generalization evoked by such tables is itself a feature of what Marx is criticizing—they have a poetic effect, making a point in the negative.

Settling upon fruit rather than Beef Wellington is apt. Writers such as Rousseau praised fruit for its naturalness, its rawness. But just as Marxism emerges from and yet critiques Enlightenment philosophes, so Marxist fruit dialectically cancels and preserves the quasi-vegetarian figuration in which it had been intricated. Enlightenment and Romantic fruit is just another form of generalization, symbolizing "nature" as opposed to "culture"—a distinction Marx himself criticized. Marx's fruit preserves nonconceptuality, nonidentity. The strawberries in Percy Shelley's "Marenghi," eaten by the republican protagonist as he gathers his energies, are not actual strawberries but a sign of his ascetic self-discipline, and of Shelley's proper consumption of the literary history of strawberries: they had come to signify the diet of a hermit, his way of life, his discipline.

Idealism wonders whether the inside could perfectly digest the outside. For Adorno idealism is "the belly turned mind," a rationalized version of appetitive rage.[38] Marx's sense is that reconciling subject and object is analogous to digestion. Postmodern critics such as Jean Baudrillard, whose account makes much of an alleged metaphysics of production, fail to acknowledge that Marx's view of production incorporates both "production" and "consumption" as commonly understood.[39] When he declares that it does not matter whether "wants" that are satisfied by commodities "spring from the stomach or from fancy," Marx assaults not only idealism, but also the crass empiricism and utilitarianism that reduces human needs to bottom lines.[40] Use-value is not about things but relationships. Certain wants cannot be expressed in solid objects. Diet studies may fruitfully deconstruct capitalist ideology's opposition between luxury and necessity, common both to economic discourse and of poetic theories such as the Coleridgean-Romantic distinction between fancy and imagination.

The concreteness of use-values is not an empirical solidity but a sociological determinacy. Eating thus becomes a focus of sociological data, an uncompromisingly stark extension of the trope of cannibalism to the silk factories: "The children were . . . slaughtered for the sake of their delicate fingers, just as horned cattle are slaughtered in southern Russia for their hides and their fat" (1.406). During the struggle for a shorter working day capitalism squeezed more value out: "Every new trick the capitalist hit upon . . . for keeping his machinery going . . . without increasing the number of personnel meant that the worker had to gulp down his meals in a different fragment of time" (1.404).

Capital warped consumption in society at large: "The adulteration of bread, and the formation of a class of bakers who sell bread for less than its full price, are developments which have taken place . . . as soon as the corporate character of the trade was lost, and the capitalist stepped behind the nominal master baker in the shape of a miller or a flour factor." This led to "the unlimited extension of the working day," since bakers were compelled to toil long hours (1.361). Marx equates this with philosophy: "this kind of 'sophistry' understands better than Protagoras how to make white black, and black white, and better than the Eleatics how to demonstrate before your very eyes that everything real is merely apparent" (1.358). The very food we put in our mouths has become an unstable trope, an adulterated materiality.

Against this giddy tropology Marx pits his expanded, humanized view of production. This is not simply a question of the pot calling the metaphysical kettle black. In his remarks on Adolph Wagner's economics Marx explicitly associates production with "consumption": "Men do not in any way begin by 'finding themselves in a theoretical relationship to the things of the external world.' Like every animal, they begin by *eating, drinking* . . . not by 'finding themselves' in a relationship, but by behaving actively, gaining possession of certain things in the external world by their actions, thus satisfying their needs. (They thus begin by production.)"[41] Marx's "production" includes the sensation of eating a nectarine, something that might surprise postmodern readers of Keats, let alone Baudrillard. Eating becomes praxis, a term suggesting the fusion of the theoretical with the practical.

To understand the "external world" is to grasp ideology itself: as Žižek wittily parodies the byline of the TV series *The X-Files*, "The Truth is Out There."[42] Or as Max Horkheimer put it: "It is not that chewing gum undermines metaphysics but that it *is* metaphysics"—a mass culture in which people get too little, not too much.[43] An eighteenth-century delicacy called the "surprize" incarnated human power: "cooked rabbits were stripped, and the flesh mixed with forcemeat fitted neatly back over their skeletons and browned with a salamander. They were carried to the table with their jaw-bones stuck into their eyes, and bunches of myrtle in their mouths, looking very surprised indeed."[44] Who is really surprised here? The dish is nonaristocratic game, a miniaturized simulation of the grandiose violence of medieval fare. But the jaw-bone piercing the rabbit's own eyes also embodies the existential punch of empirical evidence, that characteristic Enlightenment fantasy object: one is necessarily surprised if "seeing is believing"; the *consumer's* eyes are punctured. The self-evidence of empiricism is embodied in the rabbit's grotesque reflexivity: the jaw-bones in its eyes suggest a link between being seen and being eaten. In its very disembodiment the rabbit embodies the idea of analysis—dissolution and reconstitution. The dish symbolizes the secret connection between Kant and de Sade; it seems part of a ceremony of initiation into shocking knowledge. The "surprize" demonstrates that ideology contains an inconsistent fantasy kernel of enjoyment, establishing a basic fixation around which ideological language agglutinates. When analysis focuses on these "sinthomes" as Lacan called them, the surrounding ideological view can be undermined. Two centuries later this fantasy image has been relegated to the horror movie screen. Imagine it being brought to table, as a delicacy!

Why would Jean-Anthelme Brillat-Savarin so provocatively have entitled *The Physiology of Taste* (1825)? Why else other than to ground a mode of class consciousness in nature while simultaneously making that nature itself the object of a tortuously refined gaze? Brillat-Savarin's rational–sensual approach displays every aspect of appetite, digestion, and taste under the aegis of a progressive, Enlightenment foray into the world of the senses, through the rhetoric of a thorough, penetrating gaze. In his analysis of sophistication Litvak demonstrates how Brillat-Savarin reveals the ugly flip-side of taste, "the implicit cannibalism of sophistication," a sadist's delight in lips, teeth, mouth, and saliva. Taste must spit out the tasteless: "the whole machinery of nourishment is set in motion; the gastric juices rise, the internal gases are noisily displaced; the mouth fills with saliva; and all the digestive powers are up in arms, like soldiers only waiting for the word to go into action" (57).[45] Brillat-Savarin connects the voracious appetite with colonization:"When the Britons, the Teutons, the Cimmerians, and the Scythians poured into France, they brought with them a rare voracity and stomachs of uncommon capacity . . . These intruders ate in hotels, in taverns, at street-stalls, and even in restaurants." This was all to boost abstract capital, the balance of payments (135). One discerns the inverse image of the French bourgeoisie as colonizers of social space. The modern restaurant was itself a product of reverse colonization: Mennell notes that the business, which started two decades before the Revolution, was advanced by chefs fleeing aristocratic kitchens and revolutionary deputies flooding Paris (136–9).

Brillat-Savarin's chapter titles fuse the body and the mind: "The Theory of Frying," the "Philosophical Reflection" on fish (114–18, 89–90). Their coyness does ideological work. Bourgeois normalcy "knows very well" that philosophizing could never be equated with eating a piece of fish; the standard view represses a contemplative form of republicanism celebrated in the English Interregnum in figures such as Richard Franck's angler.[46] But the delicious sophistication of Brillat-Savarin's prose relies upon the playful acceptance of just such a juxtaposition. We proceed "as if" eating and thinking *were* equivalent. The distinction has been abolished at one level and preserved at another. Capitalist economics likewise "knows very well" that labor is the source of value. The trick of ideology is to act cynically as if this were not so (Žižek, *Sublime Object*, chapter 1).

Brillat-Savarin's self-reflexive series of "meditations" may at any moment enframe a narrative or dialogue. In addition to its Enlightenment voracity, it Romantically evokes something ever more about to be, displacing its authorial voice in paradoxical acts of self-grounding irony. The familiar modern ideological process of interpellation, posited by the Lacanian Marxist Louis Althusser, appears in Brillat-Savarin's literary technique. Strictures on cooking, serving, eating, and diet are rendered more powerful through their displacement onto discursive processes with which a reader can "identify." To match this diet studies must move beyond discovering how certain phenomena seem to fall outside the text, a ironically textualist obsession. How are diet and textuality *more* deeply implicated than the "sophisticated" postmodern image of shit falling on the book in Peter Greenaway's *Prospero's Books*? Diet studies risk repeating gestures of sophistication, the studied crudity of mentioning the unmentionable. Materialism is not necessarily a discourse of the unmentionable.

For Marx, "*eating, drinking*" do not preclude theory but invites it, as in Plato's *Symposium*. Satisfying one's needs might incline one to look further than one's nose. Where did your breakfast come from? To consider this is to uncover global networks of trade and power. The world may be real, but it is far from prepackaged: we do not necessarily "find ourselves" anywhere in particular, unless we are the victim of oppressive conditions and have been led there blindly.

Notes

1. Ludwig Feuerbach, *Gesammelte Werke II, Kleinere Schriften*, ed. Werner Schuffenhauer (Berlin: Akadamie-Verlag, 1972), 4.27.
2. Jean-Anthelme Brillat-Savarin, *The Physiology of Taste*, tr. Anne Drayton (Harmondsworth: Penguin, 1970), 13.

3. Charles Pigott, *A Political Dictionary: Explaining the True Meaning of Words. Illustrated and Exemplified in the Lives, Morals, Character and Conduct of the Following Most Illustrious Personages, among Many Others . . .* (London: 1795).

4. Terry Eagleton, *The Ideology of the Aesthetic* (Oxford: Basil Blackwell, 1990), introduction.

5. Jacques Derrida, *Of Grammatology*, tr. Gayatri Chakravorty Spivak (Baltimore and London: the Johns Hopkins UP, 1987), 162. I am grateful to David Clark for discussing this with me.

6. In "Violence and Metaphysics," *Writing and Difference*, tr. Alan Bass (London and Henley: Routledge and Kegan Paul, 1978), 79–153 (151–2).

7. See Denise Gigante, "After Taste: The Aesthetics of Romantic Eating." (Princeton: Ph.D. dissertation, 2000).

8. See for example Sian Griffiths and Jennifer Wallace, eds., *Consuming Passions: Food in the Age of Anxiety* (Manchester and New York: Mandolin, 1998).

9. Colin Campbell, *The Romantic Ethic and the Spirit of Modern Consumerism* (Oxford and New York: Basil Blackwell, 1987); Pierre Bourdieu, *Distinction: A Social Critique of the Judgement of Taste*, tr. Richard Nice (London: Routledge, 1989).

10. Marx, *Capital* 1.376.

11. See Margaret Visser, *The Rituals of Dinner: The Origins, Evolution, Eccentricities, and Meaning of Table Manners* (Harmondsworth: Penguin, 1991); Peter Stallybrass and Allon White, *The Politics and Poetics of Transgression* (Ithaca: Cornell UP, 1986).

12. Hannah Glasse, *The Art of Cookery Made Plain and Easy; Excelling Any Thing of the Kind Ever Published* (Alexandria: Cottom and Stewart, 1805), 235–7. On the history of carving see Keith Thomas, *Man and the Natural World: Changing Attitudes in England 1500–1800* (London: Allen Lane, 1983; repr. Penguin, 1984), 26–7; Timothy Morton, *Shelley and the Revolution in Taste*, 73, 93–6, 147–8; Norbert Elias, *The History of Manners* (*The Civilizing Process*, vol. 1), tr. Edmund Jephcott (New York: Pantheon, 1978), 118–21.

13. Raymond Williams, *The Sociology of Culture* (New York: Schocken, 1982), 209–10.

14. Jean-Paul Sartre, "Intentionality," in *Incorporations* (*Zone* 6), ed. Jonathan Crary and Sanford Kwinter 387–91 (387).

15. Pierre-Jean-George Cabanis, *On the Relations Between the Physical and Moral Aspects of Man*, tr. Margaret Duggan Saidi, ed. George Mora, 2 vols. (Baltimore: Johns Hopkins UP, 1981), 1.116.

16. Mary Shelley, *Frankenstein or the Modern Prometheus: The 1818 Text*, ed. James Rieger (Chicago and London: University of Chicago Press, 1974, 1982), 142.

17. Slavoj Žižek, *The Sublime Object of Ideology* (London and New York: Verso, 1989, 1991), 95–7.

18. Jocelyne Kolb, *The Ambiguity of Taste: Freedom and Food in European Romanticism* (Ann Arbor: The University of Michigan Press, 1995), 1–3.

19. See Timothy Morton, "In Your Face," in *Thomas Chatterton and Romantic Culture*, ed. Nicholas Groom (London: Macmillan, 1999), 79–95.

20. Milton's figuration of eating has recently been analyzed by Denise Gigante in "Milton's Aesthetics of Eating," *diacritics*, 30.2 (Summer 2000), 88–112.

21. Kolb, *The Ambiguity of Taste* 2–4.

22. Jamie Oliver, *The Naked Chef Takes Off* (New York: Hyperion, 2000), 159.

23. See Susan Sontag, "Notes on Camp," in *Against Interpretation and Other Essays* (New York and London: Anchor Books, 1990 (Farrar, Straus and Giroux, 1966), 275–92; Andrew Ross, *No Respect: Intellectuals and Popular Culture* (London and New York: Routledge, 1989), 135–70.

24. Timothy Morton, *The Poetics of Spice: Romantic Consumerism and the Exotic* (Cambridge and New York: Cambridge UP, 2000), 153–4.

25. Benjamin Robert Haydon, *The Autobiography and Memoirs of Benjamin Robert Haydon (1786–1846)*, ed. T. Taylor, 2 vols. (London: Peter Davies, 1926), 1.253.

26. Maggie Kilgour, *From Communion to Cannibalism: An Anatomy of Metaphors of Incorporation* (Princeton: Princeton UP, 1990), 210.

27. Georg Wilhelm Friedrich Hegel, *Lectures on the Philosophy of Religion*, ed. Peter C. Hodgson, tr. R. F. Brown, P. C. Hodgson, and J. M. Stewart, with the assistance of H. S. Harris (Berkeley, Los Angeles, and London: University of California Press, 1988), 252.

28. See Slavoj Žižek, *The Fragile Absolute: Or, Why is the Christian Legacy Worth Fighting For?* (London and New York: Verso, 2000), 21–40.

29. Alan Liu, "Local Transcendence: Cultural Criticism, Postmodernism, and the Romanticism of Detail", *Representations*, 32 (Fall 1990), 75–113 (86).

30. Terry Eagleton, *Ideology: an Introduction* (London and New York: Verso, 1991), 40; Žižek, *Sublime Object* 21–3.

31. Laurie Anderson, "Smoke Rings," *Home of the Brave* (Warner Brothers, 1986): "When I was a Hershey bar in my father's back pocket."

32. The allure of Coke as a eloquent expression of the commodity form is reflected in the elaborate lengths to which the Corporation has gone to create the illusion of a top-secret formula, carried around the world by a man with a briefcase handcuffed to his wrist. The substance supposed to have the ultimate "taste" turns out to have no taste at all, insofar as it merely stands in for a lumpen version of Kantian taste. Jeremy Braddock, "Coke as *Objet Petit a*" (unpublished essay); Žižek, "Coke as *Objet Petit a*," in *The Fragile Absolute* 21–4 (21–40).

33. See for example Judith Butler, *Bodies that Matter: On the Discursive Limits of "Sex"* (New York and London: Routledge, 1993); Julia Kristeva, *The Kristeva Reader*, tr. Toril Moi (New York: Columbia UP, 1986), 24–33, 34–61.

34. See for example Franco Moretti, *Signs Taken for Wonders: Essays in the Sociology of Literary Forms* (London: Verso, 1983); Jennifer Wicke, "Vampiric Typewriting: Dracula and its Media," *ELH*, 59.2 (1992), 467–93.

35. Karl Marx, *The German Ideology*, in *Selected Writings*, ed. David McLellan (Oxford and New York: Oxford UP, 1977; repr. 1987), 173–4.

36. Plato's *Phaedrus* stipulates that the *eidos* not be butchered by a bad rendition (Plato, *Phaedrus* 265e; *Phaedrus*, ed. J. Burnett (Oxford: Clarendon Press, 1901)).

37. Mark Rowlands, *Animals Like Us* (London and New York: Verso, 2002), blurb.
38. Theodor Adorno, *Negative Dialectics*, tr. E. B. Ashton (New York: The Seabury Press, 1973), 23.
39. Jean Baudrillard, *The Mirror of Production* (St. Louis: Telos Press, 1975).
40. Marx, *Capital, Selected Writings* 421. Fowkes's Penguin translation has "needs" for "wants" and "imagination" for "fancy" (1.125). This itself reproduces within Marxist theory a binary opposition constructed in capitalist ideology between necessity and luxury: some Marxists phrase this as the opposition between true and false needs. See Jonathan Hughes, *Ecology and Historical Materialism* (Cambridge and New York: Cambridge UP, 2000), 172. For a contrary view see A. Heller, *The Theory of Need in Marx* (London: Allison and Busby, 1976); Patricia Springborg, *The Problem of Human Needs and the Critique of Civilization* (London: Allen and Unwin, 1981), 106.
41. Marx, "Comments on Adolph Wagner," *Selected Writings* 581.
42. Slavoj Žižek, *The Plague of Fantasies* (London and New York: Verso, 1997), 3.
43. Max Horkheimer in Theodor Adorno, *Prisms* (Cambridge, Mass.: MIT Press, 1981), 109.
44. C. Anne Wilson, *Food and Drink in Britain: From the Stone Age to the 19th Century* (Chicago: Academy Chicago Publishers, 1991), 102.
45. See Joseph Litvak, *Strange Gourmets: Sophistication, Theory, and the Novel* (Durham and London: Duke UP, 1997), 9–10.
46. See Nigel Smith, *Literature and Revolution in England, 1640–1660* (New Haven and London: Yale UP, 1994), 320–36.

Index